Stanislavsky in the World

Stanislavsky in the World

The System and its Transformations Across Continents

Edited by
Jonathan Pitches and Stefan Aquilina

Bloomsbury Methuen Drama
An imprint of Bloomsbury Publishing Plc

BLOOMSBURY
LONDON · OXFORD · NEW YORK · NEW DELHI · SYDNEY

Bloomsbury Methuen Drama
An imprint of Bloomsbury Publishing Plc

Imprint previously known as Methuen Drama

50 Bedford Square, London, WC1B 3DP, UK
1385 Broadway, New York, NY 10018, USA
29 Earlsfort Terrace, Dublin 2, Ireland

www.bloomsbury.com

BLOOMSBURY, METHUEN DRAMA and the Diana logo are trademarks of Bloomsbury Publishing Plc

First published 2017

© Jonathan Pitches, Stefan Aquilina and contributors, 2017

Jonathan Pitches, Stefan Aquilina and contributors have asserted their right under the Copyright, Designs and Patents Act, 1988, to be identified as editors of this work.

All rights reserved. No part of this publication may be reproduced or transmitted in any form or by any means, electronic or mechanical, including photocopying, recording, or any information storage or retrieval system, without prior permission in writing from the publishers.

No responsibility for loss caused to any individual or organization acting on or refraining from action as a result of the material in this publication can be accepted by Bloomsbury or the author.

British Library Cataloguing-in-Publication Data
A catalogue record for this book is available from the British Library.

ISBN: HB: 978-1-4725-8787-9
PB: 978-1-4725-8788-6
ePDF: 978-1-4725-8790-9
ePub: 978-1-4725-8789-3

Library of Congress Cataloging-in-Publication Data
A catalog record for this book is available from the Library of Congress

Cover design: Eleanor Rose

Typeset by RefineCatch Limited, Bungay, Suffolk

To find out more about our authors and books visit www.bloomsbury.com. Here you will find extracts, author interviews, details of forthcoming events and the option to sign up for our newsletters.

Contents

Acknowledgements	viii
Translation Credits and Notes on Transliteration	ix
List of Figures	xi
Introduction	1
Context 1 Well-trodden Paths: US, UK, Russian and Soviet Perspectives on Stanislavsky's Transmission *Stefan Aquilina*	1
Context 2 A System for all Nations? Stanislavsky's Transmission in the World *Jonathan Pitches*	12

Part 1 Europe

Introduction *Stefan Aquilina*	27
1 Three Periods of Stanislavsky in Italy *Franco Ruffini*	35
2 Stanislavsky and French Theatre: Selected Affinities *Marie-Christine Autant-Mathieu*	63
3 Between Nationalism and Ideology: Stanislavsky in Lithuania *Ina Pukelytė*	87
4 An Amateur Processing of the System: Stanislavsky in Malta *Stefan Aquilina*	105
5 Moments of Transition: Stanislavsky in Greece *Maria Gaitanidi*	124

Part 2 China and Japan

Introduction — Jonathan Pitches — 143

6 Towards a Chinese School of Performance and Directing: Jiao Juyin *Siyuan Liu* — 149

7 Stanislavsky with Chinese Characteristics: How the System was Introduced into China *Jonathan Pitches and Ruru Li* — 166

8 A Producer's Perspective: Stanislavsky in Contemporary Japan *Kaori Nakayama* — 196

Part 3 Latin America

Introduction — *Stefan Aquilina* — 207

9 Stanislavsky in Brazil: Territories and Frontiers *Arlete Cavaliere* — 213

10 Stanislavsky's Legacy in Cuba *Yana Elsa Brugal* — 238

11 A Teacher's Perspective: Stanislavsky at the Escuela de Teatro de Buenos Aires in Argentina *Raúl Serrano* — 261

Part 4 Africa

Introduction — *Stefan Aquilina* — 271

12 Stanislavsky in Nigeria: Convergences and Counterpoints in Actor Training and Practice *Kene Igweonu* — 277

13 Stanislavsky in Tunisian Theatre: a Heritage in Progress *Moez Mrabet* — 290

14 A Director's Perspective: Stanislavsky in South Africa   309
    David Peimer

Part 5 Australasia

Introduction   319
Jonathan Pitches

15 Theatrical Bowerbirds: Received Stanislavsky and the
    Tyranny of Distance in Australian Actor Training   325
    Ian Maxwell

16 Acting Idealism and Emotions: Hayes Gordon,
    The Ensemble Theatre and Acting Studios in Australia   347
    Peta Tait

17 Stanislavsky in Aotearoa: The System Experienced
    through the Māori World   367
    Hilary Halba

Part 6 India and Bangladesh

Introduction   393
Jonathan Pitches

18 Between Stanislavsky and Bharata: Actor Training at the
    National School of Drama in New Delhi   399
    JooYeoul Ryu with Stefan Aquilina

19 Stanislavsky in the Modern Theatre of Bangladesh:
    A Mapping of Postcolonial Appropriation and Assimilation   417
    Syed Jamil Ahmed

Notes on Contributors   445
Index   453

Acknowledgements

This book has been in gestation for four years, and the result of a countless number of discussions via emails and Skype calls. Many individuals have contributed in their own way to the project, offering advice and encouragement. Gratitude needs to be extended, first of all, to the fantastic group of authors who contributed to this volume. They have embraced the concept enthusiastically and provided the expertise and critical thinking which form the beating heart of this volume. Thanks also to the team at Bloomsbury and specifically Jenny Ridout, for immediately seeing worth in the project, and John O'Donovan, for his meticulous work during the production phase. Our gratitude also goes to all the reviewers who commented so favourably on the project, both at proposal stage and on the final manuscript.

With a project so long in the making many people have offered feedback along the way; colleagues who have genuinely helped us refine and improve the material. Most recently these include the conference delegates at the 2016 Stanislavsky Symposium in Rose Bruford, Sidcup, who responded to our Keynote presentation on historiography and cultural transmission. We are also grateful to the support offered by Christopher Balme, Paul Fryer, Peta Tait, Maria Kapsali, Brad Haseman, and Vera Pavlova. We would also like to thank the University of Malta Research Grant Committee and colleagues in the Performance Training, Preparation and Pedagogy Research Group at the University of Leeds who have supported the research going into the writing of our respective chapters.

Every effort has been made to trace copyright holders in all copyright material in this book. Any omissions brought to our attention will be rectified in future editions.

Finally, we would like to thank our families, Ceri, Harri, George; Yulia, Matthew, and Daniel, for their love and support.

Translation Credits and Notes on Transliteration

Three periods of Stanislavsky in Italy by Franco Ruffini; translated by Stefan Aquilina.

Stanislavsky and French Theatre: Selected Affinities by Marie-Christine Autant-Mathieu; translated by Victoria Sammut.

Stanislavsky with Chinese Characteristics: how the System was Introduced into China Class transcripts translated by Huimin Wang, Siyuan Li, Shengnan Guo, and Ruru Li.

Stanislavsky in Brazil: Territories and Frontiers by Arlete Cavaliere; translated by Leonor Cione.

Stanislavsky's Legacy in Cuba by Yana Elsa Brugal; translated by Alba Florian Viton and Lucía Piquero.

A Teacher's Perspective: Stanislavsky at the Escuela de Teatro de Buenos Aires in Argentina by Raúl Serrano; translated by Alba Florian Viton and edited by Stefan Aquilina.

Stanislavsky in Tunisian Theatre: a Heritage in Progress by Moez Mrabet; translated by Vicki Ann Cremona.

Names have been transliterated in ways that are easily apprehended by an English-speaking reader. Similarly, the spelling of names already familiar in English (e.g. Stanislavsky, Meyerhold, Chekhov) has been retained.

As editors, we have made the decision not to standardize the writing of 'system' or 'System' throughout the book, to reflect the different approaches in different countries to Stanislavsky's work. This is a central theme of *Stanislavsky in the World*.

List of Figures

1 *Stanislavsky in the World* identifies the presence of Stanislavskian practices in Australia, New Zealand, Japan, China, Bangladesh, India, Lithuania, France, Italy, Greece, Malta, Tunisia, Nigeria, South Africa, Cuba, Brazil, and Argentina. These practices join those of the USSR and the US to suggest an extended map of Stanislavsky's transmission in the world.   7
2 Stanislavsky in Europe.   25
3 Silvio d'Amico and Vittorio Gassmann in 1952. © Accademia d'Arte Drammatica.   39
4 Gerardo Guerrieri. © Selene Guerrieri   50
5 Grotowski in about 1971. Photo Marianne Ahrne. © Odin Teatret Archives.   55
6 Stanislavsky playing Maigrillot in the vaudeville *Le Secret d'une femme* (this is the Russian title of the vaudeville *Les Femmes et le secret* by Saint-Yves et Léon de Villiers), Alekseev Circle, 1881. © The Museum of the Moscow Art Theatre.   65
7 Stanislavsky playing Argan in Molière's *The Imaginary Invalid*, Moscow Art Theatre, mise-en-scène by Alexandre Benois and Stanislavsky, 1913. © The Museum of the Moscow Art Theatre.   67
8 Stanislavsky playing Count Lioubine and Maria Lilina as Daria Ivanovna in Ivan Turgenev's *A Provincial Lady*, Moscow Art Theatre, mise-en-scène by Stanislavsky, 1912. © The Museum of the Moscow Art Theatre.   74
9 Stanislavsky in the role of Baron Ripafratta in *La Locandiera* by Carlo Goldoni, Moscow Art Theatre, mise-en-scène by Stanislavsky, 1914. © The Museum of the Moscow Art Theatre.   75
10 Alla Tarassova playing Anna Karenina and Mikhail Proudkine as Vronski in Lev Tolstoy's *Anna Karenina*, Moscow Art Theatre, mise-en-scène by Vladimir Nemirovich-Danchenko, 1937. © The Museum of the Moscow Art Theatre.   79

11	*Šarūnas*, directed by Andrius Oleka-Žilinskas. © Lithuanian Museum of Theatre, Cinema and Music.	92
12	Andrius Oleka-Žilinskas and Mikhail Chekhov. © Lithuanian Museum of Theatre, Cinema and Music.	94
13	Giuseppe Schembri-Bonaci's production of Dario Fo's *Gli Arcangeli non Giocano al Flipper (Archangels Don't Play Pinball)* at the Simonov Theatre in Moscow (1997). © Giuseppe Schembri-Bonaci.	110
14	Frank Camilleri in *Id-Descartes*, MITP Theatre, Valletta, Malta, November 1996. Photo by Jeremy De Maria. © Frank Camilleri.	111
15	Karmen Azzopardi and Paul Xuereb in *The Aspern Papers*, an Atturi Theatre Productions of 1976. © Paul Xuereb.	116
16	Stanislavsky in China and Japan.	141
17	Jiao Juyin (left) with Kulnyov (second from right) during a design session for *Egor Bulychev and Others*. Photo courtesy of Beijing People's Art Theatre.	155
18	A scene in *The Tiger Tally* with the principal actors. From left to right: Zheng Rong (as Hou Ying), Yu Shizhi (Lord Xinling), Zhu Lin (Lady Ruji), Dai Ya (King of Wei). Photo courtesy of Beijing People's Art Theatre.	157
19	Leikov in trench coat, centre. By kind permission of STA archive.	174
20	Chen Mingzheng demonstrating an object exercise in his flat in Shanghai. Photo by Jonathan Pitches.	179
21	Nicholas Barter leading a Stanislavsky intensive workshop for students from five drama universities, Tokyo (May 2014).	197
22	Bella Merlin and Kaori Nakayama, at Meiji University, Tokyo (June 2006).	202
23	Stanislavsky in Latin America.	205
24	*Santa Camila de La Habana Vieja* (1962). Director: Adolfo de Luis, for Teatro Milanés. Photographer: Unknown.	246
25	*Las tres hermanas* (1972). Director: Vicente Revuelta for Teatro Estudio. Photographer: Unknown.	251
26	*El tío Vania* (2014). Director: Carlos Celdrán for Argos Teatro. © Alina Morante.	256

27	Raúl Serrano. © Escuela de Teatro de Buenos Aires.	265
28	Stanislavsky in Africa.	269
29	Stanislavsky in Australasia.	317
30	Gregan McMahon, 1905–6.	331
31	Doris Fitton, in the 1930s.	333
32	Peter Finch with Diane Cilento, 1955.	336
33	Stanislavsky in India and Bangladesh.	391
34	The NSD first year Acting class focusing on the actor's work on self (Lecturer: Abdul Latin Khatana, 2005).	404
35	The NSD second year Improvisation class (Lecturer: Tripurari Sharma, 2005).	407
36	Solo performance, 'Karna' of a NSD student (the present writer) for his final examination (Duration: 90 minutes, 16 May 2004, NSD).	411
37	A scene from *A Doll's House* (Act 1), showing Golam Farida as Mrs Linde (far left), Sahana Ferdous as Nora (right of centre) and Nurur Rahman as Dr Rank (far right). Photograph by Altaf Hossain.	424
38	Abdul Halim Pramanik as Andrei in *The Three Sisters* (Act 4). Photograph by Kamaluddin Kabir.	429
39	A scene from *Behular Bhasan* showing Farida Akhter Lima as the narrator (top), and Tania Sultana as Behula (bottom). Photograph by Kamaluddin Kabir.	434
40	Farida Akhter Lima as the narrator (left), Nahida Sultana Sati as the charlatan sage (centre) and choral singers in the fourth episode of *Behular Bhasan*. Photograph by Kamaluddin Kabir.	436

INTRODUCTION: CONTEXT 1

Well-trodden Paths: US, UK, Russian and Soviet Perspectives on Stanislavsky's Transmission

Stefan Aquilina

Remapping Stanislavsky's transmission

One consequence of the 1922–4 tours which Stanislavsky himself had understood was that America was going to play a significant role in his own future as a theatre-maker. His letters indicate how he and the Moscow Art Theatre became caught within the exigencies of both American and Soviet theatres. For example, while yearning for his return home, Stanislavsky recognized the necessity to develop a concrete link with America because '[w]ithout American support, I do not see the existence of theatres and studios in Russia possible, at least for many years' (Stanislavskii, 1961, p. 59). The diplomatic dimension of the tours did not escape Stanislavsky, with one letter to Nemirovich-Danchenko pondering the Moscow Art Theatre's position as 'the first and most eloquent and persuasive ambassador of Russia, who did not bring commercial items to trade but the living Russian soul, to which America felt an attraction' (Stanislavskii, 1961, p. 43). In these letters Stanislavsky might have drafted an image of US–USSR relationships based on reciprocal support, but what emerged from those tours – the creation of two Stanislavsky-informed but distinct and conflicting acting traditions – was far removed from that utopia. Sharon Marie Carnicke, whose recent work on Stanislavsky has uncovered a mine of new material and generated innovative insights, describes Stanislavsky's centrality to both Russian and American theatres as follows:

> A map that traces the migration of Konstantin Sergeevich Stanislavsky's System throughout the world [...] would show two major points: New York and Moscow. In both cities, actors seized upon Stanislavsky's work as primary and essential. In both, teachers who had studied with the master passed their understanding of his practice on to the next generation of teachers.
>
> Carnicke, 2009, p. 7

While America and Russia are indeed important centres of Stanislavskian practices, an overemphasis on these two contexts tends to simplify the complexity inherent in the transmission and transformation of a live practice like Stanislavsky's system. Other possible and equally engaging transmission lines become obfuscated, and the aim of *Stanislavsky in the World* is to uncover some of these lesser known paths through which Stanislavsky's ideas and practices were disseminated, adopted, resisted and ultimately changed. This part of the Introduction outlines and critiques the overreliance on America and Russia as seats of Stanislavskian transmission in order to pave the way for the various case-studies that are at the heart of this present volume. The idea here is not to refute the existence of these two seats – their profile makes that impossible – but to underline the American and Russian positions as the two 'well-trodden paths' in the transmission of Stanislavskian practices and its scholarship.

Stanislavsky's position in the former USSR was intimately linked to the political scenario that enveloped him, where Joseph Stalin's strategy to create models for every aspect of Soviet life led to the regime's appropriation of Stanislavsky's work. The Moscow Art Theatre became a model of Socialist Realism, while a Materialist version of the system was used as the official training model in theatre academies across Russia and its satellite countries. Reverential accolades were common, with Stanislavsky called 'The Genius of Theatre' (1938, quotation in Carnicke, 1993, p. 22), 'an artist genius, a teacher and warrior, whose creative legacy enriches our art' (1950, in Toporkov, 1979, p. 18) and 'the outstanding reformer of theatrical art' (in Stanislavskii, 1958, p. 5). Stanislavsky's centrality survived Nikita Khrushchev's destalinization to remain the main training kernel for actors and theatre workers during the second part of the twentieth century. Ekaterina Kamotskaia, for example, remarked that the training she received during the 1970s at the Youth Theatre

Studio and at Vakhtangov's School was still based on 'exercises [taken] directly from [Stanislavsky's] books' (Kamotskaia in Pitches, 2012, p. 169). Other approaches, such as those of Vakhtangov, Meyerhold, and M. Chekhov did enter Russian actor training during the 1990s, in a way that questioned Stanislavsky's supposed realistic tendencies, but Stanislavsky's centrality was not displaced. Stanislavsky's supremacy in Russia during the latter part of the twentieth century emerges from the way that Andrei Goncharov, Secretary of the Theatre Union, articulated the enduring scope of Stanislavsky's system. While addressing a 1991 delegation of American theatre workers, Goncharov 'extoll[ed] Stanislavski's approaches to personality and the subconscious as major paths for expressing one's individuality. Ultimately, in his [Stanislavsky's] view, the actor must be trained to reveal imaginative thinking onstage so that the audience perceives a human being' (Rotté, 1992, p. 88). Stanislavsky's prominence is clear even today, as Anatoly Smeliansky, current Moscow Art Theatre Associate Artistic Director, remarks: '[t]here isn't any [contemporary] serious theatre school in Russia that isn't using it [the System] in one way or another. It is our main methodology of acting training' (in Dacre and Fryer, 2008, p. 30).

A similar scenario developed in America, as '[t]he Stanislavsky System and the practices descended from it continue to dominate American actor training' (Malague, 2012, p. 21). Different reasons are posited to explain the impact which Stanislavsky and the system had on American theatre. Keith Walden, for example, says that Stanislavsky's 'ideas caught on quickly in a foreign setting [i.e. America] because in many ways they were not foreign at all' (Walden, 2003, p. 319). He argues that a number of Stanislavskian ideas, especially his tenet that an actor must live out his role, were alien to the theatre of the time but familiar to other spheres of American life. A case in point was sales training, which at the beginning of the twentieth century was written about in a way that shared acting's 'intent on eliciting convincing performance' (Walden, 2003, p. 319). Marie-Christine Autant-Mathieu gives other reasons to explain the American receptivity to Stanislavsky's teachings. First, the United States 'did not have theatrical traditions that had been passed down from generation to generation' (in White, 2014, p. 174). A number of theatrical milestones were evident, of course, and a director like David Belasco had already made a reputation for realistic production. On his part, Stanislavsky identified talented actors like Joseph Schildkraut and David Warfield to dispel the idea that there were no talented American actors (Benedetti, 1999, p. 286). However, certain work conditions, including a domination by business firms, increased ticket prices and competition from film, prevented the development of American acting and playwriting (see Brockett, 1995, pp. 461–4).

The second reason Autant-Mathieu gives is more cultural, in the sense that 'the country was open to innovation, and its social ideal affirmed the worth and importance of each individual' (in White, 2014, p. 174). Stanislavsky struck a major chord with the imagination of a young group of theatre makers like Lee Strasberg, Harold Clurman, Stella Adler, Sanford Meisner, and others, individuals who as young practitioners were demanding attention and recognition and who would grow to then train generations of actors and actresses. The result was that Stanislavsky's name became interwoven with American theatre, to the extent that the System and the Method are to this day often taken to mean the same approach. Most revealing is how Smeliansky speaks about 'Stanislavski's "System" or "Method" as it is called in the English-speaking world' (in Dacre and Fryer, 2008, p. 30). An apparent congruency between the System and the Method is also commented upon by Jean Benedetti and Carnicke who, however, underline the problems of such whitewash assimilation. Benedetti remarks on 'the widespread confusion between the "system" and the Method as defined by Lee Strasberg at the Actors Studio in New York' (in Stanislavski, 2008, p. xx), while Carnicke warns that '[i]t is time to dispel the Method's hegemony over the interpretation of the System in the West' (Carnicke, 2009, p. 14). Both Benedetti and Carnicke agree that a clearer delineation between the System and the Method is necessary to the process of rehabilitating Stanislavsky for the twenty-first century.

Claims about an American bias in the transmission of Stanislavsky's practices tend to be articulated in two ways. First, there is an absolute assertion that America 'owns' this transmission. The most unequivocal voice in this case is that of Mel Gordon, who asserts that 'the *true* work of Stanislavsky could be found *only* in the studios and stages of New York City and in the backlots of independent Hollywood' (Gordon, 2010, p. v; emphasis added, see also p. xiv). Such reading presents the United States as a flowing pool from which Stanislavsky's ideas then dissipate to other parts of the world, a prism through which modern and contemporary readings of Stanislavsky are channelled.

Carnicke, for instance, concedes that '[d]rawing a map of the System's migration throughout the world calls visual attention to this unexpected but highly charged Americanization of Stanislavsky's work' (Carnicke, 2009, p. 11). A second set of literature presents the American line within a comparative setup from which it emerges as the context where 'Stanislavsky's legacy is *best* measured' (Zarrilli quoted in Pitches, 2012, p. 2; emphasis added). Other transmission lines are not negated, but the American prominence is reasserted by marginalizing alternative routes. Such a comparative approach is evident in Carnicke's assertion that New York has a 'unique place on the map of migration, second only to Moscow' (Carnicke, 2009, p. 10). Interestingly, the comparative emphasis on the American line finds support even from certain Russian circles. For example, Sergei Tcherkasski says that '[t]he strongest influence of Stanislavsky's ideas was experienced by the American theatre' (Tcherkasski, 2013, p. 94), and quotes a comparison between Europe and America which Smeliansky makes to point out how '[i]n many European countries Stanislavsky is just a legendary yet remote historical landscape. As for the Americans, not only do they constantly publish Stanislavski, but also present the main source of knowledge about Konstantin Stanislavski' (in Tcherkasski, 2013, p. 96). Underpinning these statements is a sense of hierarchy, of one context being the 'best' measuring gauge amongst a number (Zarrilli), the 'main' source as opposed to possible lesser ones (Smeliansky) and a 'first' or 'second' placement (Carnicke).

Such formulations are inevitable if seen through the lens of an overwhelming competitive thinking, but they do give rise to suspicion when juxtaposed with what Dick Hebdige sees as the postmodern 'replacement of unitary power axes by a plurality of power/discourse formations [...] [and] the collapse of cultural hierarchies' (in Kershaw, 1999, p. 6). Hebdige here signals a more inclusive attitude which questions singular and totalizing metanarratives and/or any propensity to delineate phenomena according to 'a scale of values' (Pickering, 2010, p. 267). The application of Hebdige's plural frame-of-mind opens wide the study of Stanislavskian lineages, in two ways. First, alternative routes of transmission of Stanislavsky's practices are identified. The immediate consequence here is that the American and Soviet/Russian hegemony on Stanislavskian transmission is diluted. Second, the object of transmission becomes pluralized in itself, becoming 'objects' and 'practices' rather than one definite and invariable system. In other words, the transmission of Stanislavsky's system(s) is problematized in terms of both locations on the migration map as well as the knowledge that is transferred.

Both considerations are at the heart of the book *Stanislavsky in the World*, as the various case-studies will show. *Stanislavsky in the World* builds on a number of recent statements which, though stating the existence of valid transmission lines beyond the US and the USSR, rarely expand upon the alternative routes. For example, Carnicke says that the system's dissemination 'spanned the globe' (Carnicke, 2009, p. 7), but does not elaborate beyond listing major theatre centres where this took place, like Eastern Europe, Germany, Great Britain, Scandinavia, and Japan. Rose Whyman similarly says that 'over the twentieth century Stanislavski-based methods have dominated Western acting, and in other parts of the world – Japan, for example – the work was increasingly recognized and used' (Whyman, 2013, p. 138). Her case studies to discuss Stanislavsky's influence and legacy, however, then support the common known paths of the US, USSR and, to a lesser extent, the UK. She also adds a brief reference to Poland and Grotowski (Whyman, 2013, pp. 160–1). It is Autant-Mathieu who offers a more detailed exposition, and argues that whereas the influence of the First Studio in America is widely known, 'one often overlooks the role played by certain other emigrant actors affiliated with the Moscow theatre, those who were either trained within it or reproduced its work methods throughout Europe' (in White, 2014, p. 168). She constructs short references on Prague, Berlin, Paris, Sofia, the Baltic Countries, and Italy (White, pp. 168–72). The UK has also been given some attention as a transmission seat of Stanislavsky's practice. For instance, Kathy Dacre outlines this transmission in her introductory report on the teaching of Stanislavskian practices in the UK, in which she identified the pre-Second World War years as an under-researched area of investigation (Dacre, 2009, p. 6). David Shirley has investigated that terrain by highlighting the contributions of Michel Saint-Denis, to which he adds the subsequent training at the London Drama Centre and the more recent developments at Rose Bruford College and RADA. Shirley's study points out how Stanislavsky's transmission in the UK has been 'more erratic and piecemeal' than in the US, but nonetheless present and palpably felt (Shirley in Pitches, 2012, p. 40). *Stanislavsky in the World* answers directly this gap in the field, and expands markedly the discussion on the transmission of Stanislavsky's practices, beyond the US, USSR, and the UK, by being the first work that takes as its

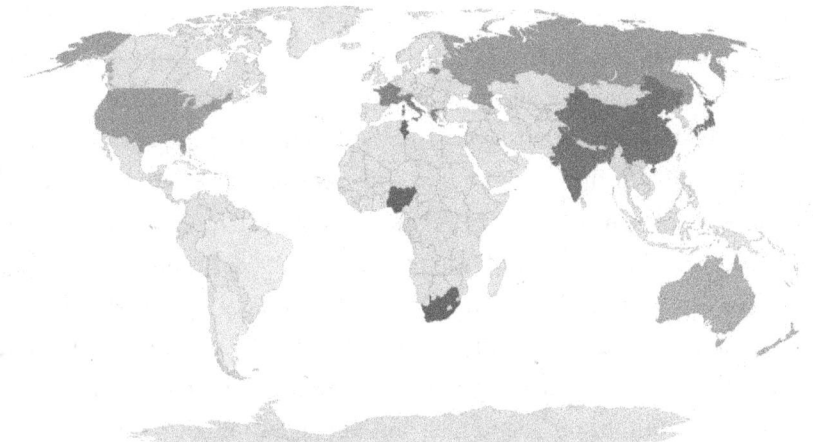

Figure 1 *Stanislavsky in the World* identifies the presence of Stanislavskian practices in Australia, New Zealand, Japan, China, Bangladesh, India, Lithuania, France, Italy, Greece, Malta, Tunisia, Nigeria, South Africa, Cuba, Brazil, and Argentina. These practices join those of the USSR and the US to suggest an extended map of Stanislavsky's transmission in the world.

subject matter the transmission of Stanislavsky across the rest of the world. It suggests a redrawing of Stanislavsky's transmission map proposed above by Carnicke, where Stanislavsky's world journey and resettlement is less rooted in American perspectives. A more complex picture of the Stanislavsky acting tradition, as well as its dissemination and scholarship, is revealed, one which, as it will be discussed below, reflects current twenty-first-century thought.

Twenty-first-century Stanislavsky

The premise behind recently published sources on Stanislavsky is that his work and ideas have been generally misunderstood, and that their restoration is, therefore, necessary. For example, Bella Merlin says that 'Stanislavsky is much quoted but little understood in this country [England] either by students or by actors' (Merlin, 2001, p. xi). Laurence Senelick, on his part, mentions 'adaptations that blurred his [Stanislavsky's] intentions and imbalanced his emphasis' (Senelick, 2014, p. 10).[1] Misunderstandings surrounding Stanislavsky are unsurprisingly framed around the two images that have been constructed in America and the USSR, images which R. Andrew White describes as Stanislavsky 'the father of the Method, an image fashioned by enthusiastic Americans, and the "scientist-artist", an image manufactured in the USSR by the Marxist materialism and Socialist Realism of Stalin's regime' (White, 2014, p. 1). The problematic gestation of Stanislavsky's books, both in editing and translation, fuelled the creation of these two images, with Senelick, for example, saying that *My Life in Art* 'exists in two distinct versions that reflect, in their separate ways, different stages of Stanislavski's life' (in Stanislavski, 2008a, p. xiii).

Both American and Soviet images of Stanislavsky are now seen with scepticism and treated as reductive myths that need demythologizing. Each negates the psychophysical integration that was so crucial to Stanislavsky, with the American branch emphasizing the psychological dimension of Stanislavsky's earliest theories, as opposed to the Soviet's weight on the physical aspects of his last phase. In a way, the US and USSR images of Stanislavsky were products of their time. With the world seemingly organized in terms of such binary oppositions like East and West, Left and Right, and Communism and Capitalism, reconciliation between these two different readings of Stanislavsky seemed impossible. Carnicke again makes this clear: 'While both centers [US and USSR] tapped the same source, their creative readings of Stanislavsky proceeded along different lines, establishing not only competing traditions but competing truths about the master's work' (Carnicke, 2009, p. 8). The Lee Strasberg–Stella Adler conflict of the 1930s was symptomatic of this discord: Strasberg's predilection for Affective Memory had, in his eyes, no space for the more physical approaches that Adler had practised with Stanislavsky in Paris. He even considered such physical approaches as 'heretical' (in Gordon, 2010, p. 60).

Twenty-first-century Stanislavsky studies are concerned with displacing these two images, and it is within these efforts that *Stanislavsky in the World* can be placed. The post-1991 opening of Soviet archives has been central to our contemporary readings of Stanislavsky's work. These new sources can also be processed through renewed historiographical and archival methodologies which question the archive as a repository of historical truths. Maggie Gale and Ann Featherstone, for example, have provided insights into the '*creative* archival process' (in Kershaw and Nicholson, 2011, p. 37; emphasis in original), which they locate in the encounter between the researcher and the material itself. The researcher is not a neutral being but an interpreter of the archival material. S/he uses his or her own ideological views, intentions, and background, generating in turn research outputs that are constructed accounts rather than conclusive certainties. Therefore, while we can doubt that archival records are ever 'documenting the authentic Stanislavsky', or that they can give access to the 'real Stanislavsky', we can be assured that Stanislavsky's figure as a 'seductive [...] "grand narrative" of history and of theatre history' (Davis in Kershaw and Nicholson, 2011, p. 90) – a trap which the American and Soviet contexts have fallen into – is at least constantly kept in check.

Former images of Stanislavsky are also questioned by the bringing to light of Active Analysis, a practice which Stanislavsky was working on during the very last years of his life. Active Analysis encourages the actor to use active improvisation in working on a role, while harnessing holistically 'all the available avenues of investigation – mental, physical, emotional, and experiential' (Merlin in Carnicke, 2009, p. 192). Active Analysis has strong supporters today, practitioners and scholars like Merlin and Carnicke who not only transmit this practice around the world but also defend it with an enthusiasm that recalls that of Stanislavsky's first Russian and American students. Active Analysis is championed as a 'liberating' practice (White, 2014, p. 5) that empowers actors to become 'the creators of their own choices, and not moveable blocks of wood' (Merlin in White, 2014, p. 331). Carnicke also describes it as 'a flexible rehearsal technique for the full range of today's performance styles' (http://www.sharoncarnicke.com/).

At first glance, the contemporary attention to Active Analysis might be seen as an attempt to displace the practices of Affective Memory and the Method of Physical Action. Merlin, for example, says:

> I am strongly aware that in the USA (where I work at the time of writing) a rather straightjacketed, dogmatic approach to Stanislavsky's teaching still persists in many quarters. The majority understanding of his 'system', it would seem, is clearly rooted in his early work, and is – to my mind – old fashioned, if not obsolete.
>
> Merlin in Pitches, 2012, p. 189

Carnicke gives a similar reading of the Method of Physical Action:

> No other period of state control impacted the practice of Stanislavsky's System more than the 1930s, when Soviet censorship turned his multi-pronged acting method for mind, body, and soul (now widely known as

Active Analysis) into a single-minded, materialist approach (called the Method of Physical Action).

in White, 2014, p. 255

However, Active Analysis has little of the irreconcilability that was at the core of Stanislavsky's twentieth-century images because it does not negate his previous experiments but actually seeks to incorporate them within a baggage of practices which the actor can call upon to navigate specific rehearsal and training situations. The starting point for Active Analysis improvisation could be anything from physical work, imagination, intuition, emotional and intellectual work because '[a]nything provided the actors with valuable clues' (Merlin, 2003, p. 34). Active Analysis, in other words, offers various options for the actor to tap into when working on a performance. The multiplicity of Active Analysis on one hand and creative archiving on the other, therefore, help to create a more open-ended picture of twenty-first-century Stanislavsky, and it is to this picture that *Stanislavsky in the World* contributes.

Notes

1 The misunderstandings surrounding Stanislavsky are also mentioned in Benedetti, 1998, p. vii; Hornby in Dacre and Fryer, 2008, p. 55; and Gordon, 1987, p. xi.

References

Benedetti, J. (1998), *Stanislavski and The Actor*. London: Methuen.
Benedetti, J. (1999), *Stanislavski: His Art and Life*. London: Methuen.
Brockett, O. G. (1995), *History of the Theatre 7th ed*. Massachusetts: Allyn and Bacon.
Carnicke, S. M. (2009), *Stanislavsky in Focus 2nd ed*. Oxon: Routledge.
Carnicke, S. M. (1993), 'Stanislavsky: Unabridged and Uncensored', *The Drama Review*, Vol. 37, No. 1: 22–42.
Dacre, K. (2009), 'An Introduction', in *Teaching Stanislavski*, A research project initiated by SCUDD (the Standing Conference of University Drama Departments) in conjunction with PALATINE (the Higher Education Academy Subject Centre for Dance, Drama and Music) and funded by a PALATINE Development Award.

Dacre, K. and Fryer, P. (2008), *Stanislavski ON STAGE*. Sidcup: Stanislavski Centre Rose Bruford College.
Gordon, M. (1987), *The Stanislavsky Technique: Russia*. New York: Applause.
Gordon, M. (2010), *Stanislavsky in America*. Oxon: Routledge.
Kershaw, B. (1999), *The Radical in Performance*. Oxon: Routledge.
Kershaw, B. and Nicholson, H. (eds) (2011), *Research Methods in Theatre and Performance*. Edinburgh: Edinburgh University Press.
Malague, R. (2012), *An Actress Prepares*. Oxon: Routledge.
Merlin, B. (2001), *Beyond Stanislavsky: The Psycho-Physical Approach to Actor Training*. London: Nick Hern Books.
Merlin, B. (2003), *Konstantin Stanislavsky*. Oxon: Routledge.
Pickering, K. (2010), *Key Concepts in Drama and Performance*. London: Palgrave Macmillan.
Pitches, J. (ed.) (2012), *Russian in Britain*. Oxon: Routledge.
Rotté, J. (1992), 'Theatre Training Moscow Style', *TDR*, Vol. 36, No. 2: 81–96.
Senelick, L. (ed.) (2014), *Stanislavsky – A Life in Letters*. Oxon: Routledge.
Stanislavskii, K. (1958), *Sobranie Sochinenii Tom. 5* (Collected Works Vol.5). Moscow: Iskusstvo.
Stanislavskii, K. (1961), *Sobranie Sochinenii Tom. 8* (Collected Works Vol. 8). Moscow: Iskusstvo.
Stanislavski, K. (2008a), *My Life in Art*, trans. J. Benedetti. New York: Routledge.
Stanislavski, K. (2008b), *An Actor's Work*, trans. and ed. J. Benedetti. New York: Routledge.
Tcherkasski, S. (2013), 'The System Becomes the Method: Stanislavsky – Boleslavsky – Strasberg', *Stanislavski Studies*, Issue 3: 92–114.
Toporkov, V. (1979), *Stanislavski in Rehearsal*, trans. C. Edwards, New York: Theatre Arts Books.
Walden, K. (2003), 'Whose Method? Culture, Commerce, and American Performer Training', *New Theatre Quarterly*, Vol. 19, No. 4: 318–35.
White, R. A. (ed.) (2014), *The Routledge Companion to Stanislavsky*. Oxon: Routledge.
Whyman, R. (2013), *Stanislavski: The Basics*. Oxon: Routledge.

Websites

http://www.sharoncarnicke.com/ [accessed 1 February 2015].

INTRODUCTION: CONTEXT 2

A System for all Nations? Stanislavsky's Transmission in the World

Jonathan Pitches

Stanislavsky's universalism

There is little doubt that Stanislavsky was a universalist. Though radically different in other ways, his thinking was very much in line with other universalist practitioners operating in Europe in the twentieth century: Antonin Artaud, Peter Brook, Jerzy Grotowski and Eugenio Barba (Knowles, 2010, p. 16). Unlike these four Europeans, Stanislavsky did not base his universalism on modernist notions of the primitive, on what may be thought to *precede* culture, but he did share with them a belief in what Ric Knowles calls the 'elementally human' (Knowles, 2010, p. 16), braided together with a career-long commitment to creative nature. As he asserted in a notebook from 1936:

> My system is for all nations. All peoples possess the same human nature.
> Stanislavski, 1968, p. 170

He had been arguing the point in print for over a decade. In his memoir, *My Life in Art*, revised and rewritten for Russian audiences in 1926 after a rather shambolic and hurried version was put out in the US in 1924[1], he ascribed this universality to both sides of his system, inner and outer:

> In rhythm, movement, speech, voice training and breath there is much that is common and therefore incumbent upon all. The same is true of the mind, the creative process, since all actors without exception need to feed the mind according to the laws of nature.
> Stanislavski, 2008a, p. 347

The urge for commonality is evident, too, in his quest for a *grammar* of acting (Stanislavsky, 2008b, p. xv) – a transcendent language designed to surmount the individual problems experienced by actors and to achieve a cohesive approach, a system. This set of overarching laws was considered by Stanislavsky to be pan-cultural, informing a global compact of 'artist actors of all nations' tasked with working out the details of the psychotechnique (Stanislavsky, 1968, p. 2). In fact, his attitude to the dissemination and transmission of his system was even more ambitious: it was to position the system as a culture in and of itself, as he argued in the final fragments of *An Actor's Work*:

> The system is not an all-purpose reference book but a whole *culture* which must be cultivated and nurtured over many long years.
>
> Stanislavski, 2008b, p. 612, emphasis in original

Viewed as such the system loses its boundedness, its nationality, allowing Stanislavsky to mobilize its powers across nations, setting a common agenda for actor training without borders – a kind of United Nations of acting.

The universal, essential or 'elementally human' are now commonly discredited terms, following a robust debate fuelled by, amongst others, Rustom Bharucha (1993), Bonnie Maranca and Gautam Dasgupta (1991) in the early 1990s, continued by Helen Lo and Jacqueline Gilbert (Lo and Gilbert, 2002) in the early 2000s and more recently elaborated by Ric Knowles (in Knowles, 2010). Whilst these debates are wide ranging and layered, they nevertheless have common characteristics and themes: a critique of the geo-political binaries of West and East, North and South; an interrogation of the power relations embedded in cultural exchange particularly in relation to empire; and a renewed focus on cultural specificity and locatedness – a preference towards materialist rather than essentialist approaches (Knowles, 2010, p. 13). On the latter theme others have argued against Bharucha's cultural materialist critique of Brook and his production of *Mahabharata*, identifying the virtues of a *trans*cultural perspective – for all its romanticism – (Shevtsova, 1997, p. 99) and for the value of identifying similarities as well as differences in intercultural performance. For Julie Peters, writing in the collection *Imperialism and Theatre*:

> The critique of productions with universalist overtones fails to acknowledge that communication across distances relies on a recognition not only of differences, but also of samenesses ... when the critique of 'universalism'

extends itself to the critique of all identification of samenesses across distance, the notion of difference itself becomes meaningless.

Peters, 1995, p. 207

This simple dialectic of difference and similarity is helpful in the current context of a global view of Stanislavsky's impact on acting. For although he could not have had any idea of the extent to which his ideas would migrate, relocate and transform across all the major continents of the world (represented here as the Americas, East and South Asia, Australasia, Africa, and Europe) he did nevertheless have a strong sense of the internationalism of his system. This was stimulated by several factors. As Dan Rebellato identifies in his *Theatre and Globalisation*, the end of the nineteenth century was a period of exponential growth in communication and transport and one of the theatrical manifestations of this rapid globalisation was the speed in which premieres of new plays were staged outside a playwright's native country – Ibsen's *A Doll's House* was produced in twelve countries in the first ten years of its life, for example (Rebellato, 2009, p. 20). This 'becoming worldwide of things' (Rebellato, 2009, p. 4), as Rebellato defines the term globalisation, would have been evident to Stanislavsky in his increasingly cosmopolitan correspondence with artists around the world, as well as in the movements of theatre people in and out of Moscow. Visiting Stanislavsky's Moscow Art Theatre (MAT) was a pilgrimage for numerous artists, directors and actors. Sergei Melik-Zhakarov and Shoel Bogatyrev list 28 actors, directors, and artists from ten different countries in their early collection of translated essays (Melik-Zhakarov and Bogatyrev, 1965), all of them moved to describe the influence of the Russian director on their practice. Polish actor, director and teacher, Alexander Zelwerowicz's[2] account is illustrative of the general spirit:

> A young actor and a still younger stage director of the Lodz theatre, I went to Moscow with an express purpose. I went there, to this mecca, well prepared having read studiously everything I could get about the work and character of the Moscow Art Theatre [...] At the end of our talk Stanislavsky asked with the cordiality of a hospitable man whether I would like to stay the rest of the season at the Art Theatre as an associate to supplement the group of about a dozen Russians, Swedes, Bulgarians, Serbs, Germans, Hungarians, and Englishmen who was something like 'assistants' at the Art Theatre at that time.
>
> Melik-Zhakarov and Bogatyrev, 1965, pp. 201–3

In addition to the visitors coming into Russia, the MAT also went abroad, on tour in 1906, 1922, 1923–4 and 1925–6.[3] As Marie-Christine Autant-Mathieu argues: 'During the first quarter of the twentieth century, the Art Theatre had a widespread and diverse influence thanks to its renown, its tours and its diaspora' (Autant-Mathieu, 2014, p. 167).

These natural migrations of the system and its productions must be viewed alongside the altogether more instrumentalist dissemination of Stanislavsky's ideas: the determination of the system as the only state sanctioned approach to deliver Socialist Realism, 'the sole artistic law of the land' (Carnicke, 2014, p. 256), and the subsequent impact on actor training after the Second World War across the Warsaw Pact countries. As I have argued elsewhere (Pitches, 2006, p. 49) Stanislavsky's personal zealotry for the system's internationalisation was uncomfortably aligned with the Soviet state's ideological push to globalize socialism, even though that endorsement came at significant cost in terms of the system's articulation, as Sharon Carnicke has pointed out in several publications (Carnicke, 2009, 2010, 2014).

But while, as Anatoly Smeliansky has suggested, in the last years of his life Stanislavsky 'addressed [his system] to the nation, to the world' (Smeliansky, 1991, p. 13), the Russian practitioner's universalism was more nuanced and differentiated than at first may seem evident. He might have considered 'all nations' to be ripe for systematisation in acting terms but he recognized that there would be necessary local 'adaptations', to use his own acting grammar:

> Let each nation, each people, reflect in its heart its most subtle, national, human traits, and let each art preserve its own national colouring, tones, and distinctive features and let this be the way to disclose the soul of each and every nation.
>
> Stanislavsky, 1968, p. 2

This collection of essays, drawn from the local perspectives of academics and practitioners in seventeen different countries, aims to echo that sentiment, to point out the differences as well (as some of the samenesses) in the system when it migrates over distances Stanislavsky would not have been able to conceive – even with his internationalising urge. In doing so we aim to bring out the 'national colouring and tones' of the cities and countries included in this book, challenging any notion of a single system for all nations. But the essays will also identify what commonality of purpose there is between Stanislavsky's project and the numerous and seemingly antithetical contexts dealt with in *Stanislavsky in the World* (the modern spoken drama of China or the Natyasastra-inspired training in Delhi, for instance).

Such an approach echoes the cultural analysis suggested by David Oswell in his influential *Culture and Society*. 'To study a culture', he argues:

> Means not to analyse the habits, customs, beliefs, ideas and arts in an enclosed and isolated place, but to investigate the connections and disconnections, the circulations and movements, the ups and downs that make a culture a living culture above and beyond its singular location.
>
> Oswell, 2006, p. 9

From Oswell's perspective, Stanislavsky's positioning of the system as a *culture* itself, does nothing to impede an analysis which is both located and migratory. Culture is dynamic, transformative and, if not entirely borderless, certainly fluid in spatial terms. This is a position we share as editors and one which will become evident in each of the ensuing essays.

The system: a case study of cultural transmission?

In histories of actor training questions of transmission are always near to the surface. These have been debated and modelled in different ways: in generational terms (Watson, 2001), in cultural, aesthetic and socio-economic terms (Evans, 2009), in methodological terms (Schechner, 2006), and in political and ideological terms (Kapsali, 2014). But until now the transmission of acting knowledge and skills has not been considered under the interdisciplinary banner of cultural transmission research, perhaps because the latter's roots are in (social) scientific, rather than arts-based, enquiry. This is a missed opportunity. Even though it draws on the disciplines of psychology, sociology, and anthropology, cultural transmission theory offers to 'help clarify how a given culture is maintained or transformed' (Schönpflug, 2009, p. 475), a promising framework in the context introduced above of the *system as a culture itself*. This section will consider whether cultural transmission offers a profitable structure for understanding acting transmission and will introduce some of its key terms to provide a backdrop to the ensuing chapters. This is not to imply that the contributors in this volume would consider themselves researchers in cultural transmission or use the term in their own work but that some of the terminologies associated with the field may help bring definition to the examples of global Stanislavskian transmission below.

Cultural transmission is the passing on of information from person to person *non-genetically*, that is to say by learned processes not inherited ones that include 'imprinting, conditioning, observation, imitation, or as a result of direct teaching (Schönpflug, 2009, p. 24). As such the content of cultural transmission covers a very wide range of possibilities: the transmission of values, skills, knowledge, and behaviours (Schönpflug, 2009, p. 9), either deliberately or unintentionally. From the perspective of Stanislavsky's transmission we might consider all of those categories as being relevant: skills, knowledge, and behaviours, most certainly, but also values. Since the very beginning of the MAT, Stanislavsky's work was imbued with a set of values that remained remarkably consistent over his career. As Benedetti notes in his biography of Stanislavsky, he and Nemirovich, 'agreed to create an ensemble which would place artistic aims above individual vanity' (Benedetti, 1990, p. 61). Along with the pragmatics associated with delivering this vision – longer rehearsal times, respectful analysis of text, detailed character and scenographic work – these were core values for the MAT and have proved to be equally influential in other cultural contexts too – as the system and its ethos migrated abroad.

In the language of cultural transmission there are three kinds of transmission: vertical (parent–offspring), horizontal (peer–peer) and oblique (teacher–mentor) (Schönpflug, 2009, p. 5). In actor training theory *verticality* is less tightly defined and includes generational influence and transmission from an older teacher to a younger tutee, beyond the family – what would be known as oblique transmission in cultural transmission theory (Watson, 2000, p. 6).[4] Setting aside these terminological nuances, what is worth noting is that diachronic (influence over time) and synchronic (simultaneous influence) perspectives often combine and *both* aspects must be considered in any balanced assessment of the processes of transmission. This marriage of historical and contemporary influence has been modelled in business as a 'T-profile', after CEO, Tim Brown's, coining of the term: a combination of depth of skill inherited in training (the down stroke) and openness to collaboration with peers (the cross stroke). Brown argues that too many graduates emerge overly dependent on their inherited or learnt skills and bereft of collaborative capacity in the here-and-now.[5] He is effectively suggesting that the transmission mechanism of direct teaching is too strong (at least for young graduates in North America) and occludes an individual's capacity for peer–peer transmission and exchange.

In the context of *Stanislavsky in the World*, the idea of a T-profile is thought-provoking. It synthesizes past and present and chimes with other ideas such as the balance of tradition and innovation in theatre making. It also brings to the surface the important and often dismissed element of performer training analysis – that the trainee (or transmission recipient) is not (and never could be) a blank slate, shorn of any previous learning. In any skills training the participant is a walking palimpsest of previous teachings, which, either explicitly or implicitly, consciously or unconsciously, play a role in the absorption of new ideas, skills, and behaviours. With its focus on the global transmission of Stanislavsky's ideas this T-shaped hybridity is a notable feature amongst the essays in this collection, but with the added complexity brought about by *intercultural* exchange. Collectively, the contributions in this book illuminate how local practitioners' previous learning and traditions from their home culture (the vertical or oblique) come into contact with new Stanislavskian ideas in the 'here, today, now' – to borrow a term of immediacy from the Stanislavsky lexicon (Merlin, 2015). There is often an imbalance of value in this exchange as old traditions and paradigms of learning are upset by (or merged with) new immigrant ideas. This balance of value can be weighted either way – a recognized need by an indigenous theatre culture to reinvent itself in response to outside influences, or active resistance to the alien imposition of a particular system. And of course there is no guarantee that such facilitative or resistant attitudes are homogenously shared across the group concerned. Richard Schechner has analyzed these forces in terms of 'integrative' and 'disruptive' interculturalism. In the former, 'different cultures work together successfully but can also harmonize different aesthetic, social, and belief systems, creating fusions or hybrids that are whole and unified'. The latter, 'refuses utopian schemes, uncloaks and parodies power relations, and promotes critical ideological perspectives' (Schechner, 2006, p. 304, 310). The extent to which the absorption of embodied principles from another culture might create 'a whole and unified' new product must be up for debate in any context but certainly there are gradations of disruptive and integrative exchange throughout the essays which follow in this book.⁶

The final concept to consider is the idea of 'transmission mechanisms' or 'transmission belts' – 'conditions or factors that enhance transmission' (Schönpflug, 2001, p. 175). In *Russians in Britain* (2011) I formulated these conditions into three categories: training places; theatre spaces; and documentation sources, to try to explain the spread of Russian training into the UK (Pitches, 2011, p. 3). In *Stanislavsky in the World* it is necessary to expand this formulation and also to offer a word of caution. The assumption beneath the idea of 'enhancement' in cultural transmission theory is that the closer the repetition of content is between transmitter and recipient, the better. This linearity is illustrated with reference to the vertical tradition of Noh Training in Japanese theatre, exemplifying a model of 'repetition of cultural practices' (Trommsdorff, 2009, p. 138). But this idealized notion of repetition is seldom realized when embodied ideas of training are being transmitted, even those which fit the vertical model of cultural apprenticeship as closely as Noh training. Indeed in actor training, and in Stanislavskian transmission specifically, *enhancement* of transmission, is not best exemplified in how 'in tact' the form of the training remains but in how effective it is in realising the theatrical aspirations of the local practitioner. Enhancement is thus a signifier of cultural adaptation – what Senelick has translated as 'adjustment' or 'the way in which an actor adjusts to the given circumstances of a stage situation' (Senelick, 2014, p. xiv). Indeed, this idea of adjustment at the level of character (*priposoblenie*) may be scaled up to give us a working analogy for this book as a whole: *Stanislavsky in the World* shows in multiple contexts how the system itself 'adjusts' to local circumstances.

Whilst it remains true that training institutions, performance spaces and documentation are key facilitators of Stanislavskian transmission in the examples which follow, this collection of essays highlights more nebulous 'factors and conditions'. Government policy, national ideology, and local legislation figure strongly as mediators or 'filters', 'which may influence the intensity of the transmission' (Schönpflug and Bilz, 2009, p. 230). The thick residue of empire and colonialism, differing understandings of amateur and professional practice and shifting ideas of national identity, are similarly important. The appropriation of an ill-defined but highly influential 'scientific method' looms large as well – the tradition of laboratory work and of practice-based longitudinal enquiry being absorbed as a working ethos. Perhaps most fundamentally, the inflection of the system by individual pedagogues with their own time-specific understanding of Stanislavsky's practice, itself mediated by other teachers and diverse forms of documentation, is a leitmotif throughout. Such complexity leads not to transmission, as we might understand it from the literature, but to dispersal, migration, and relocation. As such Stanislavsky's system may be one of the most provocative and generative of case-studies from the perspective of cultural transmission as it illustrates so many of its limitations and challenges as a theoretical domain.

The structure of the book

Decisions relating to structure are unavoidably invidious – we need only to consider the (not unreasonable) criticisms of Patrice Pavis's *Intercultural Performance Reader* (1996), based on a pivot of 'Intercultural Performance from the Western Point of View' (Part II) and 'Intercultural Performance from Another Point of View' (Part III) (Pavis, 1996, pp. v–vi).[7] In this book we have tried to evoke the dispersal, migration, and relocation of Stanislavsky by assembling it in the order of the system's transmission history as it is evidenced in the essays, maintaining geographical borders and country associations as sections for clarity and navigability. Thus we begin with Europe with five essays ranging from Northern Europe (Lithuania) to Western Europe (France), to Southern Europe (Italy, Malta, and Greece). This is not to imply any postcolonial priority to the work emerging in this continent but to mark it as the first site of transmission (after the MAT tour in 1906 discussed above). We move then to China and Japan, the transmission dated to Osanai Kaoru's founding of the Stanislavsky-inspired Free Stage (Jiyu Gekijo) in Tokyo in 1909. Our third section is Latin America (Cuba, Brazil, and Argentina) marked by the arrival of Polish director and actor trainer, Zbigniew Ziembinski, to Brazil in 1941. Section four identifies routes of transmission in Africa (in the far North, Tunisia; in the West, Nigeria and in the Far South, South Africa). Here the marker point is the founding of Ibadan University in

1948 then as a college of London University, creating the ground for Stanislavsky-influenced productions in the mid-1950s. Hayes Gordon's arrival in Australia in 1952 established what has since become a deep and institutionalized appropriation of Stanislavsky on the huge island, in contrast to the blended biculturalism expounded in the essay on Stanislavsky in Aotearoa. There are three essays in the fifth section: Australasia. Finally, in the sixth section we conclude with India and Bangladesh using the first experimentation with Stanislavsky at the National School Drama in the 1959 curriculum as a historical anchor point. Each section of the book is headed with a short introduction by one of the editors pointing out productive connections and collisions amongst the essays.

This structure does not claim to represent a definitive historical tracing of Stanislavsky's global transmission – if indeed that were ever possible. Even these dates, based solely on the materials we have gathered here and intentionally not drawing on other histories, indicate the challenges of doing so, based as they are on such different transmission mechanisms: international tours, individual mediators, institutional beginnings, and published curricula. But in arranging things in this manner we do hope to build a cumulative picture of the extent to which the system has migrated from its first home in Moscow, a city which, appropriately, seems to occupy a contingent space in the often binary constructions of the world and its cultures.

Ironically, then, for all Stanislavsky's universalising tendencies it is the pluralism of the system that presents itself so palpably through the pages of this book. This diversity does not constitute any kind of dilution of an archetypal or original system, as such a unitary system does not and never has existed – witness the many revisions Stanislavsky himself contemplated. But it does symbolize the continued currency of the system *as a living culture,* by definition thriving in its own immediate surroundings.

Notes

1 Which is not to imply that the Russian version is without its flaws. See Laurence Senelick's introduction to Jean Benedetti's translation of the 1926 version (Stanislavski, 2008a, pp. xiii–xxv) for details.

2 The National Academy of Dramatic Art in Warsaw, Poland, is now named after Zelwerowicz (1877–1955), after he founded the State Institute of Theatrical Arts in 1932.
3 To Germany (Berlin), Czechoslovakia (Prague), Austria (Vienna), and Poland in 1906; to Europe again, taking in Paris in 1922, on the way to the famous tour of the United States in 1923 and 1924; and to the US East coast for the almost forgotten Musical Studio trip, headed by Nemirovich-Danchenko from December 1925–May 1926 (Autant-Mathieu, 2014, pp. 157–78).
4 Horizontalism, though not mentioned by Watson explicitly, is understood in the same terms as cultural transmission theory suggests (cf. Pitches et al., 2011).
5 http://chiefexecutive.net/ideo-ceo-tim-brown-t-shaped-stars-the-backbone-of-ideoae™s-collaborative-culture/ [accessed 29 February 2016].
6 Schechner suggests Suzuki Tadashi from Japan, Chandralekha from India, and Phillip Glass from the USA, as examples of integrative interculturalism (Schechner, 2006, p. 306).
7 See Lo and Gilbert, 2002, p. 37.

References

Autant-Mathieu, M. C. (2014), 'The journey of the Moscow Art Theatre and its Disciples through Europe and the United States (1906 to 1937): Dissemination of an Acting Theory and Work method', in *The Routledge Companion to Stanislavsky*, ed. R. A. White. Abingdon: Routledge.

Benedetti, J. (1990), *Stanislavski: a Biography*. London: Methuen.

Bharucha, R. (1993), *Theatre and the World: Performance and the Politics of Culture*. London: Routledge.

Carnicke, S. M. (2009), *Stanislavsky in Focus*. Abingdon: Routledge.

Carnicke, S. M. (2010), 'Stanislavsky and Politics: Active Analysis and the American Legacy of Soviet Oppression', in *The Politics of American Actor Training*, eds E. Margolis and L. T. Renaud. Abingdon: Routledge.

Carnicke, S. M. (2014), 'The Effects of Russian and Soviet Censorship on the Practice of Stanislavsky's System', in *The Routledge Companion to Stanislavsky*, ed. R. A. White. Abingdon: Routledge.

Evans, M. (2009), *Movement Training for the Modern Actor*. Abingdon: Routledge.

Kapsali, M. (ed.) (2014), *Theatre, Dance and Performance Training Special Issue: Training, Politics and Ideology*. Abingdon: Routledge.

Knowles, R. (2010), *Theatre and Interculturalism*. Basingstoke: Palgrave.

Lo, J. and Gilbert, H. (2002), 'Toward a Topography of Cross-Cultural Theatre Praxis', *TDR*, Vol. 46, No. 3: 31–53.

Marranca, B. and Dasgupta, G. (1991), *Interculturalism and Performance: Writings from PAJ*. New York: PAJ Publications.

Melik-Zhakarov, S. and Bogatyrev, S. (1965), *Konstantin Stanislavsky*. Moscow: Progress Publishers.

Merlin, B. (2014), 'Here, Today, Now: Active Analysis for the twenty-first century Actor', in *The Routledge Companion to Stanislavsky*, ed. R. A. White. Abingdon: Routledge.

Oswell, D. (2006), *Culture and* Society. London: Sage.

Pavis, P. (ed.) (1996), *The Intercultural Performance Reader*. London: Routledge.

Peters, J. (1995), 'Intercultural Performance, Theatre Anthropology and the Imperialist Critique: Identities, Inheritances and Neo-orthodoxies', in *Imperialism and Theatre: Essays in World Theatre, Drama and Performance*, ed. J. Ellen Gainor. London: Routledge.

Pitches, J. (2006), *Science and the Stanislavsky Tradition*. Abingdon: Routledge.

Pitches, J. (ed.) (2011), *Russians in Britain: British Theatre and the Russian Tradition of Acting*. Abingdon: Routledge.

Pitches, J., Murray, S., Worth, L., Poynor, H., Richmond, D. and Dorey Richmond, J. (2011), 'Performer Training: Researching in the Theatre Laboratory', in *Research Methods in Theatre Studies*, eds B. Kershaw and H. Nicholson. Edinburgh: University of Edinburgh Press.

Rebellato, D. (2009), *Theatre and Globalisation*. Basingstoke: Palgrave.

Schechner, R. (2006), *Performance Studies: an Introduction*. Abingdon: Routledge.

Schönpflug, U. (2001), 'Intergenerational Transmission of Values: The Role of Transmission Belts', *Journal of Cross-Cultural Psychology*, Vol. 32, No. 2: 174–85.

Schönpflug, U. (ed.) (2009), *Cultural Transmission: Psychological, Developmental, Social, and Methodological Aspects*. Cambridge: Cambridge University Press.

Schönpflug, U. and Bilz, L. (2009), 'The Transmission Process: Mechanisms and Contexts', in *Cultural Transmission: Psychological, Developmental, Social, and Methodological Aspects*, ed. U. Schönpflug. Cambridge: Cambridge University Press.

Senelick, L. (ed. and trans.) (2014), *Stanislavsky – A Life in Letters*. Abingdon: Routledge.

Shevtsova, M. (1997), 'Interculturalism, Aestheticism, Orientalism: Starting from Peter Brook's Mahabharata', *Theatre Research International*, Vol. 22, No. 2: 98–104.

Smeliansky, A. (1991). 'The Last Decade: Stanislavski and Stalinism', *Theater*, Vol. 12, No. 2: 71–3.

Stanislavski, C. (1968), *Stanislavski's Legacy*, trans. E. Hapgood. London; Methuen.
Stanislavski, K. (2008a), *My Life in Art*, trans. J. Benedetti. Abingdon: Routledge.
Stanislavski, K. (2008b), *An Actor's Work*, trans. J. Benedetti. Abingdon: Routledge.
Trommsdorff, G. (2009), 'Intergenerational Relations and Cultural Transmission', in *Cultural Transmission: Psychological, Developmental, Social, and Methodological Aspects*, ed. U. Schönpflug. Cambridge: Cambridge University Press.
Watson, I. (ed.) (2001), *Performer Training: Developments Across Cultures*. London: Routledge.

Part One

Europe

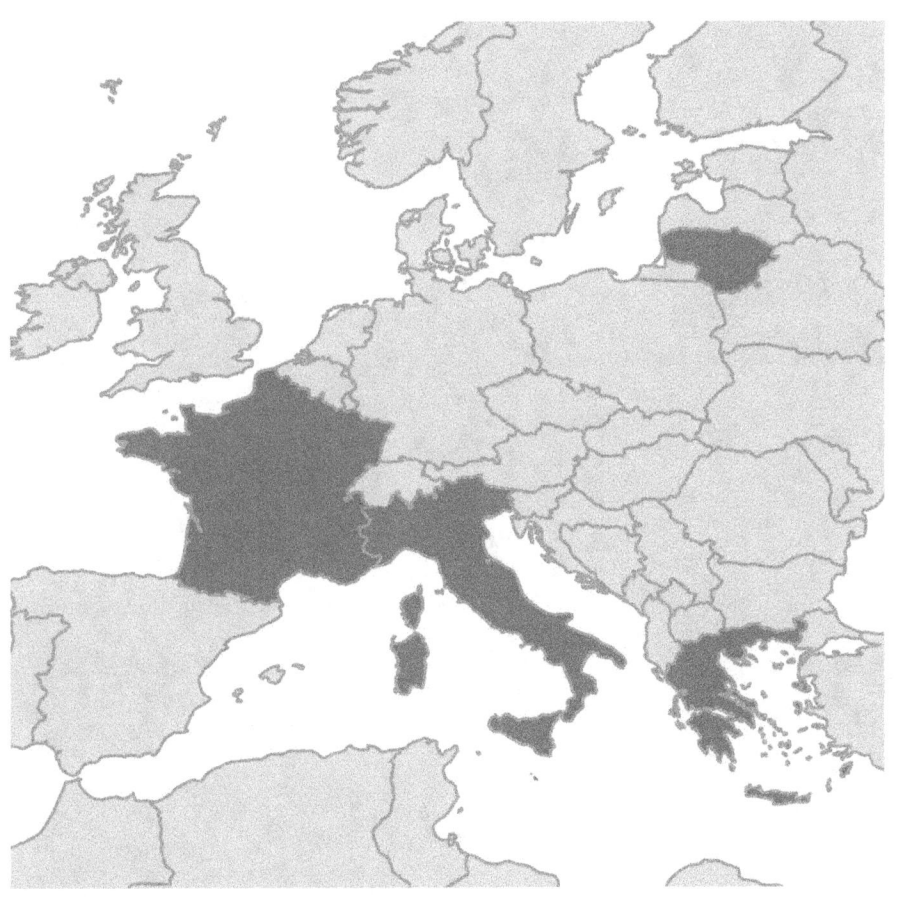

Figure 2 Stanislavsky in Europe.

Part One: Introduction

Stefan Aquilina

Contextualization of tradition and transmission processes

The essays in this Part about the transmission of Stanislavskian practices in Europe offer an insightful reminder of the role which contextualization has in the study of theatre and performance. This is not to say, of course, that contextual considerations are pertinent only to the five case-studies collated here. An effort to situate a practice within its context is a recurring motif in this volume, as contextual considerations become necessary when unpicking the creation of hybrid forms (see, for a clear example, how elements from Stanislavsky's system have been synthesized in New Zealand with Māori customs – Part Five). The European essays found here, however, do manifest to different degrees the four frames which Thomas Postlewait identifies when he problematizes historiographical contextualization, namely the relationships which a particular theatre phenomenon has with its surrounding world(s), agents, reception, and artistic heritage (Postlewait, 2009, pp. 11–18). The case-studies in question tackle the diffusion and implementation of Stanislavsky's system in France (by Marie-Christine Autant-Mathieu), Italy (Franco Ruffini), Lithuania (Ina Pukelytė), Malta (Stefan Aquilina) and Greece (Maria Gaitanidi).

Public and peer reception, for example, are central to Autant-Mathieu's essay on Stanislavsky in France, where she discusses the reaction which Stanislavsky and the Moscow Art Theatre received in Paris during the 1922–4 tours. The essay draws attention to what happens when two theatre and acting traditions encounter each other. In heading the tours, Stanislavsky was not only serving as the leader of a troupe in search of greener pastures and better work conditions, but also as a representative of the Russian tradition of psychological realism. In fact, Stanislavsky consistently 'reaffirm[ed] his intention of continuing in the path laid down by Shchepkin. In doing so he placed himself firmly side by side with Gogol, Ostrovski and the Realist tradition' (Benedetti, 1982, p. 11). On the other hand, French acting practice as theorized upon by Diderot and developed by such actors as Coquelin and Sarah Bernhardt was cultivated into a parallel tradition, one that stressed how 'acting was essentially a rationalistic process, a study of the technical means for obtaining a graceful depiction of idealized reality' (Carlson, 1984, p. 162). It is this acting tradition that Autant-Mathieu underlines when she quotes Coquelin's statement that art is representation rather than identification (p. 68), to show how the MAT's tours were confronting a context that was already defined by a rich artistic tradition of its own.

The encounter between the Russian realistic tradition and the French tradition of technical playing produced a stalemate. Techniques practiced in the two contexts were ill-suited for mutual transmission. Therefore, the longstanding tradition of French theatre leads Autant-Mathieu to assert that the system and its development 'had little lasting impact on French theatre practice' (p. 63). This particular case-study of Stanislavsky in France, however, does draw attention to the more liminal and perhaps unstable end of transmission, one which is less inclined to foreground technique but which heightens the more 'attitudinal' aspects to training. I use 'attitudinal' in the way that Robert M. Gagnè places 'attitudes' as one of the five varieties of what can be learned, the others being intellectual skills, cognitive strategies, verbal information, and motor skills. Training in attitudes fits with difficulty in such criteria as 'learning outcomes', 'aims and objectives', and 'learning assessments', because it is ingrained in nuance and subtlety rather than clear-cut schemas. Examples include training in the 'attitude of precision', the 'attitude of carefulness', 'competition', 'compromise', and so on (Gagnè, 1977, p. 232). Stanislavsky's and the MAT's influence on French theatre was similarly attitudinal rather than technical or aesthetic and, according to Autant-Mathieu, underscored ethics and the organization of a troupe as an ensemble rather than Emotion Memory, Concentration, Characterization or any other aspect of the system as practiced in the early 1920s.

The French case also draws attention to another aspect of tradition building, namely the issue of validation that arises in being associated with carefully chosen theatre agents. Ethics and ensemble were qualities which Jacques Copeau was searching for himself at the Vieux-Colombier (Evans, 2006, p. 45). Juxtaposing Stanislavsky's and the MAT's models with Copeau's own research suggests that in his endorsement of Stanislavsky, Copeau was also underlining his own practices and attempts to bring to the theatre of his time a renewed energy and focus. This is evidenced by John Rudlin and Norman H. Paul, who argue that Copeau wrote his manifesto for an acting school '[w]ith the model of Stanislavsky's Moscow Art Theatre in mind' (Rudlin and Paul, 1990, p. 3).[1] The desire to validate one's practice by linking it to the Stanislavsky's acting tradition resurfaces also in my own essay about Stanislavsky in Malta. Interviews with several Maltese theatre-makers – which have been indispensable to tackle a context whose theatre and performing arts histories have not been researched yet with the rigour required – show various examples of practitioners who reference Stanislavsky's name in order to consolidate their own intuitions about acting and theatre. Such consolidation is important because, although a professional ethos as a necessary condition for skill and quality is starting to (slowly) seep in, the majority of theatre practice in Malta is still predominantly amateur in nature.

The case-study on Stanislavsky in Malta has other parallels with that of Lithuania: both essays tackle the role which theatre institutions have in tradition building and transmission processes. Jaan Whitehead offers a helpful rationalization of theatre institutions, in which he underlines the role which they play in shaping theatre practitioners and the reception of their work: 'the theatre institutions we create are not a neutral means for doing this [connecting with audiences], [and] [...] the institutes themselves affect not only what art is presented to what audience but which artists create the art and how it relates to the wider community' (Whitehead, 2002, p. 232). The absence of stable and large-scale theatre institutions in Malta has prevented holistic applications of the system, with theatre-makers having no option but to exercise a sense of reductionism to Stanislavsky's training models wherein very specific elements of work (e.g. Imagination and Emotion Memory) are highlighted over others. Such reductionism is a contextual necessity when one contends with short rehearsal times, as is still the case in Malta.

Lithuania, on the other hand, can be situated on the other end of the institutionalization line: if theatre institutions in Malta were absent, in

Lithuania they pervaded theatrical consciousness. Postlewait argues that a necessary factor when contextualizing a theatre practice involves a consideration with surrounding political milieus (Postlewait, 2009, pp. 195–222). What is 'political' is conceived here to include social life in its broadness, ranging from the minuscule power games which people engage in as part of their daily life, to the 'higher realms' (Lefebvre, 2008, p. 45) of political institutions that are responsible for the running of the economic, educational, military, diplomatic, and cultural spheres of a nation. Whilst turn of the twenty-first century globalization critiques narrow definitions of nationhood that focus on *zeitgeist* and its accentuation of difference, Lithuania's search for a National theatre institution – boosted by the work of personalities like Andrius Oleka-Žilinskas and Balys Sruoga – found in Stanislavsky a theatre vehicle on which the 'vivid affair of our life, coming out from our conditions of life and of our experiences' (Sruoga quoted on p. 88) could be constructed. In the second part of her essay Pukelytė then argues that an ideological application of Stanislavsky's system in Lithuania was fuelled by the (Lithuanian and Soviet) state-sanctioned training which a number of Lithuanian theatre-makers received at GITIS (The Russian Academy of Dramatic Art).[2] Such training took place after the Second World War when Lithuania was incorporated in the USSR, and depended on models that drew explicitly from Soviet interpretations of Stanislavsky.

The case of Stanislavsky in Italy offers a different reading, or rather application, of contextualization. In Italy, Stanislavsky became entangled in cultural rather than political and ideological issues. With the figure of the Director emerging later in Italy than it did in other European contexts, Stanislavsky's persona fuelled a discussion on director–actor relationships and their respective positioning within theatre hierarchies. However, beyond narrow studies about Stanislavsky, Ruffini's essay also offers one exemplification of what I refer to as 'artistic contextualization', i.e. the creation of a snapshot or map of concurrent artistic practices.[3] Italian scholars such as Gerardo Guerrieri, Fabrizio Cruciani, and Ferdinando Taviani can be seen to adopt artistic contextualization as a tool to deconstruct the mythology surrounding the system (see Part One Well-trodden Paths).[4] Ruffini's essay is rich in detail, and describes the 1960 court case in Bari that questioned the reach of Elizabeth Reynolds copyright claims on Stanislavsky's books. However, the exposition on the court case serves as a prelude to other Italian readings of Stanislavsky which took place, roughly, from the 1980s onwards, wherein Stanislavsky was treated as one voice within the much broader picture of twentieth-century theatre, and hence contextualized in 'a space next to deserving others, a small entry but within a large world' (p. 53).

The essay about Greece also draws on Stanislavsky's contextualization within what in Italy has been referred to as the twentieth-century theatre tradition but which the English speaking world calls modern theatre and performance (Milling and Ley, 2000). Maria Gaitinidi, in fact, notes that some recurring principles can be discerned between early Modern Greek theatre-makers and Stanislavsky, without, however, the former having any knowledge of the Russian's work. Among these recurring principles Gaitinidi discusses the role of the actor as creator and the contrast between detailed naturalism and emotional realism. Both principles are evidenced in the work of Thomas Oikonomou and Fotis Politis. Underlining the recurrence of these principles in two disparate contexts such as modern theatre in Russia and in Greece has two advantages. First, attention is drawn to their role in paving the way for the implementation of the system in Greece, which Gaitinidi credits to Karolos Koun and his formation of Theatro Technis on the MAT's ensemble model. Secondly, highlighting recurring principles between different modern theatre contexts accentuates the awareness that, while turn of the twentieth-century theatre practitioners often presented their ideas in short and polemic manifestos that argued in favour of what they felt were unique contributions to the theatre world, the benefit of hindsight allows an alternative focus on what brought these practitioners and theorists closer to each other, on their points of convergence:

> For contemporary observers in the 1920s, or even in the 1960s, what is central was often obscured by the rhetoric of manifestos claiming uniqueness. But from today's perspective shared concerns stand out clearly because they recur. And this recurrence is even more significant since, although it is obviously a response to the ethics of the age it by no means reflects popularly accepted ideas or the dominant ideological assumptions.
>
> Innes, 2004, p. 2

Discerned here is a balance between case-specific investigations and a broader thinking that shifts attention to that which, though invariably coloured by specific, context-based factors, can be seen to recur to some degree or other, and is, therefore, common and shared. The transmission of Stanislavskian practices across a number of borders such as those evident on the European continent therefore chimes with readings that are both context sensitive but also attentive to bigger theatre pictures.

Notes

1. See also Copeau's letter to Stanislavsky where he called him 'my master' (quoted in Rudlin, 1986, p. xiii).
2. Pukelytė refers to GITIS as the State Institute for Arts (p. 97). For a brief reference to the use of GITIS as the appellation for this training context see Brown, 2013, p. 177.
3. The term 'artistic contextualization' draws from Postlewait's fourth and final consideration when unpicking context, namely that of 'artistic heritage' (Postlewait, 2009, p. 14). It is being suggested here as an alternative to Postlewait's term because 'artistic contextualization' looks at connections between contemporaneous rather than with historical and inherited precedents.
4. Moez Mrabet's essay on Stanislavsky in Tunisia also hints at contextualization as a possible tool to critique and deepen one's understanding of a theatre reality (see Introduction to Part Four).

References

Benedetti, J. (1982), *Stanislavski: An Introduction*. London: Methuen.

Brown, B. (2013), 'As Important as Blood and Shelter: Extending *studiinost* into *obshchnost*', in *Encountering Ensemble*, ed. J. Britton. London: Bloomsbury, pp. 172–81.

Carlson, M. (1984), *Theories of the Theatre*. New York: Cornell University Press.

Evans, M. (2006), *Jacques Copeau*. London: Routledge.

Gagnè, R. M. (1977), *The Conditions of Learning*. New York: Holt, Rinehart and Winston.

Innes, C. (2004), *Avant Garde Theatre: 1892–1992 2nd Edition*. London and New York: Routledge.

Lefebvre, H. (2008), *Critique of Everyday Life Vol. 2*. trans. G. Elliot. London: Verso.

Milling, J. and Ley, G. (2000), *Modern Theories of Performance*. Basingstoke: Palgrave Macmillan.
Postlewait, T. (2009), *The Cambridge Introduction to Theatre Historiography*. Cambridge: Cambridge University Press.
Rudlin, J. (1986), *Jacques Copeau*. Cambridge: Cambridge University Press.
Rudlin, J. and Paul, N. H. (eds) (1990), *Copeau: Texts on Theatre*. London and New York: Routledge.
Stanislavski, K. (2008), *My Life in Art*, trans. J. Benedetti. Oxon: Routledge.
Whitehead, J. (2002), 'Art Will Out', in *The American Theatre Reader*, ed. The Staff of the American Theatre Magazine. New York: Theatre Communication Group.

1

Three Periods of Stanislavsky in Italy

Franco Ruffini

The diffusion of Stanislavsky in Italy can be analysed in three periods. The first period is between the arrival of Tatiana Pavlova, at the beginning of the 1920s, and 1956. This period is characterized by Stanislavsky's 'science', real or presumed, and the problem of theatre direction. The second period is between 1956, the year of the first Italian edition of *Lavoro dell'attore* (*An Actor's Work*), and 1968. These are the years when the real tradition of Stanislavsky was confronted. Gerardo Guerrieri was without doubt the main protagonist here, and Italy has to be credited for bringing, for the first time and internationally, this fundamental problem of Stanislavsky's tradition to the attention of theatre research and practice.[1] The third period starts from 1968, the year of *Towards a Poor Theatre* when, thanks to the awareness that had matured and to Grotowski, Stanislavsky is rethought in light of the great theatre tradition of the twentieth century.

1922–56: Stanislavsky's 'science'

In his *Tramonto del grande attore* (The Twilight of the Star Actor), Silvio d'Amico (1929) foretold the advent of what would become theatre direction. D'Amico wrote in contraposition but also resigned nostalgia to that brilliant disorder which had given Italian theatre its vitality, but also its misery. Direction was then moving towards a sometimes inglorious normalization, at least in the countries where it had emerged. In Italy, three more years had to elapse before the term *regia* (direction) was even coined by the linguist Bruno Migliorini.

The Italian problem concerning theatre direction is very complex because it is intertwined with other theatrical and socio-political issues. Whether it was because of the star actors, or the way theatre companies were organized, or even the fascist ideology, the fact remains that theatre direction entered Italy much later than it did in the rest of Europe and, as a result, in different ways.[2] In Italy, theatre direction was linked to organic life – of the actor's body and of the performance – which called for a system of norms through which it could be shared and taught.

Stanislavsky, for whom direction was only the name given to a broader pedagogy towards life on stage, was longed for and welcomed as the creator of a science. Which science, however? Was it the science of the actor or of theatre direction? The aim during these years was to answer these questions through an understanding of Stanislavsky. Two phases can be discerned: before and after the books. The transition from one to the other is located to the years between 1934 and 1936, the years when, respectively, *Ma vie dans l'Art* (*My Life in Art*) and *An Actor Prepares* were published. The former was translated from the Russian edition while the latter constituted the American version of the first part of *Lavoro dell'attore su se stesso* (*An Actor's Work on Himself*). The beginning of this phase coincided with the European and American tours of the Moscow Art Theatre (1922–4), which solicited and provided a first direct evaluation of Stanislavsky's legend.

Stanislavsky before the books

Tatiana Pavlova arrived in Italy in what is generally recorded as 1922. As she herself acknowledged, she was not Stanislavsky's direct student, but was aware of and shared his understanding of theatre. At least, this is what she asserted and what was believed. Pavlova gave rise to a debate about direction, through her acting rehearsals and as a director *ante litteram* and through the promotion given by her collaborator, the Russian Giacomo Lvov. For many years she became the obligatory reference point for theatre direction.[3] Following d'Amico's book and Migliorini's coinage of the term, direction became the flag training at the Accademia d'Arte Drammatica (The Academy of Dramatic Art). This Academy was founded in 1935 on the instigation of d'Amico, who also served as its director. Pavlova was a teacher during the Academy's first three years, where she was considered the repository of Stanislavsky's science, whatever that was.

In 1931 Pavlova invited Vladimir Nemirovich-Danchenko to Italy to direct her company in a production of Danchenko's own play *Il Valore della vita* (Life's Worth). This was seen as an opportunity to acquire direct knowledge of the Art Theatre but also, and more importantly, of Stanislavsky. In this way it was possible to understand Stanislavsky's science and its nature.

The expectations behind this visit were as high as the unsatisfactory results generated. In a long 1931 interview, in actual fact an uninterrupted monologue, Danchenko retold the history of the Art Theatre from its very inception. He presented himself as holier than the Pope, notwithstanding the problems which had underlined his life with Stanislavsky. Theatre was 'life itself', with a mission to represent human souls. He often repeated that the actor is the king of the theatre, before the playwright, the mise-en-scène, and the director. If Stanislavsky was master of a science, then this science was the actor's. This was considered a meagre result, because the expectation was that Danchenko would have detailed ways to limit the actor's sovereignty.[4]

D'Amico tried in vain to shift Danchenko towards direction. In an earlier meeting they had in Berlin, Danchenko had already reiterated that the king of the theatre was the actor. The director's task was to disappear behind the interpreter's performance if the actor has indeed arrived to that state where the words of a part are 'believed' to have become his own. D'Amico, understandably, insisted in asking for a definition of the director's work: is he the creator of performance or the interpreter of texts? Danchenko replied that the director was none of these, as he is only the actor's servant. D'Amico had no other option but to conclude that, at the end of the day, every theory is limited to the expression of a partial truth (d'Amico, 1931).[5]

To interrogate again the nature and role of the director attention was reverted to the person who was considered Stanislavsky's official ambassador in Italy – Pavlova. By 1934 the director had emerged, through this Pavlova channel, as a despot who reduces to his own personality the content and spirit of a text, and who essentially conceives the performance as a visual choreography. This is the director who harmonizes all theatrical elements and who is an active collaborator of the author (Casella, 1934). Was this Stanislavsky's science of theatre direction? Such a conception of theatre direction marked the official training which Pavlova opened a year later.

Whatever it was, this was not what Stanislavsky had developed. Clearly, this was only a conception with nothing of the day-to-day practical complexities and consistent challenges which the mature Stanislavsky developed to guide the actor through a technical and inner exercise that, at the same time, rendered the participant worthy of dominating the stage, including the director.

Stanislavsky after the books

The publication of Stanislavsky's books allowed the verification of those concepts which had been attributed to him. In 1937, Paolo Milano – a then noted literary critic and journalist in d'Amico's circle – published the first extended summary of Stanislavsky. Milano quoted and commented upon extracts from *Ma vie dans l'Art* and *An Actor Prepares*. Stanislavsky's autobiography was first published in 1924 in its first American edition, but this does not seem to have generated any interest in Italy. More than the fact that it was translated from Russian, or that it featured an introduction by Copeau, the attention on the autobiography was probably solicited because it could be read alongside the account on the system in *An Actor Prepares*, even though the latter was limited to the first part of Stanislavsky's book and in the dubious American translation. Milano immediately clarified the previous dilemma about the work of the actor and, consequently, the director's role. There is no conflict between the director and the actor, as the matter is one of priority. Milano opened with Stanislavsky's crisis 'on a rock in Finland', from which the fundamental distinction between the 'creative state' and the 'actor's state' is taken. Stanislavsky's approach is thus configured as a preparation for the actor to believe in what he does and say on the stage as if these were true. What follows is that training cannot be solely technical or physical, but also psychological and spiritual. The greatest among Stanislavsky's discoveries is that the body and soul are intimately linked. Or more than a discovery, a verification, because the great actors of the Italian tradition intuitively knew of this link without, however, articulating it. Stanislavsky's approach was invested – as he himself asserted – in reaching their intuition through a conscious exercise.

Milano (1937) also faced the dilemma between experiencing and technique. Or, to put it in another way, between Stanislavsky and Diderot, placed face to face as two contrasting scientists of the actor's art. In the next three years, the journal *Il Dramma* (The Drama) would host a debate on what were known as the 'imitative' and cold actor on one side and the 'natural' and temperamental actor on the other, between the actor who feigns emotional experiencing and the actor who experiences the emotions that he theatricalizes on the stage (*Il Dramma*, 1940).

The debate was resolved in 1940, when the director Nicola De Pirro defined theatre direction as the work of an artist who penetrates the text 'line by line' in order to render it in 'its proper light' on stage (De Pirro quoted in Meldolesi, 1987, p. 117). This position can be substantially traced to d'Amico, who introduced such a position at the Academy and in a paragraph on the Moscow Art Theatre in his *Storia del teatro drammatico* (History of the Dramatic Theatre, 1940). In fact, d'Amico credited Stanislavsky with the fundamental disciplining of the actor's excessive power, by putting him at the service of the drama's spirit and under the director's guidance.

Figure 3 Silvio d'Amico and Vittorio Gassmann in 1952.
© Accademia d'Arte Drammatica.

The Second World War muted any cultural debate. In 1947, the Piccolo Teatro was inaugurated in Milan at a time when the Actors Studio was emerging in America. The book *La regia teatrale* (Theatre Direction, 1947), edited by Silvio d'Amico, was also published. It was time for a balance. Among the most important contributions in d'Amico's book was an eponymous entry by Ettore Lo Gatto on the Moscow Art Theatre. Lo Gatto was a passionate Slavic scholar whose contribution followed Milano's by ten years. He also offered a detailed analysis of the so-called Stanislavsky's 'system', starting from the 'creative condition' as the system's central motor. Lo Gatto also tackled the second part of *Lavoro dell' Attore* (*An Actor's Work*), on character work, which, it has to be reiterated, was still unavailable in American translation.

The year 1953 was an important one for the understanding of Stanislavsky in Italy. This was when Gerardo Guerrieri published an article on *Attualità di Stanislavskij* (Stanislavsky Today) in which he spoke explicitly of Stanislavsky's 'science of the actor'. An important contribution of Guerrieri was that he removed Stanislavsky from the sterile counter-positioning to Diderot. In the same magazine (Guerrieri, 1953) three reviews of Russian books were also published. Particularly important was the one on Vasily Osopovich Toporkov's book *Il sistema di Stanislavskij durante le prove. Ricordi* (Stanislavsky in Rehearsal: The Final Years), edited by Pietro Zveteremich. This volume is considered till this day as the most significant volume on the direct transmission of the 'method of physical action', an approach that can be considered beyond the system but within the holistic trajectory of Stanislavsky's research.[6]

At this point it is clear that the debate on Stanislavsky has developed on the direct knowledge of his books and of those who had witnessed directly his work. Symptomatic of this development was a 1953 colloquium held in Germany on Stanislavsky. The then prevalent ideology was juxtaposing Stanislavsky not to Diderot but to German playwrights. In preparing for the colloquium Brecht 'invited directors, dramaturges and a number of actors to his home. On the table there was a heap of publications by and on Stanislavsky'. When asked questions about Stanislavsky, Brecht always underlined that only a limited number of books were available and that, moreover, these were often unreliable, to the extent that he could not answer concretely the questions that were posed to him (Brecht, 1975, p. 227).

1956–68: The Stanislavsky tradition

Stanislavsky's productions as an actor and director are described and commented upon in his books in a way that they seem to make the main argument. But this is only in appearance, because when laid down on paper, these productions are detached from their ephemeral dimension and assigned a permanent one. For Stanislavsky, the stage was the site of time which passes, while the books were the site of time that endures, and an experience that transforms into a tradition. Stanislavsky's tradition – including the performances staged – is the tradition of his books.

This is particularly the case with *La mia vita nell'arte* and *Il lavoro dell'attore su se stesso*, even if the latter is often limited to the first part on the 'art of experiencing'. Stanislavsky died in 1938 without seeing the publication of the second part on the process of embodiment. The question about the nature of Stanislavsky's tradition is a question of which books did he actually write. This is not a rhetorical question because two versions exist of Stanislavsky's books, the American and Russian ones.

Stanislavsky's tradition becomes a problem when these two versions are considered the same, as current studies tacitly do. The problem is more than a philological one, and it is necessary to frame it around certain details.

Stanislavsky's books

At the end of his autobiography, Stanislavsky compared himself to a gold digger who extracts grains of precious minerals from tons of sand. These grains, Stanislavsky concluded, were nothing but the 'so-called "system"' (Stanislavskij, 2009, p. 410).[7] This was the problem which Stanislavsky faced as a writer: how can my knowledge be organized without it being reduced to a system? The 'so-called' and the quotation marks were intended to exorcize the danger of turning his grains into cooking recipes, which occurs when their use is not backed by research.

Stanislavsky started facing this problem in 1906, the year of that faithful 'rock in Finland', when he started writing *A Draft Manual for Dramatic Art* (Benedetti, 1982, p. 30). This draft manual remained unpublished, as he prohibited recipes even to himself. Years later, and riding on the wave of the

First Studio's success (1912–16), there were others who published on the 'system', with limited knowledge and without his explicit consent. It became urgent for Stanislavsky to start writing himself. He understood the need, but initially he did not know how to carry out the task. With this problem in mind, he set off on the 4 September 1922 for the Euro-American tour. After a stop in Paris, where Copeau delivered a speech in his honour, he arrived in New York in January 1923. A second American tour started in November 1923. On the 20 March 1924 he was received, with the rest of the Moscow Art Theatre, by President Coolidge.

The productions' success demanded a book for the American market. Stanislavsky returned to his worry, but his proposal for a book on the system was rejected. He was told that the public wanted an autobiography dense with the artist's aura. Stanislavsky was not interested in this, but he was not in a position to refuse. He was in urgent need of hard currency to support his son Igor's treatment in a Swiss sanatorium. The Soviet Union had not signed the International Convention on author's rights and, therefore, he could not collect royalties for the foreign sales of his books, despite his fame which would have guaranteed the book's wide circulation. The only option was to publish in America. This was a book he never expected to write. He took this American option but then resorted to less improvisatory plans for other publications. These would be properly planned, as we will see.

The team working on this first project was both eclectic and ambiguous. It was formed as follows: a demotivated author who was dictating to his secretary; a Russian émigré – Aleksandr Koiransky – on whom little is known but who, on his own admission, helped the selection and systematization of the material; J. J. Robbins, a self-styled student of the Russian actor Aleksandr Lensky and of Richard Boleslavsky, who translated the texts as he received them. It seems that some pages of the book were actually written by Koiransky. In any case, *My Life in Art* was published in April 1924.[8] Apart from the income generated, Stanislavsky was unhappy. Even the sequence of the events in the book was hurried and incorrect, conditioned by the needs of a public with whom he was unfamiliar, as unfamiliar was the English language itself. Even during the voyage home Stanislavsky started restructuring the text for a Russian edition. He continued to do this with the competent and passionate Liubov Gurevich, a friend and critic, as well as a theatre scholar. Some parts were removed, others rewritten, new parts added, the order of the chapters was settled, certain anecdotes eliminated and critical reflections added instead. The work continued till the first months of 1926 and the book was then published in the September.

Stanislavsky himself confirmed that the Russian edition was much more than a simple translation of the American version. In a correspondence with Karl Kersten, who was asking permission for a German edition, Stanislavsky was as early as September 1924 exercising the veto and saying that the Russian edition was close to completion. That edition would cover the artistic problems in more depth. The same answer was given to Gaston Gallimard in 1928.[9]

While they do have the same title and the same author's name appears on their covers, one cannot in any way say that *My Life in Art* and *Moja žizn v iskusstve* are the same book. And it is even more imperative to compare the second book that was in gestation.

The years that followed the Euro-American tours were difficult ones. While revered internationally, back home Stanislavsky was reduced to a monument of the so-called 'Socialist Realism'. Nothing was more alien to him than being fixed into an icon. His presence at the Art Theatre consistently became more marginal and indirect. On the Theatre's thirty years anniversary (29 October 1928), he suffered a heart attack while performing in some scenes of *Three Sisters*. He finished the scene without the audience realizing, but from that day he also gave up acting. Pedagogy became his main acitivity, face to face with students who came together to his own home and through the books. And first among these books was the one on the system which he had been proposing since the 'rock in Finland'.

For that which will become *Il lavoro dell'attore su se stesso*, Stanislavsky collaborated with Elizabeth Reynolds and her husband Norman Hapgood. They had met in 1924 in America. Elizabeth was a theatre expert with knowledge of Russian, while Norman was a critic experienced in book preparation. They met again in 1929 at Badenweiler, where Stanislavsky was convalescing and decided to work together on the book. The intention then was not to work on a manual. Work started in 1930. For this book Stanislavsky signed a legal document that gave Reynolds all the translation and publication rights of his works, in any language. In effect, she became a 'co-author' (see

Carnicke, 1993).¹⁰ Financial difficulties were still present and these became more pressing because of his health. These matters were solved at root by the contract signed with Reynolds because the American version became distinct and autonomous from its Russian counterpart. The collaboration with the 'co-author' and her husband proceeded as follows. Reynolds translated Stanislavsky's texts, on which she also provided some suggestions. Hapgood proposed cuts and edits himself which were then given consent and included in the American edition. For the Russian edition, Stanislavsky reserved, on the other hand, absolute freedom with respect to editorial and market requirements. Their direct collaboration ended in October 1930. They did not meet again for seven years, when Reynolds visited Russia in March 1937 and worked for some days with Stanislavsky on the volume's second part (Benedetti, 1990b, p. 345).

Following Reynolds' departure in 1930, Stanislavsky continued to prepare the material for the first part even if he had reluctantly opted out of a single volume publication. The book came out in 1936 with the title of *An Actor Prepares*. The Russian version followed two years later. The second part, as we said above, was not prepared entirely by the author. In Russia it came out in 1948, and a year later in America with the title of *Building a Character*.

The two versions of the book on the system cannot in any way be considered the same, as we have concluded for the autobiography. But it is even more so in this case. At least, it cannot be said *a priori*.

Reynolds' disinterested availability in resolving Stanislavsky's financial problems needs to be lauded, but ulterior motives exist not only in politics. Despite the good intentions, the American version eclipsed the Russian one, and the latter became a glorious heirloom for bibliophiles which is notoriously referred to without ever becoming obligatory reading. Reasons cited for this are comprehensible and valid: the increased availability of the English language and the shrewd marketing strategies as opposed to the closed Soviet market. But the result was that the American edition was transformed into the sole depository of Stanislavsky's thought.

In light of the facts, the question on the true tradition of Stanislavsky becomes inevitable. Are the books in English the same as the Russian editions? And if not, what is the difference? In the case of the autobiography, it was Stanislavsky himself who answered, as we have seen; for the second part of the book on the system the question will remain unanswered, as even the Russian edition did not receive the author's decisive stamp. However, one can answer for the first part of the book by comparing it to *An Actor Prepares*.

This is exactly what the Court of Bari asked for with the ordinance of the 11 June 1960.

In the name of the law

In 1956, Stanislavsky's book *Il lavoro dell'attore* (*An Actor's Work*) – inexplicably without the *su se stesso* (on himself) part – was published by Laterza of Bari. The book was edited and introduced by Guerrieri and translated from Russian by Elena Povoledo. It ran for almost 600 pages and collected in a single volume, as Stanislavsky had wanted, the two parts that had been recently issued in Russia (in 1954 and 1956) as the second and third volume of Stanislavsky's Collected Works. The book did not initially bear the copyright of Theatre Arts Books and of Elizabeth Reynolds.

The 'plaintiff' – in the bureaucratic jargon this is the person submitting a dispute before legal institutions – wanted to claim the royalties from the 'defendant', in this case Laterza, in accordance to the agreement signed in 1930 between Reynolds the 'co-author' and Stanislavsky the author. The hearing was convened at the Court of Bari and it was concluded on the 11 June 1960 with the aforementioned ordinance. It should be noted that the ordinance is not a judgement but only a call for a further investigation – in this case, an expert's opinion or 'expertise' – which the Court calls for in order to pronounce its judgement. The plaintiff, who from now will be referred to as the Reynolds, referred to the Italian law on authors' rights which, in article 4, says:

> The remaking of a work which constitutes a substantial creative re-elaboration of the original is protected without detriment to the original work's existent rights.

The summary of the judicial procedure cannot pretend to have a narrative *appeal*, but the process at Bari is an ideal starting point to tackle the problem of Stanislavsky's real tradition. Scholarly opinions, already authoritative, gain potency when they are sifted through the rigours of the law.[11]

In accordance with article 4, the Italian legislation on authors' rights safeguards both the original works as well as their re-elaborations, on condition that the latter present characteristics that make them unmistakably recognizable with the original work. The legal dispute focused on the first part of Stanislavsky's work, for reasons already explained. Reynolds argued that the first part of the book published by Laterza corresponded, 'with the exception of minor modifications', to *An Actor Prepares*. The other side argued that the text was a faithful translation from the original Russian which contained 'changes and additions' that shaped it in a way that it could not be mistaken for the American edition. Initially, Reynolds asked that the copyright in her possession was extended separately to include the parts that were changed and/or added, but the Court decided that the protection generated from a re-elaboration of a text referred to a work in its totality and not to individual parts.

At this point, Reynolds referred to article 4 of the Italian law. She interpreted the article as follows. The article affirmed that the expected protection for a 'substantial re-elaboration', which it had to operate 'without detriment to the original work's existent rights', had to be included in the protection of the original work. Therefore the copyright in her possession of *An Actor Prepares* should have been deemed operational even for Laterza's 'substantial re-elaboration'. The Court again had a different opinion. It clarified that article 4 simply affirmed that the protection of a 'substantial re-elaboration' does not diminish the protection of the original work. Both works are protected, even in the event where the re-elaboration constitutes such an improvement on the original work that it would thwart the latter's literary and scientific value.

Reynolds attempted two other offensives. She included in the deliberations the original Russian text, of which the Italian edition had declared that it was a faithful translation. Reynolds underlined that the text which Stanislavsky gave the Theatre Arts Books was actually that Russian one. While it was true that the text translated as *An Actor Prepares* contained cuts and changes, which were in any case agreed upon with the author, but the copyright – according to her – was to be referred to the original Russian text, the same one, in other words, which would give rise to the Italian edition. The Court, however, objected. The copyright covered the text that was eventually given for publication and which was then legally registered, irrespective of the text forwarded to the editor.

At this point, Reynolds only had one card left. She affirmed, and rightly so, that Stanislavsky, through a specific 1936 agreement, had given Theatre Arts Books the rights for all his present and future books, including 'the substantial re-elaborations', on which he had reserved an option. In view of this, even taking in consideration that the original Russian was a 'substantial re-elaboration' of *An Actor Prepares*, Theatre Arts Books had claim over the royalties for any translation, in any other language and including, of course, Italian. The Court conceded that this was true, but that fact authorized Theatre Arts Books to proceed against (the heirs of) Stanislavsky since they did not specifically cede to the American editor the rights for the Russian re-elaboration of *An Actor Prepares*, as he had committed to do. That eventuality would not have had, in any case, any relevance to the dispute at hand.

All options exhausted, the original starting point was therefore reached again. Was the Italian text – and by implication the one in Russian – a 'substantial re-elaboration' of the American version? If it was, then the Reynolds was in the wrong and, on the basis of article 4, had no claim on the royalties. If not, Laterza was at fault. The Court had no other option but to commission a literary critic to provide an expertise so that a decision could be reached.

This contentious event was concluded in that manner, without anything resolved. The ordinance is not a sentence. In addition, an expert's judgement is not binding in any way on the judgement that is to be delivered. The Court, even after requesting it, can decide against taking it into consideration, or even resolve against it. Therefore, in requesting an expertise on a matter that was in itself difficult to assess and, moreover, even reserving the right to not consider it, the Court of Bari was actually encouraging the parties to reach an agreement and avoid a repetition of the process that would in all probability reach the same conclusion. That was what actually happened. The second Laterza edition of *Lavoro dell'attore* was published in 1968 and it came out with the American copyright, 'under arrangement with Theatre Arts Books, Proprietors'. It included some variations from the previous edition which were, however, mainly cosmetic.

So who won? There is no doubt that Reynolds was the formal winner because of the level of agreement reached. However, the victory that counts in certain cases is to avoid going to trial rather than to win it. Even though the Court of Bari had not sentenced, a sentence had been issued: the American edition and, through the Italian one, the Russian edition of Stanislavsky's books are not legally assimilated.

This was the result that Reynolds had stubbornly and confidently – but also unsuccessfully – tried to avoid. All the arguments invoked were rejected without appeal. Through the decision taken by the Court of Bari the problem of Stanislavsky's true tradition was concretely assigned to the scholars' hands.

In the name of the law.

Gerardo Guerrieri's expertise

The Introduction to the incriminated volume could also be read as the expertise that the Court had asked for. It extended to Stanislavsky's two – or three – books. Guerrieri then supplemented it with two appendices, namely the Introduction to the second edition of Laterza's *Lavoro dell'Attore* and the Preface of *La Mia Via nell'arte*.

On the autobiography, Guerrieri wrote that '*My Life in Art* was written in such a hurry that the Russian edition, published two years later, was almost something else' (Guerrieri, 1956, p. XXXVIII). This was nothing new, as Stanislavsky himself had already said so; and it was also nothing particularly negative, as the autobiography was not a book about the system. Guerrieri then moved on to the book on the system, with particular attention to the first part, i.e. the American *An Actor Prepares*. He wrote that Stanislavsky

> feared and wanted to avoid at all costs that which very often happens: when his book would be treated as a sacred text, an actor's Bible. It was for these reasons that he did not write in the rigid and dogmatic form of a treatise, but opted for the fluidity of a diary. A diary is experimental, undefined, a draft, a series of notes which can be cancelled and corrected at any time.
>
> Guerrieri, 1956, pp. XL–XLI[12]

It is worth remembering that the choice of a diary over a treatise was made against Gurevich's advice. It is also to be noted that the diary form – apart from having a 'fluid' style that was inherently sensitive to 'corrections' and full of passages that were to be eventually 'cancelled' – was continuously reaffirmed by the increasing date that opens every section, as it is done in the daily drafting of one's work logbook.

All these implicit and explicit signs disappear in the America edition. There are no increasing dates, corrections to be made are made and passages to be cancelled are cancelled. The form of the diary vanishes and the one of the treatise is imposed. Regarding the repetitions, which Reynolds had deemed unnecessary and which were therefore 'cancelled', Stanislavsky wrote the following in the Introduction of the Russian edition: 'Frequent repetition of the same ideas, which I consider important, is done deliberately. Let the readers forgive me for this reiteration' (in Hobgood, 1991, p. 231).[13]

In obliterating the nature of a diary, Guerrieri accused Reynolds of having distorted the book and turned it into the 'sacred text' which Stanislavsky had feared. As if such a change could be considered 'a modification of little consequence'! The change of the form impacts the content and what can be gained from a diary is very different from what is gained from a treatise.

Finally, Guerrieri wrote on the second part of the book on the system that *Building a Character* was 'an incorrect title because it was nothing but the second part of *An Actor's Work*' (Guerrieri, 1956, p. XLIII). Even Reynolds, in the 'Explanatory Note by the Translator' admitted that *Building a Character* was the 'sequel', 'the continuation' of *An Actor Prepares* within one holistic work on the 'actor's inner preparation and the external technical means to bring a character to life before an audience' (Reynolds in Stanislavski, 1949, pp. VIII-IX). By then, however, the horses had already bolted out of the stables. Thirteen years had passed since *An Actor Prepares* had first come out, and the Stanislavsky which had affirmed itself in both the practice and reflection of American theatre and beyond was that of the 'sacred text' on psychotechnique, as if physicalization was separate to the 'actor's work'.

Objectively, Guerrieri's Introduction brings to light the pedagogical project which Stanislavsky had entrusted to his books. It is only in this way that the anomaly of this text can be explained, because it introduces one book but its content is in reality about another. In fact, in introducing the book on the system, Guerrieri speaks about Stanislavsky's autobiography. He follows it faithfully, and from the *Artistic Childhood* he moves to *Adolescence* and *Maturity*, reflecting the Russian edition of *My Life in Art*. Guerrieri gives an account of the various difficulties which Stanislavsky encountered in each of these phases, and identifies practices from *An Actor's Work* through which

Figure 4 Gerardo Guerrieri.
© Selene Guerrieri

these difficulties could be confronted and overcome. The two books become transparent, as if placed one on top of the other.

Guerrieri had intuited that the autobiography and the book on the system were in reality the same book. It was one diary of Stanislavsky 'the student', with one section giving the sequence of the events while another parallel section presents the daily work that emerges from those events. The signs disseminated in the Russia edition of *An Actor's Work* served – and still do – to remind that the main objective behind reading the book was to compose in practice one's own 'life in art', apart from understanding acting techniques. In eliminating these signs, even if in good faith, the extensive American editing overshadowed that particular pedagogical project, and almost cancelled it completely.[14]

Guerrieri further fine-tuned his reading of Stanislavsky's books when in 1968 he introduced the second Laterza edition of *An Actor's Work*, the one that was agreed upon with Reynolds. He repeated the Introduction's scheme of the first edition. He spoke of another book. If before he had spoken of the book that had preceded *Il lavoro dell'attore*, he now spoke of the book that followed it: the fourth volume of the *Collected Works* (1956) that was dedicated to *The Work of the Actor on the Role*. The Italian title of this volume is *Lavoro dell'attore sul personaggio* (The work of the actor on the character), which Laterza published in 1988, evidencing an incautious betrayal of the original Russian which was titled *Rabota aktera nad rol'jui*, i.e. an actor's work on a role, which is very different, even and especially to Stanislavsky, from the 'character'.

After quickly fulfilling the obligatory rites of an Introduction, where he spoke of the 'I' and of truth on stage, Guerrieri developed, with ample supporting documentation, the first critical exposition of the 'method of physical actions', which constituted the kernel of the Russian edition. He reproduced the complete set of twenty-four stages which Stanislavsky had proposed for *The Inspector General* and, through timely commentary, analysed *Othello*'s Act III, Scene 3. The latter scene also featured in the Russian volume.

With the first and second Introductions, Guerrieri positioned *Il lavoro dell'attore* between the autobiography – which Stanislavsky himself had intended as a sort of introduction – and the work on the role. In this way he destabilized the image of a Stanislavsky who was exclusively concerned with the technique of experiencing and, subsequently, with the actor's work that was only directed on 'himself'. The Stanislavskian actor which emerges from the two introductions has two defining characteristics. First, he does not apply recipes but undertakes experiential research in his 'life in art'. Second, he understands that his work on himself must be placed at the service of a production's process. No systematic rules and no tension between the actor and the direction: this was Guerrieri's answer to the question which had characterized the encounter with Stanislavsky in Italy and beyond.

La mia vita nell'arte was published in Italy in 1963, on the centenary of Stanislavsky's birth. It was published by the prestigious publisher Einaudi. Guerrieri included, on a last minute request of the editor, a brief Preface of six pages. He did not treat the autobiography as an introduction but as a summation of Stanislavsky's complete work opus, in his books and on the stage. The Introduction describes Stanislavsky's autobiography as 'a method to control oneself, to structure the chaos of experience', which is 'Stanislavsky's whole life, a sort of ascending [...] towards the awareness of the organism's actions and reactions' (Guerrieri, 1963, p. XIII and p. XV). The organism in this sense is not only the physical body but all that it contains within, the soul and mind. Returning to the original principle, Guerrieri crafted the extreme version of his reading of Stanislavsky, recognizing him as a master of life. In theatre and through theatre.

The battles and the war

Like *Il lavoro dell'attore*, *La mia vita nell'arte* was also translated from Russian and did not bear the American copyright, even though the 'co-author' – thanks to the retroactive agreement of 1930 – could have acquired the right in 1948. Reynolds seems to have not disputed this, as the outcome of the Bari trial had evidently served as a deterrent. And it was by then evident that the Russian edition of the autobiography was 'something different' to the American version, which meant that *My Life in Art*'s copyright did not cover it.

A contention was, however, evident with the Italian publisher. It did not take place at the Court, but in the correspondences that underlined the difficult relationship between Guerrieri and Einaudi. The conflict – for it was a real conflict – took off during the first years of the 1950s when Einaudi entrusted the theatre series *Collezione di teatro* (Theatre Collections) to Guerrieri. Einaudi expected a series of dramatic texts linked to the great theatres. Guerrieri, on the other hand, envisaged a series of dramatic texts with an extensive number of essays on theatre culture, with emphasis on the masters of twentieth-century theatre. The publisher did allow courteously some concessions but essentially remained opposed to Guerrieri's proposal since such texts on theatre culture could be placed in another series titled *Saggi* (Essays). This contention might look as an issue of little importance, but not to Guerrieri. He believed that the issue was not on the value of certain essays on theatre but in rethinking the identity and relevance of theatre culture itself.[15]

Einaudi already had plans for the publication of Stanislavsky's autobiography and Guerrieri had been since 1940 working independently on it. However, the two initiatives did not converge. Apart from the incomprehension and latent hostility, Guerrieri's relationship with Einaudi was fraught further by his dealings with Laterza. Had Guerrieri edited Stanislavsky's autobiography, which was close to his heart, he would have expected its publication in

Collezione di teatro. In all probability the publisher decided to cut the Gordian knot and excluded Guerrieri from this project. *La mia vita nell'arte* was published as part of the series *Saggi* and without Guerrieri's involvement. But there are battles, and there is the war.

Concurrent with these skirmishes with Einaudi and the soon to be publication of *Lavoro dell'Attore*, the monumental *Enciclopedia dello Spettacolo* (The Encyclopedia of Performance) was published in 1954. It was conceived and coordinated by Silvio d'Amico. Guerrieri's position on theatre culture found its greatest fulfilment in the Enciclopedia. The breadth of theatre culture was evidenced over those nine studious volumes, where it was presented as going beyond its own dramatic and scenic works, in a way that theatre could be tackled without a sense of restrictive barriers. In the various sections of the Enciclopedia literature, art and the work of the actor, but also commercial strategies, sociology, anthropology, and psychology interact. This was a whole world which Einaudi only wanted dramatic literature to appear as its centre and, moreover, that dramatic literature which had been produced already. Guerrieri authored, amongst many others, the section *Attore* (Actor), in which Stanislavsky occupied a space next to deserving others, a small entry but within a large world. Angelo Maria Ripellino, then a debutant writer in his early thirties, wrote in his section *Stanislavskij*:

> Whoever studies Stanislavsky today must in a first place liberate him from those common nets in which he has been imprisoned by zealous interpreters. Stanislavsky was one of the most restless and dynamic Russian theatre-makers and not a bundle of prefabricated formulas or an arid supporter of Coherence. He was a passionate researcher of new paths.
>
> Ripellino, 1954, p. 266

Between Guerrieri and Ripellino, it is clear that theatre scholarship had become intransigent towards compartmentalization and superficial readings.[16]

Who had won? As in the dispute with Reynolds, it has to be said that Guerrieri had again lost the match with Einaudi. His work on *La mia vita nell'arte*, with the exception of that short Preface, had to find place in the introductions to other books. The *Collezione di teatro* remained as the publisher had conceived it. But if the higher stakes were those pertinent to the autonomous status and dignity of theatre culture, than it was Guerrieri who had won the war, in spite of and also as a result of the lost battles.

After 1968: The twentieth-century tradition

Coincidences, by themselves, mean nothing. However, they strengthen one's thoughts. The year 1968 saw not only the second Laterza edition of *Lavoro dell'attore* and the recuperation of Stanislavsky's true tradition, but also the publication of Jerzy Grotowski's *Towards a Poor Theatre*. The Italian edition was published two years later. Stanislavsky passed on the testimony to Grotowski, even if in reality it was only a coincidence. But, through this coincidence, the publication of *Towards a Poor Theatre* can be read 'as if' Stanislavsky was passing the testimony to Grotowski.

In 1980 the book *L'attore creativo* (The Creative Actor) was published. The title was short for *Conversazioni al Teatro Bol'šoj (1918-1922)* (Lectures at the Bolshoi Theatre), sessions which Stanislavsky had given and which were transcribed by Konkordia Antorova. The Italian translations of the lectures are followed by Grotowski's text *Risposta a Stanislavskij* (An Answer to Stanislavsky), where he writes:

> Some questions are meaningless. 'Is Stanislavsky important to the new theatre?' [...] If he is important to you, then ask: why? Do not ask if he is important to others or to theatre in general. 'Is *An Actor's Work on Himself* relevant today?' This question is meaningless for the same reason. What is today's practice? This in fact means that there is today's practice which is necessarily different to yesterday's. But is today's practice the same for everyone? There is your own specific practice. Therefore you can ask if this book is important to you within your practice. But do not ask me. One cannot answer in someone else's place.
>
> Grotowski in Stanislavskij, 1980, p. 191

This official certification is a late one, but the original text of the *Risposta* was from 1969. Even then it was 'as if' Stanislavsky's words had become a dialogue, as if Grotowski had transformed Stanislavsky in a reference point to find answers to the questions which he was posing to himself, questions on his own time and identity, but answered through Stanislavsky's own time and identity.

In Italy this was immediately the case. With the aura of Grotowski's productions in memory, the capacity of his book to be read as a battle flag rather than a manifesto of a poetics, Grotowski set theatre practitioners and scholars the task to clarify their position within the tradition of twentieth-

Figure 5 Grotowski in about 1971.
Photo Marianne Ahrne © Odin Teatret Archives

century theatre. In this tradition, Eugenio Barba and Odin Teatret were at the time showing, especially in Italy, an active and living presence.

It was understood that Grotowski represented the ultimate synthesis of this tradition and, because of this, the harbinger of its end, and that there was the danger of losing that inheritance. Stanislavsky lost the sharp and exclusive position of a protagonist in an exclusive story. He became interspersed within a movement that was animated by the anxiety to establish a new theatre tradition. New monographs were published that brought in precious new knowledge.[17] However, the most interesting line of study became the one where Stanislavsky was inserted in the tradition of the twentieth century. In the following part I will outline the main stages of this movement.

Fabrizio Cruciani (1985) assigned the title of 'Founding Fathers' to twentieth-century practitioners like Copeau, Appia, Craig, Meyerhold, and others, including, of course, Stanislavsky. He titled their followers as 'theatre communities'. A book can become influential through its name, which was the case with Cruciani's book *Teatro nel Novecento. Registi pedagoghi e comunità teatrali del* XX *secolo* [Twentieth-Century Theatre. Director-pedagogues and theatre communities in the 1900s]. These Founding Fathers were not directors *and* pedagogues but director-pedagogues whose groups became – in reality or in their utopian vision – 'theatre communities', as the book proceeded to confirm on a case by case basis.

Fabio Mollica (1989) was a student of Cruciani who, after learning Russian in order to read for a doctorate on Stanislavsky, developed a passionate and highly informed book on the First Studio. The book was edited by him, even though in reality it was Mollica's, and till today it is an essential volume to understand Stanislavsky as 'a director-pedagogue of a theatre community'.

Mirella Schino (2003) used the Founding Fathers and their visions to provide the first synthesis on early theatre direction. She identified the heart of the twentieth-century tradition in theatre's aspirations to create an equivalent to life that was based on the same organic principles. Schino presented performance as an organic body, not only in Craig's utopia which had postulated it, but also in Stanislavsky's work with Chekhov, which had forever been relegated to the cage of naturalistic psychology and the emphasis supposedly placed on the 'soul', to the extent that this, almost in principle, was extraneous to the concreteness of the physical and scenic body.

A parallel discussion was developed by Marco De Marinis (2000). He used – implicitly or explicitly – Schino's discussion on the director-pedagogues and their theatre communities' 'hunger for life' to analyse the 'new actor' as the backbone of twentieth-century tradition.

Ferdinando Taviani had co-written with Cruciani an Introduction for *L'attore creative*, titled *Sulla scienza di Stanislavskij* [On Stanislavsky's Science]. This was identified not in the actor/director alternative but in the intricate relationship in a novel's text and subtext. The extemporaneousness of that text did not do justice to Taviani's importance in Stanislavsky studies. It was exercised in an indirect manner, from the outside so to speak, through his fundamental contributions on Barba and Grotowski.

It is difficult to give an account of Grotowski's contribution from the books written. His influence in Italy was very profound, especially after his final 1986 settlement in Pontedera's Workcentre. Grotowski's contribution developed, first and foremost, through personal contacts with theatre-makers and scholars. Traces of published material about the argument which concerns us here can be found in *Al lavoro con Grotowski sulle azioni fisiche* (At Work with Grotowski on Physical Action), written by Thomas Richards (1993), Grotowski's 'fundamental collaborator' and heir. This book was published two years after Toporkov's book *Stanislavskij alle prove* (1991), which it implicitly confronts. Grotowski declared that he had gathered Stanislavsky's inheritance through the work experiences described by Toporkov, while Richards' book tells of the questions which Grotowski was asking and which he searched for answers through Stanislavsky.

I owe a lot to these scholars, especially to Taviani. After the 1991 text *Romanzo pedagogico* (A pedagogical novel), where a parallel between Stanislavsky's two books was identified and documented, my most recent volume titled *Stanislavskij* (Ruffini, 2005) is a reading of the so-called 'system' in the light of Theatre Anthropology as developed by Barba. This reading also deepened Grotowski's answer to Stanislavsky. However, Stanislavsky is present in all my research about twentieth-century theatre, to the extent that my closest collaborators call it 'Ruffini's obsession', an opinion which this essay will not dispel. In this essay I have restricted myself to the books, with good reason. But there is more. Theatre walks on two legs, the books and the stage, but I have not spoken about 'Stanislavskian theatre', of its actors and performances.[18] What is a Stanislavskian actor? What is a Stanislavskian performance? Practical research is necessary to answer these questions, but there is one mainstay: the 'I believe' when faced with a result, whichever path used to reach it.

Notes

1 Gerardo Guerrieri (1920–86) was a director, dramaturg, scenographer, translator and theatre critic and essayist. Apart from the various entries in *Enciclopedia dello Spettacolo* (The Encyclopaedia of Performance), his texts also appear in *Lo spettatore critico* (1987). The material in his archives are extensive and in part unexplored. See Geraci, 1990.
2 On the problem of theatre direction in Italy, apart from Claudio Meldolesi's essential *Fondamenti del teatro italiano. La generazione dei registi* (The foundations of Italian theatre. The generation of theatre directors, 1984), see also Mirella Schino (2011), *Storia di una parola. Fascismo e mutamenti di mentalità teatrale* (The History of a word. Fascism and changes in theatre mentality).

3 Giacomo Lvov has to be credited with the first contribution in Italy on Stanislavsky, albeit a generic one. This work was titled *Il teatro russo contemporaneo* (Contemporary Russian Theatre), and it came out in 1927.
4 The interview was titled *Il credo teatrale di Nemirovič* (Nemirovich's theatrical credo), and given in December 1931 to Eugenio Bertuetti, journalist, critic, and playwright.
5 On Danchenko's presence in Italy also see M. Schino, Carla Arduini, Rosalba De Amicis, Eleonora Egizi, Fabrizio Pompei, Francesca Ponzetti, Noemi Tiberio, 2008 and Malcovati, 2010.
6 The other two books reviewed are *Il sistema di Stanislavskij e il teatro sovietico* (Stanislavsky's system and Soviet Theatre), by Nikolai Abalkin (ed. Pietro Zveteremich) and *Lezioni di regia di K. S. Stanislavskij. Colloqui e appunti nelle prove* (*Stanislavski Directs*), by Nikolai Gorchakov (ed. Ignazio Ambrogio).
7 This quotation is taken from the new translation from Russian of Stanislavsky's autobiography.
8 For more details see Senelick, 1981 and Benedetti, 1990a.
9 On Stanislavsky's relations with foreign editors see Benedetti, 1990a, p. 270.
10 For details on the contract see Benedetti, 1990b, pp. 316–17.
11 The ordinance of the Court of Bari is published in 'Il Foro italiano', Vol. LXXXIII, parte 1–117. This was brought to my attention by Dr Viviana Casini, who I thank for the exhaustive work which she carried out for her 2002–3 dissertation. It is worth explaining the reasons behind the plaintiff's appeal to Italian law. They could not appeal to the Bern Convention (9 September 1886), which had institutionalised 'The International Union for the protection of literary and artistic work' because both the US and the USSR did not adhere to it. Nor could they appeal to the 'International Convention on author's rights' (Geneva, 6 October 1952), because in Italy this came in effect only after the publication of the Laterza edition. They could only appeal to the bilateral convention between the US and Italy, signed on the 28 December 1892, which established equality of treatment of Italian citizens in the US and vice-versa. According to that Convention Italian citizens could appeal the 'Copyright Act' operative in the US, while American citizens could appeal to Italian laws (of 22 April 1941, no. 633) on the author's rights.
12 In the 'Explanatory Note by the Translator' of *Building a Character*, Reynolds is late to depict a Stanislavsky who was preoccupied that his so-called 'system' was treated as 'a kind of Bible'. This was not the opinion shared in 'Note by the Translator' of *An Actor Prepares*, where the book was presented as 'a grammar of acting'.

13 Jean Benedetti's recent English translation of *An Actor's Work* does not publish the full version of Stanislavsky's Introduction and among the passages omitted is the quoted part on the repetitions.

14 This is what I have analytically demonstrated in *Romanzo pedagogico. Uno studio sui libri di Stanislavskij* (A pedagogical novel. A study on Stanislavsky's books). See Ruffini, 1991.

15 On the relationship between Guerrieri and Einaudi, especially as it relates to the series *Collezione di teatro*, see Guerrieri, 1992. A developed commentary by Stefano Geraci is included. Guerrieri was not alone to emphasise theatre culture. He was part of a movement in which many participants of the 'critical direction' and of 'the youngest ones', as Meldolesi called them, took part. The critical direction refuted tradition without however having an alternative reference. It had to create its tradition by referring to book culture more than stage practice. This explains why the main exponents of critical direction – from Giorgio Strehler to Luigi Squarzina, Vito Pandolfi and Gerardo Guerrieri – were all personalities with multiple characteristics. They were directors, but also scholars, critics, dramaturges, and translators. The book culture was their main tool and weapon, even more than the academic.

16 Ripellino would publish in 1965, with Einaudi, one of the most important books on Russian theatre direction of the first decades of the twentieth century, titled *Il trucco e l'anima* (The make-up and the soul). In that book he expressed his admiration for the dynamite that was Meyerhold, which he contrasted to Stanislavsky to whom he expressed no particular affection. However, the picture that he traces of that patient master, at work on minute details, is among the most perceptive, documented, and passionate that can be read.

17 Fausto Malcovati's work needs to be particularly signalled here. Malcovati was a relentless and refined researcher of Stanislavsky's world. He was in charge of the numerous other Laterza editions of *Il Lavoro dell'Attore* which followed Guerrieri's 1968 edition. The 1997 version and its Preface were particularly important. In 1988 Malcovati had published, again with Laterza, a critical biography titled *Stanislavskij. Vita, opere e metodo* (Stanislavski. Life, work, method). That same year he edited and introduced *Il lavoro dell'attore sul personaggio* (*The Work of the Actor on the Role*), IV volume of Stanislavsky's Collected Works. In 2009 he edited the new Italian translation of *La mia vita nell'arte*, which was enriched with precious new Appendixes and a new Introduction. For other books edited by Malcovati see the References.

18 Regarding the training for a Stanislavskian actor one can note the Libera Accademia di Teatro (Free Theatre Academy), founded at the end of the 1940s by

Pietro Sharoff, who had been a student of Stanislavsky and acting teacher at the National Centre of Cinematography. There is also the Studio di Arti Sceniche (Studio for Scenic Arts), founded in 1957 by Alessandro Fersen, where the system was at the basis of the advancement in theatre direction that had been indicated by Grotowski. Dominique De Fazio, who for many years was a student and collaborator of the Actors Studio, disseminated in various seminars Stanislavsky's ideas with renowned charisma and pedagogical efficiency. We will limit ourselves to these cases not only because of their notoriety but also because their reference to Stanislavsky is officially recognised. But the so-called 'system' is present, under various titles and in different dosages, in all theatre schools. And more than in any other case the 'so-called' and the quotation marks are necessary here.

References

Benedetti, J. (1982), *Stanislavski. An Introduction*. London: Methuen.

Benedetti, J. (1990a), 'A History of Stanislavski in Translation', *New Theatre Quarterly*, Vol. 6, No. 23: 266–78.

Benedetti, J. (1990b), *Stanislavski. A Biography*. London: Methuen.

Brecht, B. (1975), 'Studi su Stanislavskij', in *Scritti teatrali II*. Torino: Einaudi.

Carnicke, S. M. (1993), 'Stanislavsky. Uncensored and Unabridged', *TDR*, Vol. 37, No. 1: 22–37.

Casella, A. (1934), 'Tatiana Pavlova: Regista', *Comoedia*, 10.

Cruciani, F. (1985), *Teatro nel Novecento. Registi pedagoghi e comunità teatrali del XX secolo*. Firenze: Sansoni.

d'Amico, S. (1929), *Tramonto del grande attore*. Milano: Mondadori.

d'Amico, S. (1931), 'Dančenko e l'arte teatrale', *Comoedia*, Yr. XIII, no. 9.

d'Amico, S. (ed.) (1947), *La regia teatrale*. Roma: Angelo Belardetti Editore.

De Marinis, M. (2000), *In cerca dell'attore. Un bilancio del Novecento teatrale*. Roma: Bulzoni.

De Pirro, N. (1940), 'Nascita della regia in Italia', *Scenario*, January Issue.

Geraci, S. (1990), A note to G. Guerrieri 'Pagine di teatro', *Teatro e Storia*, Vol. 8: 11–14.

Grotowski, J. (1968), *Towards a Poor Theatre*. Odin Teatrets Forlag.

Grotowski, J. (1970), *Per un teatro povero*. Roma: Bulzoni.

Guerrieri, G. (1953), 'Attualità di Stanislavskij', *Arena*, 3, Oct-Dec.

Guerrieri, G. (1956), 'Introduzione', in K. Stanislavskij, *Il lavoro dell'attore*. Bari: Laterza.

Guerrieri, G. (1963), 'Prefazione', K. Stanislavskij, *La mia vita nell'arte*. Torino: Einaudi.

Guerrieri, G. (1987), *Lo spettatore critico*. Roma: Levi.

Guerrieri, G. (1992), 'Lettere sulla <<Collezione di teatro>> Einaudi', *Teatro e Storia*, Vol. 12: 3–18.

Hobgood, B. M. (1991), 'Stanislavski's Preface to *An Actor Prepares* and the Persona of Tortsov', *Theatre Journal*, Vol. 43, No. 2: 219–28.

Il Dramma, 15, Apr. 1940.

Lwow, G. (1927), 'Il teatro russo contemporaneo', *Nuova Antologia*, 334.

Malcovati, F. (ed.) (1986), *Tre Sorelle, Il giardino dei ciliegi, Zio Vanja – mises-en-scène*. Milano: Ubulibri.

Malcovati, F. (ed.) (2002), *Il gabbiano – mise-en-scène*. Milano: Ubulibri.

Malcovati, F. (2010), 'Un épisode italien resté confidentiel. Les mises en scène de Nemirovitch-Dantchenko en Italie', *Teatro e Storia*, Vol. 31, New series no. II: 237–61.

Meldolesi, C. (1984), *Fondamenti del teatro italiano. La generazione dei registi*. Firenze: Sansoni.

Meldolesi, C. (1987), *Fra Totò e Gadda. Sei invenzioni sprecate del teatro italiano*. Roma: Bulzoni.

Milano, P. (1937), 'Il metodo di Stanislavskij e il mito dell'attore italiano', in *Il Dramma*, 3, Vol. I.

Mollica, F. (ed.) (1989), *Il teatro possibile. Stanislavskij e il Primo Studio del Teatro d'arte di Mosca*. Firenze: La casa Usher.

Nemirovich-Danchenko, V. I. (1931), 'Il credo teatrale di Nemirovič', an interview given to E. Bertuetti, *Il Dramma*, 1, December.

Richards, T. (1993), *Al lavoro con Grotowski sulle azioni fisiche*. Milano: Ubulibri.

Ripellino, A. M. (1954), 'Stanislavskij', in *Enciclopedia dello Spettacolo Vol. IX*. Roma: Sadea, pp.263–72.

Ripellino, A. M. (1965), *Il trucco e l'anima*. Torino: Einaudi.

Ruffini, F. (1991), 'Romanzo pedagogico. Uno studio sui libri di Stanislavskij', *Teatro e Storia*, Vol. 10: 3–55.

Ruffini, F. (2005), *Stanislavskij. Dal lavoro dell'attore al lavoro su di sé* 2nd ed. Roma-Bari: Laterza.

Schino, M. (2003), *Nascita della regia teatrale*. Roma-Bari: Laterza.

Schino, M. (2011), 'Storia di una parola. Fascismo e mutamenti di mentalità teatrale', *Teatro e Storia*, Vol. 32, New series no. III: 169–212.

Schino, M., Arduini, C., De Amicis, R., Egizi, E., Pompei, F., Ponzetti, F., Tiberio, N., (eds) (2008), *L'anticipo italiano. Fatti, documenti, interpretazioni e testimonianze della grande regia in Italia tra il 1911 e il 1934*, *Teatro e Storia*, Vol. 29.

Senelick, L. (1981), 'Stanislavsky's Double *Life in Art*', *Theatre Survey*, Vol. 22, No. 2: 201–11.

Stanislavski, K. (1924), *My Life in Art*. Boston: Little, Brown & Co.

Stanislavski, K. (1936), *An Actor Prepares*. New York: Theatre Arts Books.

Stanislavski, K. (1949), *Building a Character*. New York: Theatre Arts Books.

Stanislavskii, K. (1926), *Moia zhizn' v iskusstve*. Moscow. Subsequently this book was included as the first volume (1954) of *Sobranie Sochinenii* (Collected Works) in eight volumes. Moscow: Iskusstvo.

Stanislavskij, K. (1934), *Ma vie dans l'art*, trans. N. Gourfinkel, eds N. Gourfinkel and L. Chancerel. Bruxelles: La Renaissance du Livre.

Stanislavskij, K. (1980), *L'attore creativo. Conversazioni al Teatro Bol'šoj (1918–1922). Etica*, eds F. Cruciani and C. Falletti. Firenze: La casa Usher.

Stanislavskij, K. (2009), *La mia vita nell'arte*. Firenze: La casa Usher.

Toporkov, V. O. (1991), *Stanislavskij alle prove. Gli ultimi anni*, ed. F. Malcovati. Milano: Ubulibri.

Vakhtangov, E. (1984), *Il sistema e l'eccezione*, ed. F. Malcovati. La casa Usher: Firenze.

2

Stanislavsky and French Theatre: Selected Affinities

Marie-Christine Autant-Mathieu

Konstantin Stanislavsky/Alekseev had 'French Theatre blood' in his veins: his maternal grandmother was an actress from Paris who played at St Petersburg's Mikhailovsky Theatre during the 1846–7 seasons. *Theatre News* commented on her performance as follows: 'Madame Varley, hired to act as a maid, is a second-class actress, but has received good training' (Stanislavskii, 1994, t. 6, p. 588). Over time, this remark acquired a certain irony since it is precisely against that kind of training that Stanislavsky would build his System.

This blood relationship that ties Stanislavsky to French Theatre leads us to examine not only Stanislavsky *in* France – that is to say the impact of the Moscow Art Theatre's (MAT) three tours in Paris (1922, 1923, and 1937) – but more generally, Stanislavsky *and* France. First this study will present what the Russian artist owes to French Theatre, particularly the influence of the French School on his training as an actor and a director of an amateur troupe. Then an examination of his challenges to the French approach to acting and the creation of the System based on very different grounds will follow. Finally, the analysis of the different tours of the Art Theatre in Paris will highlight the importance of 'the horizon of expectations' (Jauss, 1978) and the political context of the reception. The Russian performances, though discovered very late (twenty-four years after the founding of MAT, and twelve years after the first European tour), were welcomed with triumph but had little lasting impact on French theatre practice. French artists, especially those in favour of reforms, admired the organization and the ethics of the Russian company, but were unconvinced by the aesthetics (realism) or acting style, which was emotional and oriented towards experiencing. André Antoine, the members of the Cartel, and the many opponents to theatre as a commercial industry, were fascinated by the idea of an *art theatre* with a director as the head of a *permanent company*, the conductor of an *ensemble*. Jacques Copeau would go on to admire Stanislavsky as the founder of the studios – small pedagogical and experimental cells on the fringe of institutional theatre (Autant-Mathieu, 2014). But Stanislavsky's System only had a few followers, not only because of the late translation of *An Actor Prepares* in 1958, but also because theatre practitioners were attached to the art of 'representation' and preferred playing 'with their heads', as stated by Denis Diderot (Diderot, 1995, t. 2, p. 72). They did not believe that the actor's work needed a special method. Despite Copeau's efforts in writing his foreword to *Ma vie dans l'art* (*My life in Art*) in 1934, and those of Jean Vilar in his foreword to *La formation de l'acteur* (*An Actor Prepares*) in 1958, Stanislavsky will remain a revered artist in France, but not the one who has disciples. In contrast, French artists enthusiastically adopted Brecht's 'Distancing Theatre', following the triumphal tour of the Berliner Ensemble in Paris in 1954.

French Melodrama as a training school for novice actors

At the opening of the Art Theatre's tour in Paris in December 1922, Stanislavsky told the audience that he had started his acting career by playing in French operettas and vaudevilles (Stanislavskii, 1994, t. 6, p. 185). Indeed, in the 1880s, and within his circle of amateur artists, Alekseev/Stanislavsky was fascinated by musical comedy, brought to fashion by the famous actress Anne Judic.[1] With his fellow performers, he experimented in order to gain the vocal and rhythmic fluidity of French operettas.

Working in 1886 on the Russian translation of Florimond Hervé's *Lili*, Stanislavsky wrote that '[u]sually, when French is translated into Russian, the result is long, complex sentences with subordinate clauses. But we decided to write the script in short sentences only, no longer than the French' (Stanislavski, 2008, p. 69). By imitating the French style, the Russian text would become lighter and more incisive, and would favour the development of technical virtuosity, vocal range, speech delivery, gestures, and embodiment of a fast

Figure 6 Stanislavsky playing Maigrillot in the vaudeville *Le Secret d'une femme* (this is the Russian title of the vaudeville *Les Femmes et le secret* by Saint-Yves et Léon de Villiers), Alekseev Circle, 1881.
© The Museum of the Moscow Art Theatre.

tempo-rhythm. Moreover, French light plays like *La Corde sensible*, *Le Secret d'une femme*, *Nitouche*, and especially *Lili*, allowed Stanislavsky to create characters endowed with subtleties, as one can see in his many transformations in the role of soldier Planchard. As a result, melodrama, vaudeville, and operetta were for Stanislavsky real and valuable training, as they had been for Gémier and Dullin (Dullin, 1985, pp. 33–5).

After the years of apprenticeship, where imitation took over method, Stanislavsky went through a critical turning point. In 1897, one year before the creation of the Art Theatre, Stanislavsky was in Paris and saw the performances of *L'avare* (*The Miser*) and *Le Misanthrope* (*The Misanthrope*) at the Comédie-Française. His impression was very negative, and he shared it with journalist

Lucien Besnard in an invaluable letter offering his point of view on the concept of tradition:

> I revere the French for their tradition, which, by the way, has now become a simple uninteresting routine in the realm of light comedy and drama. [...] I was just in Paris last spring and saw *The Miser* and *The Misanthrope* at the Comédie. [...] Do you know what my conclusions were? The greatest foes of Molière are the actors of the Comédie. This is not tradition but simply idiotic obstinacy – to desiccate such a great author the way they do. [...] The actors in the roles of Molière are not living people, but mannequins. This is why the best Tartuffe I have ever seen was our Russian actor Lensky[2]: he did not act according to tradition but created the role and was interesting.
>
> Senelick, 2014, pp. 78–81

This is why, when Stanislavsky produced and played the lead in *Le Malade Imaginaire* (*The Imaginary Invalid*) in 1913, he rejected this way of playing Molière, and tested his first discoveries on how to approach acting. He had many challenges in order to reach the heart of the character. How to personify a seventeenth-century French man? According to the System that he created in 1906 and had been testing since 1912 at the First Studio, he needed to 'experience' this character of an invalid. He started with imitation, hoping to create the role from the outside, so to arrive to the inside. But this approach did not let him get into Argan's psychology. It was necessary to lure himself in experiencing the egoism and despotism of his character within himself (Stanislavskii, 1986, t. 2, pp. 22–3).

Thus, Stanislavsky, as a youth, started imitating French actors' performances in lighter pieces through exterior characterization, to borrow a term from the System, and as he matured he succeeded in experiencing his characters from the inside. Even as he disputed the principles of the French School in building his System, Stanislavsky remained tempted by French Theatre throughout his life. In the 1920s, while actors of his System and his studios could control the work on themselves according to the process of experiencing, Stanislavsky realized that an established routine was settling, sinking the acting into a stagnant and passive psychological realism. He then made use of two French comedies (*Marchands de gloire* – *The Merchants of Glory*, by Marcel Pagnol and Paul Nivoix, and *Le Mariage de Figaro* – *The Marriage of Figaro*, by

Figure 7 Stanislavsky playing Argan in Molière's *The Imaginary Invalid*, Moscow Art Theatre, mise-en-scène by Alexandre Benois and Stanislavsky, 1913.
© The Museum of the Moscow Art Theatre.

Pierre-Augustin Caron de Beaumarchais) and a melodrama (*Les Sœurs Gérard*, adapted from *Les Deux Orphelines* – *The Two Orphans*, by Adophe d'Ennery and Eugène Cormon) to intensify rhythm, stimulate physical expression, and galvanize the vivacity of speech. Beaumarchais' play will be remembered in the Art Theatre's history as one of the most beautiful successes (Otan-Mat'e (Autant-Mathieu), 2006, pp. 81–98).[3]

Dispute with Diderot and Coquelin

Stanislavsky also used works from French artists and scientists in his research and development of an innovative and universal acting system. When he started writing his System, he looked for examples to back up his intuition with practical observations. He used the performances of French actors he saw in Paris and on tour in Moscow before 1917 to illustrate three trends in the art of theatre. He strongly condemned routine acting that uses clichés, the theatre craft (*remeslo*), but he judged estimable the French approach as described by the actor Benoît-Constant Coquelin in 1894. Stanislavsky read and made notes on *L'Art du comédien,* extracts of which were first translated into Russian in 1908 (Stanislavskii, 1993, t. 5/1, p. 613). He approved the starting premise: the actor does not simply demonstrate but he is also a creator of his role. Like Coquelin, he believed that technical skills for all actors were a necessity, and that they had to be acquired through constant training (one cannot rely on inspiration). But he had a different analysis of emotion and nature. For French actors, pure and simple nature only makes a mediocre theatre impact. 'The pig can scream well, but he screams without art', Coquelin writes (Coquelin, 1894, p. 56). Art is not identification but representation (Coquelin, 1894, p. 56). Stanislavsky borrows this term to name the second trend of theatre acting, the art of representation (*predstavlenie*), admirable for its preparation techniques that allow a real mastery of gesture and diction. But he argued against the control of emotion, simply imitated on stage and not really felt, in acting that is 'cold as ice while the role is on fire' (Stanislavskii, 1993, t. 5/1, pp. 419–20). He refused to support acting that relies on the division between the 'first', the instrumentalist, and the 'second', the instrument. The 'first' conceives the role to create, and constitutes a model that the 'second' executes 'until the moment when the critic in his "first" is satisfied' (Coquelin, 1894, p. 5).[4]

From the middle of the nineteenth century, the Russian actor Mikhaïl Shchepkin (1788–1863) had already developed an emotive and natural acting. Claiming sensitivity and sincerity in acting, and condemning the art of pure entertainment, the 'cult of form', Stanislavsky placed himself as his heir and he also supported the Tolstoian thesis for an art that would be serious, educational, and ethically influenced (Tolstoy, 1897). For him, the Russian School relied on the fusion between the actor and the role in the creative state (*samočustvie*) and on the research for stage equivalence to the natural state. Relying on emotionally controlled work, established by the links between the conscious and the unconscious, and on sensitive acting justified from the inside, the art of *emotional experiencing* (*perezhivanie*) is the third trend of acting whose fundamental mechanisms Stanislavsky theorized on.[5] Stanislavsky clarified that 'emotional experiencing' existed also in the art of representation (Stanislavskii, 1986, t. 2, p. 21): the actors of this latter school also live and embody their roles. However, they do not do it on stage, in front of the audience, but at home, when they are alone or during closed rehearsals. The role is only 'experienced' to find a form for the effect. Whereas the art of representation would be content with the plausibility of feelings, Stanislavsky, after Pushkin, also claimed the truth of passions in the given circumstances (Stanislavskii, 1994, t. 6, pp. 68–9).

To locate his approach in a critical reading of the French model, Stanislavsky relied on the new Russian translation of the *Paradoxe sur le comédien* (*Paradox of the Actor*) published in Moscow in 1923.[6] Denis Diderot's theories were well known in Russia since the end of the nineteenth century, but Stanislavsky insisted on reading the whole text again in order to give a solid basis to his arguments. Thanks to his friend Liubov Gurevich, a famous literary critic who was also, until the 1930s, his adviser for documentation and writing, Stanislavsky knew and approved of Alfred Binet's refutation of Diderot (Gurevič, 1926). This psychologist, who worked on hypnosis, exceptional memories, split personalities, and hysteria, became interested in the behaviours of playwrights and in the emotions of actors. His investigations, with the participation of Jean Mounet-Sully, Julia Bartet, Coquelin, Gustave Worms, and others, invalidated Diderot's conclusions. The actors always feel the emotions of their role and can do two things at the same time: 'Being affected and controlling oneself at the same time does not imply any contradiction' (Binet, 1896, p. 295).

Binet is a disciple of Théodule Ribot, who was the father of French psychology. Stanislavsky read and took careful notes on four of his books. A revered scientist by the end of the nineteenth century, and student of Claude Bernard and Jean-Martin Charcot, Ribot was interested in the unconscious activity that he studied through dysfunctions and pathologies. He focused his research on issues of will, memory, feelings, and personality. Most of his books were translated into several languages as soon as they were published, including in Russian. Stanislavsky borrowed from Ribot the notion of 'reviviscence' (Ribot, 1931, p. 78), literally in Russian *perezhivanie*, which serves as a foundation for his System. Without entering into the details of all the terms Stanislavsky took from Ribot's thinking – given circumstances, generic images, subtext, radiation, adaptation – it is mainly 'affective memory' that cements the System, because it is that memory that lets the actor activate, during each performance, the emotional mechanisms that work by analogy with the emotions of the character. The affective memory brings back to life a former emotional event, like Proust's madeleine: it colours, animates, arouses, directs the sentiments, but it only appears to the conscious on an exceptional basis, under the shape of the emotion that created it (Ribot, 2007, p. 56).[7] The System, exported in the United States, and transformed into the 'Method' at the Actors Studio, will keep this key notion of sense or affective memory (Cohen, 2010, p. 146).

Ribot's theses were condemned by Ivan Pavlov at the beginning of the 1930s, which led Stanislavsky to give another scientific basis to his research. He relied on conditional reflexes to explore the 'line of physical actions' (Autant-Mathieu, 2007). At first glance, the inner work goes to second place behind a work through improvisation, etudes (*etiudy*), that allow the actor to reach the emotion, not with the activation of past emotions, but through actions that act from the outside (like stimuli) towards the inside.

Despite the recurrent attacks against his System – by the avant-gardists in the 1920s and the defenders of a materialistic art that condemned the work on the unconscious and on spirituality – Stanislavsky kept his acting principles based on experienced emotions. In October 1927, an actress of the Second Moscow Art Theatre, directed by Mikhail Chekhov,[8] asked Stanislavsky: 'is it correct to represent the role by keeping it at a distance and then imitate it by trying, as much as possible, to merge with it [...]?'(Stanislavskii, 1999, t. 9, p. 731). Stanislavsky answered that only manners, walk, and appearance could be imitated. But outer imitation does not show the emotions inside. This observation did not reduce his admiration for the virtuosity of the French actors, playing according to the art of representation, as he emphasized in his reply to her correspondent:

The art of the French school [...] is very complex and very difficult. I was trained in it, was at the Paris Conservatoire and therefore I have the right to speak. [...]. Such actors as Sarah Bernhardt know how to work in a way not one Russian actor can.

Senelick, 2014, p. 494

If numerous French actors' tours in Russia in the nineteenth century, such as Sarah Bernhardt, Mademoiselle George, Rachel, Coquelin, and Mounet-Sully, contributed to the spreading in Russia of an acting model based on refined diction and the search of effect, an opposite movement started after October 1917. Then, it was the Soviet companies like The Moscow Art Theatre (1922–24), the Tairov's Chamber Theatre (1923 and 1930), the Vakhtangov Theatre (1928), and the Meyerhold Theatre (1930) which were travelling to the West, showing the vitality of pre-revolutionary Russian art and also demonstrating, through diverse productions of avant-garde theatres, the creativity brought about by the Revolution.

The French stopovers during the Moscow Art Theatre tour

In September 1922, the Bolshevik government authorized the Moscow Art Theatre's tour in the United States, via Berlin, Prague, Zagreb, and Paris. They left for one season, but the triumphal welcome they received everywhere led them to extend this trip: they only returned to Soviet Russia in the spring of 1924.

This tour arrived in Paris after two missed opportunities: in 1906, during the first extensive European tour, and in 1912, when the Art Theatre had intended to alternate with the Russian ballet of Serge Diaghilev.[9] The revival of Maurice Maeterlinck's *L'Oiseau bleu* (*Blue Bird*) in Paris at the Théâtre de Réjane on 27 February 1911, based on the Arts Theatre's mise-en-scène, cannot be considered as a first introduction of the Russian principles on the French scene. The show was performed in a private theatre, in front of a public eagerly expecting effects. This was a traumatizing experience for Leopold Sulerzhitsky, Stanislavsky's confidant and representative. The lack of discipline, the actors' turnover, the amateurism stunned him (Suleržickij, 1970, p. 480) and convinced Yevgeny Vakhtangov, who accompanied him, that they should not act like the French. 'Only technique. And a bad one' (Vakhtangov, 2000, p. 52).

After the Revolution, the new State, which nationalized the MAT, took an opportunity of the tours to prove to the world that the Russian heritage was alive and to underline 'the universal importance of Stanislavsky' (Sibirakov, 1974). Nevertheless, the actors of the company did not leave as 'emissaries for their homeland, to glorify it' (Šverubovič, 1990, p. 425) but more simply to be able to survive in the years of civil war chaos. At that time, the Art Theatre was criticized as a symbol of bourgeois art (Meyerhold, quoted in Senelick, 1992, p. 75),[10] and was weakened by an internal crisis. One part of the troupe that gave performances in Ukraine during the summer 1919 was cut off from Moscow by the White Army and could not return to Moscow. They then started wandering through Europe under the name of Kachalov Group. This separation deprived the Theatre of some of its best actors during the very difficult years of political upheaval. As the living conditions were deteriorating, they started imagining great tours abroad, where the Theatre was still highly esteemed. But, the government in 1920 and 1921 refused to let them go, and demanded that the Kachalov Group return to Moscow as an act of loyalty. A majority of its members returned in the spring of 1922, making the great international tour possible.

It is for personal reasons that Stanislavsky took the lead of the company when abroad. Expropriated of his flat and factories, he was relocated in such unsanitary conditions that his son's health seriously deteriorated. Stanislavsky needed money in order to be able to send Igor to a sanatorium in Switzerland to be treated for tuberculosis. (Stanislavskii, 1999, t. 9, p. 136.)

Thus, the main objective of this first tour of the Art Theatre (now Soviet) was to restore a company threatened by implosion, weakened by the lack of funds, and the difficult living and working conditions. Thanks to 'the pumping of dollars'(Stanislavskii, 1999, t. 9, p. 83)[11] and by showing performances, but also by taking some engagements like writing books and presenting his System, Stanislavsky tried to ensure the financial survival of the theatre: 'Outside America, there is no place to earn money. In Europe, you can only spend it', he says, and he adds with lucidity or cynicism that there is nothing to expect from Europe 'except successes and good reviews' (Stanislavskii, 1999, t. 9, p. 100, p. 138). Europe, and more particularly France, were no more than stopovers, used by the company as promotion for their 'road to Eldorado' (Smeliansky, 1991, no. 11 and no. 12).

An Odyssey

Organizing the tour was a real challenge, as it meant travelling to the United States from Russia with about sixty people and seven wagons of material, across central Europe which was in enormous political, economic, and social turmoil, during a season known for its stormy weather. With the exception of Germany and Turkey, no country had diplomatic relations with the USSR. England and Canada even refused the entrance of a 'Bolshevik' theatre on their territory.

The authorization to tour was subjected to drastic controls and conditions. The requirements to travel were to be addressed directly to the GPU[12] (the state political directorate) and each participant had to make a specific request to the Special Committee for artistic tours abroad. In order to keep their apartments, each traveller had to pay the rent during the whole time they were away. Despite many incredible adventures and internecine strife, and thanks to strict disciplinary conditions, together with a rather coordinated and efficient material organization, the company was able to survive for two seasons: the Bolshevik government accepted the tour's extension because a part of the income would be used to fight against the rampant starvation of the civil war.

The first Art Theatre tour in Paris at the Théâtre des Champs-Élysées presented between 5–20 December 1922: Alexei Tolstoy's *Tsar Fiodor Ioannovitch*, Maxim Gorky's *The Lower Depths*, and Anton Chekhov's *The Cherry Orchard*, seventeen performances in all, and a special night on the 24 December which included Ivan Turgenev's *A Provincial Lady* and three extracts from Fyodor Dostoevsky's *The Brothers Karamazov*.

The French discovered an art that had been praised in central Europe since 1906. The company was fresh, it had triumphed in Berlin, Prague, Zagreb, and was now preparing for the United States. The American correspondents were on the alert. The impresario Morris Gest, to further promote the Theatre, kept sending gifts. The team was inspired by the success and excited to conquer the new world, united under one banner, one 'brand', the MAT.

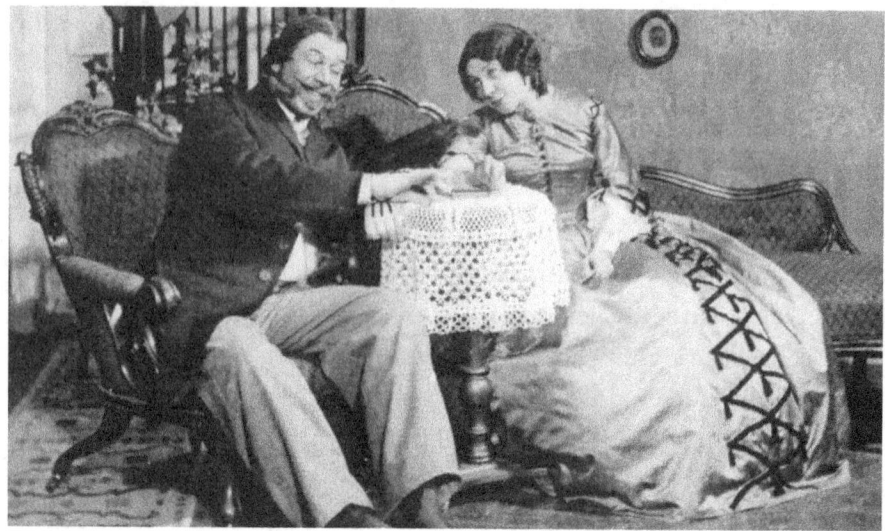

Figure 8 Stanislavsky playing Count Lioubine and Maria Lilina as Daria Ivanovna in Ivan Turgenev's *A Provincial Lady*, Moscow Art Theatre, mise-en-scène by Stanislavsky, 1912.
© The Museum of the Moscow Art Theatre.

But when the company returned to Paris in October 1923, (this second tour was again scheduled before the next American stop), the circumstances had radically changed. They had to flee the German Revolution, the shows in Berlin were cancelled, train ticket costs were one thousand times more expensive, and sixty people had to stay in Paris for one and a half months when the dollar rate had just collapsed and President Raymond Poincaré had blocked their visas. Moreover, one performance had to be postponed because the set was late, and the compensation had cost them dearly. Not only were they already in debt, but they also had to create new costumes because some had been stolen. The troupe was exhausted from never-ending travel and, overwhelmed by this avalanche of misfortune, they feared overwork and tensions. The repertoire had been modified: to *Tsar Fiodor* and *The Cherry Orchard* they also added Goldoni's *La Locandiera* (*The Mistress of the Inn*), Chekhov's *Ivanov*, Ibsen's *An Enemy of the People*, and the stage adaptation of *Brothers Karamazov*, this time in full. But the presentation of non-Russian plays was an obstacle for the French spectator. What they had appreciated in acting Tolstoy, Gorki, or Chekhov, they disliked for Goldoni or Ibsen.

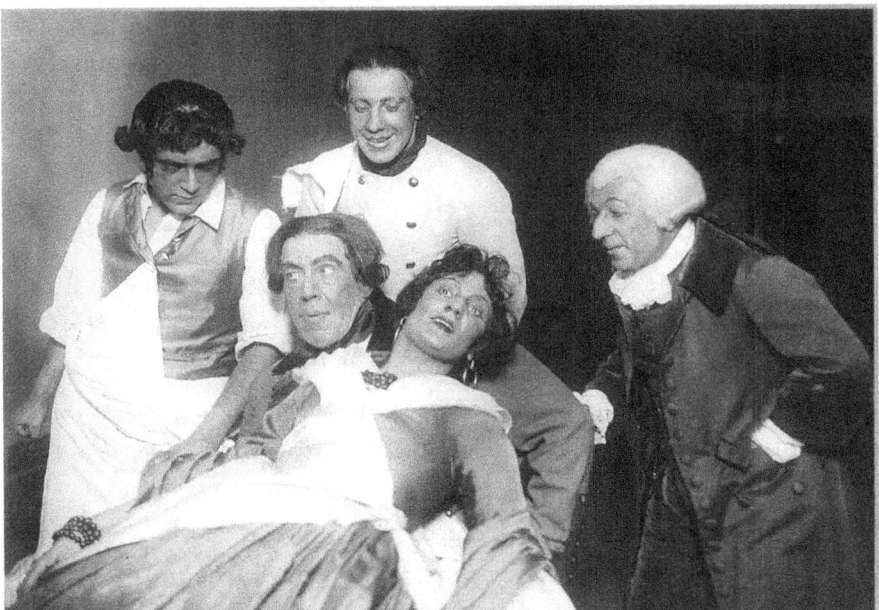

Figure 9 Stanislavsky in the role of Baron Ripafratta in *La Locandiera* by Carlo Goldoni, Moscow Art Theatre, mise-en-scène by Stanislavsky, 1914.
© The Museum of the Moscow Art Theatre.

A compilation of the reviews the company received in Paris during its *first tour* can provide an overview of its reception. André Antoine expressed his admiration for a disciplined theatre that played truthfully and as an ensemble. He even wished to have discovered the MAT earlier (Antoine, 1922). The company was also compared to a religious brotherhood that was at the service of art, while Stanislavsky was compared to Saint Joseph: 'he carries his genius like the carpenter carries his planer' (Kessel, 1922). Louis Jouvet related in detail Stanislavsky's visit to Jacques Copeau at the Vieux-Colombier (a small community impelled by devoted disciples), and expressed his admiration for the Stoicism of the Russian director who, in respect of the theatrical art, stayed level-headed on the stage of the windy Théâtre des Champs-Élysées while the set was being rapidly moved (Jouvet, 1954, p. 287, p. 290). The unanimous feeling was that a lesson had been received.

A few discordant voices were heard, however, in this choir of praises. Some noted that the exceptional success of the tour was to be expected and that the work of the actors from Moscow was not new. This opinion prevailed during the *second tour* in autumn 1923. With the element of surprise gone, the reception was tainted with remarks that were more about ideology rather than aesthetics.

The political weight

As the 1920s progressed, the French press and a majority of the audiences welcomed performances from abroad with more and more hostility. This kind of cultural nationalism crystallized around the respect of the text and a mistrust regarding the mise-en-scène that could be nothing more than 'a theatrical treatment inspired by an unbridled fantasy and by the desire to shine as an individual' (Copeau quoted in Corvin, 1993, p. 14).[13] The rigour and sobriety of the French were considered an antidote to German pomposity (Expressionism) and to Bolshevik extravagance (Constructivism).

In 1922, very few conservative reactions welcomed the performances of the Moscow Art Theatre, which were quite sober in comparison to the excesses of the Russian Ballet, with its splendour, Oriental aura, and colourful folklore. The fact that the audience did not understand the Russian language was not considered an obstacle, because the 'other expressive skills the actors possess, are so eloquent' (Antoine, 1922). Nevertheless, Pierre Veber's exasperation revealed some xenophobic hints that the majority of journalists would publicly express one year later:

> From time to time, we suffer from 'exotic fever'. We need Dutch people, Spanish ones, Flemish, Germans, Russians, etc., etc. And suddenly these people are better artists, better set designers, better writers, and better musicians.
>
> Veber, 1922

Indeed, in October 1923, Paris received the MAT along with the Swedish ballet of Rolf de Maré. In March of the same year the audience had already discovered Tairov's Chamber Theatre, 'the most dangerous offensive that our Theatre has known in years', according to Antoine, who encouraged to not 'let us be more damaged' and to resist what 'disintegrates our genius and our good taste' (Antoine, 1923a). Antoine claims his admiration for Stanislavsky who does not ruin Art but improves it, and adds: 'it is high time that we give the scene back to the French taste, but let us go ahead and imitate the others [Stanislavsky and the Art Theatre] for their respect of original work, the author and the audience' (Antoine, 1923b).

This time, critics remained sceptical. To them, the MAT represented the past, its art was only one side of Russian art, and looked foreign to the 'genius of French culture' (De Schloezer, 1923). About the *Brothers Karamazov*,[14] G. Boissy claimed that 'those Russians [...] are, deep down, nothing but barbarians. Their Bolshevism was only a theory to free their primitive tempers' (Boissy, 1923).

If Stanislavsky, during the second tour, doubted the real and particular curiosity of the Parisians, he was also preoccupied with the political tensions, which were worsening and turning the company into a puppet. Provocations had started one year earlier in Berlin, when he had met actress Maria Germanova, an opponent of the new Communist regime. Some journalists had commented on the event, casting doubts on Stanislavsky's loyalty. In 1923, France was very hostile to the new Bolshevik power, and was the only country to recognize the White government under General Wrangel.[15] Could the fact that France had accepted the Art Theatre for a second tour be interpreted in Moscow as a suspicious French gesture of confidence?

Stanislavsky remained vigilant. He was in Paris for the twenty-fifth anniversary of the MAT, and felt it dangerous to celebrate the event there because Russian immigrants would have to be invited. He chose to forbid any private meetings on the 14 October 1923, and to give little significance to that night's performance by using understudies. He did not go to the Théâtre des Champs-Élysées, even though he was called there three times. Nevertheless, he failed to outsmart another provocation the day before his departure. Despite the actors being extremely tired, he accepted to support a charity event at the Lutetia Hotel, which would help starving writers and theatre people in the USSR. He realized too late that the main sponsor for the dinner was Pavel Milioukov, a former minister of the Provisional Government, who emigrated in 1918 and was now the Chief Editor of the Russian newspaper in Paris *Poslednie novosti*. Stanislavsky immediately had to send Vladimir Nemirovich-Danchenko an explanation of what happened, as the event was quickly exploited in Moscow. On the 13 November 1923, an anonymous and venomous article, entitled 'Art theatre and white immigration' was published in the Soviet press:

The applause and praises to those traitors of the working class, to those negotiators of the Russian people's successes, should horrify and disgust all those who cherish the new proletarian Russia. But apparently our actors from the Art Theatre do not feel this way; their conscience is darkened by their long stay abroad.[16]

Apparently, the proletarian press took the extension of the tour as a desertion. The enemies of the MAT did not stop there and found a new occasion to drag them through the mud. In December 1923, during a charity auction in New York, a picture appeared in the American press showing the Russian artists next to Prince Felix Yusupov. Soviet newspapers used that photo with the caption 'Expatriates have illegally taken out valuable goods and sold them abroad'. On 12 February 1924, Stanislavsky had to send another explanation to Moscow to reaffirm his loyalty (Stanislavskii, 1999, t. 9, p. 130).

Paris, 1937: The end of the old Art Theatre

The international tour of 1922–4 was important in two ways: on one side, it was well-attended both by the general public and foreign artists, thus preparing the way, for the teaching of Stanislavsky's System.[17] The second is that this tour was the turning point, once they returned to Moscow, for the reorganization of the Art Theatre. Although the original objective (coming back with a mountain of dollars) was not attained, it became clear that it was impossible to continue the way it had been till then – the repertoire as well as the actors were growing old, and the administration had been overturned by nationalization. For Stanislavsky, the real break-up did not take place during the October Revolution but upon the return from the international tour, in spring 1924. The division between those who made the international glory of the Theatre and those who had stayed in Russia was doubled by another split between the old and the young. This generational divide showed different attitudes to the new political and cultural realities. The youth did not believe in Art above all, in self-sacrifice for aesthetic and ethical ideals. They believed more in social action and the education of the masses. When he returned to Moscow, Stanislavsky realized that the founding principles of the Theatre – a dual-direction (Stanislavsky and Nemirovich-Danchenko) without interference from political authorities, a collective feeling and ensemble playing, working in close collaboration with authors and designers, who are freely chosen, training in the System and with flexibility – were over.

Thirteen years later, the Art Theatre tour in Paris in August 1937 sadly revealed what the company had become: the political display window for Stalin's theatre policy. The company included 160 people travelling with twenty-two wagons. They presented a repertoire that Stalin himself had selected. It contained one Russian classic: *Anna Karenina* by Lev Tolstoy, and two Soviet plays: *The Enemies* by Maxim Gorki, and *Lyubov Yarovaya* by Konstantin Treniov.

Figure 10 Alla Tarassova playing Anna Karenina and Mikhail Proudkine as Vronski in Lev Tolstoy's *Anna Karenina*, Moscow Art Theatre, mise-en-scène by Vladimir Nemirovich-Danchenko, 1937.
© The Museum of the Moscow Art Theatre.

All these productions were directed by Nemirovich-Danchenko who accompanied the company on his own. This time, Paris was the only destination, chosen not for France's cultural prestige, but for the international exhibition happening there, which gave Stalin the opportunity to present a 'sample' of Soviet art (Bertenson, in Arensky, 1968, p. 244).

As in the 1920s, when it had served as a step towards the American Eldorado, Paris was again just a pretext. The Stalinist USSR wanted to prove to the world that it had a great theatre, traditions that were not only preserved but also transformed. The Art Theatre's realism had become 'socialist', and the Art Theatre troupe had undergone a rejuvenation which had made it tougher, more direct and more 'popular' (Russian immigrants would find it provincial and vulgar). The slow erosion of the Theatre's founding principles was hardly masked behind the ostentatious official recognition, such as the Lenin Order, which had been attributed to the company just before the tour and which was also part of Stalin's 'gift' (Nemirovich-Danchenko, quoted in Arensky, 1968, p. 250).

At the same time when the Art Theatre made that journey for pure propaganda, the collaboration between the two founding directors came to an end, after forty years. Stanislavsky died exactly one year later, in August 1938. His old companion remained alone at the head of that enormous institution, which had become the jewel of socialist theatrical art.

At the beginning of the 1920s, the Moscow Art Theatre had exported a model of artistic work. In 1937, it exhibited a model of State theatre. France did not really witness the first stage that was revealed during the first European tour of 1906: a free, independent, innovative, and modern theatre.

Stanislavsky in France: misunderstandings

Having demonstrated the influence of French Theatre on Stanislavsky's training apprenticeship, studied his determination to find other acting approaches, and described the context of the three MAT's tours in Paris, one can conclude with a number of hypotheses on the paradoxical System's limited impact on actor training in France.

We know that Stanislavsky insisted on the practical aspects of his teaching, and was not giving an absolute value to his writings: he warned that the System was not a philosophical book, but a practice based on the experience and engagement in a work programme: 'When philosophy starts, the System stops'(Stanislavski, 1966, p. 306). The French missed that point. From the beginning, they distrusted the training that they took as a rigid theory, which they had discovered thirty-two years after the Americans and in a version which was very different from the Russian one (Benedetti, 2005). Until the first translation in French of *An Actor Prepares* in 1958, Stanislavsky was considered only as an actor and a director, and remained disassociated from his pedagogy. From the triumphal tour of the 1920s, Antoine, Copeau, Firmin Gémier, Jouvet, Charles Dullin, Jean Vilar, and Antoine Vitez became relays for the legend around Stanislavsky, a legend born at the beginning of the twentieth century with books from Jacques Rouché and Gordon Craig, and sustained by oral stories from travellers or expatriate artists (Georgy Serov, Gueorgui Serov, Vladimir Sokolov, Georges Pitoëff, Mikhail Chekhov, Grigori Chmara, Maria Germanova).

The admiration towards Stanislavsky: the man, the artist, the director of a company as an 'ensemble', and the founder of studios is unanimous (Dort, in Stanislavski, 1966, p. IX). However, it is symptomatic that Copeau and Vilar, two preface writers of the first translations of Stanislavsky's works, were not interested in the System and preferred to highlight the mystery which surrounded the creative process (Copeau, in Diderot, 1995, p. 335). While they also believed that the renewal of theatre is through the education of a new artist, they disagreed on the fact that the laws of nature could be replicated in the theatre through an inner approach that was as rigorous and progressive as a grammar. Copeau wanted to rediscover life in its natural outpouring, without theory and through improvisation (Copeau, 2000, p. 410). For Vilar, the actor who analyses the gestational process of creating a role cannot go through completely and make sense of the 'inexpressible' (Vilar, in Stanislavski, 1958, p. 13). As for Vitez, he started his career in theatre in the 1950s and 1960s as a fervent admirer of Stanislavsky. To him, the Russian artist was the man who invented the School and asked the right questions. But Vitez was against the idea of a progressive and complete pedagogy (Vitez, 1994, p. 56). To him, the great merit of the System is the provision of a vocabulary which permits the naming of the stages of the actor's psychological progression (Vitez, 1994, p. 61). As from the 1970s, Vitez turned to the teachings of Meyerhold and his overtly theatrical political theatre, experimenting with conventional forms and no more with realistic matters.

Therefore, on the one hand, supporters of the traditional theatre of 'representation' resist the Stanislavskian 'experiencing' pedagogy and, on the other hand, French stage seeks new forms which break away from mimesis, embodiment, and the 'as if' illusion.

Years have passed and nothing has changed. Stanislavsky's pedagogy still continues to arouse sceptical reactions. Without even considering the complex notions such as *emotional experiencing* or *affective memory*, the simple term 'System' creates distrust. Stanislavsky's acting is associated with psychological realism that presupposes a work that is thought of as static, introverted, as cut off from partners and deprived of spontaneity. Stanislavsky's name remains an important reference in drama classes and during rehearsals, but it has a number of biases and prejudices; perhaps it is because of the weight and scope of French tradition, with its strong attachment to the text and reliance on good diction, or perhaps because there were no direct translations of Stanislavsky's works from Russian, and perhaps finally, maybe also because of the lack of curiosity by French artists who are still inspired by the Diderot's *Paradox of the Actor*.

Notes

1 Stanislavsky attended Anne Judic's tour in Moscow in November 1883. His sisters saw her in Paris.
2 Alexandr Lensky (1847–1908), actor and director of the Maly Theatre, Moscow.
3 *Marchands de gloire* premiered on 15 June 1926. Stanislavsky was assisted in his direction by Vasili Luzhsky and Nikolai Gorchakov. *Les Sœurs Gérard* premiered on 29 October 1927. Stanislavsky was assisted in his direction by Gorchakov and Elizaveta Telesheva. *Le Mariage de Figaro* premiered on 28 April 1927. Stanislavsky was assisted in his direction by Telesheva and Boris Vershilov.
4 After the Revolution, at the beginning of the 1920s, this division that Stanislavsky contests will be taken by Meyerhold in his explanation of bio-mechanical acting. The avant-garde artists, indeed, refuse psychology and its principles and preferred a rational, materialist art, that is measured and measurable. Meyerhold also refers to the French system of the actor's emploi, which he will define in the context of Soviet Theatre of the 1920s.

5 In French theatre, Stanislavsky traced the experiencing art back to Molière dramaturgy and the correspondence and memoirs of the famous actress Adrienne Lecouvreur at the beginning of the eighteenth century. See Vinogradskaia, I., 2003, 2, p. 437.
6 Stanislavsky had read extracts from Diderot's *Paradoxe sur le comédien* during the summer of 1914, before reading the whole text in 1923. It is not insignificant that Diderot's treatise was prefaced in 1923 by the Commissar for Public Education Anatoly Lunacharsky: at that time, the revolutionary left wing was looking for theoretical support to contest psychological theatre.
7 In Russian *affektivnaya pamyat'*, Translation from French. E. Maksimova, St Petersburg, tipografija A. Lejgert, 1899.
8 Mikhail Chekhov claims that it is not the truth of the experiencing that allows the birth of the character, but the imitation of this truth. The actor 'puts on' the character as he has seen in his imagination and imitates it. Arguing with Stanislavsky for whom the actor must start from himself to go to the character, M. Chekhov chooses Coquelin's side.
9 During the summer of 1911, Nemirovich-Danchenko was in Paris hoping to organize a 1912 tour of the Art Theatre that would alternate with the Russian Ballet. He met Serge Diaghilev, but nothing ever came out of it.
10 In 1921, Meyerhold wrote: '[. . .] now we understand the predominant social composition of the MAT audience, which consists of remnants of the bourgeoisie who were too late to board ships headed for Constantinople' (quoted by Soloviova, 1992, p. 75).
11 The expression has been cut in the first edition of Stanislavsky's *Collected Works in 8 Volumes* (1954–61).
12 The request, signed by Nikolai Podgorny and Sergei Bertenson, is dated 30 August 1922 and includes a list of names of the participants and their individual requests.
13 Until the 1960s, the domination of French theatre by dramaturgy goes along with the exaltation of classical repertoire, and explains the rejection of Artaud, Claudel (whose drama does not follow the Aristotelean model) and the mistrust for surrealism.
14 In opposition to the 'farcical performance' presented by the MAT, French critics appreciated the deep and sober directing of the *Brothers Karamazov* at the Théâtre des Arts, in an adaptation of Jacques Copeau and Jean Croué in 1911.
15 France recognized the USSR in 1924, seven years after the Bolshevik Revolution.
16 *Žizn' iskusstva* in Petrograd, then *Rul'* in Berlin and in *Poslednie novosti* in Paris.

17 But France, attached to the 'theatre of representation', and Germany, attracted by Expressionism and marked by Brechtian theatre, resist the penetration of Stanislavsky's teaching.

References

It was not possible to indicate the page numbers for Newspapers articles, which were kept as cuttings at the Performing Arts department of the Bibliothèque nationale de France.

Antoine, A. (1922), 'Discipline', *Comœdia*, 7 December.
Antoine, A. (1923a), 'Il faut réagir', *Le Journal*, 22 March.
Antoine, A. (1923b), 'Des gens sérieux', *Le Journal*, 22 October.
Archive Moscow Art Theatre, Chast' IV (Part 4), KS 1712, 1 ed. hr.
Arensky, K. (ed.) (1968), *Pis'ma v Gollivud. Po materialam arhiva S. Bertensona*. Monterey (USA): K. Arensburger.
Autant-Mathieu, M. C. (ed.) (2005), *Le Théâtre d'Art de Moscou, Ramifications, voyages*. Paris: CNRS éditions.
Autant-Mathieu, M. C. (ed.) (2007), *La Ligne des actions physiques. Répétitions et exercices de Stanislavski*. Montpellier: L'Entretemps.
Autant-Mathieu, M. C. and Henry, H. (eds) (2009), *Les Voyages du théâtre Russie/France. Cahiers d'histoire culturelle* No. 22, Tours: Université François Rabelais.
Autant-Mathieu, M. C. (2014), 'Copeau se rêve en Stanislavski', *Les nouveaux Cahiers de la Comédie-Française*, No. 12, October, pp. 45–9.
Benedetti, J. (2005), 'Les éditions occidentales des œuvres de Stanislavski', in *Le Théâtre d'Art de Moscou, Ramifications, voyages*, ed. M. C. Autant-Mathieu. Paris: CNRS, pp. 79–95.
Binet, A. (1896), 'Réflexions sur le paradoxe de Diderot', *L'année psychologique*, Vol. 3, No. 3, pp. 27–95.
Boissy, G. (1923), *Comœdia*, 20 October.
Chekhov, M. (1995), *Literaturnoe nasledie*, t. 2. Moscow: Iskusstvo.
Cohen, L. (ed.) (2010), *The Lee Strasberg Notes*. New York: Routledge.
Copeau, J. (2000), *Registres VI. L'Ecole du Vieux-Colombier*, ed. C. Sicard. Paris: Gallimard, coll. Pratique du théâtre.
Coquelin, B. C. (1894), *L'Art du comédien*. Paris: Paul Ollendorff. Translated in *Russkij artist*, 1908, No.15.
Corvin, M. (1993), 'Une chance manquée de l'entre-deux guerres en France', *Confluences*, St-Cyr l'École, pp. 12–23.
De Schloezer, B. (1923), *La Nouvelle Revue Française*, 1 December.

Diderot, D. (1995), *Ecrits sur le théâtre, t. 2. L'acteur,* ed. established and presented by A. Ménil. Paris: Pocket, coll. Agora Les Classiques.

Dullin, C. (1985), *Souvenirs et notes de travail d'un acteur.* Paris: Librairie théâtrale.

Gurevič, L. (1926), *Tvorčestvo aktera, O prirode hudožestvennyh pereživanij aktera na scene.* Moscow: réed. Knižnyj dom LIBROKOM.

Jauss, H. R. (1978), *Pour une esthétique de la réception.* Paris: Gallimard, coll. Bibliothèque des idées.

Jouvet, L. (1954), 'Rencontre avec Stanislavski', *Revue d'histoire du théâtre,* Vol. IV, No. 24, pp. 287–90.

Kessel, J. (1922), *Liberté,* 22 December.

Levinson, A. (1923), *Comœdia illustrée,* October.

Otan-Maťe (Autant-Mathieu), M. K., Galcova, E. (2006), *Ot teksta – k scene.* Moscow: OGI.

Ribot, T. (1931), *Psychologie de l'attention.* Paris: Félix Alcan (first edition in 1889).

Ribot, T. (2007), *Problèmes de psychologie affective.* Paris: L'Harmattan (first edition in 1894).

Senelick, L. ed. (1992), *Wandering Stars, Russian Emigré Theatre 1905–1940.* Iowa City: University of Iowa Press.

Senelick, L. (ed. and trans.) (2014), *Stanislavsky, A Life in Letters.* London and New York: Routledge.

Sibirakov, N. (1974), *Mirovoe značenie Stanislavskogo.* Moskva: Iskusstvo.

Smeliansky, A. (1991), 'V poiskah Eldorado. Amerika v suďbe Hudožestvennogo teatra', *Moskovskij nabljudatel',* No. 11, pp. 1–6 and No. 12, pp. 9–12.

Soloviova, I. (1992), 'Do You Have Relatives Abroad? Emigration as a Cultural Problem', in *Wandering Stars, Russian Emigré Theatre 1905–1940,* ed. L. Senelick. Iowa City: University of Iowa Press, pp. 69–83.

Stanislavski, C. (1958), *La Formation de l'acteur,* trad. E. Janvier, preface by J. Vilar. Paris: Olivier Perrin.

Stanislavski, C. (1966), *La Construction du personnage,* trad. C. Antonetti, preface by B. Dort. Paris: Olivier Perrin.

Stanislavski, K. (2008), *My Life in Art,* trans. and ed. J. Benedetti. London and New York: Routledge.

Stanislavskii, K. (1986), *Iz zapisnyh knižek,* v. 2. Moscow: VTO.

Stanislavskii, K. (1988–99), *Sobranie Sochinenii,* 9 Vols. Moscow: Iskusstvo. t. 5/1, 1993; t. 6, 1994; t. 7, 1995; t. 9, 1999.

Stanislavski, C. (1934), *Ma vie dans l'art,* trad. N. Gourfinkel et L. Chancerel, preface by J. Copeau. Paris: éditions Albert.

Suleržickij, L. (1970), *Povesti i rasskazy. Staťi i zametki o teatre. Perepiska. Vospominanija o L.A. Suleržickom,* pred. E. Poljakovoj. Moscow: VTO.

Šverubovič, V. (1990), *O starom Hudožestvennom teatre*. Moskva: Iskusstvo.

Tolstoy, L. (1897/1995), *What is Art?*, trans. R. Pevear and L. Volokhonsky. London: Penguin.

Vakhtangov, E. (2000), *Écrits sur le théâtre*, trans. annotated, and preface by H. Henry. Lausanne: L'Âge d'Homme.

Veber, P. (1922), *Le Petit Journal*, 6 December.

Vinogradskaia, I. (2003), *Letopis' žizni i tvorčestva K S. Stanislavskogo*, v. 3. Moscow: Moskovskij Hudožestvennyj teatr.

Vitez, A. (1994), *Ecrits sur le théâtre, 1. L'Ecole*. Paris: P.O.L.

3

Between Nationalism and Ideology: Stanislavsky in Lithuania

Ina Pukelytė

The chapter deals with the two periods in the dissemination of Stanislavsky's theatre ideas in Lithuania. The first period relates to the development of the Lithuanian National Theatre, during the first Lithuanian independence that stretched between 1920 and 1940. The second period encompasses Soviet times, starting with 1947 and ending in 1989. The objective is to reveal how Stanislavsky's theatre ideas spread among a number of Lithuanian directors and actors and what impact they had on their artistic activities. Stanislavsky's system was introduced in Lithuania via his actors and students during the interwar period. They were escaping Soviet Russia in order to find better living and working conditions in the West. Amongst these one finds Andrius Oleka-Žilinskas and Mikhail Chekhov, who were among the most influential individuals for Lithuanian theatre. During the second, Soviet period, Stanislavsky's theatre approach was imposed on all Soviet theatres and countries by the Communist Party. During the first period Stanislavsky's ideas about theatre were considered innovative. They were developed by his students and were seen as open and progressive, whereas in Soviet times his theatre became a tool of Soviet propaganda. Nevertheless, directors like Romualdas Juknevičius and actors like Leonardas Zelčius, Laimonas Noreika, and Birutė Raubaitė, who had finished their studies at GITIS (The Russian University of Theatre Arts) after the Second World War, were able to transmit to Lithuanian actors Stanislavsky's theatre ideas and to maintain a high artistic level of acting and directing. The chapter will show that in both cases the political impact on theatre in Lithuania was of considerable importance and that the political decisions made during both periods were decisive for the dissemination and perception of Stanislavsky's ideas in Lithuania.

Striving for a National Theatre

As soon as Lithuania proclaimed its independence after the First World War in 1918, the National Theatre was created in Kaunas, the temporary capital of Lithuania.[1] The theatre was supposed to support the newly born country first of all ideologically, and therefore, discussions were started about its mission and conception. One of the outstanding individuals who was strongly engaged in creating the National Theatre was Balys Sruoga, a poet, theatre critic, and researcher.[2] In his articles of the beginning of the 1920s, Sruoga expressed the wish that Lithuanian theatre would imitate neither the Moscow Art Theatre (MAT), as its naturalistic acting was considered as having 'reached the end of its rope' (Sruoga, 1994, p. 28)[3], nor Tairov's Moscow Chamber Theatre, which at that time was staging symbolic plays. Lithuanian theatre was supposed to search for inspiration in its own cultural heritage and only then integrate modern acting knowledge derived from other countries. Its acting nevertheless was seen as a 'vivid affair of our life, coming out from our conditions of life and of our experiences' (Sruoga, 1994, pp. 28–9). Sruoga believed that the artistic force of the actor should join together with the will of the people, with the former being a moderator of the common creation. This aim, according to Sruoga, could only be achieved if the theatre was guided by artists that were seeking integration with the audience. He recognized such an artist in Andrius Oleka-Žilinskas, an actor of Lithuanian origin who was educated at the First Studio of the MAT.

Oleka-Žilinskas joined the MAT in 1913, as an associate. He stayed at the theatre for one year, after which he was recruited to serve in the army. He returned to Moscow in 1917 and was accepted as a student at the First Studio. Between 1917 and 1920 he played in several performances of the Studio, including *Twelfth Night*, *The Wreck of the Ship 'Hope'* and *Baladine*. The dream of the Studio's founders, Stanislavsky and Leopold Sulerzhitsky, was 'to create something that would be similar to a spiritual order of actors. Members of the order had to be more noble-minded, with wider horizons, perceiving human nature, being able to sacrifice themselves for a cause' (Stanislavski, 1951, p. 393). At the time when Oleka-Žilinskas was working in it, the aspirations of the Studio were starting to change, however: Sulerzhitsky had died in 1916 and Stanislavsky would soon distance himself from the Studio as it would become more of a formal theatre, with an emphasis on the production of performances rather than training. Striving for new challenges while trying to escape post-revolutionary Russia, Oleka-Žilinskas left Moscow for Kaunas in 1920, with the goal to become a leader of the newly-founded National Theatre. In the summer of the same year the Lithuanian Art Association elected him, together with Sruoga, as a member of the Theatre Council, which had to develop a unique Lithuanian theatre concept based on rituals, fairy tales, and ancient songs, or the plays of certain Lithuanian modern writers (*Menas*, 1920, p. 4). Nevertheless, the Council decided that the theatre should be led by a personality that would have stronger links with Lithuanian actors, which led to Oleka-Žilinskas' being offered to head the newly established Acting Studio rather than the National Theatre. Since the ambitions of the young leader were not met, Oleka-Žilinskas soon left Lithuania for Paris, even before the opening of the Theatre. In the summer of 1921 he joined the MAT Prague Group, led by Vasily Kachalov, and toured with it in Europe until 1922, when he returned to the First Studio in Moscow. In 1924, the First Studio became the MAT II, where Oleka-Žilinskas worked until his return to Lithuania in 1929.[4]

Meanwhile, Sruoga had assessed the first five years of the National Theatre's existence, and found that it had failed to fulfil its mission in expressing the nature of Lithuanian theatre. The performances that were shown on stage were 'anti-artistic and anti-theatrical' (Sruoga, 1994, p. 69), without depicting the nature of the nation. The latter could be achieved only when an adequate form of acting would be created, a kind of particular Lithuanian style of acting (Sruoga, 1994, pp. 76–7). Sruoga systematically criticized the repertoire and the acting style of the National Theatre. He was convinced that the theatre needed a leader who would be able to introduce the theatrical innovations that were taking place in Russia, and Oleka-Žilinskas was proposed once again as the leader of the young Lithuanian National Theatre. As the 1926 correspondence between Sruoga and Oleka-Žilinskas shows, the latter was indeed interested in heading the theatre, but was wary of finding himself in the same situation of 1920 wherein he would not be recognized again as the leader. His driving force in theatre, insisted Oleka-Žilinskas, was the search for 'a profound feeling of art and ideology, which would be above any personal matters, because it is the only thing that unites everybody and thus creates the united spirit' (Oleka-Žilinskas, 1995, p. 108). Oleka-Žilinskas specified that he would return to Kaunas only if he could work in conditions that made the revelation of this spirit possible.

Oleka-Žilinskas' ambition fitted the concept of the theatre that Sruoga had in mind and efforts were made to persuade him to come and work at the National Theatre.[5] It took three years to prepare the arrival of Stanislavsky's pupil and in September 1929 Oleka-Žilinskas disembarked in Kaunas for the second time. His first engagement was a production of the play *Šarūnas*, written by the modern Lithuanian writer Vincas Krėvė.[6] At the same time Oleka-Žilinskas also worked with the students at the Theatre's Acting Studio and at the Hebrew Acting Studio.[7] It was in February 1930 that he officially became the head of the Theatre and its artistic director. At that time he was already supported by his troupe, who admired his method of rehearsing and communicating. They distinguished three important qualities in Oleka-Žilinskas' approach to theatre. First of all, he was very much concerned with theatre ethics and often quoted Sulerzhitsky's dictum 'no aesthetics without ethics', which meant that actors were to feel part of a collective, be attentive to each other and behave themselves not only as actors but also as responsible citizens. The second quality was his capacity to help an actor find the kernel of a role and thus to achieve scenic truth, which for him originates from the plane of the imaginative and artistic fiction. This scenic truth gave actors the liberty of improvisation. Oleka-Žilinskas' third important quality was his capacity to create mass scenes, where every actor was directed to feel an important component of the performance (Oleka-Žilinskas, 1995, p. 26, p. 28, p. 44).

The success of *Šarūnas* was built on these principles. The theatre had, according to the critics, witnessed its long-awaited maturity. Oleka-Žilinskas guided not only the drama troupe of the theatre, but also its opera and ballet. In order to establish a certain order in the theatre, he wrote: 'I can admit only the same behavior in the theatre as it was in the MAT. And I will introduce here this behavior, no matter how much it costs me. I do not want people to conduct themselves as if in a public office, but to be in love and full of respect for what they are doing' (Oleka-Žilinskas, 1995, p. 136).

Šarūnas corresponded to what the Theatre Council had described, ten years before, as an authentic Lithuanian theatre. It is a dramatic poem, a song, and a fairy tale at the same time, about the heroic Lithuanian past and the ability of the people to sacrifice themselves in the name of the homeland. In interpreting the play Oleka-Žilinskas refused any illustrative or naturalistic scenes and condensed the text and the actions in a way that it started to resemble a song, thus achieving a unique form of performance. While analysing the performance in his article '*Šarūnas* at the National Theatre', Sruoga pointed out the reasons of its uniqueness. First, he emphasized that Oleka-Žilinskas had explained to the troupe as well as to the press the idea behind the performance (Sruoga, 1994, pp. 123–46). In other words, the press knew beforehand the purpose of the play and could explain it to the audience, while the actors understood the sense of their being on stage. Second, the form of the performance demanded that the troupe acted as if it was an orchestra. The actors had to coordinate their instruments – bodies and voices – in a way that the whole would again resemble a song. Sruoga also recognized Vakhtangov's influence in Oleka-Žilinskas' performance and it proves that Oleka-Žilinskas did not limit himself only to the Stanislavsky's acting approach, but integrated in his work the aesthetical findings of other Stanislavsky's pupils.[8]

With the performance of *Šarūnas* several things became evident concerning the Lithuanian National Theatre and its relationship to the theatre reforms going on in Russia. Lithuanian theatre observed the latter reforms, but did not literally transfer to its stage Stanislavsky's approaches. It was only when the creative group working on a performance could find a specific form and meaning for them being on stage, that this acting approach – the notion of ensemble and the individual work on one's voice and body – was considered as progressive. Stanislavsky's system was a flexible form; it was alive and modified according to the artistic personalities that were transmitting it to the actors. Ultimately, *Šarūnas* crowned the efforts of the Lithuanian intellectuals, especially Sruoga's, to create a National Theatre that would be relevant to contemporary society by giving rise to profound questions about the newly reborn nation. Oleka-Žilinskas finally became the leader of this theatre and was tasked with opening it to the progressive theatre movements of the time.

Figure 11 *Šarūnas*, directed by Andrius Oleka-Žilinskas.
© Lithuanian Museum of Theatre, Cinema and Music.

The Acting School

Oleka-Žilinskas' aim to achieve a new standard in the understanding of theatre was supported in two ways: first, as mentioned earlier, he offered acting courses at the Acting School of the National Theatre and, second, he invited his former colleague Mikhail Chekhov to support him both at the Theatre and the School.

Oleka-Žilinskas himself described the content of his own courses as 'Stanislavsky's system'. The courses were methodically written down by his pupil Algirdas Jakševičius. Later on, when Oleka-Žilinskas was already living in the United States, he used these notes to prepare his courses for American students (Girdzijauskaitė, 2000, p. 85).[9] The courses consisted of a theoretical background as well as practical tasks, for students to learn step by step how to react in given stage conditions, create characters, and improvise texts for their scenes. Students were introduced to Chekhov's acting practice in 1931, which corresponded to their third year of studies. Oleka-Žilinskas distinguished Chekhov's practice from that of Stanislavsky, describing it as image based, whereas for him Stanislavsky's approach was based on empathy with the character.[10] He did not want his students to limit themselves to only one acting approach, but to get acquainted with others that were developing at the time.

The students of the School would soon meet Chekhov in person. Together with other actors of the MAT –Viktor Gromov and Aleksandra Davydova – Chekhov came to Kaunas at the invitation of Oleka-Žilinskas, for a tour in May 1932. On this occasion he pronounced himself in the Lithuanian press on the mission of theatre in young countries such as Lithuania or Latvia: 'The younger the country is, the more ideas it has about culture, more willingness and determination and, therefore, it has more possibilities to create a new theatre' (*7 meno dienos*, 1932, pp. 83–8). According to his experience, the modern spectator did not want to be entertained but wanted a theatre that would make him think about what was going on, a theatre that would make him better. In this way Chekhov joined and supported the discourse that was already taking place between Oleka-Žilinskas and Sruoga.

Chekhov's visits to Kaunas were short, but significant. He combined them with his other work at different theatres in Riga.[11] In 1932 and 1933 he staged three performances: *Hamlet, A Midsummer Night's Dream*, and *The Government Inspector*, plays which Chekhov had already staged in Moscow, either at the MAT (*The Government Inspector*) or at the First Studio (*Hamlet, A Midsummer Night's Dream*). At the same time he also gave sixteen lessons to Oleka-Žilinskas' acting students[12], that were taken down as notes by the aformentioned Algirdas Jakševičius and Romualdas Juknevičius. The notes, together with his letter *On Atmosphere*, sent from Riga to Kaunas at Oleka-Žilinskas request, give an idea of Chekhov's main theatre preoccupation, which was to explore how an actor with his/her concrete actions can relay the inner spiritual life of the character and create its general image.

In spite of their intense and productive creative and pedagogical activities, both Oleka-Žilinskas and Chekhov were accused of moving away from the idea of the Lithuanian National Theatre. Indeed, the plays that Chekhov and Oleka-Žilinskas staged in Kaunas were mostly of foreign origin and their content did not correspond to the promises that Oleka-Žilinskas had started off with through the performance of *Šarūnas*. In some of his statements he even declared ironically that theatre cannot do the work of a historian and give society a substantiated picture of the country's glorious past.[13] This statement was supported by Sruoga, who declared that 'the essence of theatre expresses

Figure 12 Andrius Oleka-Žilinskas and Mikhail Chekhov.
© Lithuanian Museum of Theatre, Cinema and Music.

itself not in the choice of the plays but in its creative methods and means' (Sruoga, 1994, p. 165). In this way he was distancing himself from the national theatre idea that he had once believed in. The world economic crisis of the early 1930s caused a rise of nationalistic minded ideology, both in Lithuania and Latvia, and it was required for the theatre to stop the expansion of the Bolshevik ideology that, according to the pro-nationalist critique, was represented by the artists of Russian origin.[14] Sruoga was concerned with this simplistic approach to art and argued that 'if theatre serves the state but not art then it ends up in the same ideological place that Russia found itself in several years ago, and which is now diligently imitated by the Nazis. [...] A comformist piece of art never gives the world anything worthy or eternal' (Sruoga, 1994, pp. 163–4). Thus Sruoga supported Stanislavsky's concern for a theatre that deals with, first of all, aesthetic rather than social questions (Benedetti, 1990, p. 235).

In Latvia, as well as in Lithuania, national sensibility was in tension with what was emerging from Bolshevik Russia. This polarization, represented by pro-nationalist critique and supported by some of the actors, led Oleka-Žilinskas to leave the post of the head of the theatre in October 1933, while Chekhov left Riga towards the end of May 1934.[15] Oleka-Žilinskas tried to stay in Kaunas and create an independent theatre with his former students, with whom he created the Young Theatre (Jaunųjų teatras) in 1933. The theatre staged one play based on Harriet Beecher-Stowe's *Uncle Tom's Cabin*. However, having no state support, he abandoned the project and left the city in January 1935, in order to join Chekhov in Paris. Subsequently, both of them moved on to their subsequent destinations: Oleka-Žilinskas ended in New York in 1935, whereas Chekhov received an invitation to work in Great Britain.

Besides Oleka-Žilinskas and Chekhov, other students of the First Studio were active in Kaunas at different times, like Vera Soloviova, Oleka-Žilinskas' wife who played in some productions of the National Theatre[16] as well as supported her husband at the Acting School. Another name is that of Victor Gromov, who offered courses at the Hebrew Acting School, and Michael Gor, a former student of the Third Studio. Stanislavsky's colleague, the famous Russian set designer Mstislav Doboujinski, lived in Kaunas for a longer period and prepared stage sets for numerous performances of the National Theatre.

The above activities show that even though Stanislavsky's approach to theatre was considered as the basis of acting technique and theatre education, it was also enriched with the progressive theatre ideas that Oleka-Žilinskas and Chekhov developed during their career. Therefore, their activities, as well as those of their compatriots Soloviova and Doboujinski, promoted the Lithuanian National Theatre to the European vanguard. However, the turbulent political situation decribed above, as well as the rise of National Socialism in Europe, interrupted the intense theatrical development that was possible in Lithuania from Stanislavsky's associates. Nevertheless, it still left important imprints in the artistic formation of many of the actors and students of the National Theatre and its Acting School. Actors gave attention to the notion of ensemble, the development of their psychophysical apparatus, and an organic approach to the characters they played. Therefore, these imprints were centred on a sharp awareness of the aesthetic rather than political dimension of theatre.

Oleka-Žilinskas' and Chekhov's studies especially inspired two young men, Algirdas Jakševičius and Romualdas Juknevičius. Both found their vocation in stage directing, and after finishing their studies at the Acting School they broadened their knowledge in foreign countries – Jakševičius stayed for a year at Vakhtangov's theatre and then moved for a further year to New York, while Juknevičius stayed for two years in Moscow and worked at Meyerhold's theatre. On his return Jakševičius staged one play at Kaunas' National Theatre, Eugene O'Neill's *Marco Millions*. Unfortunately, any momentum to his career was interrupted by his abrupt death. Juknevičius, on the other hand, had a turbulent artistic career in Lithuania of more than twenty years. On his return from Moscow, he was joined by Henrikas Kačinskas and Juozas Grybauskas, two former colleagues from the School. The three were appointed by the Minister of Education to the newly created Klaipėda State Theatre. Their first task was to write a programme and send it to the authorities. This programme allows us to state that, after having observed and analysed different acting techniques in Moscow, Juknevičius had aligned himself to Stanislavsky's approaches. He declared:

> Theatre art is in its nature a collective art. [...] That is why we, the workers of the theatre, should remember Stanislavsky's words: 'I am definitely persuaded that in the theatre one should first of all create a collective that would have one aim and one idea, because without it no creative work is possible in the theatre.' A theatre collective is possible only when people involved talk in the same language. [...] If there is no common language, no system, there is no art as culture and there is no theatre.
>
> Aleksaitė, 1998, p. 81

Performances that Juknevičius staged until the Second World War in Klaipėda and later on in Kaunas and Vilnius (the latter regained the status of the capital in 1939) confirmed this belief. However, the Second World War and the political alterations again stopped the successful career of the director. After the end of the war Juknevičius was dismissed from Vilnius National Drama Theatre on the grounds of being politically unreliable and worked for seven years in the provinces. The annexation of Lithuania by the Soviet Union after the war abruptly stopped the development of the National Theatre and introduced a revised notion of Stanislavsky's system that was adapted to the needs of the Soviet Party and its propaganda in the whole Soviet territory. Thus, the discourse about the aims and means of the young Lithuanian National Theatre became obsolete.

From National to Soviet Theatre

Juknevičius closes the first period of the spread of Stanislavsky's ideas via his actors who migrated to the West. The second period relates to Stanislavsky's pupils who stayed in Russia after the Revolution and transmitted their knowledge to students that were purposely sent from different national republics to GITIS, the State Institute for Arts, in Moscow, to train in the system. This took place particularly between 1947 and 1952.

Stalin and his government recognized Stanislavsky's acting system as the only one that corresponded to the favoured Socialist Realism ideology and, therefore, it was the only one that could be taught to the younger generations of Soviet actors.[17] GITIS became a bastion of the new ideology that had to be passed on to future theatre artists of the whole Soviet Union. Therefore, groups of students of the newly annexed countries (Lithuania, Estonia, Latvia) were sent to Moscow to study acting so that on their return they would disseminate the knowledge in their own countries. Such a policy also aimed at the education of artists who would be loyal to the new regime and its ideology.

The Lithuanian group consisted of twenty-four students, amongst whom were future famous actors like Leonardas Zelčius, Antanas Gabrėnas, Laimonas Noreika, Antanina Mackevičiūtė, Regina Varnaitė, and Birutė Raubaitė, and directors like Henrikas Vancevičius and Aurelija Ragauskaitė. Most of them were fascinated by the possibility of studying in Moscow and saw it as an opportunity to acquire a deeper understanding of the system, which they previously only knew from the translations of Stanislavsky's books into Lithuanian.[18] As later interviews with these actors show, they studied the basics of acting with great enthusiasm. Lessons were given by Vasilii Orlov, a former student of the Second Studio and MAT actor, and Marja Orlova, a former student of the Third Studio. They were supported by Grigori Konski, a MAT actor of the younger generation. Closely related to the MAT, these teachers made a substantial impact on the way young actors understood their theatre mission. While trying to avoid an open confrontation with the ideological challenges of the epoch, Lithuanian pupils together with their teachers trained in how to express scenic truth, how to react in the given circumstances, how to create a character, and how to use their body and voice. The contents of the thirty-two lessons of the first year were transcribed by a secretary, in order to pass it on to later students as a system taught by Vasilii Orlov. As a copy of this report shows, the lessons were limited to technicalities related to the students' learning aims and avoided any typical Soviet language clichés which were otherwise necessary in the publications of that time.[19] The course's introduction explained why the lessons had to be recorded: Stanislavsky insisted that those pupils of his who were to transfer the system to their own students had to systematize their training, in order to find 'genuine principles for our artistic work. That would be really something fundamental.'[20] During the first lesson students got acquainted with the basic rules of the course: they had to develop respectful and trustful relationships with the teachers and with each other, be organized and disciplined, and have a general understanding of ethics. The lessons during the first semester consisted in both group exercises and the creations of small scenes. Therefore, students developed their attention, physical behaviour, memory, and imagination. During the second semester they got acquainted with the notion of rhythm, temperament, and the use of words in the scenes, which had to complement the actions rather than illustrate them. By the end of the year the students were capable of creating scenes that showed the developement of all these techniques.

During the first decade of the Soviet regime the mission of the theatre was also debated, as it had been debated in independent Lithuania. The newly instated authorities demanded theatre to serve ideological goals. However, the main difference was that Soviet theatre had to have a new, socialist, content. As the secretary of the Lithuanian Communist Party Antanas Sniečkus said: 'the wise national politics of our Leninist-Stalinist Party assures unlimited possibilities for the development of the culture of the Lithuanian nation; this culture is national in its form and socialist in its content' (Banionis and Guobys, 1986, p. 41). Lithuanian theatre had to take as an example 'the front of Russian Soviet culture', as well as the Soviet culture of other Soviet Republics, and use it to foster the development of Lithuanian culture. This discourse corresponded to the one that the Communist Party was enforcing in all of the Soviet Union Republics. It was demanded that Soviet theatres must copy the performances of the MAT. Copies of the Soviet heroes on the local stages had to be identical to the MAT originals, and therefore, even such props as wigs or moustaches had to be brought directly from the workshops which belonged to that theatre (Aleksaitė, 1998, pp. 158–9).

As in the former independent Lithuanian theatre, the national repertoire was in Soviet times also considered by politicians as an important tool to create a theatre with a new content. However, the new repertoire was not to support the search for a national identity but rather to produce socialist content that would show 'correctly the life of the Soviet society, influence the development of the best qualities of the Soviet people and educate Soviet youth in a Communist Spirit' (Banionis and Guobys, 1986, p. 34). As a result, a competition for the best Soviet plays was organized in 1947 across the whole Soviet Union. As the official reports of that time show, Lithuanian theatres and, especially, Lithuanian writers, could not easily adapt to the new demands and therefore different departments of the Lithuanian Communist Party's Central Committee took on the task to help the theatres, so that their repertoires would conform with the ideological objectives of the Soviet Union. Consequently, an order was issued in 1952 which introduced censorship in all Lithuanian theatres (Banionis and Guobys, 1986, p. 46), which was active until the collapse of the Soviet Union in the 1990s.

In spite of the strong state interference concerning the ideological matters of the Soviet theatre, the Lithuanian GITIS group in Moscow was able to produce performances of high artistic quality, which were later on brought to Kaunas Theatre and successfully performed during the years to come. Three performances, Maxim Gorki's *Barbarians*, Pierre Beaumarchais' *The Marriage of Figaro* and Jaroslav Galan's *Golden Eagle* were integrated into the repertoire of the Kaunas Youth Theatre. These three performances were directed by

Grigori Konski and they were considered as 'a threshold of a new rise of the theatre'.[21]

Stalin's death and the destalinization that followed during Khrushchev's rule, only gave little freedom to the theatre directors of the younger generation. All of them were still obliged to study in Russian schools since studies abroad were absolutely prohibited. Moscow and St Petersbourg (Leningrad in the Soviet period) were the only destinations for young people who wanted to study theatre directing. As these cities were the only places where rare artistic tours from friendly Western countries were allowed, young Soviet artists could get a glimpse of the current Western artistic trends and movements. Among such directors, Henrikas Vancevičius and his younger colleague Jonas Jurašas should be mentioned. They started introducing performing patterns, such as the Theatre of the Absurd and the Theatre of Cruelty, which were moving away from the realistic, socialist approach.[22] New trends in stage direction demanded from actors a new approach to the characters they interpreted. In the late 1960s and at the beginning of the 1970s, Stanislavsky's system started to become distanced from the professional stage, even though it still remained the main methodological tool for acting students at the Vilnius Music and Theatre Academy (former Conservatory). It was still recognized as the only theatre tool until the beginning of the 1980s. During that period, the young but already prominent director Jonas Vaitkus emerged with his own methodology. Vaitkus did not neglect Stanislavsky's approach of acting, but he also used other alternative acting methods, like Theatre of Cruelty or Grotowski's Poor Theatre style.[23]

Conclusion

Lithuanian actors became acquainted with Stanislavsky's approach at the end of the 1920s. It was presented to them not as an accomplished system, but as a work in progress, an open system that had to be complemented by Stanislavsky's students. The first people to transmit this understanding of Stanislavsky's system were Andrius Oleka-Žilinskas and Mikhail Chekhov. Both of them communicated their individual approach to acting and enriched it with their own theatrical experiences. Romualdas Juknevičius, a former student of Oleka-

Žilinskas and Chekhov, was especially inspired by the new approach to theatre art and transferred it to Lithuanian actors via the performances he staged. At the end of the 1940s and in the beginning of the 1950s Vasily and Maria Orlov introduced the system to a younger generation of Lithuanian students who were intentionally sent to study it in Moscow. Although the goal of the Communist Party was to prepare young actors who would be ideologically reliable and would serve as a tool of Soviet propaganda, the teachers tried to avoid ideological confrontations and concentrated on the transmission of the basic rules of acting, according to the teachings of Stanislavsky. Thus the quality of acting was improved in Lithuanian Soviet theatre.

Notes

1. After the First World War Vilnius was annexed by the Polish state and therefore the Lithuanian capital moved to Kaunas (from 1918 till 1938), the second largest Lithuanian city. The Lithuanian Drama Theatre was opened on 19 December 1920, with a performance of *The Feast of St John*, a play written by Hermann Sudermann. In 1922 the theatre was renamed The National Theatre of Drama and in 1925 The National Theatre. It is considered the first professional Lithuanian theatre that played in the Lithuanian language.
2. Balys Sruoga, born 1896, started to publish his poetry in 1912. In 1915 he studied Humanities in Petrograd and a year later he moved to Moscow for further studies. In 1918 he escaped the Russian Revolution and returned to Lithuania where he started to work as a teacher in Vilnius, but had to leave the city for Kaunas because of the Polish occupation. In 1924 Sruoga defended his thesis in Munich, Germany, and returned to Kaunas where he worked till 1940 as a Professor at the University of Vytautas Magnus. He was arrested by the Germans in 1943 and taken to Stutthof concentration camp. He returned back to Lithunia in 1945 and took a post at Vilnius University. Sruoga died in 1947, after having written his most famous book *Dievų miškas* (The Forest of Gods). This book was based on his reminiscences of life in the concentration camp.
3. All translations from Lithuanian are the author's.
4. A detailed Oleka-Žilinskas' biographical note was presented by Lithuanian researcher Gintaras Aleknonis. See: Aleknonis, 2001, pp. 300–4.
5. Jurgis Baltrušaitis was an important symbolist, who wrote poetry in Lithuanian and in Russian and founded the editing house Scorpion. During the period of

1922–39 he worked on a diplomatic mission in Moscow. Jurgis Savickis, a modernist writer, was also a member of the diplomatic community. He became the director of the National Theatre in 1927. Baltrušaitis and Savickis were the most important negotiators in persuading Oleka-Žilinskas to come and work in Lithuania.

6 Vincas Mickevičius-Krėvė was a writer, researcher, and political personality. *Šarūnas* is one of his first plays, written in 1911.

7 The Hebrew Acting Studio was created in 1923, by the initiative of the theatre critic Dr Alexander Mukdoni. It aspired to prepare professional actors who would be educated in the spirit of the processes that were taking place in the progressive Russian theatre. Therefore, the studio invited such teachers as Michael Gor, pupil of Vakhtangov, Oleka-Žilinskas and Viktor Gromov, a pupil of Mikhail Chekhov, among others. Oleka-Žilinskas worked at the Hebrew Acting Studio till January 1930. He was later replaced by Viktor Gromov. Oleka-Žilinskas started to rehearse with the students the play *The Mighty Castle*, which was later completed by Viktor Gromov in May and shown at the National Theatre.

8 The First Studio was created by Stanislavsky and Sulerzhitsky but it was the latter who took charge till his 1916 death. Sulerzhitsky was followed by Vakhtangov, who was to work there till his death in 1922. Afterwards Chekhov assumed leadership of the Studio.

9 Žilinskas arrived in New York in 1935 and began at once to teach acting. He created his own Actors Studio in 1940 but he had to close it during the war period. He reopened the Studio after the war and worked there until his death in 1948.

10 Jakševičius' notes *Olekos-Žilinsko vaidybos sistemos užrašai* can be found here: LTKMM, File AD466, pp. 9–10.

11 Between 1932 and 1933 Chekhov worked in Riga at the National Theatre and at the Russian Theatre.

12 The courses took place between 18 August and 2 November.

13 In the press conference presenting the 1931 season Oleka-Žilinskas noted: 'We are preparing a Lithuanian ballet that should be based on Lithuanian national dances, on movements that are characteristic only to the Lithuanian nation. [...] And what is this "past" that is characteristic to us? [...] Instead of doing creative work our theatre is forced to go to ethnographic expeditions deep into the countryside and search for this "past", since there are no other sources for it' (Česnulevičiūtė, 2012, p. 110).

14 Three important Lithuanian newspapers and magazines, namely *Naujoji Romuva*, *Židinys* and *Vairas* accused the National Theatre with the Russification of the theatre. For instance, the Theatre was reproached for giving the role of Gertrude in *Hamlet* to the Russian Vera Solvojova and not to a Lithuanian actress, and that the

production of *The Government Inspector* advocated the Bolshevik way of living. More about it in Blekaitis, 1989, pp. 158–64.

15 An article in Latvian magazine *Brivā Zeme* (*Free Land*) illustrates this national sensibility. More in: Autant-Mathieu, 2009, 313–15.
16 Vera Soloviova played the role of Gertrude in *Hamlet*, staged by Michail Chekhov, and the role of Nemeside in Byron's poem *Manfred*, both in 1932.
17 As Sharon Marie Carnicke notes: 'Correspondence between Stalin and Stanislavsky, recently unearthed in the Moscow Art Theatre archives, suggests that indeed Stalin manipulated Stanislavsky's image in the world, imposing a virtual internal exile on him during the last four years of his life. [...] Stanislavsky's writings, too, were appropriated for the cause' (Carnicke, 1993, p. 24). When the Soviet Government decided to create a model acting school adjunct to the Moscow Art Theatre, *An Actor Works on Himself* was officially seen 'as setting forth the model curriculum for this school and therefore as its primary textbook. A commision was appointed specifically to vet the book and bring it into line with dialectical materialism, which, as Stanislavsky himself put it, had become the philosophy "required of all" under communism' (Schneider and Cody, 2002, p. 30).
18 In 1936 the book *Apie aktoriaus kūrybą* (About the Creation of an Actor) appeared, edited by the former students of Oleka-Žilinskas, Juozas Grybauskas and Henrikas Kačinskas. In 1938 Algirdas Jakševičius translated into Lithuanian Stanislavsky's *An Actor Prepares*. This book was published in 1947.
19 Personal archive of Leonardas Zelčius, a member of the GITIS Lithuanian between 1948 and 1952.
20 The manuscript of the course, personal archive of Leonardas Zelčius, p. 2.
21 More about it in: Vengris, 1979, pp. 152–3.
22 More about it in: Landsbergis, 1972, pp. 153–64.
23 Further readings concerning Jonas Vaitkus include: Bajor, 1991 and Šabasevičienė 2007.

References

Aleknonis, G. (2001), *Režisierius Andrius Oleka-Žilinskas* [Director Andrius Oleka-Žilinskas]. Vilnius: Scena.
Aleksaitė, I. (1998), *Režisierius Romualdas Juknevičius*. Vilnius: Baltos lankos.
Autant-Mathieu, M. C. (2009), *Mikhail Tchekhov. Michael Chekhov de Moscou a Hollywood du theatre au cinema*. Montpellier: L'entretemps.
Bajor, A. A. (1991), *Rozmowy z Jonasem Vaitkusem*. Krakow-Wilno.

Banionis, E. and Guobys, A. (1986) *Teatras 1940-1960*. Vilnius: LTSR Mokslų akademijos Istorijos institutas.

Benedetti, J. (1990), *Stanislavski: a Biography*. London: Methuen Drama.

Blekaitis, J. (1989), *Iš mūsų teatro praeities// Metmenys*, no. 56.

Carnicke, S. M. (1993), 'Stanislavsky: Uncensored and Unabridged', *The Drama Review*, Vol. 9. No.1 Fall: 22–37.

Česnulevičiūtė, P. (2012), *Andrius Oleka-Žilinskas, Balys Sruoga ir kiti*. Vilnius: Lietuviu literatūros ir tautosakos institutas

Girdzijauskaitė, A. (2000), *Lietuvių teatro istorija* [History of Lithuanian Theatre]. Vilnius: Kultūros ir meno institutas.

Jakševičius, A. A. *Olekos-Žilinsko vaidybos sistemos užrašai*. LTKMM (Lithuanian Museum of Theatre, Cinema and Music), File AD466, pp. 9–10.

Landsbergis, A. (1972), *Avangardizmas Lietuvos Scenoje// Metmenys*, no. 23.

Markevičiūtė, E. (2010), *Kauno Valstybinis Dramos teatras 90 (Kaunas National Drama Theatre 90)*, Kaunas.

Moore, S. (1969), *The Stanislavski System*, New York: Viking Compass Edition.

Oleka-Žilinskas, A. (1995), *Vaidybos džiaugsmas* [The Joy of Acting]. Vilnius: Scena.

Šabasevičienė, D. (2007), *Teatro piligrimas*. Vilnius: Krantai.

Schneider, R. and Cody, G. (2002), *Re: Direction A Theoretical and Practical Guide*. London and New York: Routledge.

Sruoga, B. (1994), *Apie tiesą ir sceną* [About Truth and Stage]. Vilnius: Scena.

Stanislavski, K. S. (1951), *Mano meninis gyvenimas* [My Life in Art]. Valstybinė grožinės literatūros leidykla.

Vengris, A. (1979), *Lietuvos tarybinis teatras 1940-1956* [Lithuanian Soviet Theatre 1940–1956]. Vilnius: Mintis.

Internet sources

'Lietuviu Meno Kūrėju Draugijos Teatro darbu pagrindai', in: *Menas* (1920), No. 1, 4, http://www.epaveldas.lt/vbspi/biRecord.do?biExemplarId=67648&biRecordId=6663 [accessed 14 September 2016].

'With M. Chekhov' in: *7 meno dienos* (1932), no 83, 8, http://www.epaveldas.lt/vbspi/biRecord.do?biExemplarId=26482&biRecordId=3549 [accessed 14 September 2016].

4

An Amateur Processing of the System: Stanislavsky in Malta

Stefan Aquilina

Introduction

This essay discusses Stanislavsky's impact on theatre in Malta, a small island in the middle of the Mediterranean with a population of about 400,000 people. Theatre practice in Malta saw its major developments from the 1960s onwards, developments that were informed by a search for a national identity and set against a backdrop which saw the country steadily moving towards the 1964 independence from British colonialism. The impact of Stanislavsky's practice on theatre in Malta can be approached from several angles. There is no evidence to support the existence of a direct line of theatre transmission, one that would see a Maltese practitioner training with Stanislavsky himself. The Russian director did visit Malta briefly in September 1914, but no theatrical activity is recorded as he and his fellow travellers were not granted permission to disembark from their ship (in Vinogradskaia, 2003, p. 442). Several indirect lines do, however, exist. In fact, a number of Russian and Soviet practitioners who had trained within the Stanislavsky acting tradition delivered a number of workshops in Malta, or staged productions with local actors.[1]

Among these one finds Vera Vlasova, a former student at the Moscow Art Theatre Studio of Massalitinoff in Berlin and member of the Prague Group. Vlasova delivered a series of lectures and workshops in 1973. Her visit was organized by the United States Information Service and Theatre Workshop, a local theatre collective whose members, like Albert Marshall and John J. Schranz, would become prominent names in local experimental theatre.[2] Inna Soloviova, a theatre academic from the Lunacharsky State Theatre Institute and the Moscow Art Theatre Studio-School, delivered another set of workshops and lectures in 1990 to Theatre Studies students, at the University of Malta. Her focus was on the relationship between Anton Chekhov and Stanislavsky (*Times of Malta*, 1990, p. 9). Finally, a number of Soviet directors were invited by Politeatru, a left-wing theatre group, to stage productions with Maltese actors in the late 1980s and early 1990s. These included Niko Kiasashvili, who delivered sessions that outlined Stanislavsky's system, Andrei Droznin, Viktor Merezhko, and Aleksander Slavutski (Azzopardi, 2003, p. 143). To these one can also add Sergei Yashin's 1991 production of Alexei Arbuzov's *Evening Light*. Yashin was the director of the Gogol Dramatic Theatre in Moscow and he was described in the local press as 'a master of the Stanislavsky Method' (*The Sunday Times*, 1991, p. 20). This production was staged with the Atturi Theatre Productions (Actors Theatre Productions), Malta's closest attempt at a repertoire company.

Whilst these instances of Russian influence are important, my focus here is on another aspect of Stanislavsky's impact on theatre in Malta, namely the way that his ideas and practices were processed in an inherently amateur context by local practitioners who had first encountered the said practices abroad, while studying in various theatre institutions. What will emerge from this reading is a tendency to highlight individual components of the system over a more holistic application. This reductionism to a single component is a necessary practice in an amateur context like Malta which has consistently lacked both formal theatre institutions and professional opportunities. A series of interviews with about twenty local practitioners served as the main material for this essay.[3] My interview choices were dictated by a combination of factors. As stated, most of the practitioners chosen have pursued studies and training abroad. Moreover, they also shared the desire to improve the standards of the *teatrin* (Light or Diminutive Theatre). This was a widespread theatre practice that had emerged in the nineteenth century, where many companies staged undemanding and often haphazard entertainment for the common people. *Teatrin* had ceased to play a significant cultural role by the end of the 1950s, but its melodramatic scripts and acting had acquired a strong position in local theatrical memory, to the extent that many young experimental practitioners of the second part of the twentieth century still felt the need to express their unequivocal distance from it.[4] Finally, the practitioners interviewed tended to gravitate around the Manoel Theatre Academy of

Dramatic Art (MTADA), Malta's first formal theatre and acting school. The MTADA was set up in 1977 through a Technical Cooperation Agreement with Britain (Carabott, 2012, p. 67). It is still active today, under the name of the Malta Drama Centre, and offers tuition in theatre and dance to some 500 children, youngsters, and adults. Its current Principal is Mario Azzopardi, an important figure in Maltese literature and theatre. Azzopardi served, amongst others, as Artistic Director of the Soviet Cultural Centre in Malta and he was also the founder and main force behind Politeatru.

Encountering the institution

Historically speaking, the discussion that I will develop is located to the last part of the twentieth century, from the 1960s onwards. These decades saw several Maltese practitioners pursuing training abroad, within Russian acting schools and theatres (like GITIS, and the Vakhtangov, Taganka, and Simonov Theatres), English performance schools and universities (such as the Bristol Old Vic and the University of Bristol Drama Department, the Royal Central School of Speech and Drama, the Webber Douglas Academy of Dramatic Art, St Mary's University, Liverpool Institute for Performing Arts, and Rose Bruford College), and other continental spheres (e.g. the Real Escuela Superior De Arte Dramático in Madrid and the Piccolo Teatro di Milano with Giorgio Strehler).[5] Recurring throughout these training places is the encounter of one individual with the large-scale organization of a veritable theatre institution. In fact, local practitioners were quick to point out the scale of these institutions, one that revolves around an operational infrastructure, an enduring stability, large and state-of-the-art spaces, and a strong name generated through decades of practice and tradition building. For example, Giuseppe Schembri-Bonaci, a former Maltese Ambassador to the USSR, described the Vakhtangov Theatre (where he studied under the tutelage of Piotr Fomenko) as 'a machine: it employed three thousand people. [...] There is a structure [and] [a] disciplined system which I liked because [...] it let me work'. He noted how a time and space for work would be given to him with the knowledge that there are other specialists responsible for the production side of the work, the advertising, costumes, props, and so on. The theatre functioned like a factory, one which, however, also possessed a unique driving philosophy or ideology that would differentiate it from the numerous other theatres or schools in Moscow. The Taganka Theatre manifests a similar infrastructure. Stephen Florian, whose training in Moscow was made possible through a scholarship offered by the Malta-USSR Friendship Society, described it as a very stable theatre, with a repertoire running in three different halls, strong if controversial links with the government, several committees responsible for its operation, and a clear style and name of its own. In his own words:

> This is a stable theatre, with many scripts coming in, there is a repertoire going on and not just the staging of one play. There is not one hall but three. The committee must decide which plays are more compatible with the artistic style of the theatre.

These practitioners returned to Malta to find out that such institutions were missing.[6] It is around this lack of theatre institutions that I frame my use of the term 'amateur'. It is difficult to find material that tackles amateur practice on a meta-level. A reason for this is that the term 'amateur' is common parlance, in the sense that the meanings of 'an amateur photographer', of 'amateur football', and, of course, 'amateur actor' are all taken for granted. A negating approach that evidences a series of binary oppositions against professional theatre is at work here, one that relegates the existence of amateur theatre to a dependency on the professional scene. For example, amateur theatre is a non-professional activity that, consequently, does not generate financial profit to its unskilled practitioners.[7] Claire Cochrane, a theatre historian who researched the amateur practices of the smaller British nations, argues that such treatment owes its origin to the development of capitalism, which generated a desire for skill and day-to-day commitment from practitioners that rendered 'the amateur [as] non-professional and by implication incompetent' (Cochrane, 2001, p. 234). Amateur and professional theatres have consistently rubbed shoulders with each other in the histories of theatre practice, sometimes profitably, as when state-funded professional institutions developed from amateur activity, but also, and perhaps more predominantly, in conflict to one another, as when professional actors begrudge the audiences that attend amateur performances instead of their own.

The notion of what the amateur is, however, needs readdressing within the context of Malta which lacks a professional performance tradition and a professional contemporary scene. Theatre practice in Malta is still predominantly amateur in nature, and it was even more so during the years that I am surveying. Even today, very few practitioners have the opportunity to turn professional. Practitioners interviewed noted that they are indeed 'amateurs' in the sense that their work is rarely adequately remunerated, though they then seek to make up for this amateurism by instilling what they called 'a professional attitude'. This is seen in the case of Lemonhead Productions, for example, which is described as 'an amateur drama company with a professional approach'.[8] Mario Azzopardi remarks more generally: 'We are amateurs but with a professional attitude. I never staged a frivolous play. Never. [In the local scene] there is an attitude that seems to compensate for the fact that there is no financial accreditation'. This notion of a 'professional attitude' has led to the demarcation in two of the theatre scene, as seen from the reading given by Marvic Doughty, a former student of Azzopardi and his collaborator at both Politeatru and the Drama Centre:

> I am a professional banker, I can say that and I can state it because that is where I make my money. I am qualified in it, although in a certain way I am also qualified in theatre. However, professionally speaking my job is at the bank. The difference is that though we are amateurs, many of us still work in a professional manner [in theatre]. [...] There is a lot of effort involved in rehearsing long hours in the evening after a day of work. [...] Moreover, many see me as professional because I always participated in plays of a certain level, in demanding plays. The amateurs are those that participate in *teatrin*, in the villages and towns. [...] They can be very involved [...], but nobody taught them how to act. [...] The plays they stage have little depth. I believe that if I am not going to practice theatre for money, then at least I am taking something mental and cultural out of it.

This 'professional attitude' translates into a desire for more dedicated rehearsal work, more thought given in the choice of scripts, deeper characterization, and more socio-political commitment. Groups that sought to infuse their work with these practices while inevitably remaining within the constraints of the amateur context at large include the aforementioned Atturi Theatre Productions, Teatru 111, Teatru Strada Stretta, Koperatturi, Politeatru, Groups for Human Encounter, Lemonhead Productions, and Curtain Raiser Productions. It is within such groups that Stanislavsky's influence and consequent amateur processing can be discerned. Prominent among these

Figure 13 Giuseppe Schembri-Bonaci's production of Dario Fo's *Gli Arcangeli non Giocano al Flipper* (*Archangels Don't Play Pinball*) at the Simonov Theatre in Moscow (1997).
© Giuseppe Schembri-Bonaci.

groups were individuals who had either studied abroad or formed strong ties with foreign institutions. They modelled their groups on these theatre institutions but, showing an uncharacteristic pragmatic streak, opted from the outset for a more modest scale. Returning practitioners not only sought to apply the practical techniques they had studied, techniques that included but were not restricted to Stanislavsky-based approaches, but also attempted the recreation of that modus operandi characteristic of theatre institutions:

> On my return to Malta [from Moscow] I had no choice but to work as I had learned. I did not know how to work differently. I had to create my own group, one that would have a certain relationship together, a group that would know and understand each other following years of work together. A group that would share an ideological and philosophical basis.
>
> Schembri-Bonaci

These theatre groups can be considered as institutions on a 'smaller scale'. I use this appellation on purpose. Vicki Ann Cremona, Associate Professor of

Figure 14 Frank Camilleri in *Id-Descartes*, MITP Theatre, Valletta, Malta, November 1996.
Photo by Jeremy De Maria. © Frank Camilleri.

Theatre Studies at the University of Malta, describes local theatre developments as having followed European and American trends, but 'on a greatly reduced scale' (Cremona, 2008, p. 128). The discussion being developed here sheds light on the meaning of this 'smaller scale' or 'greatly reduced scale' designation and sets the ground for the local processing of Stanislavsky and the system. The standards of these small-scale institutions saw much improvement over *teatrin* groups, but they never came close to the longevity of the foreign institutions, to their consistency of production and, in most cases, to their standards. For example, the local 'mini' institutions still had to make do with much shorter rehearsal periods than their foreign models, an essential point which I shall discuss below. The major successes were in this case perhaps scored by Teatru 111 and Groups for Human Encounter. Under the direction of Stephen Florian, the former performed their works over a period of eight to ten weeks, thus giving the actors the opportunity to fine-tune their work. The latter's production of *Id-Descartes* (co-created by director John J. Schranz and performer Frank Camilleri) was presented many times over a period of eight years between 1996 and 2003, and in about ten different European contexts.[9] The 'smaller scale' factor can also be seen in the use of performance spaces. Although the awareness of having one's own space as a means of creating a sense of belonging to a particular theatre practice and ideology can be discerned, the small spaces used by many of the theatre groups mentioned above can hardly be compared to the 'monumental' theatres of, for example, Moscow.[10]

The amateur processing of the system

The transfer and processing of the system in any context out of Russia, including Malta, is one example of a much broader discourse about 'cross-border knowledge transfer'.[11] The importance attributed to the transfer of knowledge between cultures is one that increased dramatically in today's globalized world. In fact, studies like Bhagat et al. (2002) have shown the intrinsic link between the rapid globalization that marked the last fifty years or so and cross-border transactions. These transactions engage in knowledge that is defined as 'a resource that exists in an individual or a collective and is embedded in rules, processes, or routines. It is a product of human reflection and experience and *is either explicit and codified in formal rules, or tacit and not easily articulated or explained*' (Javidan et al., 2005, p. 63; emphasis is mine). Both explicit and tacit forms of knowledge chime with the transfer and dissemination of performance practices. For example, the articulation of explicit knowledge in formal rules resonates with what Dan Rebellato (2009) refers to as 'the phenomenon of McTheatre', i.e. the 'megamusicals' franchise that transfers a show across different contexts through the acquisition of very precise scores, lighting designs, movement patterns, direction plans, costumes, merchandise and so on. This result in a series of productions that 'are, to a very significant extent, identical' (Rebellato, 2009, p. 41). The more tacit forms of knowledge in theatre take the form of embodied (training) practices, of which the system is an example. Embodied practices respond to the difficulty in articulating the nature of what is being transferred and how it is being assimilated, reflecting tacit knowledge's imperative to be both 'inimitable' but at the same time also 'appropriable' (Al-Laham and Amburgey in Kohlbacher and Krähe, 2007, p. 171).

In Malta, the processing of Stanislavsky was informed by this tension between what is 'inimitable' and 'appropriable'. The 'mini' institutions referred to above did not provide the infrastructure necessary to delve in the holistic study and application of Stanislavsky and therefore Maltese practitioners tended to appropriate singular and, therefore, 'smaller' or even minor components from the system. In effect, they brought a sense of reductionism to the system, an alignment to single components of Stanislavsky's work which I would like to argue takes two forms: the technical and non-technical. Reference to *An Actor Prepares* illustrates the technical form. This reference is made here on purpose, as a number of practitioners were first introduced to Stanislavsky's theories through this book.[12] For example, Alfred Mallia, who played an important role both in acting pedagogy as well as in Theatre-in-Education, emphasized the role of Imagination in the creation of roles, particularly when the actor has to embody experiences that are alien to his experiential baggage. Mario Azzopardi underlined the Emotion Memory component and regarded this as a valuable technique to help the actor discover his or her inner self. Other practitioners referred to more general building blocks of acting technique, which they linked back to Stanislavsky. These included Characterization, make-believe, and inside-outside processes. On the other hand, several other practitioners tended to translate this singular emphasis in a less technical aspect of Stanislavsky's, such as a concern with the ethical dimension of theatre, as in theatre being a reality that deserves 'a certain respect' (Josette Ciappara) and, interestingly, the example presumably posed by Stanislavsky in the creation of a national theatre institution (Schembri-Bonaci). Stanislavsky's research in village life for the production of *The Power of Darkness*, centred as it was on the life, folklore, and customs of the traditional Russian peasant, was here cited as a model. What is most revealing to notions of amateurism, however, is not that these practitioners adopted one element from the system, but that each underlined a different aspect altogether. The amateur processing of the system reflects a uniqueness and diversity that is perhaps more synonymous with amateur theatre and which belies the institutional packaging of Stanislavsky.

The reduction of the system into a single element is necessary because theatre-makers in Malta have to consistently contend with short rehearsal periods. This lack of time, as well as appropriate rehearsal and performance spaces, has always been a hurdle for anyone doing theatre in Malta. In view of these shortcomings, the application of one component from the system becomes both a technical choice as well as an operative necessity. Schembri-Bonaci related how a director like Fomenko could take three years to stage *The Queen of Spades*, a production that would then stay in the repertoire for a further two years. This was possible because the infrastructure was in place. Such rehearsal periods are generally unheard of in Malta, and indeed the few groups which extend their rehearsals and transform them into an exploratory and devising space are generally frowned upon by the more mainstream groups. The application of a single technical aspect derived from Stanislavsky answers directly to this lack of rehearsal time and emerges again in the use made by certain practitioners of what I call 'everyday life as a space for rehearsal'. This practice sees the actor adopting in his own everyday life physical and psychological traits of the character being rehearsed. It extends the short rehearsal times at one's disposal. On a first level, the practice of using everyday life as a space to rehearse and work on a role is perhaps more easily associated with Method acting. Indeed, actors like Al Pacino have referred to it in the context of a number of movie roles played.[13] However, its origins can be traced back to Stanislavsky who first experimented with it when, most revealing, he was still a young amateur actor and lacked a formal and systematic approach to create a role. For example, he used it in 1883 when rehearsing *A Practical Man*, by performing regular improvisations and living throughout his day as the 'character within the circumstances of the play' (Stanislavski, 2008, pp. 43–4).[14] On a first level, these experiments might be seen as naïve, especially when juxtaposed with the more complex work that he would carry out in his mature years, but the reality is that the practice of using the everyday life of the actor as a space to work on a role was recalled by Stanislavsky at a crucial moment in his development, when, while rehearsing *Dead Souls* (1932), he instructed Toporkov to perform a series of improvisatory pranks in his own daily life (Toporkov, 1979, p. 102). These were seen as important material for Toporkov to strengthen his grasp on the role of Chichikov.

The use of everyday life as a space of rehearsal seemed particularly recurrent among the practitioners interviewed. Bryan Muscat, a versatile director and actor who has worked in satire, TV programmes for children, and more traditional theatre, values the reactions of other people that this practice generates. These reactions help the actor gauge how convincing he is in his playing:

> We meet new people every day and all the time something is happening. You need to observe all the time as an actor. You need to use your friends and family. [...] Once I had a role where a guy was in love. His girlfriend left him, so I created a girlfriend which I didn't have. [...] I created this girl who everyone knew about but no one ever met. They thought she was real. After four months always talking about how much I loved her, and then saying she left me. I created the feeling of how it should be felt if this girl left me and I wanted these reactions from my parents and friends. [...] Seeing people's faces will teach you a lot in how to react.

A second example revolves around Karmen Azzopardi, one of Malta's leading actresses. Azzopardi took the preparation of her roles very seriously. Lino Farrugia, who directed her in a number of performances staged by the Atturi Theatre Productions, noted how she would host dinner parties in a manner reminiscent of the character she would be preparing, including the way she dressed, the food she prepared, and the way she generally behaved. A third case revolves around an anonymous actress who had problems living

Figure 15 Karmen Azzopardi and Paul Xuereb in *The Aspern Papers*, an Atturi Theatre Productions of 1976.
© Paul Xuereb.

the part of a nun. Stephen Florian, who was directing, asked her to put on the respective dress and go out in the streets. She also had to assess her playing through other people's reactions. Florian remarked how she came back 'transformed'.

It is revealing to note what the interviewee says next. In an attempt to validate the use of this exercise, reference was made to its application by Robert De Niro. Therefore, Stanislavsky's name, or of another practitioner in his tradition, is appealed to in order to validate one's practice. Latching oneself to the Stanislavsky acting tradition becomes a matter of achieving accreditation, an important issue with amateurs who are traditionally uncertain with their doing. Two practitioners (John Suda and Karmenu Aquilina) remarked how they had come across the name of Stanislavsky when they were well into their career. They were surprised to realize that they were following, 'more or less', his approaches ever since they had started doing theatre. This realization increased their confidence, in that there was a major name in theatre history who had suggested similar practices. The desire for accreditation is perhaps most evident in the case of John J. Schranz, founder and director of Groups for Human Encounter and former Theatre Studies Lecturer. Schranz makes consistent reference to Stanislavsky in his writings and interviews.[15] Stanislavsky was also a reference point during the first years of the MTADA. This was corroborated in a number of interviews. For example, Mario Azzopardi, who also served as one of the school's first teachers, related how the student-actor would be fascinated to find out the extent of Stanislavsky's impact across the world, especially in America, and how he had influenced the Marlon Brando generation of actors. The students felt that this was giving weight to their studies and that they were not working in a vacuum.

A certain ambivalence surrounding Stanislavsky's name is, however, to be noted. On one side we have the above calls for accreditation where the name of Stanislavsky becomes synonymous with theatrical excellence. For example, Rev. Prof. Peter Serracino-Inglott, a former University Rector who also played a key behind-the-scenes role in the political arena, described the soprano Miriam Gauci as 'if [she] had been trained by Stanislavsky himself' (*The Sunday Times*, 2011, p. 13). However, Stanislavsky has also emerged in other cases as a sort of phantom, one who is only subliminally present in the practice. In such cases his name is not directly referenced, very often in order not to overladen the amateur actors with whom one would be working. The awareness is, however, that his main tenets are indeed the building blocks of theatre practice which are impossible to neglect. This is evident in

Lino Farrugia, a director and teacher who first encountered Stanislavsky's teachings in the early 1970s through the instigation of Francis Ebejer, Malta's most prominent modern playwright. Farrugia remarked how he opts not to make reference to Stanislavsky's name, especially when working with young students, so as not to turn a rehearsal into a 'study'. Shirley Blake, a former Politeatru actress and subsequent co-founder of the group Troupe 18:45, makes a similar comment: 'even if they [the Politeatru teachers] were not bombarding us with Stanislavsky, the work was obviously [informed by] Stanislavsky'.

A further ambivalence is seen in the tug-of-war that emerges between the System and the Method. There is a general confusion between the two, with a number making reference to 'Stanislavsky's Method'. Similar confusions emerge as a result of a lack of knowledge of Stanislavsky's various phases and main tenets, with a number of practitioners confusing 'inside-out' processes or significantly simplifying major acting techniques. The latter was evident in one particular case. One interviewee noted that an actress with whom he was working had problems identifying with the character of Nina in *The Seagull*. To rectify this, they 'went through the psychophysical approach workshop; sitting down with your arms tied behind you trying to express a feeling, etc. Then letting go your arms. The psychophysical approach basically.' This reading, of course, shows none of the complexities marking recent debates on psychophysicality. While it is important to note that the interviewee's comment is weak only from an academic point of view, as any practitioner is perfectly entitled to adopt practices and to refer to them in any manner that he finds suitable,[16] it is equally important to point out that such simplistic reading is symptomatic of the local scene which lacks the developed contexts and institutions necessary to allow for an in-depth study of Stanislavsky or, indeed, of any other practitioner. Consequently, the complexities of the system as well as its potential are never really disclosed to local theatre practitioners. One positive point that emerges from this situation is that Stanislavsky is consistently referred to in a critical manner. He does not become the hallmark of theatre reference or, in other words, an institution, in the manner that Rose Whyman, for example, describes Stanislavsky-based approaches to 'have dominated Western acting' (Whyman, 2013, p. 138). As Manuel Cauchi, a leading actor and Drama Teacher specialist, says: 'I still fall back to that [Stanislavsky's] approach but I don't put it as the be-all and the end-all, absolutely not. [...] Sometimes I do, most of the times I don't, it depends on the situation'. Consequently, Stanislavsky is often placed within a shallow pool of influences that include Meyerhold, Copeau, Brook, Brecht, Grotowski, and Barba (Cremona, 2008, p. 128 and Azzopardi, 2012, p. v), names used according to the individual practitioner's penchant for, to use their own words, 'physical', 'political', or 'avant-garde' theatre.

Conclusion

In this essay the processing of Stanislavsky within a context that lacks a tradition of professional theatre institutions and practice was discussed. Such a context like theatre in Malta evidences a necessary reductionism that underlines singular elements of the system over a holistic application. Interest in Stanislavsky remains strong, as evidenced by the recent 'Acting with Stanislavsky' workshop that was organized by the Masquerade Theatre and Arts School (July 2013).[17] The workshop was led by Professor Michael Earley from Rose Bruford College. The socio-political context surrounding this workshop is very different from the one expounded upon in this article. Malta has been a member of the European Union since 2004, which has opened many opportunities for local artists in terms of funding, training, and engaging performance examples. As a result, the 'professional attitude' described above is starting to become supported by more professional training, qualification, and infrastructure. In fact, reference to a shift from amateur to professional frameworks is evident in such official documents as the National Cultural Policy (Galea et al, 2011, p. 52). This shift also informs one of the objectives behind the V.18 Valletta European Capital of Culture (ECoC) 2018, which is developing 'a sustainable cultural sector by rising to the challenge that the intensity and calibre of the ECoC title brings with it, particularly in terms of human resources and their professionalism'.[18] Stanislavsky will not be necessarily referenced within these emerging contexts, but the malleability of the system should at least guarantee his phantom-like presence in the general practice of theatre in Malta.

Notes

1. Lack of space does not allow me to discuss another possible lineage linking Stanislavsky to Malta, one that revolved around professional English directors brought over by the British Council to stage productions with the B.I. Players, the Council's amateur group. These visits took place in the 1950s and 1960s, and the productions featured both Maltese and English actors (Arrigo, 1998–9, pp. 52–4). Stephen Florian argues for the existence of this line and says that these directors 'claimed to be specialists in the Stanislavsky System'.
2. See *Times of Malta*, 1973, p. 6 and the event programme.
3. The interviews were carried out over a period of eighteen months between August 2012 and April 2013. Unreferenced quotes in the essay are sourced from these interviews. I would like to thank the 2013 cohort of students enrolled for the Theatre Studies unit THS 2044 *The Stanislavsky Acting Tradition*, at the University of Malta, for their assistance with the interviews.
4. Aspects of *teatrin* practice are documented in *Kitbiet dwar it-teatrin* (Essays on *teatrin*, Azzopardi, 2010).
5. Here, I also include the research oriented postgraduate degrees followed, for example, in Italy and France.
6. Attempts to create such theatre institutions, often on a national level, were either unsuccessful (see the attempt in the early 1960s coordinated by the British Institute in Malta and the local actress Ethel Farrugia, in Arrigo, 1998–9, p. 54) or short-lived (e.g. the Kumpanija Nazzjonali tad-Drama [National Drama Company] in the second part of the 1980s, see Cremona, 2008, p. 137).
7. Amateur theatre is treated in this manner in Schoell, 1963, pp. 151–7 and Hodgson, 1988, pp. 17–18.
8. This is taken up as a sort of slogan on the group's website. See: http://www.lemonhead.com.mt/ [accessed 20 August 2013].
9. See: http://www.icarusproject.info/performances/id-descartes/ [accessed 15 August 2013]. Camilleri has gone on to set up Icarus Performance Project (Malta), his own research group, in 2001. The Project researches 'the space between training and performance processes as a self-contained and integral phenomenon', on which Camilleri has published extensively (see Publications link on the group's site). Camilleri is also the current Head of the Department of Theatre Studies and Director of the School of Performing Arts at the University of Malta.
10. The search for a defining space is particularly seen in: Stephen Florian's housing of Teatru 111 in a small performance space that had formerly served as war rooms,

retitled as Lascaris Playhouse; Atturi's failed attempts on two different occasions to secure their own permanent space (Cremona and Schranz, 1994, p. 588); Teatru Workshop's use of a space in Marsamxett harbour; A-teatru becoming synonymous with the activity at the Tigne complex; and Groups For Human Encounter leasing of a garage in Naxxar and transformation into the ActionBase Research Studio.

11 I refer here to literature from the field of Management, which in recent years has given the issue of knowledge transfer due consideration. See Kohlbacher and Krähne (2007), Javidan et al. (2005), Bhagat et al. (2002), and Gupta and Govindarajan (2000).

12 A number of interviewees, including Stephen Florian, Lino Farrugia, and Mario Azzopardi have indeed noted that *An Actor Prepares* and the other Hapgood translations of Stanislavsky's works were already making the rounds from the late 1960s onwards.

13 See: http://flickeryflicks.blogspot.com/2008/01/al-pacino-method-actor.html [accessed 23 August 2013].

14 See also the anecdote in *My Life in Art* when Stanislavsky visited a train station dressed as a beggar to investigate the technical problems he was having with 'sense of moderation' (Stanislavski, 2008, p. 39).

15 See, amongst others, *The Sunday Times*, 1999, p. 5 and 2002, pp. 54–5.

16 I am here indebted to Jonathan Pitches' similar reading when he discusses the academic shortcomings of Lee Strasberg's book *A Dream of Passion*. See Pitches, 2006, pp. 110–11.

17 See: http://www.masquerademalta.com/news.php?id=214 [accessed 26 August 2013].

18 See: http://www.valletta2018.org/about/objectives [accessed 26 August 2013]. Valletta is the capital city of Malta. It was built by the Knights of St John after the victorious Great Siege of 1565 against the Ottoman Empire. Valletta was officially recognized in 1980 as a World Heritage Site by UNESCO.

References

Arrigo, C. (1998–9), 'From B.I. Players to Atturi', *The Manoel Theatre Journal*, Vol. 1, No. 3: 51–7.

Azzopardi, M. (2003), *It-Teatru f' Malta*. Malta: PIN Pubblikazzjoni Indipendenza.

Azzopardi, M. (ed.) (2010), *Kitbiet dwar it-teatrin*. Malta: Malta Drama Centre.

Azzopardi, M. (2012), 'Preface', in *M'hemmx Bżonn Siparju*, ed. M. Azzopardi. Malta: Malta Drama Centre, pp. v–vii.

Bhagat, R. S., Kedia, B. L., Harveston, P. D., Triandis, H. C. (2002), 'Cultural Variations in the Cross-Border Transfer of Organizational Knowledge: An Integrative Framework', *Academy of Management Review*, Vol. 27, No. 2: 204–21.

Carabott, Y. (2012), 'L-Istorja tat-twaqqif taċ-Ċentru tad-Drama', in *M'hemmx bżonn siparju*, ed. M. Azzopardi. Malta: Malta Drama Centre, pp. 61–79.

Cochrane, C. (2001), 'The Pervasiveness of the Commonplace: The Historian and Amateur Theatre', *Theatre Research International*, Vol. 26, No. 3: 233–42.

Cremona, V. A. (2008), 'Politics and Identity in Maltese Theatre: Adaptation or Innovation?', *TDR*, Vol. 52, No. 4: 118–44.

Cremona, V. A. and Schranz, J. J. (1994), 'Malta', in *World Encyclopaedia of Contemporary Theatre Europe*, eds D. Rubin, P. Nagy and P. Rouyer. London: Routledge, pp. 582–92.

Galea, D., Attard, A., Bezzina, D., Giglio, J., Mercieca, C., Grima, R. (2011), *National Cultural Policy Malta 2011*. Malta: Parliamentary Secretariat for Tourism, the Environment and Culture.

Gupta, A. and Govindarajan, V. (2000), 'Knowledge flows within multinational corporations', *Strategic Management Journal*, Vol. 21, No. 4: 73–96.

Hodgson, T. (1988), *The Drama Dictionary*. New Amsterdam Books: New York.

Javidan, M., Stahl, G. K., Brodbeck, F. and Wilderom, C. P. M. (2005), 'Cross-Border Transfer of Knowledge: Cultural Lessons from Project GLOBE', *The Academy of Management Executive*, Vol. 19, No. 2: 59–76.

Kohlbacher, F. and Krähe, M. O. B (2007), 'Knowledge Creation and Transfer in a Cross-Cultural Context – Empirical Evidence from Tyco Flow Control', *Knowledge and Process Management*, Vol. 14, No. 3: 169–81.

Pitches, J. (2006), *Science and the Stanislavsky Tradition of Acting*. London: Routledge.

Rebellato, D. (2009), *Theatre and Globalization*. Hampshire: Palgrave Macmillan.

Schoell, E. R. (1963), 'The Amateur Theatre in Great Britain', *Educational Theatre Journal*, Vol. 15, No. 2: 151–7.

Stanislavski, K. (1980), *An Actor Prepares*, trans. E. Hapgood. London: Methuen.

Stanislavski, K. (2008). *My Life in Art*, trans. J. Benedetti. London: Routledge.

Toporkov, V. (1979), *Stanislavsky in Rehearsal*, trans. C. Edwards. New York: Theatre Arts Books.

Vinogradskaia, I. (2003). *Zhizn I Tvorchestvo K.S. Stanislavskovo 2 1906-1917*. Moscow: Moscow Art Theatre.

Whyman, R. (2013), *Stanislavski: The Basics*. Oxon: Routledge.

Newspaper references

Times of Malta, 1973, 2 November, p. 6.
—— 1990, 11 March, p. 9.
The Sunday Times, 1988, 18 December, p. 44.
—— 1991, 20 January, p. 21.
—— 1991, 10 March, p. 20.
—— 1999, 17 January, p. 5.
—— 2002, 4 August, pp. 54–5.
—— 2011, 30 January, p. 13.

Moments of Transition: Stanislavsky in Greece

Maria Gaitanidi

Introduction

In searching for Stanislavsky in Greece the scarce sources available have made this research extremely challenging as well as exciting; it entailed collecting and uniting the scattered pieces of a giant puzzle. This chapter will not simply offer a historical overview of Stanislavsky's influence on Greek theatre-makers. It will assess critical statements of Greek practitioners themselves, statements about the writings and works of the Russian man of theatre which open the door for a number of questions regarding transmission, pedagogy, and cultural identity. The presence of Stanislavsky's work in Greece will hopefully allow to shed some light on the current state of the Greek theatre industry at an important moment of transition.

Greece's troubled history, with its constant interchanges between peace and war, and external (shaking off four-hundred years of Turkish occupation, the First and Second World Wars) as well as internal challenges (the military junta between 1967 and 1974), has profoundly influenced the evolution of theatrical activity and its associated cultural life. Against this fraught political background, modern theatre in Greece initially revolved around practices that, like other examples of continental theatre during the second half of the nineteenth century, relied heavily on the personality and unique temperaments of particular actors and actor-teachers. In fact, actors such as Marika Kotopouli, Andrianou Kiveli, Pantelis Horn, Dimitris Rodiris, Fotis Politis, and Pelos Katselis,[1] combined passion and instinct rather than formalized or academic knowledge in order to act, direct, explore, and transmit their art by creating schools bearing their names. Stanislavsky's role within this context was one of a catalyst towards a more ensemble playing, as will become apparent when discussing the work of Karolos Koun (1908–87) and Stathis Livathinos (1962–). These two directors will be considered as case-studies aimed at highlighting a discussion about the impact of Stanislavsky's theories and practices on leading us to believe that his research provided a paradigm for action rather than a model to be applied. This is observed after the Second World War and at the turn of the twenty-first century.

Preparing the ground: Thomas Oikonomou and Fotis Politis

There is no concrete evidence of Stanislavsky-influenced work in Greece during the first part of the twentieth century. Theatre practitioners at that time explored a number of practices which, in retrospect, could be seen to have paved the way for the implementation of the System in Greece. It is in the work of Thomas Oikonomou (1864–1927) that symptoms of Stanislavskian precepts can be identified first. Between 1900 and 1927 Oikonomou developed his practice within various institutionalized theatre contexts in Athens, like the Royal Theatre, the Royal Conservatory, and then the National Theatre. His approach was naturalistic to an exaggerated extent.[2] He notoriously demanded from Marika Kotopouli, one of the National Theatre's leading actresses, a visit to mentally ill patients in order to study for her role of Marguerite in Goethe's *Faust* (Grammatas, 2002, p. 234). Theatre historian Antonis Glytzouris writes that Oikonomou saw the actor as a creator, an artist rather than simply an executor. His performances as an actor in Ibsen's plays were highly regarded as the epitome of emotional realism that went beyond the mere delivery of the words and the imitation of emotions. Below is an extract from a 1910 review of one of Oikonomou's performances:

> [A]ccuracy, depth and, if I may use the expression, soul. Measured in his gestures, controlled in his cries, he confines all his power to his facial expression, which truly becomes the mirror of the soul. He pronounces his phrases in the most evocative way and always has the perfectly suited stance or movement. His eyes speak more than his mouth. The whole is as studied as each detail. For he does not present only the general lines of the man he

paints in his acting, but even the finest shading. A suddenly rhythmic, mathematical pace he assumes as Oswald in *Ghosts* tells us more than the most frenzied, the most lunatic movements of a commonplace actor.

in Glytzouris, 2012, p. 7

While it is not clear whether Oikonomou had any knowledge of Stanislavsky's experiments, it appears however that there are indeed parallels between the way that Ibsen's play was being performed here and Stanislavsky's first experiments as a director. This parallel with Oikonomou is evident in the ways that the Greek practitioner was trying to eliminate what Stanislavsky would refer to as the 'theatre in the theatre' (Stanislavski, 2008a, p. 118), evident when in the above quotation reference is made to measure and control as antidotes to frenzied and lunatic movements. There are also traces of Stanislavsky's early approach of using the outer dimension of performance (e.g. the facial expression) to express the actor's inner work, here referred to as mirroring 'the soul'.[3]

A similar parallel between emerging practices in Greece and Stanislavsky's ideas can be discerned in the work of Fotis Politis (1890–1934). Glytzouris described Politis as the first Greek director in the modern sense of the word, who thus contributed to the end of a star-centred theatre (Glytzouris, 2001, p. 201). Politis, who had also studied with Max Reinhardt in Germany, proposed an approach to staging that would see the director's endeavour to expose the nuances of a dramatic text:

> Politis calls for a directing art which acts internally, to distinguish it from directing of the external, which limits itself to the aesthetics of a nicely staged living room. [...] The director translates the work of the poet into the language of the stage. He finds the way for the deepest meaning of the play to appear, to illuminate the characters and thus to bring the spectator closer to the author. This is his aim and in order to reach it, everything becomes simple in his hands: the actor, the scenographer, the costumes, the musician, the dancer. Everything and everyone are at the service of the poet and his work.

Bastias, 1934[4]

Observing Greek practitioners' first attempts at defining their understanding of acting and directing, we note that their main focus was on the relation between the text/author and the actor. Actors were mainly judged on their ability to express the message of the author through a detailed expression of a range of human emotions. The Greek aesthetic tendencies of that period and the literary body of work show that Greek theatre artists were navigating closely to what was soon to be called the Stanislavsky System, especially in the ways that Greek directors were looking for psychological depth, less pompous acting, and a harmonious approach to production. Such early attempts can be seen to have prepared the ground for a more direct application of Stanislavsky's techniques, which in Greece can be credited to Karolos Koun.

Karolos Koun at the Theatro Technis

In 1942, at the height of the Fascist occupation of Greece, Koun opened the Theatro Technis (Art Theatre), with very specific objectives that included the development of 'collective work, theatrical training and common artistic aims'.[5] It is within this context of work that Koun first experimented with Stanislavskian techniques. Koun's place within the Stanislavsky acting tradition speaks of what Jonathan Pitches refers to as 'debates over the purity of a source' (Pitches, 2012, p.6). While Koun was unequivocal in his assertion that '[m]y reference was Stanislavsky' (in Varopoulou, 1992), the numerous sources that he mentions belie at root any exclusive affiliation to one practice or practitioner. Stanislavsky's influence on Koun was mediated through 'an American Stanislavskian staging' to which he had been exposed in the UK through a performance of Clifford Odets' *Golden Boy* (in Varopoulou, 1992). A second channel is through the translations in Greek of Stanislavsky's books. These were carried out by George Sevastikoglou, a playwright and Koun's friend.[6] A third line of influence relates to the French theatre tradition, as Koun wrote: 'I also got to know Russian theatre and Stanislavsky through the French stage. At the National Theatre I saw students of Copeau and when I was in France I saw performances of Gaston Batti and Pitoeff's production of Tolstoy's *Living Corpse*' (in Zei, 2015, p. 136). Following Copeau's objective to cleanse the text from artificial acting, what John Rudlin refers to as 'the quest of sincerity' (Rudlin, 2010: 43–62), Koun drew new demands from the actors, beginning with a search for a more psychological approach to theatre which harks back to the first phase of Stanislavsky's experimentation with the System. This is evident from Koun's own words:

> When we created the Theatre in 1942 [...] we were immersed in Stanislavsky's teachings. We did our best to learn everything about his school. We studied his books, we analysed his method. Then we loved psychological theatre, Ibsen, Chekhov, Pirandello. We were directly influenced by it. It is one of the reasons we named our theatre after the Moscow Art Theatre.
>
> Koun, 1997, p. 92

This psychological dimension permeated rehearsals with Koun, as evident in the following quotation by Koun's student Alexis Solomos:

> The young actors, each sunk in their corner, were quite oblivious to the outer world, and lived their parts within those bleak walls; in immobility at first and with only a murmur; then, slowly, the characters of the play emerged from the book and began to stir the actors' blood like a magic potion, which flowed as far as the tips of their fingers, and formed their lips in the shape of the words. You saw young men, who as the atmosphere of the suburban home or the small coffee shop faded from them, were wrapped in the northern grayness of Rosmersholm. There was something morbid, you might even say, nightmarish, in the profound concentration of the procedure. Koun sat in his own corner like the rest [...]. He watched silently. He let the young actors mould the text, give it shape, feel it. As they played, his face mirrored the emotions of all the parts in turn, and by merely looking at him they could be helped over any difficulty they encountered.
>
> in Kiriakos, 2012, p. 27

The actors themselves were realizing a shift in their approach to the character, where they had to research in depth and embody their roles. In the words of Lykourgos Kallergis, 'they [the actors] had to become the characters and not just interpret them'.[7] Audiences also reacted positively to Koun's actors in his production of *The Cherry Orchard* (1945). He scored another Chekhovian success a year later with the staging of *The Seagull* (rehearsed over six months, a first for the Greek industry). The audiences discovered a new stage atmosphere that was permeated with silence and hidden meanings behind the words, and Koun has thus been credited with creating 'a more sophisticated public through productions of foreign plays ranging from Shaw to Albee and reinterpretations of Greek classics' (Chambers, 2006, p. 329).

Whereas the performance dimension adopted from the Stanislavsky acting tradition is certainly psychological, Koun looked for a more psychophysical equilibrium through his research in Greek folk theatre, which contributed the physical dimension. He sourced the Theatro Technis actors from within the folk culture of his time so that the raw human material could embody the liveness and the plasticity of the body and feelings, exploring the possibilities of movement and speech which had a meaning because they emerged from a concrete need. He turned to the lower social classes where the harsh living conditions 'could be sensed and seen on the skin of the human beings' (Koun, 1997, p. 22), in order to cultivate actors who were very sensitive to the reality of daily life and accompanying emotions. Koun wanted to understand this reality and discover the root of what constituted existence in its raw form, in the sense that 'hunger is hunger, thirst is thirst and pain is intense, alive, marked without pretence on the body, the muscles, the nerves' (Koun, 1997, p. 22). He introduced the creation of character whose life exists before the curtain goes up and continues well after the lights go off in the auditorium, which is another practice that Stanislavsky had developed and termed as the play's 'before-time' and 'after-time' (Benedetti, 1998, pp. 152–3). Koun's actors had to act 'honestly, simply, modestly, with a constant battle between wry sarcasm and human pain' (Glytzouris, 2012, p. 13).

Stanislavsky's influence on Koun is also evident in the importance attributed by the latter to ensemble work which, like Stanislavsky, Koun also gave an ethical underpinning.[8] Koun began by giving more rehearsal time and by creating a suitable environment for the company, one that was removed from business matters (the sponsors of theatre were influencing heavily the artistic work because they were financing it). He gave everyone equal wages and also developed the importance of dedicating oneself to 'pure' art (Glytzouris, 2012, pp. 10–11). Koun's ensemble emphasis was manifested in the status given to the tiniest roles in a play and in how an artist should work with equal pleasure on any part, be it a jeune premier, a clown, or a servant. The way he speaks about the work of the artist echoes Stanislavsky's vision in *My Life in Art*, especially when the Russian theatre-maker wrote about the formation of the Moscow Art Theatre (Stanislavski, 2008a, pp. 159–60). In this case, Koun references Stanislavsky himself:

> Stanislavsky often intervened in the personal life of his collaborators. Flirting and easy relationships were considered as distracting and perverting to the

inner world of the artist, and hence he forbid them. However, he made sure that each actor had a room full of light and a small library, in a way that the actor's hysterical nature would soften up, which would make him realise that he is a spiritual worker.

Koun, 1997, p. 17

Koun continued his research, staging more Ibsen and Chekhov, but preferred to opt for a deliberate exaggeration of the form rather than a meagre realism, resulting in a more grotesque expression and creating his own poetic realism (Kiriakos, 2012, p. 20). The reference point here became the work of Evgeni Vakhtangov on fantastic or imaginative realism, to underline again that Koun's alignment to the 'Stanislavsky reference' still allowed deviation from the original source. It is very probable that Koun accessed Vakhtangov's theories through Nikolai Gorchakov, the latter's student, who published in English *The Vakhtangov School of Stage Art* in 1959.[9] Gorchakov states that Vakhtangov privileged a justification that would create an imaginative realism, where actors were required to exercise their imagination in order to find immediate justification for their actions, what is happening in the here and now of the performance, which was not necessarily stemming from the author's text (Whyman, 2008, pp. 166–7). Underlining these inputs, however, were values which Koun had absorbed from his earlier experimentation in Stanislavskian techniques, namely those of continuous search, the faith in development and progress, and observation of the environment.

There seems to be no trace in Koun's work of Stanislavsky's last phase of research on physical actions and speech as action as described by the latter's student Maria Knebel. We could only attribute this to a lack of translations,[10] an issue that all European and American practitioners and scholars have faced and still sometimes do. Koun would talk about the biomechanics of Meyerhold and the organicity of Grotowski's bodies,[11] but his focus would always shift to ancient Greek drama, where his first love for folk art and culture found its best expression. He passed away in 1987, leaving a 'style of acting [that] was easily discernible. [...] [M]uch depended on the subtlety of each detail. [...] [T]here was always homogeneity in the acting, the results of a dedicated, disciplined and hardworking group' with whom Koun worked for more than twenty-five years (Bacopoulou-Halls, 1998, p. 282). Koun's students, such as Mimis Kougioumtzis, Giorgos Armenis, and Giorgos Lazanis, who was described as 'the eldest of Koun's artistic inheritors' (Bacopoulou-Halls, 1998, p. 423) taught and directed after his death and today his school, which has run parallel to the main Theatre right from its inception, is still one of the most highly regarded theatre establishments in the country.

The work of Stathis Livathinos

Two pedagogical contexts marked Greek theatre training in the last few decades. The only set courses on Stanislavsky are those delivered at the Drama Departments of the University of Athens, Thessaloniki, Patras, and Nafplio. Sonia Moore's book *The Stanislavski System* features among the titles suggested in these Departments. As Phillip Zarrilli mentions in his article on re-reading Moore's book, such inclusions could indicate a predominant understanding of the System through the American Method Acting lens, which can only heighten the psychological emphasis in Stanislavsky's practice that had been practiced by Koun (Zarrilli, 1989, p. 38). Another popular title is Gorchakov's *Stanislavski Directs*. Both books are based on accounts of personal practice, hinting that Greek artists tend to prefer what is based on experience rather than academic research and theory. Such an experiential approach is concretely pursued at the drama schools of the National Theatre in Athens, Koun's Theatro Technis, and the Conservatory of Athens. From my experience of participating in an Anton Chekhov Seminar in 2010 on *The Cherry Orchard*,[12] and when working with alumni of all three schools, the impression that arises is that historical research and contextualization is often left to the discretion of the student and that it does not feature in the day-to-day work of these three institutions. Therefore, there is no direct reference to any theatre practitioner of the likes of Stanislavsky, Mikhail Chekhov, or Brecht. Plays are chosen and given to the students by the tutors, scenes and monologues are then distributed or selected by the students themselves and acted out in front of the tutor(s) and the whole class. Consequently, the craft of acting is fragmented into myriad practices each representing the ideas of particular acting teachers.

It is against this background that Stathis Livathinos can be found developing his practice. My sources in discussing Livathinos will change from what Diana

Taylor calls 'supposedly enduring materials (i.e., texts, documents, buildings, bones)' to 'the so-called ephemeral *repertoire* of embodied practice/knowledge (i.e., spoken language, dance, sports, ritual)' (in Davis, 2011, p. 93; emphasis in original). More specifically, I will bring in two kinds of input from the reservoir of my own experience. The first input is from within the rehearsal room, especially when Livathinos and his ensemble worked on a production of Mikhail Lermontov's *Masquerade* (2008). The second input is a critical evaluation of the Greek contemporary scene that is based on my observations and involvement as an informed spectator, but also as an interviewer of fellow Greek practitioners. These interviews include Irini Moundraki, the dramaturge and coordinator of the Drama Department of the National Theatre in Athens, as well as former students of Greek drama schools who are now theatre professionals. Consequently, the majority of the statements here are based on the personal opinions of artists, students, journalists, and theatre administrators. In this way, this material reflects the living process of experiencing theatre and observing its processes as a theatre practitioner and researcher.

Livathinos followed his first contact with acting in Athens – he is the grandson of Manos Katrakis, a great name of the Greek stage – by studying at GITIS in Moscow, between 1984 and 1990. Upon his return to Greece he set up a permanent laboratory within the National Theatre in Athens (2001–7), on a model that was not dissimilar to the ancillary relationship which the First Studio had in its first years of operation with the Moscow Art Theatre. Here Livathinos set out to research acting processes and produce work, against a working background that privileged the creation of an ensemble of actors. This was concretely searched through the transmission of a common vocabulary that included notions such as subtext, perspective, given circumstances, and a method based on étude work. When producing plays his actors worked together for minimum of five or six months, as Koun had done fifty years before. As a pedagogue and director Livathinos was not afraid to talk about Stanislavsky, but also other theatre practitioners like Anatoli Vassiliev, next to whom he learnt his art.

I had the chance of working with Livathinos on his production of *Masquerade*.[13] Observing Livathinos' rehearsals was very instructive, as he can be seen to have used a complex process that borrowed from and combined certain techniques not only from Stanislavsky and Vakhtangov, but also from Active Analysis as developed by Maria Knebel. I participated in Livathinos' analysis of Lermontov's text, where he would question his actors on the facts of the play. At the beginning of the process he would ask everyone to read all the roles and to articulate their understanding of these. This approach can be clearly traced back to Stanislavsky's Round-the-Table analysis which similarly sought to produce 'an in-depth analysis of the play' (Whyman, 2013, p. 13). However, Livathinos also directed actors to search for parallels between Lermontov's text and contemporary Greece. This practice chimes with Vakhtangov's work after the 1917 Revolution, which was always carried out with a direct eye on what was happening out of the theatre. As Pavel Markov asserted, 'it is impossible to separate [Vakhtangov's last productions] from Moscow of the period' (in Rudnitsky, 2000, p. 53). The analytic work carried out by Livathinos on the text went beyond the cerebral by using étude work, in an Active Analysis manner, where 'cast members examine the play "on their feet," through improvisations that test their understanding of how characters on the page relate to each other and confront each other in performance' (Carnicke, 2009, p. 212). To my knowledge Livathinos is the only director in Greece to even consider working with the études, having done so before Vassiliev directed Euripides' *Medea* (2008) or ran the aforementioned workshops on Chekhov's *The Cherry Orchard*.

Livathinos' work with the études did not necessitate actors to follow the exact structure of the text, as Vassiliev would teach me a year later, and neither did he underline the importance of the encounter between an actor's own material as a human being and the material of the play given by the author. Such synergy between the actor as a distinct human being and the Given Circumstances of a play was the approach which Stanislavsky developed at the end of his career, when he asserted that before delving into psychological depth, it is the actor's responsibility to ground his work in the tangible physical actions with which the actor is most familiar with as a human being: 'Art begins when there is no role, when there is only the "I" in the given circumstances of the play' (Stanislavsky quoted in Toporkov, 1979, p. 156). In steering away from this approach, Livathinos reiterates Koun's dilution of the original (Stanislavskian) source, in this case by adding Vakhtangov's more immediate outlook on the public world and a unique take on the études work.

A further contribution of Livathinos is that in the analysis, he discussed the possible justifications of the characters' relationships and actions in advance of the actors getting up to discover through études the scenic action. This resulted in an acting approach that merged psychophysical justification, symbolism (i.e. the aesthetic input through design and choreography), and directorial vision (Livathinos had a very strong opinion about the play which drove the actors in one clear and collective direction).

Livathinos is a great supporter of theatre pedagogy and he does not miss a single opportunity to highlight how the lack of artistic education in Greece has contributed to the lack of consciousness that theatre is a craft.[14] He notices that theatre is in the hands of the self-taught and describes the Greek theatrical education as being 'anachronistic and medieval'.[15] Livathinos suggests a Stanislavskian education for the actors and directors to be, not so much in the way they produce theatre but in the way they approach their practice. An actor needs to be full of curiosity and gather material for his roles through other artistic expressions (such as painting, sculpture, music, visual arts, etc.), daily life observations, and a constant cultivation of the mind, in a way that was proposed by Stanislavsky himself (Stanislavski, 2008b, p. 156 and p. 226). Many times he told me that there is no point of imposing a personal vision on a play if you have not exhausted the possibilities emerging from the play itself. His actors talk constantly about the play they rehearse in relation to their own experiences and also to the socio-political status quo. Livathinos' actors stand far from the simple learning of their lines and neither do they stop at the mere psychological explanation of the text. A strong example of this research was seen during the rehearsal of the bracelet scene in *Masquerade*, between the actors Maria Nafpliotou and Vassilis Andreou.[16] The two actors, in their everyday clothes, tried out the scene a few times, and a real game of structure and freedom developed which for me encapsulated the possibility of a theatre as Stanislavsky foresaw it in the final years of his research and passed on to his student Maria Knebel: the power and action of the word.[17] Here lies for me the key of a transition in both Stanislavsky's application in Greece as well as Greek theatre in general, when Stanislavsky is not considered outdated but actually becomes a model for research and experimentation from which springs a new period of work that marries the cultural, the pedagogical, and the political.

Paving the way again: Stanislavsky in Greece and the future

In a recent interview Livathinos judged that formalism is in retreat on the international theatre scene, and that it is time to return to the human soul in order to make theatre.[18] I am not sure how much this is accurate when I look at the new era of Greek theatre directors who are aged under 40, directors like Katerina Evangelatou, Dimitris Karatzas, and Hector Ligizos.[19] These emerging theatre-makers have often studied abroad (Germany and/or Russia) and they look for their own style through different forms, be it Brechtian, naturalistic, or verbatim.

Opposing Livathinos' statement is Theodoros Terzopoulos, another contemporary theatre-maker, who represents in his unique way a different side of contemporary Greek theatre. Terzopoulos has a particular link with Russian theatre and Russia, where he has been invited to stage his work. For example, in 2006 he staged with Russian actors a version of Sophocles' *Oedipus Rex* at the Alexandrinsky Theatre in St Petersburg.[20] His staging of Euripides' *The Bacchae* inaugurated the 2015 opening of the Stanislavsky Electrotheater (a transformation of the former Stanislavsky Drama Theatre).[21] Terzopoulos has a unique practice that includes techniques from the Polish and Oriental theatre traditions to create his own actors' training method. He announced the death of Stanislavsky's system in Greece, as he sees the system stuck in spider nets, while a certain physical and vocal formalism is seen to be more interesting: 'The birth of physical theatre in recent decades, primarily and formally in the 1980s, is now a fact, and therefore becomes featured extensively in global conferences and festivals.'[22] Terzopoulos, however, shares with Livathinos a similar preoccupation: the absence of a theatrical tradition due to the absence of a developed pedagogical tradition. He praises the potential of Greek artists in the making but criticizes the Greek State for having forgotten the necessity for supporting the arts.[23] In fact, his work and method will be published first in Russian before appearing in his own mother tongue.

It would appear that the constant search for foreign models, by studying abroad or by aligning oneself to other theatre traditions, as has been the case with Terzopoulos' exporting of his work to Russia, are testament of the need for figures who can overturn what has been established in the Greek theatrical culture and has proved immovable till now. It seems that whereas Greek artists are willing to explore alternative theatre practices, it is not to be immediately assumed that these alternatives can be embodied by them and accepted by the wider public as valuable. There is a dichotomy between aspiration and realization. I believe this issue could be resolved either by the joining of forces between the Greek State and the wider Greek theatrical community, where a common perspective (such as the creation of a strong educational system) could be shared, or, alternatively, by fuelling again the independent establishment of theatrical ensembles who, as Koun did some sixty years ago, start from scratch the process of research into the actor's craft in a way that is threaded in the Greek socio-cultural evolution and heritage.

Heading towards the end of this short journey I would like to briefly share my work experience of Greek actors whilst they were studying with Vassiliev in Athens in order to support my statement above with concrete facts based on experience. My observations echo Livathinos' and Terzopoulos' thoughts. During the workshop on *The Cherry Orchard*, I saw only in a few instances something that could possibly be derived from Stanislavsky, or which was developed in the heritage left by Koun. Exaggeration of feeling, naturalistic pretence, and a superficial interpretation of speech were amongst the clichés I noted. However, in only ten days of work with Vassiliev, it was barely believable how the actors were able to play with such abandon, invention, freedom in the body and speech. Vassiliev himself admitted that amongst the various nationalities he had worked with throughout his long career as a theatre pedagogue, the Greeks had this special nature of organic playfulness that is combined with movement and speech and a sensitive connection to their cultural, social, and political roots. They had no limitations imposed by specific religious and/or social codes of the past or the present that would limit them in their exploration.

In this transitional moment, when Livathinos has become the new Artistic Director of the National Theatre of Athens and Terzopoulos is finding international opportunities, and when the country is about to redefine a number of its past demons, the possibilities are endless. Greek theatre-makers are ready to rediscover Stanislavsky's work as a paradigm that combines theatrical heritage and contemporary identity.

Notes

1. For extensive biographies on some of the great Greek actors visit http://koutalianossimos.wordpress.com/2013/09/29/ [accessed 29 December 2014].
2. I want to note that there was no perceptible distinction between naturalism and realism at this point in Greece, as it can be testified a text by writer Ksenopoulos http://www.arnos.gr/2011/dmdocuments/yliko/filologia/neoelliniki.filologia/Eisagogiko.simeioma.tou.komvou.gia.to.Natouralismo.pdf pp. 15, 19 [accessed 26 December 2014].
3. See also Stanislavsky's difficulties in staging Ibsen's plays, especially when 'feel[ing] [the [play's] inner content' as well as 'find[ing] a clear-cut artistic form for it' (Stanislavski, 2008a, p. 191).
4. All translations from the Greek are the author's.
5. http://www.theatro-technis.gr/greek-art-theatre-karolos-koun/ [accessed 29 May 2015].
6. Sevastikoglou appears to have translated Stanislavsky's *An Actors Prepares* and *My Life in Art* around 1942, during the German Occupation. No exact dates are available as the texts were circulated under different titles in order to avoid suspicion, and they were never published. The translation of *My Life in Art* was lost during Sevastikoglou's travels in exile (Zei, 2015, pp. 135–6).
7. Interview with Lykourgos Kallergis, member of Koun's ensemble as seen in the Karolos Koun Archives at the Ypogeio in Athens, extracts from old programmes.
8. On the role of ethics within Stanislavsky's work see Aquilina, 2012.
9. It is worth noting that the book was translated in Greek only in 1997 by Andreas Manolikakis who was Director of the Department of Directing Studies at the Actors Studio.
10. Maria Knebel's work is still not available in English; I have based my own research on the French version of her writings supervised by Anatoli Vassiliev.
11. http://youtu.be/wDjbNjUzmgg [accessed 9 November 2014].
12. This workshop seminar was led by Anatoli Vassiliev. Further reference to this workshop will be made later in this essay. My link to the Russian tradition of actor training is via Vassiliev, with whom I trained in acting, directing, and theatre pedagogy for 6 years.
13. There is nothing written about his work if not various articles in newspapers, including reviews of this plays and interviews. I will use here some personal notes from my conversations with him and the rehearsals I attended as participant and observer.

14 http://www.theaterinfo.gr/theatreauthors/interviews/livathinos/index.html [accessed 11 November 2014].
15 http://www.theaterinfo.gr/theatreauthors/interviews/livathinos/index.html [accessed 28 April 2015].
16 From personal notes during the rehearsals of *Masquerade*, Athens, April–May 2008.
17 For more about this subject see Maria Knebel's book *L'Analyse-Action* (2003).
18 http://www.athinorama.gr/theatre/article/o_stathis_libathinos_mila_sto_a-11194.html [accessed 24 August 2015].
19 http://m.athensvoice.gr/index.php?r=site%2Fpage&view=article&id=80558&cat=thepaper [accessed 14 November 2014].
20 http://www.attistheatre.com/en/%CE%99%CE%A3%CE%A4%CE%9F%CE%A1%CE%99%CE%9A%CE%9F/terzopoulos.html [accessed 4 June 2015].
21 http://www.themoscowtimes.com/article.php?id=515059 [accessed 1 June 2014].
22 http://www.theaterinfo.gr/abouttheatre/theatretheory/terzopoulos/index.html [accessed 13 November 2014].
23 http://www.avgi.gr/article/3762628/thodoros-terzopoulos-to-kainourgio-gennietai-apo-ti-sullogikotita [accessed 13 November 2014].

References

Aquilina, S. (2012), 'Stanislavsky and the impact of studio ethics on everyday life', *Theatre, Dance and Performance Training*, Vol. 3, No. 1: 302–14.

Bacopoulou-Halls, A. (1998), 'Greece', in *Theatre Worlds in Motion: Structures, Politics and Developments in the Countries of Western Europe*, eds H. van Maanen and S. E. Wilmer. Amsterdam, Atlanta: Rodopi B. V., pp. 259–308.

Bacopoulou-Halls, C. (ed.). (2006), *Continuum Companion to Twentieth Century Theatre*. UK: Continuum.

Bastias, K. (1934), 'The new period of the National Theatre', in *Estia* (newspaper, 20 September 1934). Athens.

Benedetti, J. (1998), *Stanislavski and the Actor*. Great Britain: Methuen.

Carnicke, S. M. (2009), *Stanislavsky in Focus, 2nd ed*. Oxon: Routledge.

Chambers, C. (ed.) (2006), *The Continuum Companion to Twentieth Century Theatre*. London and New York: Continuum.

Davis, J. (2011), 'Research Methods and Methodology', in J. Davis, K. Normington, G. Bush-Bailey, with J. Bratton, 'Researching Theatre History and Historiography', in *Research Methods in Theatre and Performance*, eds B. Kershaw and H. Nicholson. Edinburgh: Edinburgh University Press, pp. 89–98.

Georgousopoulos, K. (2008), 'Speech hides the drama', in *Ta Nea* (newspaper, 4 January 2008).

Glytzouris, A. (2001), *Stage Direction in Greece: the Rise and Consolidation of the Stage Director in Modern Greek Theatre*. Heraklion: Crete University Press.

Glytzouris, A. (2012), 'Henrik Ibsen: the quest for Realism and the rise of Greek theatrical modernism', *Ibsen Studies,* Vol. 12, No. 1: 3–26.

Gorchakov, N. (1959), *The Vakhtangov School of Stage Art.* Moscow: Foreign Languages Pub. House.

Grammatas, T. (2002), *Greek Theatre of the 20th Century Vol. A.* Athens: Eksanta.

Kiriakos, K. (2012), 'The young director Karolos Koun', in *Skene*, 4.

Knebel, M. (2003), *L'Analyse-Action*. Paris: Actes Sud Papiers.

Koun, K. (1997), *We make theatre for our soul*. Athens: Kastaniotis.

Pitches, J. (ed.) (2012), *Russians in Britain*. Oxon: Routledge.

Rudlin, J. (2010), 'Jacques Copeau: The Quest for Sincerity', *Actor Training 2nd ed.*, ed. A. Hodge. London and New York: Routledge, pp. 55–78.

Rudnitsky, K. (2000), *Russian and Early Soviet Theatre*, trans. R. Permar, ed. L. Milne. New York: Thames and Hudson.

Stanislavski, K. (2008a), *An Actor's Work*, trans. J. Benedetti. Oxon: Routledge.

Stanislavski, K. (2008b), *My Life in Art,* trans. J. Benedetti. Oxon: Routledge.

Toporkov, V. (1979), *Stanislavski in Rehearsal*, trans. C. Edwards. London and New York: Routledge.

Varopoulou, E. (1992), 'Our life is a rehearsal', in *To Vima* (newspaper, 22 November 1992).

Whyman, R. (2008), *The Stanislavsky System of Acting: Legacy and Influence in Modern Performance*. Cambridge: CUP.

Whyman, R. (2013), *Stanislavski: The Basics*. Oxon: Routledge.

Zarrilli, P. (1989), 'Thinking and Talking about Acting: Re-reading Sonia Moore's Training an Actor', *Journal of Dramatic Theory and Criticism*, Vol. III, No. 2: 37–51.

Zei, A. (2015), *Me molivi Faber n.2*. Metaihmio: Athens.

Part Two

China and Japan

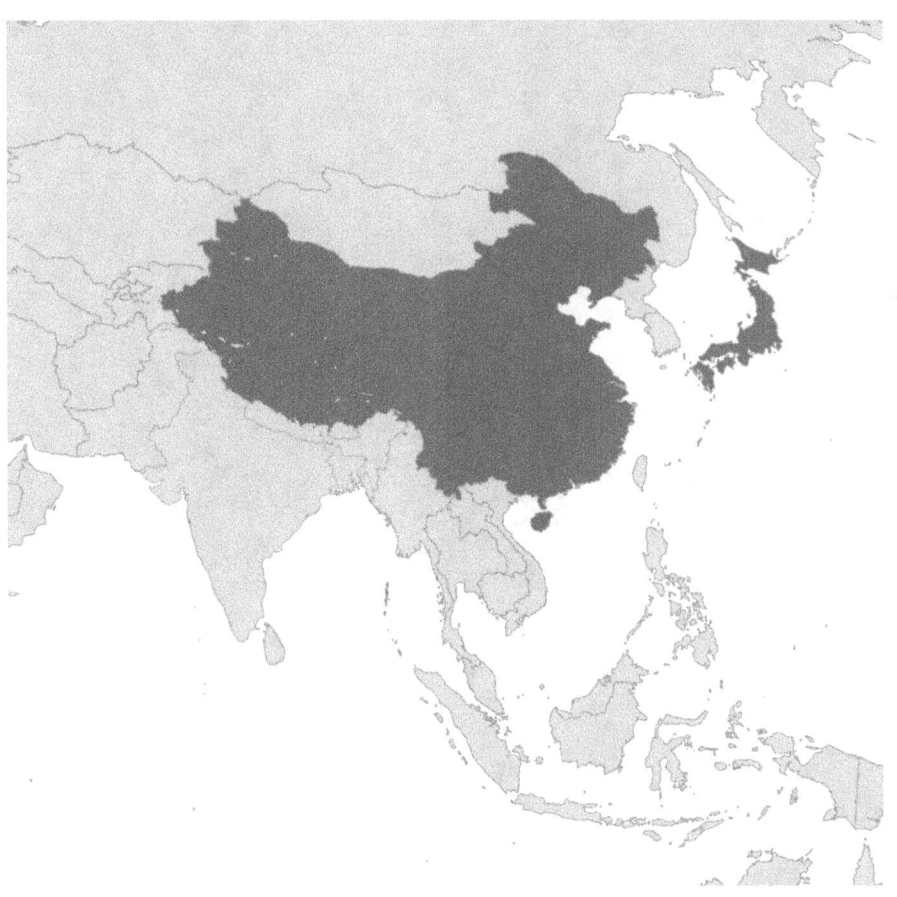

Figure 16 Stanislavsky in China and Japan.

Part Two: Introduction

Jonathan Pitches

Shifting alliances: Stanislavsky in China and Japan

That the influence of Stanislavskian realism had spread to Tokyo as early as 1909[1] – the year Stanislavsky was experimenting with an embryonic version of his system in the production of *A Month in the Country* – is testament to the forces of globalization which intensified at the turn of the century. Japan had been forced to open up its doors to foreign influence by the US in 1853 after two hundred years of self-enforced isolation, in the so-called 'Black Ships' incursion into the bay of Tokyo, then Edo. This action culminated in a trade treaty with America in 1854 and with several other countries in the ensuing years, including Russia, France, England, and Holland, ushering in a 'new imperial policy, the aim of which was the complete renewal of the Japanese government and economy according to Western principles' (Savarese, 2010, p. 294). Originating also in Tokyo, China's first foray into Western-style realism is traditionally dated as 1907 with the Chinese-speaking production of *Lady of the Camellias* by the Spring Willow Dramatic Society (Rubin et al., 1998, p. 105; Brandon, 1997, p. 37). Maturing into the genre of spoken drama, *huaju*, Chinese audiences finally had an alternative to their long-standing traditional forms of theatre – *xiqu* – a development which was buttressed by the New Cultural Movement between 1917 and 1919 and its associated publications. As Siyuan Liu argues in the chapter on 'Modern Chinese Theatre' in *Modern Asian Theatre and Performance 1900-2000*: 'the only path to achieving this function [of social enlightenment] was to remove the "vestiges" of the old society and adopt new concepts, methodologies and forms from the West, particularly realist theatre' (Wetmore, Liu and Mee, 2014, p. 80).

The three essays in this part, focusing respectively on the work of the director, teacher, and producer, are very much about 'concepts, methodology and forms', offering a series of practical perspectives that are sometimes overlooked by concentrating primarily on the literature of the period. What grass-roots influence has the work of Stanislavsky had on China and Japan? How have theatre *practices* been affected by his thinking and who is responsible for this transmission of embodied knowledge in both countries? Siyuan Liu (on Jiao Juyin's hybrid approach), Jonathan Pitches and Ruru Li (on the Soviet Experts at the Shanghai Theatre Academy), and Kaori Nakayama (on contemporary training in Tokyo) help to answer these difficult questions in the following essays. Indeed, viewed collectively they help dig beneath the catch-all term 'Stanislavskian realism' itself, which in the context of China and Japan necessarily references other European practices, specifically Henrik Ibsen's playwriting (the *New Youth* magazine of the New Cultural Movement had a whole issue dedicated to the Norwegian's dramaturgy in 1918 as Li identifies below) and André Antoine's directing (the Free Theatre in Tokyo – Jiyo Gekijo – was named after Antoine's Théâtre Libre in Paris). As producer, Kaori Nakayama, outlines in her shorter examination of Stanislavsky in Japan, the modern theatre movement, known under the umbrella term of *shingeki* in Japan, was 'inspired by Antoine and Craig in direction and took the English Stage Society as its organisational model'. In fact, the supposed 'turn to realism' reflected in the repertoire of *shingeki* and *huaju* plays of the early to mid-twentieth century is also potentially misleading as many other genres were drawn on for inspiration, including Eugene O'Neill's and Georg Kaiser's expressionism, Maurice Maeterlinck's symbolism, and Oscar Wilde's comedy of manners (Wetmore, Liu and Mee, 2014, p. 83). Just as it is important not to pigeonhole Stanislavsky as a one-trick-realist so it is true of the early experimentations in non-traditional East Asian theatre. Equally, the essays in this section debunk any suggestion that Western theatrical influences remained unscathed or generically dominant in their translation into Eastern contexts; hybridity and adaptation are key themes.

Although the beginnings of this Part's story are in the first years of the 1900s, the histories outlined in the essays are firmly in the middle of the twentieth century (for the Chinese chapters) and in the beginnings of the twenty-first (for Japan). As such they outline a picture of Stanislavskian transmission that stretches from its most intensive period (in the mid-1950s in

China) to one in decline (in contemporary Japan). So why did it take half a century for Stanislavsky's System to be fully appropriated into this region? The answers to this question are indicative of a number of issues ranging across this book: developments in the political context; the delay before embodied, face-to-face teaching was possible; problems with translated sources; cultural imperatives and industrial 'need'. Let us deal with these in turn.

The political context behind these case-studies is complex and highly volatile, bridging two world wars, one civil war, and direct conflict between Japan and China. As Pitches and Li outline in *Stanislavsky with Chinese Characteristics: how the System was Introduced into China* the aftermath of this history of conflict – the communist revolution in China and the creation of the People's Republic of China in 1949 – led to a short but highly influential window of opportunity, where strategic collaboration between China and the Soviet Union was possible. Using new archival sources Pitches and Li bring to the fore the human figures who would otherwise be dwarfed by this massive political picture: Russian teachers from Moscow and St Petersburg (Boris Kulnyov and Yevgenia Lipkovskaya) working with Chinese students and tutors in the Shanghai Theatre Academy. This brief flowering of activity was quickly curtailed by the advent of the Cultural Revolution (1966–76) and both spoken drama and traditional theatre were 'virtually devastated' (Rubin et al., 1998, p. 105). But, as Li points out in the second part of this co-authored chapter, with nothing else to draw on as a methodology for directing and training, many practitioners emerging out of the Cultural Revolution were quick to return to Stanislavskian practices, in parallel, that is, with the rise of Brecht, whose influence had been initiated by Huang Zuolin as early as 1951 (Fei, 2006, p. 243). Revered in the 1950s, reviled in the 1960s and revived in the late 1970s, Stanislavsky's reputation was indelibly tied to the political landscape of China and its shifting alliances.

As with other contexts in this book – in Latin America for instance and across Europe – the relationship between the publication of Stanislavsky's ideas and any direct teaching of his work is fundamental to the way in which his ideas have been transmitted. For Nakayama in Japan, innovations in Stanislavskian training were hampered by poor translations from English and German in the 1950s and 1960s (with the definitive translation from the Russian only appearing in 2009). The result is a lack of a 'standard for actor training in Japan', she says, as '[t]here is no common language among actors' (p.201). In China there was a long delay between the first interest in Stanislavskian aesthetics and ethics from the early part of the twentieth century and any clarification of the system in writing. Of course this is true even in Russia, with the first part of *An Actor's Work on Himself* emerging in the same year Stanislavsky died in 1938. Relatively speaking, China was quick to publish his work – with extracts from *My Life in Art* and *An Actor Prepares* appearing in 1938 and 1939 respectively (Li, 2003, p. 250) and a full translation (from English) of the latter in 1943. But it was not until the arrival of Boris Kulnyov and his colleagues from the Soviet Union in 1954 that a direct or embodied link with Stanislavskian practices was established, making him a central figure both to Li and Pitches' essay and to Siyuan Liu's detailed examination of Jiao Juyin's directorial career at the Beijing People's Art Theatre in the essay *Towards a Chinese School of Performance and Directing*.

Finally, there is the question of need – what is it that led these countries to espouse and adapt Stanislavskian principles in their local contexts? This, of course, is an almost impossible question to answer – at least in a short introduction – as the key factors playing a role in these motivations (put simply in Li and Pitches essay as 'Why?') are constantly in flux. Japan and China both started their relationship with Stanislavsky driven by a wider cultural imperative to 'open up' and modernize. But over a hundred years later with both countries having undergone enormous modernization programmes, the lure of Stanislavsky today has to be radically different. In reading these three essays there is an underlying sense that for all the government enforcement and policy decisions first backing and then denouncing Stanislavsky it is the local variations of his practice which have found most purchase: Jiao Juyin's hybrid approach and Hirata Oriza's 'quiet theatre' for instance. It is these 'adaptations', as we term them in the main introduction, which are indicative of a practitioner's own adjustment to context (artistic *and* political) and it these culturally-located innovations which have endured thus far and which will surely endure in the future.

Notes

1 This is the date of the founding of the Little Theatre in Tokyo by Osanai Kaoru and Sadanji Ichikawa II and their inaugural production of Ibsen's *John Gabriel*

Borkman. Osanai then visited the Moscow Art Theatre in 1912 and saw Craig's *Hamlet*. See Oya (2013) for details of Craig's influence and for illustrations of Osanai's tendentious *Lower Depths*, modeled on Stanislavsky's production.

References

Brandon, J. R. (ed.) (1997), *The Cambridge Guide to Asian Theatre*. Cambridge: Cambridge University Press.

Fei, C. F., (2006), 'Huang Zuolin: Michael Chekhov's Link to China's Modern Theatre', *New Theatre Quarterly*, Vol. 22, No. 3: 235–48.

Li, R. (2003). *Shashibiya: Staging Shakespeare in China*. Hong Kong: Hong Kong University Press.

Oya, R. (2013), 'Kaoru Osanai and the impact of Edward Gordon Craig's theatrical ideals on Japan's *shingeki* (new theatre) movement', *Shakespeare,* Vol. 9, No. 4: 418–27.

Rubin, D., Pong, S. C., Chaturvedi, R., Majumdar, R., Tanokura, M., and Brisbane, K. (eds.) (1998), *The World Encyclopedia of Contemporary Theatre: Asia/Pacific*. London: Routledge.

Savarese, N. (2010). *Eurasian Theatre,* trans. R. Fowler. Holstebro: Icarus Publishing.

Wetmore, K. Jr, Liu, S., and Mee, E. B. (2014), *Modern Asian Performance 1900-2000*. London: Bloomsbury.

6

Towards a Chinese School of Performance and Directing: Jiao Juyin

Siyuan Liu

Between 1951 and 1963, the modern Chinese spoken drama (*huaju*) director Jiao Juyin (1905–75) staged a number of realistic and classical-costume plays that established his place as China's most creative director who successfully blended Stanislavsky-based realistic performance techniques with Chinese theatrical aesthetics. In his realistic plays, he used the concept of 'mental image' (*xinxiang*) that blended Coquelin the Eldest's outside-in technique with the state-sanctioned practice of Stanislavsky's experiencing the role, creating, among other plays, the tremendously successful *Longxu gou* (*Dragon Beard Ditch*, 1951) as the inaugural production of the Beijing Renmin Yishu Juyuan (Beijing People's Art Theatre, BPAT). After alternating experiments in internal and external approaches in different productions and observing the Soviet expert Boris Kulnyov[1] direct Gorky's *Yegor Bulychov and Others*, Jiao chose the historical play *Hufu* (*The Tiger Tally*) in 1956 to introduce *xiqu*[2] aesthetics and techniques to the *huaju* stage. He continued to experiment with Chinese theatrical concepts and techniques in follow-up productions of classic-costume plays and modern realistic dramas, including the highly acclaimed *huaju* classic *Chaguan* (*Teahouse*, 1958). While his experiments were curtailed in 1963 by the radical buildup towards the Cultural Revolution, his productions as well as his acting and directing theories have made significant contributions to a Chinese style of spoken theatre.

Modern Chinese theatre started at the turn of the twentieth century and went through hybrid and amateur stages in its first three decades. Professional and semi-professional actors imitated Hollywood stars in the 1930s. After the Chinese version of *An Actor Prepares* was published in 1943, many *huaju* actors and directors attempted to apply the system, which became the officially sanctioned method of dramatic creation after the establishment of the People's Republic of China in 1949. In the 1950s, five Soviet experts taught in the Central Academy of Drama in Beijing and its counterpart in Shanghai (see essay by Jonathan Pitches and Ruru Li in this Part), which solidified the dominance of the system in actor training and performance.

However, Jiao Juyin approached the system from two different angles than other Chinese directors and actors, namely traditional Chinese theatre and Stanislavsky's partners at the Moscow Art Theatre – Nemirovich-Danchenko and Chekhov. Both starting points proved essential to his directorial practice and theorization during his eruptive creative decade of the 1950s and early 1960s. Jiao was first a scholar and translator with considerable first-hand experience in traditional theatre before becoming a professional *huaju* director in his late forties. Consequently, his decades of preparation significantly shaped his relations with the system as well as his open embrace of *xiqu* aesthetics after 1956.

To start with, while Jiao majored in political science at Yenching University in Beijing between 1924 and 1928, he was active in student dramatics and prolific in writing and translation, including publishing two substantive essays on Ibsen and Molière and translating *Shakuntala*, Goldoni's *Mistress of the Inn*, Molière *Tartuffe*, and Chekhov's *Swan Song* and short stories. In 1930, he was tapped to establish the Chinese Xiqu School (Zhonghua Xiqu Xuexiao) in Beijing, the first modern training school for *jingju* (Beijing opera) actors and actresses, a four-year experience that provided him with rare hands-on knowledge of Chinese theatrical aesthetics and performance techniques. This knowledge formed the foundation of his PhD dissertation at the University of Paris in 1938 titled *Le théâtre chinois d'aujourd'hui* (The Chinese Theatre Today), a substantive study of Chinese theatre's dramaturgy, performance, organization, training, technology, and twentieth-century reforms, including the introduction of spoken theatre (Tchiao, 1938). After returning to China in the same year in the middle of the War of Resistance against Japan, he went to the southwest interior to join mainstream *huaju* artists, first spending three years in Guilin, Guangxi Province when he started to direct *huaju* plays occasionally while continuing publishing articles on traditional theatre and its reform. He then had a short, ill-fated stint (1941–2) teaching at the National Drama School in

Jiang'an, Sichuan Province. This was followed, between 1943 and the end of the war in 1945, by an economically strained period that was nevertheless pivotal to his directorial eruption, as he translated Nemirovich-Danchenko's *My Life in Russian Theatre* and Chekhov's plays and wrote insightful analyses of these works that became his gateway to the Stanislavsky system.

Jiao believed Nemirovich-Danchenko and Chekhov influenced Stanislavsky's emphasis on the inner world, who 'was able to create great and incisive tones with image, sound and color, but his starting point was not the inner world,' which was changed after Nemirovich-Danchenko introduced *The Seagull* to Stanislavsky and Chekhov demanded 'acting without acting anything' during its rehearsal (Jiao, 2005b, Vol. 2, p. 155). Nemirovich-Danchenko also influenced Jiao's understanding of the director's function as an interpreter of the playwright, mirror for the actors, and organizer of the production. In addition he was credited by Jiao as influencing the system's focus on experiencing the character with a system focusing on the actor's intuition, infection, the law of inner justification, the simplicity of supreme art, and natural revelation instead of 'acting' (Jiao, 2005b, Vol. 2, pp. 152–4). Furthermore, Jiao started using the concept of '*mental* image' during this period as he often (but not always) translated the term 'image' in the English *My Life in Russian Theatre* into 'mental image' (*xinxiang*) in Chinese instead of the standard *tuxiang* or *xingxiang*.[3]

For example, Danchenko argues in defence of intuition: 'But as it lends itself only with difficulty to analysis, as "images" prompted by intuition do not allow license and demand a rigid control in the selection of theatrical resources, so to this day the lords of theatrical undertakings are afraid of it and avoid it' (Nemirovich-Danchenko, 1936, p. 157). Here, as in several other places, Jiao translated image into *xinxiang* (Jiao, 2005b, Vol. 7, p. 295), which Jiao later viewed as the first stage of creating a character, telling his actors during the *Dragon Beard Ditch* rehearsal that 'there is no image (*xingxiang*) without mental image (*xinxiang*)' (Yu, 1983, p. 3).

It is also intriguing to note that Jiao's mental image seems to be unrelated to Stanislavsky's use of 'inner vision' or 'mental picture' in Hapgood's English *An Actor Prepares*, rendered as *neizai de xingxiang* and *neixin de xingxiang* respectively in Chinese (Zhang, 2011, p. 46, p. 108). It is possible that the five characters of the latter phrase can be shortened as *xinxiang*, Jiao's mental image. However, this logic is belied by the fact that Jiao's 1951 lecture on Chapter 8 of *An Actor Prepares* ('Faith and a Sense of Truth'), in which 'mental picture' is discussed, does not mention the phrase or concept (Jiao, 2005b, Vol. 2, pp. 213–20), suggesting Jiao did not see any connection between Stanislavsky's 'mental picture' and his 'mental image.'

Regardless of entry point, there is no doubt that by the time Jiao returned to Beijing in 1946 to teach at Beijing Normal University, he started applying the system to semi-professional productions, including a sinicized and naturalistic version of Gorky's *The Lower Depths* renamed *Yedian* (*The Night Inn*) in which he demanded bedbug stains being painted on pieces of the set to help the actors' memory recall. After the establishment of the People's Republic of China (PRC) in 1949, Jiao finally got his chance to apply his unparalleled knowledge of the Moscow Art Theatre model and the system in the newly established BPAT. He was first invited as a guest director in 1950 to direct *Dragon Beard Ditch* and its tremendous success won him a place at the reorganized BPAT in June 1952 as its First Deputy Artistic Director and General Director (*zong daoyan*). As the legend goes, Jiao and the other three 'founders' of the theatre – its Artistic Director and China's most famous playwright Cao Yu, the Party Secretary and Jiao's ultimate political and artistic protector Zhao Qiyang, and another director Ouyang Shanzun – spent the first week in a 'forty-two-hour conversation' that, much like the historical 'eighteen-hour meeting' between Stanislavsky and Nemirovich-Danchenko, set the theatre's goals as modelling itself after the Moscow Art Theatre and developing the Chinese style of *huaju*. Eleven years later, when Jiao finished directing his last play in August 1963, he had led the theatre's significant advance in both directions. A 1980 restaging of his 1958 *Teahouse*, with the same cast and his co-director, shocked Europe and prompted Peter Brook to tell the actors: 'Your performance is of the realistic school, which generally suffers from two problems, overacting or lacking in expressive power. You have perfectly overcome both' (Shihua and Xiaogu, 1980).

His endeavour with his core group of actors started with the successful production of *Dragon Beard Ditch*, a play the novelist Lao She wrote in 1950 to commemorate a municipal construction project that covered up an open drainage system in a poor neighbourhood in southern Beijing.[4] Jiao was invited to direct the play as a result of his naturalistic hit *The Night Inn*. These two plays represent Jiao at his most dedicated stage to Stanislavsky's *experiencing* the character, although he stressed experiencing life rather than the self. He started the rehearsal by asking the mostly inexperienced young actors without formal training to observe local residents for two months and write daily journals. Each was given two notebooks, so that he could check one of them, write comments, hold weekly discussions, and advise individual actors every night. This is the stage for the actors to form their rudimentary mental images. When he finally started rehearsals, he devoted the first phase to discovering and practising the mental images so that the physical characteristics blended with internal motivations to become the actors' 'second self'. Next, he helped the actors merge their mental images with their characters and given circumstances. Instead of pre-blocking for specific stage pictures, he encouraged the actors to move about following the inner rhythm of their characters until they 'gradually lost the sense of acting and merged into life' (Jiao, 2005b, Vol. 2, p. 239).

In reality, Jiao followed both Stanislavsky's inside-out and Benoît-Constant Coquelin's outside-in methods: 'The actor's creative process this time should start from the outside-in method and then inside-out; create a mental image first and then delve deeper to find its emotional basis.' 'When preparing for a character, it is possible to use Coquelin's method. After that, proceed to experiencing' (Yu, 1983, p. 3).[5] While Jiao did not ignore seeking the emotional basis of the characters, his mental image was designed to counter *huaju's* predominant misunderstanding of the system that, unaware of Stanislavsky's physical system in *Building a Character*, only emphasized experiencing the characters' inner world and deemed the emphasis on physical actions 'formalism'. For Yu Shizhi, who played the lead Cheng the Madman, and his fellow young actors, the 'mental images' they culled from observation gave them concrete movements and gestures. It is in fact through Yu's effort in the 1980s to convincingly demonstrate the concept's instrumental significance to the BPAT actors that 'mental image' has become known as one of Jiao's signature contributions; Jiao certainly used the concept during rehearsals, but did not elaborate it in his writings.

Despite the success of *Dragon Beard Ditch*, Jiao was not completely satisfied with his approach and in 1954 tried (but largely failed) to apply an overtly outside-in approach in his next major production, Cao Yu's *Minglang de tian* (*The Bright Sky*), an awkward attempt to document the ideological transformations of a group of doctors in PRC. The shift was prompted by Jiao getting hold of a copy of the Russian equivalent of *Building a Character* titled *Rabota aktera nad soboj: Čast' II, Rabota nad soboj v tvorčeskom processe voplošeniâ dnevnik učenika* (*An Actor's Work on Himself: Part II, Work on the Creative Process of Embodiment, A Student's Diary*), which was published in Moscow in 1948 and brought to China by someone who had been to the Soviet Union (Su et al., 1985, p. 56; Stanislavskii, 1948).[6] He was able to read it with the help of a Russian dictionary and used the example of a student's transformation into a sinister critic through costume and makeup, which appears in Chapter 7 of the Russian version and Chapter 2 of the English version, as early as Autumn 1951 in a lecture at the Central Academy of Drama (Jiao, 1951, p. 58).

Therefore, by 1954 Jiao was ready to use an entirely physical approach to combat the lethargic performance on Chinese stage, a phenomenon succinctly summarized by the actor Lan Ma: 'We were actually able to act; learning from Stanislavsky sometimes messed us up!' (Zheng, 2009, p. 182) For *The Bright Sky*, Jiao pre-blocked all movements, provided detailed physical description for each character and declared at the onset: 'The director has constructed the design based on the script's characters and lines. The task now is to inspire the actors to align their understanding of their character images with the inner and outer worlds designed by the director' (rehearsal record, quoted in Su et al., 1985, p. 60). However, such a drastic change from his previous emphasis on inner experience frustrated his actors, who called his method 'molding dough figures' and themselves 'super-marionettes' (Su et al., 1985, p. 62). Once Jiao heard such name-calling, he refused to show up at the rehearsal. It took the Party Secretary Zhao Qiyang three visits to his home and sitting next to Jiao through the rest of the rehearsal for the rehearsal to proceed. In the end, while the production won first-place awards for playwriting and directing at the 1956 National *Huaju* Festival, Jiao never repeated the approach. Instead, he turned his attention to observing the Soviet expert Boris Grigorievich Kulnyov (1896–1959) from Moscow's Vakhtangov Theatre who directed Gorky's *Egor Bulychev and Others* at BPAT in 1956. Unlike Jiao's grand visions, Kulnyov's rehearsal started with a brief discussion of the characters and their given circumstances. It quickly transited to the improvisation phase during which the Bulychevs set up their own rooms with attention to minute details of the props and interactions, which naturally led the actors to using lines from the

Figure 17 Jiao Juyin (left) with Kulnyov (second from right) during a design session for *Egor Bulychev and Others*.
Photo courtesy of Beijing People's Art Theatre.

script, thus starting the formal rehearsal phase with scripts. Kulnyov also explained that he preferred the phrase 'script and character analysis through action' over the more commonly used 'method of physical action' in order to accurately capture Stanislavsky's belief in the unity of psychophysical actions in his final years (Su et al., 1985, p. 62).

Seeing a Soviet expert in rehearsal using psychophysical actions may have convinced Jiao of the system's affinity with Chinese theatre. Another contributing factor to his nationalist turn in 1956 was the often-languid performance in the year's *huaju* festival, which triggered calls for a Chinese system of *huaju* performance. In May 1956, when *The Tiger Tally* was already in rehearsal, Premier Zhou Enlai praised the newly adapted *kunqu*[7] play *Shiwu guan* (*Fifteen Strings of Cash*) and encouraged *huaju* artists to learn from it: 'Our *huaju* generally lacks *xiqu*'s strong indigenous style. Some foreign friends think Chinese *huaju* has not absorbed the characteristics of indigenous *xiqu* [...]. The advantage of Chinese *huaju* lies in its strong sense of life, but it is not mature yet' (Zhou, 1980, p. 5). All these factors provided impetus to Jiao's bold experiment.

And bold he certainly was. Using a play written in 1942 by the historian and playwright Guo Moruo on palace intrigues during the Warring States period (476–221 BCE), Jiao's production of *The Tiger Tally*, which debuted in January 1957 after eight months of rehearsal, used extensive *jingju* role-type-specific speech patterns and eye, hand, and body movement techniques as its essential performance vocabulary. It was aided by an open (not box) set design with strategic set pieces, a *jingju* percussion orchestra, and traditional costumes with water sleeves, which the actors used for a wide range of expressions. At first, Jiao's experiment met stiff resistance from the actors who viewed *xiqu* performance as formalist (an ideological taboo), especially after Kulnyov's *Egor Bulychev and Others*, which they deemed the authentic way of performance: 'Start from the self, use the character's logic to create vibrant images; search for the through line of actions, use endlessly rich inner monologues to truly think and act on stage' (Zhu, 1959, p. 27). Again, Zhao Qiyang intervened to guarantee the continuation of the rehearsal.

Eventually, the actors were persuaded of *xiqu*'s equally rich inner experience, as expressed in the saying *xinliyou* ('having it in the heart') that performs interiority through exquisite and accurate physicality acquired through extensive practice (Zhu, 1959, p. 28). To reach this level, Jiao organized the actors to watch *xiqu* performances and asked them to demonstrate one acquired technique the following day (Zhao, 1994, p. 43). He also invited *jingju* actors to tutor the physical lessons, helping the actors to endow their inner world in water sleeves, eye movements, and gestures.

Jiao extensively discussed the experiment in a post-mortem after the play's enthusiastic reception as a significant step in *huaju* sinification: First, 'devote to the fullest degree where needed.' This concerns *xiqu*'s philosophy of devoting attention to minute details of dramatic highlights while touching lightly insignificant events, in contrast to *huaju*'s tendency indiscriminately to stage events in sequence. Second, 'demand the fullest truth, predominantly the truthfulness of thoughts and emotions.' Jiao argues that 'all *xiqu* techniques are subservient to the depiction of the inner world, existing entirely for the sake of

Figure 18 A scene in *The Tiger Tally* with the principal actors. From left to right: Zheng Rong (as Hou Ying), Yu Shizhi (Lord Xinling), Zhu Lin (Lady Ruji), Dai Ya (King of Wei).
Photo courtesy of Beijing People's Art Theatre.

expressing the inner truth.' While *huaju* acting emphasizes real listening, watching, and feeling between the performers, *xiqu* stresses revealing the characters' inner deliberations and preparations *to the audience*. Consequently, he followed *xiqu*'s convention of having the actors face the audience, not the acting partner, when listening so that the audience could see their reactions through their eye movements. Third, '*xiqu* uses a series of connected, logical, reasonable, correct, but also extremely concise physical actions to express inner actions.' *The Tiger Tally* adapted some *jingju* action routines (*chengshi*) with varying success, but Jiao was convinced of their efficacy and continued experimenting in ways to hybridize them with *huaju*. Fourth, *xiqu* is both spatial and temporal, and the latter is especially useful for *huaju* actors' sense of tempo in actions and speech. Fifth, speech delivery in the production was a mixture of heightened and everyday patterns and would take more plays to arrive at the right balance. Sixth, mime performance in the production was a combination of onstage props and offstage imagined objects such as clouds and faraway carriages, performed with the committed devotion of the actors' minds, eyes, and hands (*xindao, yandao, shoudao*) and their trust in the audience's imagination. Seventh, the production used a suggestive and poetic set design. Finally, the use of percussion music was the least satisfactory element of the experiment due to insufficient rehearsal time (Jiao, 2005b, Vol. 3, pp. 47–52).

Jiao continued his experiment in 1959 with *Cai Wenji*, which Guo Moruo wrote for him, about the return to the central kingdom of the Han Dynasty poetess Cao Wenji with a heavy ransom by the warlord Cao Cao (155–220). Her conflicted decision of leaving her husband and children in the north, deeply touching poems, and Cao Cao's statesman-like appreciation of a rare talent provide a poetic backdrop for a more mature fusion production by Jiao and his actors, now fully committed and much more proficient in *xiqu* vocabulary. Jiao followed up with two more classic-costume productions. The first was the 1962 *Wu Zetian*, again by Guo Moruo, about China's only female ruler, although the production was much more realistic, with full palace settings and restrained (though no less elegant) acting. So was his 1963 restaging of *Guan Hanqing* by Tian Han. Fully at ease with nationalized *huaju*, Jiao used this play of the Yuan Dynasty (1271–1368) playwright, originally staged in 1958, for a seamless fusion of *xiqu* and *huaju* in both dramaturgy and performance, moving, for example, an offstage performance onstage as *xiqu* performance within the *huaju* frame and adding two transitional scenes in *xiqu* fashion (Su et al., 1985, pp. 153–4; Jiao, 2005b, Vol. 3, pp. 293–4).

His adoption of *xiqu* aesthetics also applied to realistic plays and was a critical reason behind the success of *Teahouse* as well as the revolutionary play *Zhiqu Weihushan* (*Taking Tiger Mountain by Strategy*), both in 1958. The former, written again by Lao She, uses a big teahouse in Beijing as a backdrop to three cross-sections in the first half of the twentieth century – the end of the Qing Dynasty (1898), the warlord era of the 1920s, and the late 1940s before the Communist takeover. The latter is about the adventures of a Communist army hero amongst a gang of bandits in the northeast. While both were still realistic plays, what sets them apart from *Dragon Beard Ditch* is Jiao's distance from naturalist staging: '"A slice of life" does not equate a work of art. What the audience wants to see is theatre, which means concentrated, refined, and typified life' (Beijing renmin yishu juyuan *xiju yanjiu ziliao* bianjizu, 1980, p. 199).

He elaborated on *huaju*'s *xiqu*-inspired theatricality in a 1959 article (Jiao, 2005a, p. 554). First, use actions that are specific to the Chinese nation, for example, do not shrug. Second, while *huaju* does not demand direct physical actions to correlate with internal monologues or subtexts, *xiqu* applies physical movements directly to and simultaneously with primary stage actions and dialogue in order to reveal the variegated and swift twists and turns of the characters' inner reactions, as 'it is imperative that the scene of their mutual conflict, influence, and inspiration be played out with extremely robust rhythm' (Jiao, 2005a, p. 559). Third, while *xiqu* pays special attention to expressing the characters' individualized attitude towards given circumstances and conflicts, similar to Stanislavsky, it also endows the actors with far more techniques than *huaju*. Fourth, *xiqu* only performs what the audience is interested in through broad strokes and meticulous delineations. Finally, on the issue of 'for whom do I act,' instead of Stanislavsky's 'solitude in public,' *xiqu* actors intentionally involve the audience and seek their support and sympathy, resulting in the audience's constantly active imagination that enriches and supplements life on stage. 'Consequently, while *xiqu* performance involves a much stronger sense of theatricality, its truthfulness is much more marked as a result, not lessened' (Jiao, 2005a, p. 562).

Jiao's emphasis on performing for the Chinese audience with their familiar stage vocabulary and his open embrace of theatricality is clearly evident in his 1958 productions. By then, as he and his core group of actors had gone through the 'mental image' stage of *Dragon Beard Ditch*, the physical phase of *The Bright Sky* and the first *xiqu* experiment of *The Tiger Tally*, they were able to hybridize these techniques and aesthetics. To start with, Jiao applied Stanislavsky's directing techniques where applicable, including asking his co-director Xia Chun to lead the actors to experience the life of teahouses and using copious live sound effects, resulting in a complicated and well-coordinated offstage chorus with those not onstage at the time. But he had also reached a level of artistic freedom that was no longer bound by any theoretical dogma. In contrast to his previous practice, and possibly influenced by Kulnyov, he did not give an overriding directorial concept at the onset of the *Teahouse* rehearsals even as he meticulously planned certain scenes, especially the opening that involves eight tables, each with multiple customers with their own stories and motivations, creating a raucous opening of a late Qing teahouse at its zenith.

The two productions benefited extensively from the *xiqu* concepts and techniques Jiao discussed in his 1959 article, particularly theatricality, a tempo of extending dramatic highlights and gliding through insignificant moments, and performing for the benefit of the audience. He asked his actors to remember that 'although the stage and audience section are usually separate, they are in reality "two halves" that become a unified space during performance, a sacred space "jointly created" by the audience and actors!' (Jiao and Yu, 1995, p. 29) For the tragi-comic final scene of *Teahouse*, in which three old men reminisce their futile struggles for the country and themselves, Jiao simply told them to deliver many important lines directly to the audience. According to Yu Shizhi, who played the manager of the teahouse Wang Lifa: 'We tried it accordingly. Unexpectedly, this minor adjustment gave us great excitement. Not only was there no reduced truthfulness as a result of less communication between us, but our emotions flew more freely' (Yu, 1987, p. 85).[8]

In terms of learning from *xiqu*'s usage of tempo control, Jiao later summarized the issue as two sides of the coin. On the one hand, the director should '[a]chieve the most with the least' by keeping 'actions that are not related to the characters' thought and inner conflict [...] as brief as possible.' On the other hand, 'pay great care to actions that are central to the portrayal of the characters and do not leave out any minute dramatic conflict' (Su and Zuo, 2003, p. 35). One example of playing out dramatic conflict takes place in Act One of *Teahouse* in which an imperial wrestler Erdezi attempts to beat another customer Master Chang for poking fun at his inability to fight the English and French armies who had burned down the Summer Palace. Just as they are about to fight, a voice calls out: 'Erdezi, you're quite an important person, aren't you?' Hearing the voice, Erdezi stops and respectfully approaches and courteously addresses the person (Master Ma), who tells him: 'Settle your disputes in a reasonable way. Must you always resort to violence?' Erdezi eagerly agrees, offers to pay for Ma's tea and goes to the back of the teahouse for another fight. Master Chang walks up to thank Ma, who abruptly gets up, says, 'I'm busy. Goodbye!' and moves to the door at upstage centre when a church bell strikes, prompting Ma to stop, take off his hat, solemnly cross himself and quickly exit (Lao, 2010, pp. 552-3; Liu, 2007, pp. 333-5; Lao, 2008, 9'-12').[9] With only three lines, the playwright masterfully delineates the supposedly powerful position of a Christian who, because of his relations with Westerners, cowed an official hooligan but also rebuffed Chang for his denigration of the British and French armies. But it was Jiao's masterful control of the rhythm and dynamic sequence that reveals Ma's condescension to Erdezi, contempt for Chang, and humility in front of the church bell – an action Jiao added – that lucidly performed the distorted power dynamics in late Qing.

Jiao also used many of *jingju*'s formalized performance conventions known as *chengshi* in movement and dialogue. One such technique is a heightened pose known as *liangxiang*, especially when used during a character's initial entrance to enhance the first impression. This is the case for two contrasting characters in Act One of *Teahouse*, the young industrialist Qin Zhongyi and the aged Eunuch Pang, favourite of the Empress Dowager Cixi, who comes to the teahouse to buy a wife right after Cixi has suppressed the Hundred Days' Reform and executed its leaders. Qin, who is one of the three disillusioned old men in the final scene, makes his entrance as the landlord of the teahouse and a brash capitalist ready to sell his land and save the nation with new factories. Preceded by the crisp effect of horse taps, bells, and his call to stop the horse, Qin strides in holding a horsewhip, makes a *liangxiang* in his dazzling outfit and haughty confidence, before addressing Wang the manager and walking quickly downstage to inspect his property (Liu, 2007, pp. 343-4; Lao, 2008, 22'25"–22'35"). Similar treatment is used for Eunuch Pang's entrance just as Qin is ready to leave, starting from the sounds of a slow, stately horse carriage and then fawning greetings to Pang, who then enters looking down for the door step and helped by young eunuch, before turning to face the audience with a puffy face without eyebrows and speaking with an effeminate eunuch voice. Their contrast is then heightened by a battle of the tongues, ending in a stalemate: 'Qin Zhongyi: What little influence I may wield won't go far in your presence. / Eunuch Pang: Well said. Let's both try our best, and see what happens. Ha, ha, ha!' (Lao, 2010, p. 558) In performance, the actors enact the final laughter using a *jingju chengshi* to highlight a stasis of power usually used at the end of a mental battle. One character would lean forward to say 'ah', and the other will do the same. Then the first would lean back to utter another 'ah', again followed by the second with the same movement and utterance. Finally, they both would burst out laughing 'ha, ha, ha . . .,' slowly at first, building up to a crescendo and then denouement. This is exactly what happened during this scene between Qin and Pang, thus perfectly capturing the battle of the new and old forces before the fall of the Qing Dynasty (Liu, 2007, pp. 347–9; Lao, 2008, 27'45"–30').

More importantly, this representative sinicized gem in *Teahouse* is a clear testament to Jiao's success in bringing the Western-oriented *huaju* to the Chinese audience. Without sacrificing *huaju*'s internal and external realism in the Stanislavskian sense, Jiao's later productions were well aligned with the Chinese term for theatre, *xi*, which also means play, show, trick, joke, or sport, as opposed to *ju*, a new term used in the twentieth century as equivalent to drama, as in *huaju* – spoken drama. It is the playfulness, fun, excitement, knowing laughs and chuckles that frequently arose during the *Teahouse* performance that bonded the actors and audience who together made the production the crown jewel of Jiao's endeavour to nationalize *huaju*.

Unfortunately, Jiao was not allowed to finish his experiment after 1963 because of radical arts policies that led to the Cultural Revolution, during which he died of cancer in 1975. Nor was he allowed to finish a nine-point outline titled 'Lun minzuhua' (On Nationalizing Spoken Drama) that would have provided a systematic theorization of his experiments. Nevertheless, his tremendous contribution to BPAT and modern Chinese theatre through his acting system that blended Stanislavsky, Coquelin, and *xiqu* as well as his unparalleled achievement in hybridizing Western and Chinese aesthetics in *huaju* have created some of the best productions in modern Chinese theatre and provided to the world a major case-study of the dynamics between Stanislavsky's system and indigenous theatre.

Notes

1 Kulnyov is known to have performed the role of Doctor in the 1932 premiere of *Egor Bulychov and Others*. He also served from 1945 till 1959 as 'Deputy Director of the Theatre School named after BV Shchukin' (Ying and Conceison, 2008, p. 221, n. 23).

2 *Xiqu* is the collective term for traditional Chinese theatre.
3 *Xinxiang* literally means 'heart image' because to the Chinese mentality, heart is linked with mind. Therefore, an alternative name might be 'heart/mind image'.
4 For more background of the circumstance of Lao She's authorship of the play, see Chapter 1 of Braester, 2010.
5 Jiao wrote these lines in the journal by Yu Shizhi, who played the protagonist in *Dragon Beard Ditch*. Jiao never discussed how he had accessed Coquelin; the most likely possibility is that he had studied the famous French actor during his PhD studies in France.
6 This version is missing in Jean Benedetti's discussion of the versions of *Building a Character* in his 'Translator's Foreword' to *An Actor's Work*. See (Stanislavsky, 2008, p. xix).
7 *Kunqu* (kun opera) is the oldest existing form of traditional Chinese theatre. It was developed during the early Ming Dynasty (1368–1644).
8 Yu remembered this event in a 1983 article as happening in the 1962 restaging of *Teahouse*. However, according to a Match 1958 report before the play's opening, Jiao already asked the actors to open up directly to the audience, 'although the actors are not completely accustomed to it yet' (Zhu, 1958, p. 23).
9 Of the three sources, the first is the English script translation, the second is the 1979 restaging prompt book with the original cast and Jiao's co-director Xia Chun, and the third is the 1992 stage recording of the 1979 version.

References

Beijing renmin yishu juyuan *xiju yanjiu ziliao* bianjizu (ed.) (1980), *Chaguan de wutai yishu* (The Stage Art of *Teahouse*). Beijing: Zhongguo xiju chubanshe.

Braester, Y. (2010), *Painting the City Red: Chinese Cinema and the Urban Contract*. Durham: Duke University Press.

Jiao, J. (1951), 'Daoyan ruhe yunyong Sitannisilafusiji tixi' (How Does a Director Use the Stanislavsky System), *Renmin xiju*, 3, (6): 56–9.

Jiao, J. (2005a). *Beijing renyi yanju xuepai chuangshiren: Jiao Juyin lun daoyan yishu* (Founder of Beijng People's Art Theatre Style of Performance: Jiao Juyin on the Art of Directing). Beijing: Zhongguo xiju chubanshe.

Jiao, J. (2005b). *Jiao Juyin wen ji* (Collected Works of Jiao Juyin), ed. Beijing renmin yishu juyuan xiju bowuguan. Beijing: Wenhua yishu chubanshe.

Jiao, J. (original text), and Yu, S. (annotation) (1995), 'Lun minzhuhua (tigang)' (On Nationalizing Spoken Drama (Outline)), *Zhongguo xiju* (1), (8): 28–31.

Lao, S. (2008), *Chaguan* (Teahouse, DVD, 1992 Stage Recording. Directed by Jiao, J. and Xia, C.). Beijing: Beijing wenhua yishu yinxiang chubanshe.

Lao, S. (2010), *Teahouse*, trans. by Ying, R., revised by C. Conceison, in *The Columbia Anthology of Modern Chinese Drama*, ed. X. Chen. New York: Columbia University Press, pp. 547–97.

Liu, Z. (ed.) (2007), *Chaguan de wutai yishu* (The Stage Art of *Teahouse*). Beijing: Zhongguo xiju chubanshe.

Nemirovich-Danchenko, V. I. (1936), *My Life in the Russian Theatre*, trans. J. Cournos. Boston: Little, Brown and Company.

Shihua, Y. and Xiaogu, L. (1980), 'Lao She mingju *Chaguan* zaiyu Xi'ou (Lao She's Famous Play *Teahouse* Victorious in Western Europe), *Renmin ribao* (People's Daily), November 15.

Stanislavskii, K. (1948), *Rabota aktera nad soboj.: Čast'* II, *Rabota nad soboj v tvorčeskom processe voploŝeniâ dnevnik učenika* (An Actor's Work on Himself: Part II, Work on the Creative Process of Embodiment Student's Diary). Moscow: Iskusstvo.

Stanislavsky, K. (2008), *An Actor's Work: A Student's Diary*, trans. J. Benedetti. New York, London: Routledge.

Su, M. et al., (1985), *Lun Jiao Juyin daoyan xuepai* (On The Jiao Juyin School of Directing). Beijing: Wenhua yishu chubanshe.

Su, M. and Zuo, L. (2003), 'A Chinese Director's Theory of Performance: On Jiao Juyin's System of Directing.' Translated by Shiao-ling Yu, *Asian Theatre Journal*, Vol. 20, No. 1: 25–42.

Tchiao, T. (1938), *Le théâtre chinois d'aujourd'hui* (The Chinese Theatre Today). Paris: E. Droz.

Ying, R. and Conceison, C. (2008), *Voices Carry: Behind Bars and Backstage During China's Revolution and Reform*. Lanham, MD: Rowman and Littlefield.

Yu, S. (1983). 'Jiao Juyin xiansheng de "xinxiang" xueshuo' (Mr. Jiao Juyin's Theory of 'Mental Image'), *Xiju bao*, (4): 305.

Yu, S. (1987), *Yu Shizhi lun biaoyan yishu* (Yu Shizhi on the Art of Acting). Beijing: Zhongguo xiju chubanshe.

Zhang, M. (2011), *Zhang Min wenji* (Collected Works of Zhang Min). Vol. 5. Beijing: Zhongguo dianying chubanshe.

Zhao, O. (1994). 'Shiyan: pailian huaju *Hufu* yinqi de yichang zhenglun – wo zai Beijing Renyi gongzuo ershiwu nian sanyi (zhi 3)' (Experiment: A Debate Instigated by the Huaju Production of *The Tiger Tally* – Reminiscence of My Twenty-Five Years Working at the Beijing People's Art Theatre (3)), *Xin wenhua shiliao* (1): pp. 39–47, 60.

Zheng, R. (2009), *Jingdian renwu Zheng Rong* (Classic People: Zheng Rong). Beijing: Zhongguo xiju chubanshe.

Zhou, E. (1980), Guanyu *kunqu Shiwuguan* de liangci jianghua (Two Speeches Concerning *Kunqu Fifteen Strings of Cash*). *Wenyi yanjiu* (1): pp. 4–7.

Zhu, L. (1959), 'Xiqu biaoyan zai huaju zhong de xiaohua he yongyun chutan' (Preliminary Discussion on the Digestion and Utilization of Xiqu Performance in Huaju), *Xiju bao* (12): 27–31.

Zhu, Q. (1958), *Chaguan* daoyan tan *Chaguan* (*Teahouse* Directors on *Teahouse*). *Xiju bao* (6): 22–3.

7

Stanislavsky with Chinese Characteristics: How the System was Introduced into China

Jonathan Pitches and Ruru Li

Introduction

For four short years, from January 1954 to January 1958, training in modern Chinese theatre (called *huaju* or spoken drama in Chinese) witnessed an unprecedented programme of Stanislavsky-based teaching, centred in the two main centres of cultural activity in China: Beijing and Shanghai. There had been earlier incursions of Stanislavsky's ideas into China, in written form through the translation of *An Actor Prepares* (from the English version, in 1943) and the publication of Boleslavsky's *Acting: the First Six Lessons* in 1937 and through practice in the teaching of Huang Zuolin[1] and his wife Dan Ni. The couple had returned to China in 1937, having steeped themselves in Michel St Denis's work at the London Theatre Studio and to a lesser extent, Michael Chekhov's in Dartington, England (Fei and Sun, 2006).[2] Although these early transmission routes were important and complemented China's enduring interest in realist theatre sparked by the birth of the Western-inspired *huaju*, it was not until the 1950s that the Sino-Soviet planets became fully aligned and a concerted effort to introduce Stanislavsky's System into the key training institutions in China was made by the Ministry of Culture. This was one strand of Mao Zedong's fledgling policy of 'leaning to one side' or *yibiando*, as we discuss later. Outside the Soviet Union and its Warsaw Pact neighbours, no other country has undertaken such a concerted and strategic effort to introduce Stanislavsky's practice into its native theatre. Yet, such political enthusiasm to create a new Eastern orthodoxy in Stanislavskian practice, did not avoid some significant limitations and distortions in its transmission into China. This seeming paradox, which we are calling 'Stanislavsky with Chinese characteristics',[3] is a key discussion point for this chapter, one which we seek to place in context, with reference to newly translated archival documents from the period.

The theatre was only a small part of the influence of the Soviet Union in the 1950s, as Edward Wang points out:

> This was indeed the honeymoon period [1950s] in Sino-Soviet relations, in which the Soviet influence touched almost every corner of Chinese society, ranging from economics, social life and gender relations to scientific research, higher education and literature and art.
>
> Wang, 2010

Douglas Stiffler offers some sense of the scale of this influence in quantitative terms: 'approximately 11,000 Soviet experts – advisors, teachers, and technical specialists' with 861 working in Higher Education alone (Stiffler, 2010, pp. 304–5). It was a truly monumental effort designed to build China's economic, scientific, and educational infrastructure on similar ideological foundations as Communist Russia and at great pace. Ironically, it was this shared ideological basis for collaboration that scuppered the honeymoon between the two massive countries and which led to the Sino-Soviet split of 1960. As Fairbank and Goldman succinctly put it in their *China: a New History*: 'In short, the Sino–Russian linkup was tenuous and could dissolve as soon as the CCP began to develop its own style of national communism' (Fairbank and Goldman, 2006, p. 379).

The Soviet Experts' influence on Chinese culture was, then, short-lived and from the perspective of theatre and actor training the window is even smaller (1954–8). As the uncontested orthodoxy in Soviet actor training (after the birth of Socialist Realism and Zhdanov's 'First All-Union Congress of Soviet Writers' in 1934),[4] it was inevitable that Stanislavsky's System was the chosen form of training to be exported to China – the orthodoxy was simply extended to East Asia. However our research indicates that the teaching of Stanislavsky in China was much more flexibly delivered than the idea of an orthodox System implies. The Experts were chosen to represent a multi-faceted and variegated Stanislavsky – one more commonly associated with contemporary criticism of his work. This, according to one of the recipients of the Soviet teaching in Shanghai, was a tactical decision from the Soviets:

> Why did the Russian Government send those three people [to China]?
>
> Because those three people [Lesli, Kulnyov, and Lipkovskaya] represented the development of Stanislavsky's System. They taught us with different emphases. They didn't really say there was one Stanislavsky. Instead they wanted Chinese people to see the whole thing.[5]

A detailed analysis of this period is, then, very valuable and for several reasons: firstly because it brings a new focus to the blurred picture we have of Stanislavsky in China currently; secondly because it exemplifies in concrete terms at a local level the much larger cultural strategy adopted by the People's Republic of China; thirdly because it helps us understand the routes of Stanislavskian transmission up to present day China, the long view adopted in the second part of this chapter.

In terms of the current understanding of Chinese Stanislavsky, there is very little published research in English and nothing from within Stanislavsky studies. William Huizhu Sun's essay, 'Mei Lanfang, Stanislavsky and Brecht' (Sun, 1987) gives a sweeping account of what he sees as the three phases of Chinese theatre development (Sun, 1987, p. 147), helpfully describing some of the precursors of a Stanislavskian training in China. His analysis of the work itself is restricted to a sentence and he describes the job of the experts as leading 'refresher courses [...] to train an army of artists and teachers well versed in the Stanislavsky system' (Sun, 1987, p. 141). Our research indicates that the workshops were a much more sustained and pivotal experience for the participants than the term 'refresher course' suggests. Min Tian's monograph *The Poetics of Difference and Displacement* (2008) offers a far more extended discussion of what he calls 'Wiping Real Tears with Water Sleeves' – a reference to the fusion of traditional Chinese theatre techniques with Western emotional realism. He identifies the 'profound and pervasive influence' (Tian, 2008, p. 160) of Stanislavsky during the 1950s and attributes this to the visits of Soviet teachers to the Central Academy of Drama (CAD) in Beijing and the Shanghai Theatre Academy (STA).[6] However, his analysis of the *practices* involved is purely theoretical – a comparison of the 'significant convergences between Stanislavsky's theory and the art of *xiqu*' (Tian, 2008, p. 168). In addition, only two experts are named. Li Ruru's *Shashibiya: Staging Shakespeare in China* offers the only concrete example of the practical work of the Experts – *Much Ado About Nothing* directed by Lipkovskaya with the Advanced Acting Training Class in 1957 (Li, 2003, pp. 54–6). In her analysis Li makes the fundamental point of legacy:

The impact of Soviet ideology and Stanislavskianism on *huaju* was far-reaching. Lipkovskaya's *Much Ado* set up a model adopted in China for the next 40 years.

Li, 2003, p. 61

Given the scarcity of critical literature in English relating to Stanislavsky in China, there remain some key questions, both at the level of the work itself and its far-reaching impact: who were the Experts and with whom did they work? What did they actually do with their students? How did they achieve such a long term, if uneven, impact on Chinese theatre?

Using newly gathered data from the archives of the STA, supplemented by interviews with participants who experienced the work first hand, this chapter will answer these questions directly.[7] It will focus on one extended example of Stanislavsky teaching in Shanghai but will place this illuminating practical documentation in context with references to the wider 'given circumstances' of the Soviet Experts' contribution to Chinese actor training in China. To achieve this dual perspective, the chapter is structured following the six famous questions designed by Stanislavsky in *An Actor's Work*:

Ask yourself questions and answer them honestly, sincerely: the *who, what, when, where, why, wherefore* of what you observe happening.

Stanislavski, 2008, p. 116

Just as they are core to the first year of training in Stanislavsky's *An Actor's Work*, these questions also formed an essential part of the teaching of Stanislavsky in Shanghai. For one interviewee, for instance, they provided 'the key to the treasure'.[8] We do not subscribe to a strict chronology in the narration of this case, therefore, but instead attempt to reveal the key players and their practices, alongside the cultural and political conditions and motivations bearing down on Stanislavsky's System in China.

Who?

The question of who delivered the training in the period would seem to be one of the easiest to answer for this chapter. Yet this ostensibly simple detail has been missing from other published research or only vaguely identified as, for instance, 'numerous experts' (Fei and Sun, 2006) or 'Soviet Experts' (Sun, 2012).

As already noted, Min Tian names two experts – Lesli and Gureev – and Li Ruru's exposition of Lipkovskaya's direction has also been mentioned. In fact, there was a minimum of five specialists given the title of 'Expert' who taught at both sites over the period of four years. They were:

- Platon Vladimirovich Lesli (1905–72)
- Boris Grigorievich Kulnyov (1896–1959)
- G. N. Gureev (1890–?)
- Yevgenia K. Lipkovskaya (1901–89)
- Y. W. Leikov (No dates)

There is more sketchy evidence in the STA archives of other unnamed experts: a makeup artist, a lighting expert, a film expert based at the Shanghai Film institute, and a request for a theatre historian to be sent from the USSR, but even though there was evidence of their lecture materials, the Chinese protocol of not naming experts directly as a gesture of respect at the time has the unwanted result of affirming their anonymity in the documentary record today. The status of the specialist is also decisive as Lesli's wife (Galina Ivanovna) taught at the CAD, arriving in Beijing in May 1954, but slipped through the net as someone without the designation 'Expert'; she was only an 'Appointed Teacher'.[9]

For nearly forty years Lesli was a director and acting teacher at the Moscow Art Theatre itself. In 1923, he was an assistant director at the Second Moscow Art Studio and after 1936 also worked at GITIS. His remit at the Moscow Arts was to oversee the System's transmission across the USSR through a web of National Studios and this was extended to foreign countries, with China the most prominent example.[10] Of all the Experts, he was the most feared, taking a dictatorial approach to his teaching of directing that was widely resented.[11] His blinkered approach was such that he pointedly walked out of Mei Langfang's demonstration of *jingju* in Beijing, showing no respect for traditional Chinese theatre arts, as they did not comply with what he saw as realistic norms.[12]

Kulnyov's contribution to teaching in Shanghai and Beijing is almost entirely unknown outside of China and Russia, a gap in the record that this chapter will rectify with an analysis (in the 'What?' section) of his 16-session introduction to Stanislavsky, recorded in minute detail in the STA archives. Director of the Boris Shchukin Institute, after Boris Zakhava was removed in 1948, Kulnyov was celebrated as a talented teacher, altogether more humble than Lesli and sensitive to the audiences with whom he was working. As a satellite of the Vakhtangov Theatre, the Shchukin Institute was removed from the Moscow Arts Theatre and Lesli's domain, and the work there drew on a creative fusion of Stanislavsky and Meyerhold: what Boris Zhakhava called a synthesis of 'content and form, truth of feeling and theatricality' (in Edwards, 1965, p. 125).

Lipkovskaya came to China from St Petersburg (then Leningrad). She was Assistant Professor of Dramatic Art at LGITMik – the State Institute of Theatre, Music, and Cinematography – and had considerable experience working with non-Russian students. Unlike Lesli and Kulnyov, Lipkovskaya was based in Shanghai as her main working environment, following a request from STA to have their own Soviet Expert. She directed productions during her stay as well, most famously *Much Ado About Nothing* (1957), stressing the importance of the superobjective and of *experiencing* through a characteristically long period of rehearsals – up to six months (Li, 2003, p. 65).

Gureev, a directing expert and outstanding theorist, was based in Beijing during the period of the Soviet Experts' visits and Leikov was a theatre designer, also based in Beijing but working alongside Lipkovskaya in Shanghai for some of his time in China. Whilst there is very little material on the latter, Gureev's work has been relatively well documented, including his contribution to the China Theatre Association conference in January 1958. There he made the puzzling assertion that: 'the Stanislavsky system has in reality existed in Chinese classical *xiqu*' (Tian, 2008, p. 164), rewriting the ancient history and legacy of Chinese theatre in a sentence. Gureev's texts (published in Chinese) were *Seminars on Stanislavsky's System* (Gureev, 1957)[13] and *On Directing: an Essential Guide* based on his work at the CAD (Gureev, 1960). They have proved to be some of the most influential written texts in China relating to Stanislavsky's practice and to theatre directing in general.

This expanded picture of the Soviet Experts is only half of the picture, of course. We have yet to consider who were the beneficiaries of the Experts' teaching. The answer to this question is instructive and offers tangible evidence of how the emergent People's Republic of China, 'conscientiously applied Stanislavski's psychological realism to their traditional theatre both in theory and practice' (Tian, 2008, p. 159). We will focus on the classes Kulnyov led at the STA, firstly because this is the most detailed record so far uncovered and secondly because his sixteen classes were designed as a pilot for a full two-year programme taught in Beijing. It is reasonable, therefore, to assume that the teaching experienced by the chosen participants in STA had similar characteristics to the more extensive training in the nation's capital.

Kulnyov worked with two layers of 'students': a core of seven carefully chosen participants, all just graduated and newly appointed teaching assistants, and a group of established tutors:

Participants: Chen Mingzheng, Guo Dongli, Liu Kecheng, Song Shunjin, Song Tingxi, Xu Qiping, Zhou Bing.
Teachers: Hu Dao, Luo Sen, Tian Jia, Wang Qi, Xue Mu, Zhang Junchuan, (plus the STA President, Xiong Foxi).

Thus in his classes we see him constantly moving between the direct transmission of Stanislavskian principles to the participants and reflective commentary for the teachers about how to realize this transmission in future classes: a startling mix of teaching and coaching-teaching. This example from his 11 November class is indicative:

> Then the Expert said to Comrade Wang Qi 'you should tell your students what you are going to talk about at the beginning of class. Today, you did not make clear which Unit of exercises you are going to do. You are like a young horse and want to run from the start. I understand that you are enthusiastic. But you should tell them the content of the class calmly, arouse their interests in the content of the class and then you can begin the teaching'.
>
> Kulnyov, 1954

As seven graduate actors, already employed as future teaching assistants at STA, the participants were carefully chosen to maximize the dissemination of Kulnyov's ideas. By guaranteeing the future employment of the young students the School made strategic decisions to ensure that none of the ideas would be lost or exported to other training centres. Each of them went on in later seasons to teach Stanislavsky-based classes in STA and as we shall see later, some of them became part of the leadership team at the Academy. In our research we interviewed three of the seven participants, now all retired: Chen Mingzheng, Guo Dongli, and Song Tingxi in order to 'triangulate' the relatively dry descriptions of the studio stenographer with the felt experiences of the students. Fragments of these interviews are embedded in the analysis of the classes, which appears below.

When and where?

Focusing on the temporal movements of the Experts gives us a good indication of the relative statuses of the two main sites of transmission – Beijing's CAD and STA. In other words: the details of 'Where' are entirely wrapped up in 'When'. It also helps us understand how the programme of Stanislavsky training grew and spread from its central hub in Beijing.

According to the *Cultural News Dispatch* (Wenhua tongxun published in June 1954), three Experts arrived in Beijing at the beginning of 1954 and started working at the CAD, the Musical Conservatory, and the Dance School, respectively. They arrived in Beijing as the primary city for training in the whole of the country – indeed at that time STA was still known as the East China College of the CAD, only attaining full independent status in 1956. Whilst we do not know the names of these first three Experts, we do have evidence that Lesli transferred from Beijing and arrived in Shanghai before any of the other Experts at STA, leading ad hoc masterclasses in the spring of 1954.[14] This led to a much more organized period of training starting in October 1954 taught by Kulnyov, who also transferred from Beijing for the period. As we will see in the 'What' section, these classes began on 22 October and ran until the 13 November 1954 and, as stated, were designed to offer an overview of a two-year training programme in Stanislavsky. Kulnyov then returned to Beijing in December and started a full, two-year training course with thirty participants and as many as fifty observers back at the CAD from January 1955–January 1957. Lesli, for his part, began his teaching in Beijing in November 1954, after leading the pilot sessions in Shanghai.[15]

The STA's experience with Kulnyov led the administrators there to make a request to the Ministry of Culture to invite an Expert to work with them directly, someone who was not simply moonlighting from Beijing. That Expert was Lipkovskaia and she arrived in the October of 1955, staying for two years and working both within and beyond the confines of STA in Shanghai. Working alongside her but flitting between the two cities, was Leikov but his movements are less clear in the archival record, even if there is photographic evidence of his presence at STA.

The directing Expert Gureev arrived in Beijing in September 1956, remaining mainly in Beijing. He taught classes until the end of 1957 and, as we have seen, attended the China Theatre Association conference in January 1958.

Figure 19 Leikov in trench coat, centre.
By kind permission of STA archive.

What?

These pencil sketches offer us an overview of what kind of teaching was undertaken in the period by the five Experts: Lesli, working both with Russian scene studies and traditional Chinese repertoire, Leikov with design students, Gureev theorizing the processes of direction, and Lipkovskaya teaching through her own direction of major pieces, including Shakespeare's *Much Ado*. A particularly rich source of 'what', however, is in Kulnyov's classes taught in Shanghai in the autumn of 1954 before he started his formal Advanced Acting Course at the CAD in January 1955. These classes were run as a pilot, and formed the framework for his full course in Beijing. Whilst they took less than three weeks to deliver, they nevertheless constitute an important overview of the extended formal training Kulnyov was to design for Beijing and they highlight his priorities as a Stanislavsky teacher. The first archival record of his lessons begins with the following words:

Class One (Afternoon, October 22, 1954)

At 2 PM, the Expert walked vigorously into the classroom and said hello to everyone kindly. Then he asked everyone to sit round to be closer to each other. He was very modest and said 'Your President, Mr Xiong Foxi and I have made such a decision: during our stay here, we will not only watch students' practice, but also give teachers some lessons'.

Kulnyov, 1954

In the STA archive there are over three hundred pages of detailed stenographic notes, chronicling each of the sixteen classes led by Kulnyov in immense detail. An appendix of over 150 discrete exercises concludes the record, giving a snapshot of the work he introduced to the seven graduate actors:

- Concentration of Attention (1–36) [Unit 1]
- Relaxation of muscles (37–48) [Unit 2]
- Imagination (49–61) [Unit 3]
- [Memory of Physical Actions using] Imaginary object exercises (1–36) [Unit 4]
- Bodily self-perception and belief (37–79) [Unit 5]
- Changing attitudes [Unit 6]:
  - to imaginary space. Imagination exercises (80–92)
  - to real objects (93–106)
  - towards facts and their judgement (107–27)
  - to other actors on stage (128–38)
- Objectives/Action/Adaptation (139–51)

In his last class (13 November 1954) Kulnyov refers to this appendix of exercises, explaining the relationship between what he called separate Units (of teaching material) and the exercises themselves, encouraging a healthy independence and pedagogical autonomy redolent of Stanislavsky's oft-quoted observation: 'the System is not a cookery book [...] but a whole *culture* which must be cultivated and nurtured over many long years' (Stanislavski, 2008, p. 612; emphasis in original):

I have given you the exercises of each Unit to print. However, when the teachers accept this method, you should not take it as a prescription. You should do them in your own way. You should do everything in your own way. These exercises may inspire your thoughts. You can create your own exercises. With your classmates, you should try to solve problems in the creative work. Teach the students to really listen and see and teach them to act in logical sequence. In this way, they could find more thoughts involved and explore people's psychological aspects. Otherwise, it will be nonsense.

Kulnyov, 1954[16]

Recorded as a dialogue between Kulnyov, the Expert, the seven newly appointed teaching assistants, and a handful of STA established tutors, the whole document is reminiscent of the fictional classes Stanislavsky had created for both parts of his *Actor's Work on Himself*. There are similar successes and defeats for Zhou Bing, Guo Dongli, and Chen Mingzheng as there are with Stanislavsky's Kostya, Grisha, and Varya, the same patient probing from the master, the same progression from basic tasks to complex training. But one thing was radically different: Kulnyov was teaching his classes for real – and on the East Coast of China.

In the space afforded to us in this chapter, there is only scope to analyse the overall shape of the classes, to offer one or two examples of Kulnyov's practice, and to assess its relationship to principles of Stanislavsky. But even in this preliminary analysis it should be evident how profound was the impact of his work on his individual students, on the STA and, by extension, on the subsequent development of spoken drama in China.

The extent to which Kulnyov ranges across the first two of these perspectives – impact on students' individual creativity and on STA's organizational strategy – is evident in the very first class led by the Soviet Expert. In this opening class Kulnyov outlines the relationship between the first three foundation Units of practice: Concentration of Attention, Relaxation, and Imagination, stressing their integration and mutuality:

> The three units of 'Attention Focusing', 'Muscle Relaxation' and 'Imagination' are connected with each other. They are an organic whole. First practise them respectively, and then combine them.
>
> Kulnyov, 1954[17]

His way into this simple point is perceptive relating to the dual focus he takes throughout. Asking for a STA teacher to come forward he begins his class quizzing the tutor Tian Jia about how he would start a programme of training with first years:

> Now you are the teacher. The seven people are your students. They have just passed the entrance examination and been accepted as the students of Level One. How are you going to give them the first lesson?
>
> Kulnyov, 1954[18]

Tian Jia suggests that they should begin with Concentration exercises, and sends the seven students off to observe the room in all its detail. Kulnyov's empathetic response is typical of his general approach across the sixteen classes. Recognizing that in their first-ever class, Level One students would be nervous and unable to concentrate deeply, he shifts the atmosphere from serious and high focus to light and relaxed, asking Xu Qiping to play the accordion and the rest of the class to join him in a rousing Soviet Song, 'conducted' by Kulnyov himself:

> The classroom was full of merry songs and the atmosphere was also more active. The Expert said to the faculty, 'We need to make students forget the tension of entrance examination and arrange such a learning environment to make them enjoy talking about what they know and show what they have learnt!'
>
> Kulnyov, 1954[19]

The Soviet Expert's attention then shifts from establishing an environment conducive to creative work to teasing out the STA tutors' approach to Imagination: 'the Expert asked Comrade Hu Dao, "Are there any other exercises developing the imagination?"' Hu Dao then confirms that he 'provide[s] the students with three nouns and ask[s] them to link them with a series of coherent actions', a suggestion which meets with Kulnyov's approval. After exploring a number of exercises designed to test actors' imagination, the Expert widens his focus to the rest of the tutors and begins to generalize about future admissions policy:

> I suggest that your admission committee should manage to involve an examination to test the imagination of new students, because imagination and rhythm are equally important. We should learn how to develop students' ability to imagine.
>
> Kulnyov, 1954[20]

This prompt is then sanctioned by the President of STA in his summing up after the day's work, addressing his staff: 'You'd better divide into groups to discuss and study [the Expert's suggestions] seriously'.

This pattern of developments is suggestive of a number of things. Firstly it clarifies the power Kulnyov had in the room – as a State-sponsored visitor no one was able to challenge his suggestions and the most senior STA representative was duty bound to accept the Expert's organizational proposals as well as his practical ideas. Secondly and relatedly Kulnyov is able to move from student-focused teaching, to tutor training, to policy recommendations for the Academy, all in the one day. Thirdly Kulnyov's credo that the System must be flexibly delivered is backed up by his actions in the classroom – relaxation, imagination, and concentration all play a part in his teaching during this session but he sometimes finds creative and indirect ways into these principles, without losing the integrity of the terms.

Two other examples serve to illustrate the impact of the work on the students, both seen through the eyes of Chen Mingzheng.

The first example is the shift in the depth of understanding of the System prompted by Kulnyov's teaching. The transcripts reveal that a Stanislavsky curriculum was already being taught at STA, reconstructed from books, but the ideas were not sufficiently organized by the native tutors and none of them had encountered teachers with an embodied understanding of the System:

> LR: So what had happened before [Kulnyov taught you]?
> CM: We had a Concentration training, looking at one object, so we did it. But we had not been told why we should do it – so we were looking at it without knowing why. We also went out to the factories and to the streets and afterwards we did the imitation. [But] we were pretending. So for me the work [with Kulnyov] was kind of transformational.[21]

Kulnyov's ability as a teacher was twofold – to set individual exercises in a wider logical sequence of development and thus to engender a deeper understanding in the participant of the efficacy of the exercises. Interestingly this move to *experiencing* from imitating (in Chen's words) was partly encouraged by mixing up the demands made on the participants and by knitting in elements of surprise as Kulnyov explained in his ninth class: 'when we assign tasks to students, it is better to embed some "unexpected" things in

Figure 20 Chen Mingzheng demonstrating an object exercise in his flat in Shanghai. Photo by Jonathan Pitches.

these tasks [...] you need to act as if the thing happens to you for the first time and that this thing never happened before' (Kulnyov, 1954).²²

The second example relates to the exercise devoted to the 'memory of feelings', as prominent, perhaps surprisingly, in the Chinese teaching of Stanislavsky in 1954 as it was in the American manifestations of Stanislavsky teaching collectively known as the Method (Krasner, 2000). Again this exercise was considered transformational by the participant bringing about a theatrical epiphany of sorts for Chen. Speaking fifty years later from when he was first asked to recount the story of his lost dog, Chen was still visibly moved by the experience. Forced to relocate, and commanded to leave his pet dog behind, he and his family were sailing down the river to their new home in a bamboo raft. Chen had concealed the dog in his suitcase but it was discovered once the boat set off. Rather than running off the dog followed Chen for several miles, along the bank of the river. Only after another tributary joined the main river, cutting off the dog's route, were master and animal finally separated, leaving the dog to fend for himself and the twelve-year-old Chen to deal with his loss. Li Ruru interpreting for Chen explains:

> When he told this story the sad feelings of separation were remembered. He had already studied acting for four years but he had never ever been touched like he was when telling this story. After this simple, five-minute exercise he realised the memory was there and he could remember the feelings. He used [the power of] that [discovery] in his work as an actor, a director and a writer.²³

This revelation illustrates how emotion memory can shorten historical time dramatically as Chen experienced once again the pain of that moment in his modest front room, sixty years later. But it also indicates how this early formative moment influenced his practice as an artist in the years that followed Kulnyov's short introductory classes. It is to this long view that this chapter turns in the following sections, looking back to 'Why' and forward to 'Wherefore'.

Looking back: Why?

In order to answer why in the early 1950s the Chinese government invited the Soviet Experts to come to teach at both the CAD and STA, the only two conservatoires that trained modern spoken drama actors, and why

Stanislavsky's System has had such an unusual impact on Chinese theatre (both modern and traditional song-dance theatres), we need to examine the root of Chinese theatre itself, the reason why the modern spoken drama emerged and developed quickly for a nation that had its own strong theatrical tradition, and the political and ideological demands after the People's Republic was founded in 1949.

The indigenous theatre is called *xiqu* in Chinese, literally meaning 'theatre of [sung] verse', which indicates the importance of the musical component and its association with classical poetry. Chinese theatre did not emerge until the middle of the twelfth century, yet it soon reached its unique and highly-developed form and has continued to evolve since, maintaining the same integral aesthetic features; nearly three hundred regional theatres are scattered across the country using different levels of stylization. *Jingju* (known in the West as Beijing Opera) is normally taken as a representative of the *xiqu*, because it is a total theatre borrowing and absorbing elements from a diversity of pre-existent theatres. Conventionalization (*chengshi*) is the key to the understanding the theatre: every aspect – singing, speaking, dance-acting, combat, costuming, and makeup – has to follow certain modes, patterns, or rules. Central to the system is the categorization of role types; each role type is codified by specific requirements for every aspect mentioned above.

If *xiqu* emphasizes stylization over realism, the modern spoken drama was born to fight against such a formalized song-dance theatre, and its commencement in 1907 was a response to the spirit of the time when China had suffered a series of military defeats at the hands of foreign powers. Advocating the adoption of Western knowledge as a means to eradicate the decadence and backwardness of the country, leading intellectuals called for a new realm of Chinese literature and art, which, they believed, would help reform the nation. At that time, theatre was central in the nation's culture, because it was the most popular entertainment enjoying a wide range of audiences from the court, high-ranking officials, rich merchants to the peasants, peddlers, and even beggars in the street. It was also the place illiterate people received their education. Rejecting Chinese cultural superiority, young radicals found the traditional song-dance theatre so ornamental that it was unable to carry out any social function to inspire its audiences to be transformed into 'new citizens' (Liang, 1973, p. 3). Finally, in 1907 a group of young Chinese students studying in Tokyo organized the first performance of a new theatre that contained only dialogues and monologues without song or dance. Their work was inspired by the European-influenced modern Japanese theatre. In the same year the new-style theatre also appeared in Shanghai. Modern Chinese drama was thus an imported theatrical genre from the West via Japan.

The impact of the newly born modern drama on the intellectual life can be seen in two special issues published by *New Youth*, the influential and iconoclastic journal of the era that advocated Mr Science and Mr Democracy in order to establish a completely new culture for China. The two issues, one on Ibsen (4:6, June 1918) and one on theatre reform (5:4, October 1918), made it clear that the modern drama was a powerful disseminator of radical thought, while 'the old drama' (referring to *jingju* and the indigenous song-dance theatre) could not fulfil the same mission. This was because it used neither 'the typical actions of human beings' nor the 'people's typical language', and consequently it 'could not evoke human feelings even if it wanted to' (Fu, 1918, 5:4, p. 324). For both didactic and aesthetic reasons, radicals considered Western realistic spoken drama superior to the Chinese sung theatre. 'Theatre' thus became unprecedentedly ideological, representing new or old, progressive or backward, naturalness or falseness. The debate on the value and quality of the naturalistic modern spoken drama versus the non-mimetic traditional song-dance theatre could be seen as a prelude to the 1919 May Fourth Movement and later became a decisive reason for the introduction of Stanislavsky's System to China.

Despite the modern spoken drama being advocated by the radicals, people had little knowledge about how to perform it, because they were introduced to the new style of drama through written summaries and translated play texts. Apart from those Chinese students in Japan who saw Japanese actors performing *shinpa* (a Japanese hybrid form of *kabuki* and Western-style spoken theatre) and a small number of Chinese people in Shanghai who saw foreign performances, including those staged by the international settlers' own amateur drama clubs and touring performances,[24] most actors who devoted themselves to the new style of drama had no idea about how to act in the new style. They either used the familiar acting conventions of the traditional theatre, or they had no acting skills at all. Later Hollywood films became useful learning resources, because people believed that since spoken drama was an imported form from the West, it was natural to learn from anything produced in the West.

With this situation, we can understand the words 'great surprise, captivation, charm, fascination' (Zhang, 1981, p. 2) that Zhang Geng used to describe the impressions and feelings when he and other modern drama activists first read the descriptions of the Moscow Art Theatre and of Stanislavsky and his System in the 1930s and 1940s. Practitioners enthusiastically used what they had heard or read on the stage. For example, in order to represent realism on the stage, director Zhang Min (also the later co-translator of the first Chinese version of *An Actor's Work on Himself* Part I [1943][25]) invited a Russian fencer to teach actors fencing skills for about two months for his 1937 *Romeo and Juliet*. The fencing episodes were so true to life that actors kept injuring themselves with the real swords they used. Yet, the acting was criticized for being as dull as 'reciting a book of classical Chinese', because Zhang had requested actors to lay emphasis on their characters' psychological dimensions (Li, 1937, p. 14). Lü Fu and Zhao Ming write in their memoir that when the Theatre Team No. 9[26] rehearsed a newly written play by a Chinese playwright in 1942, they put Stanislavsky's words on the wall in the rehearsing room and spent a long time on character and play analysis. But, as they point out, the work was 'based only on the fragments of Stanislavsky which it was possibly to get hold of; we only gained half-baked knowledge and often interpreted the meaning out of the context' (Lü and Zhao, 1985, p. 229). When it came to the real rehearsals, actors seemed to have forgotten what they had analysed and did not know what to do in a scene; even the learned lines were quickly forgotten. Later, the two writers used the term 'half-cooked rice' to describe the production they staged. Chinese actors realized that reading alone was not enough to support their acting; they were eager to have teachers who could teach them Stanislavsky through practice.

Theatre practitioners' fervent aspirations for learning the authentic Stanislavsky System, which was the 'crystal of the world theatre, the correct artistic requirement and the correct road-sign for Chinese future theatre' (quoted in Hu, 1995, p. 155), were finally realized when the newly established people's government followed Mao Zedong's policy of 'leaning to one side' (*yibiandao*). This policy encapsulated the doctrine that 'the Communist Party of the Soviet Union is the best teacher and we must learn from it' (Mao, 30 June

1949). Alongside industries, agricultures and militaries, the arts and education took the Soviet Big Brother's work as a model. It should also be noted that those who had been eagerly involved in establishing the new spoken drama or were in the May Fourth Movement all played an important role in politics and culture in the new People's Republic. For example, Ouyang Yuqian (1889–1962), who had been an active member of the first Chinese student group in Tokyo in 1907, led the debate about the modern drama and constructed the narrative of its history, holding many important cultural positions including the president of the CAD since it was established in 1950 until his death. And Lü Fu, one of the writers quoted above, was the Deputy Head of the Shanghai Cultural Bureau and the Deputy President of the Shanghai People's Art Theatre for many years. These people controlled the discourse at the time, another important factor in the comprehensive introduction of Stanislavsky and socialist realist theatre to China.

The 1950s and on: Wherefore?

Contradictory findings are discovered when examining how Stanislavsky's System embedded itself in Chinese theatre culture. The following four areas of enquiry may help summarize the complexity: Stanislavsky's absolute authoritative power; confusion caused by arbitrary implementation; the impact of the Cultural Revolution; and the current multiplicity of acting and directing schools.

Stanislavsky's absolute authoritative power

Mao's slogan that the whole nation and the Party should thoroughly lean to the side of the Soviet Union transformed the original artistic pursuit of improving spoken drama acting methods into an ideologically driven political correctness stamped with a powerful Communist force. In the early 1950s it was decreed that Stanislavsky's System would become the sole method that the Chinese theatre *including* the indigenous song-dance theatre should use. Apart from the CAD and STA who had the privilege of having Soviet Experts working there, Beijing and Shanghai organized various workshops and seminars to learn from Soviet theatre's advanced experiences.[27] Those, who did not completely agree with the methods used in the two academies became the target for attacks during the Anti-Rightist campaign (1957). Xue Mu, a young lecturer in his twenties at STA, exemplified the situation. In an article published in the 1957 May Issue of the *Academy's Bulletin* (Yuanbao),[28] Xue questioned some points in the USSR-style acting curriculum that had been implemented at the STA since 1953, and made comparisons between the traditional theatre training and Soviet Expert Lipkovskaya's methods used in both teaching and rehearsing. Not long after this article, Xue was labelled as a Rightist, removed from the Academy and not rehabilitated until 1979. His fellow colleagues were forced to denounce him publicly through writing.[29]

The Experts' work in CAD and STA had a great impact on the students who attended the courses, not only on what they taught but also on their personal working style. *Cultural News Dispatch*, internal documents edited and distributed by the Ministry of Culture in the 1950s, recorded the Soviet Experts' 'diligent and conscientious work' (Ministry of Culture, 1954a, p. 16) and encouraged the whole arts sector to adopt their practices as models. The fact that, even after the Sino-Soviet split, the USSR drama curriculum and Stanislavsky's approaches were still used by the two academies clearly illustrates their profound influence. Those who attended the Experts' courses all became key teachers in the two academies, producing generations of students for the next forty years. For example, among those who attended Kulnyov's sixteen classes, Song Tingxi and Xu Qiping worked respectively with three Tibetan classes (in 1959–62, 1964–6, and 1977–81), Guo Dongli was the Deputy Head of the Department of Directing at STA for decades, while Chen Mingzheng, as an educator and director, was Head of the Department of Acting for a similar length of time, directing over sixty stage productions for students and professionals, up until his last work, *The Government Inspector*, in 2010.

Confusion of implementation

Meanwhile the imposition of Stanislavsky's System caused much confusion in Chinese theatre. Xue Mu's questions demonstrate part of this problem. More difficulties occurred among the large number of traditional song-dance theatre practitioners who were trained since childhood in stylized singing, speaking, dance-acting, and combat as we have discussed. Their training and Stanislavsky's methods belonged to two different schools of aesthetics. Stanislavsky's System emphasizes experiencing and inner motivation to represent a piece of real life, while the Chinese song-dance theatre pays no attention to naturalistic details on the stage. Instead, the expressions of feelings and emotions of the characters are supported by a large acting vocabulary of colourful and codified movements and gestures. Writings by those from the traditional theatre who attended the Advanced Directing Course[30] and the class notes published in CAD's journal, *Drama Studies,* at the time reveal that the arbitrary implementation of Stanislavsky's System in the traditional song-dance theatre led to great confusion.[31] Further, Lesli's severe criticism of the traditional Chinese theatre's stylization, and his view that there was no justification for showing contemporary audiences a theatre that lived a thousand years before, heaped more pressure onto the song-dance theatre practitioners. Lesli's speech was published in *Cultural News Dispatch* (Ministry of Culture 1954b, 7:77–82) as a document that all levels in the cultural sector should study; the Cultural Ministry's editorial note stated: 'We should pay attention to these opinions. We hope that every level of cultural departments will pass this document to the traditional song-dance theatres and leading practitioners to study. For those aspects that can be improved straightaway, all levels of cultural departments should work out plans and put them into practice' (Ministry of Culture 1954b, p. 77).

Whilst these confusions and problems occurred in the Chinese acceptance of Stanislavsky's System they also encouraged more practitioners to consider how to approach Stanislavsky and to digest his methods more organically in the Chinese context. Between 1958 and 1960 Ouyang Yuqian organized a number of fora at the CAD about how to learn from the indigenous theatre, and the published articles show that Gureev made a good contribution to the discussions. For example, he spoke highly about CAD's decision that the newly written speech curriculum would 'select teaching materials from the rich indigenous resources and China's own genres'. Gureev pointed out that 'this practice demonstrates that the curriculum has not only developed USSR's experience but also made its own creative contributions' (Gureev, 1958: p. 114). Around this time, China witnessed a heated debate on spoken drama Sinicization, in both academic writing and creative work.[32] Jiao Juyin's directing work best exemplifies how spoken drama integrated song-dance theatrical components, while the acting experiences documented by actors from the song-dance theatre also illustrate the benefit they gained from learning modern drama and Stanislavsky's ideas.

The impact of the Cultural Revolution and current multiple schools of training

During the Cultural Revolution, Stanislavsky and his System were described as the 'deadly foe' of the proletarian culture and were severely denounced.[33] Because he had enjoyed his authoritative power since the 1950s (maintaining his authority even after the Sino-Soviet split), Stanislavsky had the 'privilege' of being criticized systematically. A special group named 'Denouncing Stanislavsky's System' was organized to edit a book focusing on the criticisms. Not only were some of Mao's quotations printed at the beginning of the book, but a few lines specifically referring to Stanislavsky by Madam Mao (Jiang Qing) were also quoted. In a talk held at the Forum on Literature and Arts in the Armed Forces, she pointed out that Stanislavsky belonged to 'the Russian bourgeoisie', and thus his ideas were 'not Marxism but bourgeois thoughts'.[34] The book contains twenty-one articles, covering a wide range of subjects criticizing the 'reactionary nature' of Stanislavsky and his System (Shanghai Cultural System, 1971, p. 54), which 'weakened people's revolutionary will to fight and sabotaged the proletarian revolutionary movement' (Shanghai Cultural System, 1971, p. 12). There is also an appendix of Stanislavsky's quotations which are used as a target to be 'thoroughly critiqued using Mao Zedong's thoughts' and a postscript that articulates the purpose of the book. Yet, when spoken drama productions gradually appeared again in the late 1960s after a period when the stage of the whole country had been occupied solely by model revolutionary pieces (*yangbanxi* including both *jingju* and ballet), directors and actors still adopted some of Stanislavsky's methods to approach the rehearsals. They had been taught through the System and there was no other way for them to approach a play.

Immediately after the Cultural Revolution, the whole of China was in a mood to put the clock back ten years and to make up for the incalculable losses.[35] Stanislavsky's System regained some of its power, but not for long because new ideas and thoughts swarmed into the country. The decisive turning point that opened theatre practitioners' minds was the early 1980s debate about 'the conception of theatre' (*xijuguan*).³⁶ Although the term was first raised in 1962 by Huang Zuolin after he directed the first Brecht play in China, it did not attract people's attention when the whole theatre was 'leaning to the one side' of Stanislavsky. After experiencing the criticism of Stanislavsky's System during the Cultural Revolution and as Chinese theatre was absorbing a diversity of new styles,³⁷ people realized the value of Huang's discussions about the differences and overlapping ideas among Stanislavsky, Brecht and, Mei Lanfang. In addition, more non-realistic foreign play texts were available in Chinese and Chinese playwrights started employing new methods in writing. Directors came to realize, for example, that the given circumstances or the conventional order of time and space may be interrupted and consequently, they started seeking new inspirations.

Conclusion: Stanislavsky with Chinese characteristics

Discussing the dissemination of Stanislavsky in China we need to note the 'Chinese characteristics' in the dissemination and implementation of his System across this vast land. In a recent essay Taiwan-based theatre researcher Lin Wei-yu observed:

> Virtually everyone in the *huaju* world talks about Stanislavsky, their understanding and practice (even those who strongly defend the orthodoxy of Stanislavsky) are in many ways tinged with Chinese characteristics.
> Lin, 2015, p. 50

Her words echo British director Gail McIntyre's comments when she first encountered the Chinese theatre in Chengdu, the capital city of Sichuan province. She found Stanislavsky in China was very different from her own understanding although at the seminar during the day everyone quoted Stanislavsky's terms such as 'experience' and 'emotional memory'.

There are several reasons for this confusion of interpretations. Firstly, those who attended or observed the Soviet Experts' teaching were, after all, a small number compared to the huge number of theatre practitioners in the country. Secondly, the Experts' work in China only lasted four years and after the Sino-

Soviet split, there was no further contact between the theatres of the two countries until the 1990s. The Experts' students eagerly disseminated what they had learned but the individual disseminator's understanding and preference would unavoidably affect the original materials. Thirdly, the strong tradition of the Chinese indigenous theatre inevitably influenced ideas about 'what theatre should look like' for both practitioners and audiences. It is understandable that a new graduate from one of the academies though vigorously trained within the System would bend him/herself to the overall acting style of the theatre company to please audiences. Finally, the physical condition of the theatre buildings also contributed greatly to these 'Chinese characteristics'. Before the 1990s most theatres were built for the purpose of the song-dance theatre; facing an auditorium of about 2,000 seats often in two to three storeys, actors would subconsciously exaggerate. The situation is changing. More blackbox style theatres and studios have been built; more practitioners have become fascinated by the intimate relationship between actors and audiences. Today Stanislavsky is taught together with other acting approaches, not only in the two drama academies but also in drama disciplines in universities[38] and in the National Academy of Chinese Theatre Arts which is specialized for training the traditional song-dance theatre practitioners (Jia, 2006, p. 162). The routes of further developments in the Chinese relationship with Stanislavsky are for future research.

In terms of the period in Chinese theatre history dealt with here we can conclude by observing that the colouring of Stanislavsky with 'Chinese characteristics' is best explained with direct reference to the practices shared during this short-term alliance of nation states, an alliance which for all its brevity had demonstrable and long-lasting effects. Using Stanislavsky's prompts for character analysis as a structural device, this chapter has revealed the given circumstances of a pivotal moment in the development of Chinese *huaju*, drawing on the first-hand testimony of those who experienced the transmission of practice, on detailed transcripts of the practice itself and on policy documents. In doing so we have revealed the individual, institutional, and national adaptations needed to make Stanislavsky's System work on home ground. They are testimony to the inventiveness and impact of the expert teacher Boris Kulnyov, whose sixteen lessons in the autumn of 1954 became a 'system in microcosm' for the carefully selected beneficiaries. But, equally, they speak to the openness and receptiveness of those beneficiaries, Kulynov's students, who embody to this day the meeting of two systems.

Notes

1. Further discussion on Huang Zuolin can be seen in Li, 2003, pp. 121–7.
2. Extracts of *An Actor Prepares* were translated by Zheng Junli as early as 1937 according to William Sun (1987, p. 139) and the same translator also produced the first Chinese version of Boleslavsky's *Acting* in that year.
3. A phrase borrowed from the famous Deng Xiaoping's slogan that through the radical economic reforms and adoption of the market economy, China was to become 'socialism with Chinese characteristics' (Deng, 1991, p. 4).
4. Anatoly Smeliansky dates the beginning of this national orthodoxy at December 1931 and the advent of the Gorky Moscow Arts Academic Theatre (Smeliansky, 2014, p. 91).
5. Interview with Prof Chen Mingzheng, 15 April 2014.
6. Following the structure of the Soviet drama schools, each academy started from four departments: acting, directing, dramatic literature and playwriting, and stage designing, although more departments have been added since the late 1990s including TV presenting, musical theatre, and arts management. Except for acting, all departments train students for indigenous song-dance theatres. The two academies also run advanced courses for professionals.
7. The full range of sources comprises: archival documents from the STA from 1954–60, the published journals of the CAD and STA, newly conducted interviews with the three out of seven of the chosen 'transmitters' of the work in Shanghai (Prof. Guo Dongli, Prof. Chen Mingzheng, Prof. Song Tingxi, and renowned *jingju* director Mr. Ma Ke, the original Dogberry in Lipkovskaya's production of *Much Ado*), plus additional literature identified in the references.
8. Prof Song Tingxi, interview 16 April 2014. For Prof Song, though, there were only five questions – and no 'wherefore?'
9. STA Archive, 1956 – 1.0002. Another example is Natalia, who according to Prof. Guo Dongli, was the wife of a military expert working in the Military Academy. Natalia was a graduate of Lunacharsky Institute of Theatre. She taught at Nanjing Military Huaju Company, and at STA.
10. Stanislavsky had a plan as early as 1917 to create a network of up to 15 studios –a so-called Theatre Pantheon – drawing on his international connections with Copeau and Craig (cf. Benedetti, 1990, p. 234).

11 For instance Prof. Guo stated: 'Zhou Bing acted the main character in the scene study [led by Lesli in spring 1954]. I was the understudy. I felt I was lucky that Lesli didn't work on me because he was fierce and was always cursing people, and I didn't really like it'. (Interview, 17 April 2014).
12 A male actor playing female roles, Mei toured Japan, USA, and USSR before 1949 and caused great sensation among non-Chinese theatre practitioners, scholars, and general public, including Stanislavsky, Meyerhold, Brecht, Chaplin, and others.
13 Based on his public lectures organized by the China Theatre Association (held in Beijing, Nanjing, and Shanghai).
14 Prof. Guo confirmed that Lesli led two scene studies at STA: one (*Morning Sunrise over Moscow*) with the finalists group (Level 4) which made up Kulnyov's later class and the other with Level 3 students on a Chinese play.
15 From CAD Xiju xuexi, No. 2, (September 1957) p. 13.
16 Class 16: 13 November 1954.
17 Class 1: 22 October 1954.
18 Class 1: 22 October 1954.
19 Class 1: 22 October 1954.
20 Class 1: 22 October 1954.
21 Interview, 15 April 2014.
22 Class 9: November 2 1954.
23 Interview, 15 April 2014.
24 Siyuan Liu *Performing Hybridity in Colonial Modern-China* offers a good discussion of the theatre at the time. Basingstoke: Palgrave Macmillan, 2013; Xu Banmei vividly records his own experience of working in the early spoken drama: *Reminiscences of Spoken Drama in Its Initial Period* (Huaju chuangshiqi huiyilu), Beijing: Zhongguo Xiju Chubanshe, 1957.
25 Stanislavsky, C. translated by Zheng Junli and Zhang Min, 1943. Chinese translation titled: Yanyuan ziwo xiuyang (An actor's self-cultivation), Chongqing: Sanlian Shudian.
26 A theatre company led by the Communist Party working in the Nationalist-controlled areas from 1938–49. Chinese name: Yanju dui.
27 According to the Chinese publication of Gureev's seminar notes, he also gave public lectures in Nanjing, the capital city of Jiangsu province.
28 In Xue's published article 'A Few Questions Occurred When Implementing Soviet Union's Drama Curriculum', after emphasizing that both the traditional Chinese song-dance theatre and Stanislavsky's System possess the nature of realism, he pointed out the differences in training. He raised three aspects: students' stage experience, the meaning of truth ('truth in everyday life' or 'artistic truth'), and external techniques where he quotes Stanislavsky's idea about the importance of

techniques (in *An Actor's Work on Himself*, Volume II) and criticized that the Soviet Drama Curriculum for the first and second years only stressed the importance of 'experiencing' (1957, No. 18: 19–20).
29 A few articles can be seen in the issue No. 23 of the Shanghai Theatre Academy's Bulletin (Yuanbao).
30 Daoyan ganbu xunlianban, literally: 'directing cadres training class'.
31 The language barrier was another issue. Hu Dao notes a conflicting situation between Lesli and A. Jia caused by how to translate the Russian phrase into the Chinese words 'action' or 'movement' (Hu, 2002, pp. 5–6).
32 See Li, 2015, pp. 11–14.
33 Zheng Xuelai, one of the translators of Stanislavsky's works in China wrote an article recounting briefly how the Russian practitioner was denounced during the Cultural Revolution. See Zheng, 1978: 7; and also Shanghai Cultural System – 'Denouncing Stanislavsky's System' Group ed., *Chedi pipan Sitannisilafusiji tixi* (Thoroughly Denouncing Stanislavsky), Shanghai Renmin Chubanshe, 1971.
34 Shanghai Cultural System – 'Denouncing Stanislavsky's System' Group ed., 1971: np.
35 Li Ruru's discussion of the revival of *Much Ado About Nothing* by Hu Dao, one of the assistants to Lipkovskaya, best exemplifies the situation. See Li, 2003: 56–9.
36 More information about this period can be seen in Ferrari 2012 and Bianweihui 1988–9.
37 For instance symbolism, cubism, structuralism, Existentialism, post-modernism, Theatre of the Absurd, Artaud's Theatre of Cruelty, Grotowski's Poor Theatre.
38 The monopoly of the CAD and STA in drama education was stopped from the 1990s. A large number of national and provincial universities and colleges offer drama or combined degree with the arts.

References

Bao, W. 24 July 1969 'Buyao qingyi fangguo Sitanni zhege fanmian jiaoyuan' ('Do Not let the "Negative Teacher" Stanislavsky Escape Easily'), in *Wenhuibao* (Wenhui Daily).
Benedetti, J. (1990). *Stanislavski: a Biography*. London: Methuen.
Bianweihui (Editorial Board) (1988–9), *Xiju guan zhengming ji* (Debates on the conception of theatre, 2 Vols). Beijing: Zhongguo Xiju Chubanshe.
Deng, X. (1991), 'Build socialism with Chinese characteristics', in *Major documents of the People's Republic of China—selected important documents since the Third*

Plenary Session of the Eleventh Central Committee of the Communist Party of China (December 1978 and November 1989), ed. Research Department of Party Literature, Central Committee of the Communist Party of China. Beijing: Foreign Languages Press, pp. 1–5.

Edwards, C. (1965), *The Stanislavsky Heritage*. London: Peter Owen.

Fairbank, D. K. and Goldman, M. (2006), *China: a New History 2nd ed.* Boston: Harvard University Press.

Fei, C. F. and Sun, W. (2006), 'Othello and Beijing Opera: Appropriation as a Two-Way Street', *TDR*, Vol. 50, No. 1: pp. 120–33.

Ferrari, R. (2012), *Pop goes the avant-garde: experimental theatre in contemporary China*. London: Seagull Books.

Fu, S. (1918) 'Various perspectives on theatre reform', in *Xin qingnian* (New Youth), 5:4 (October).

Gu, C. (2011), *Tade wutai: Zhongguo xiju nv daoyan chuangzuo yanjiu* (Her Stage: Chinese Woman Directors and Their Creativity). Shanghai: Yuandong Chubanshe.

Gureev, G. N. (1957), *Sitannisilafusiji tixi jiangzuo* (Seminars on Stanislavsky's System), translated by W. Sun, S. Zhang, A. Wang, and S. Zhang, proofread by S. Zhang. Beijing: Zhongguo Xiju Chubanshe.

Gureev, G. N. (1958), 'Fayan' (Talk at the Forum of Speech Curriculum), *Xiju xuexi* (Drama Studies), No. 3: pp. 113–33.

Gureev, G. N. (1960), *Daoyan xue jichu* (Directing: An Essential Guide), trans. S. Zhang. Beijing: Zhongguo Xiju Chubanshe.

Hu, D. (2002), *Xiju biaoyanxue: Lun Sishi yanju xueshuo zai woguode shijian yu fazhan* (On Acting: Practice and Development of Stanislavsky's System in China). Beijing: Zhongguo Xiju Chubanshe.

Hu, X. (1995), 'Sitanni tixi zai Zhongguo' ('Stanislavsky's System in China'), *Nanjing Daxue xuebao* (Nanjing University Journal), No. 3: 153–73.

Jia, J. (2006), *Ershi shiji Zhongguo xiandai jiaoyu shigao* (History of Drama Education in the Twentieth Century). Zhongguo Xiju Chubanshe.

Krasner, D. (2000), 'Strasberg, Adler and Meisner: Method Acting', in *Actor training*, ed. A. Hodge. Abingdon: Routledge, pp. 144–63.

Kulnyov, B. (1954), 'Transcript of 16 classes taught at Shanghai Theatre Academy', translated by Guo Shengnan, Li Siyuan and Wang Huimin. Shanghai Theatre Academy Archive: Shanghai.

Li, M. (1937), 'Luomiou yu Zhuliye, gongyan hou de pingjia' ('Romeo and Juliet – Evaluation on Its Performance'), *Da gong bao zengkan* (The Ta Kung Pao Supplement), 9 June.

Li, R. (2003), *Shashibiya: Staging Shakespeare in China*. Hong Kong: Hong Kong University Press.

Li, R. (ed.) (2015), *Staging China: New Theatres in the Twenty-First Century*. Basingstoke: Palgrave Macmillan.

Liang, O. (1973), *Yinbingshi quanji* (Complete works of the ice-drinkers' studio). Taipei: Wenhua Tushu Gongsi.

Lin, W. (2015), 'Lin Zhaohua's Innovation of *Huaju* Acting in *The Master Builder*', in *Staging China: New Theatres in the Twenty-First Century*, ed. L. Ruru. Basingstoke: Palgrave Macmillan.

Liu, S. (2013), *Performing Hybridity in Colonial Modern-China*. Basingstoke: Palgrave Macmillan.

Lü, F. and Zhao, M. (1985), 'Yanju Jiudui shiyi nian' (Eleven Years of the Theatre Company No. 9), in *Zhongguo huaju yundong wushinian shiliaoji (1907– 1957)* (Historical Materials Concerning the Chinese Spoken Drama Movement over 50 Years, 1907–1957), ed. Editorial Committee of Historical Materials Concerning the Chinese Spoken Drama Movement over 50 Years. Beijing: Zhongguo Xiju Chubanshe, pp. 202–39.

Mao, Z. (Mao, T.) (1949). 'On the People's Democratic Dictatorship', https://www.marxists.org/reference/archive/mao/selected-works/volume-4/mswv4_65.htm [accessed 31 October 2015].

Ministry of Culture (1954a), 'Nuli xuexi Sulian xianjin yishu jiaoyu jingyan' (Learn hard from the USSR about Their Advanced Experience in Arts Education), in *Wenhua tongxun* (Cultural News Dispatch), Issue 6: 16–20.

Ministry of Culture (1954b), 'Zhongyang Wenhuabu guanyu Sulian Minzhu Deguo xijujia dui woguo xiqu gaige wenti ji juchang zhixu deng fangmiande yijiande tongbao' (A circulated report by the Ministry of Culture about comments given by theatre experts of the USSR and German Democratic Republic on issues of theatre reform and the audience's conduct in the theatre auditorium) in *Wenhua tongxun* (Cultural News Dispatch), Issue 7: 77–84.

Shanghai Cultural System – 'Denouncing Stanislavsky's System' Group (ed.) (1971), *Chedi pipan Sitannisilafusiji tixi* (Thoroughly Denounce Stanislavsky). Shanghai: Renmin Chubanshe.

Smeliansky, A. (2014), 'Silhouette of a Destiny: the Letters of Stanislavsky', in *The Routledge Companion to Stanislavsky*, ed. A. White. Abingdon: Routledge, pp. 82–100.

Stanislavski, K. (2008), *An Actor's Work*, trans. J. Benedetti. Abingdon: Routledge.

Stiffler, D. (2010), ' "Three Blows of the Shoulder Pole": Soviet Experts at Chinese People's University 1950-7', in *China Learns from the Soviet Union 1949-Present*, eds T. P. Bernstein and H. Y. Li. New York: Lexington Books, pp. 303–26.

Sun, W. H. (1987), 'Mei Lanfang, Stanislavsky and Brecht on China's Stage and their aesthetic significance', in *Drama in the People's Republic of China*, eds C. Tung and C. Mackerras. New York: Suny Press.

Sun, Y. (2012), 'Shakespeare reception in China', in *Theory and Practice in Language Studies*, Vol. 2, No. 9, pp. 1931–8.

Tian, M. (2008), *The Poetics of Difference and Displacement*. Hong Kong: Hong Kong University Press.

Wang, E. (2010), 'Review of Bernstein, Thomas P.; Li, Hua-Yu, *China Learns from the Soviet Union 1949-present*'. H-Soz-u-Kult, H-Net Reviews. December.

Xu, B. (1957), *Huaju chuangshiqi huiyilu* (Reminiscences of Spoken Drama in Its Initial Period). Beijing: Zhongguo Xiju Chubanshe.

Zhang, G. (1981), *Xiju yishu yinlun* (Introduction to the Dramatic Art). Beijing: Wenhua Yishu Chubanshe.

Zheng, X. (1978), 'Lun Sitannisilafusiji tixi' ('On Stanislavsky's System'), *Xiju Yishu* (Dramatic Art), 4, pp. 5–18.

A Producer's Perspective: Stanislavsky in Contemporary Japan

Kaori Nakayama

How have you encountered Stanislavsky in Japan and in what capacity?

Since 1998 I have been involved in actor training and drama/theatre in education as a producer and/or an interpreter with many foreign directors and trainers. Originally I did not have any particular idea about Stanislavsky – I had not trained in the Stanislavsky system, but learnt through working with foreign directors and trainers.

My first encounter with actor training can be traced further back to 1995, when I conducted an interview with Nicholas Barter for a magazine, featuring foreign trainers in the performing arts. Barter was then the Principal of RADA who, since 1993 (and up until 2012) was also involved in intensive acting workshops in Japan, appropriately entitled 'RADA in Tokyo'.

In his interview, Barter pointed out what he perceived to be some of the problems with Japanese actors and their training: 1) each drama school has been providing different actor training; 2) there is a lack of qualified trainers; 3) the closed nature of theatre organization; and 4) the importance of new good plays for good actors (Geidankyo, 1996, pp. 5–7).

Based on his insights, my objectives have developed in the course of my own research and business, and could be summarized as: 1) to release actors from the limitations of organizational politics through experiencing the theories and practices of various artistic influences; 2) to foster intelligent actors with critical thinking and spontaneity; and ultimately 3) to change the definitions of what is a 'good' actor as well as what is a 'good' play. My task is to

Figure 21 Nicholas Barter leading a Stanislavsky intensive workshop for students from five drama universities, Tokyo (May 2014).

question some of the peculiar theatrical conventions and unholy traditions in Japanese theatre by providing different contexts and practices. This has been my role and responsibility as someone educated abroad – especially as my study abroad was made possible by performers' rights money.

Shingeki – the modern theatre movement – was launched by the rejection of the traditional acting and dramaturgy of Kabuki during the process of modernization and Westernization of society after the Meiji Restoration of 1868. Can you expound more on this movement, and the role that Stanislavsky played in it?

The Modern theatre movement began in the earliest years of the twentieth century. It was an earnest effort to replace Japan's traditional theatre of entertainment with contemporary plays derived from the European stage that contained symbolic meaning (Havens, 1982, p. 145). In practice, in 1909, a kabuki actor-manager Ichikawa Sandanji II launched 'Jiyu Gekijo' (the Free Stage) with the director Osanai Kaoru, as a non-commercial experimental venture. Prior to this, Sadanji had travelled to Europe and had experienced three weeks training at RADA. Inspired by Antoine and Craig in direction and took the English Stage Society as its organization model (Miyake, 1942, p. 150), they staged Ibsen's *John Gabriel Borkman*. This event heralded the arrival not only of naturalism as a *style* of theatre but also of 'translated drama' as a *genre* of theatre. In addition, it proved the importance of drama rather than the individual actor's art – *gei*. Kabuki depended on trained gestures known as *kata* – according to Watanabe, a sequence of visible and invisible languages, a kind of second script (Watanabe, 2004, pp. 6–11). The raising of the status of drama was an epoch-making discovery for Japanese theatre.

Osanai played an important role in introducing Stanislavsky's practices into Japan. In 1912–13, Osanai travelled to Russia and met Stanislavsky in person. However, he could not find any opportunity to attend any rehearsals or to see the scripts with Stanislavsky's directorial notes (Hatta, 1976, p. 97). Through seeing the performances, though, Osanai intuitively understood an actor's active creativity and he mimicked Stanislavsky's staging in his own production of *The Lower Depths* in 1913.

In 1924, Osanai and the director Hijikata Yoshi set up a company at Tsukiji Little Theatre. In its five stormy years, they produced 114 plays – eighty-nine were foreign, translated dramas. In terms of actor training, it mostly relied on the directors' demonstrations – visual mimicry from acting in films, especially for translation drama (Sugiyama, 1957, pp. 161–2), in addition to on-the-job training, use of the Dalcroze method and voice training (Hatta, 1976, p. 102). Although Stanislavsky was a kind of symbolic icon of Western progressive theatre in pre-war *shingeki*, nobody knew exactly what his practices were until his publications became available in the early 1940s. There was no clue or vocabulary for understanding the Stanislavsky system in Japanese theatre earlier than that.

Stanislavsky developed his system in tension between a formal theatre company (with all its concerns of repertoire and finances) and smaller, more intimate studio work. Is such a tension evident in any way in Japan?

Post-war *shingeki* enjoyed its heyday in the 1950s to 1960s and could be characterized by '*Gekidan*', a membership body of theatre-makers, which has been mostly self-governed and self-financed: there was no government funding until 1990. Some *gekidan* have more than 100 members and about 80 per cent of them are actors and actresses. Major *gekidan* can offer full seasons and tour the country each year, and smaller professional or quasi-professional groups perform regularly. However, even major groups pay only a pittance and employ much of their talent only part-time (Havens, 1982, pp. 158–9).

They are, to a certain extent, democratic in their operation, because all members are traditionally involved in the decision-making process, including the selection of plays and new members. However, actors step back during the creative process and are obedient to a director (Nakayama, 1998, p. 23). That is to say that Japanese contemporary theatre is a director's theatre, despite its organizational structure.

Gekidan often have a *yoseijo* – drama school – attached to them. A limited number of graduates from the *yoseijo*, selected by the existing members, can acquire *gekidan* membership, and as their member-directors teach at the *yoseijo*, the relationship between director-as-teacher and actor-as-student can be sustained even after the students acquire *gekidan* membership. All members must be loyal to their *gekidan* – when actors work outside of the *gekidan* as actors for film, TV, or commercial theatres, they contribute 30 per cent or more of their earnings to their *gekidan* for its running costs. Their 'outside' work turns them into popular figures and promotes their national touring.

Within the emerging movement of *shingeki*, the Stanislavsky system was seriously investigated and incorporated into actor training in the 1950s to 1960s. This was possible due to the arrival of many publications on actor training from abroad. The investigations of the Stanislavsky system by Shimomura Masao, Hatta Motoo, and Okakura Shiro particularly influenced many *gekidan* and *yoseijo*. However, these investigations were in some ways bound to be unsuccessful. Firstly, Stanislavsky was transformed into an ideological figure by his association with 'socialist realism' (Kan, 1981, p. 123). Secondly, the translations of *An Actor Prepares* by Yamada Hajime in 1954–6 from English and by Senda Koreya from German in 1968–71, were not completed properly. These translations promoted an understanding of a US-biased Stanislavsky in Japan (Horie, 2014, p. 6). It was not until the full translation from Russian of *An Actor Prepares* by Horie Shinji arrived in 2009 that this bias was finally addressed. Thirdly, in my view, the accelerated commercialization of *shingeki*, despite its artistic or political beliefs, distanced it from Stanislavskian principles. As a popular form, but lacking funding, the self-financed *shingeki* had to stage large-scale productions with star actors at larger theatres rather than intimate studio spaces; audience expectations and the compromises of *shingeki* alienated Stanislavsky from their practices.

What would you say were the main elements from Stanislavsky's practices that were taken up by *gekidan* groups?

Judging from their writings, I found that the investigations in the 1950s to 1960s were closest to a 'genuine' Stanislavsky. However, in the course of the *shingeki* development, Stanislavsky was almost forgotten and 'Method Acting' was introduced instead. Although *shingeki* was often associated with socialism or communism, at the same time post-war Japan was heavily Americanized. Information via the media was mostly biased towards the US. In addition, the idea of 'emotional memory' was relatively easy to accept for Japanese practitioners. However, being 'in character' has sometimes been over-interpreted as assimilation or even spiritual possession. This is partly promoted by a long-lasting popular manga, 'A Mask of Glass' (since 1976) by Miuchi Suzue: a heroine who tries consistently to assimilate into her different roles through experiencing highly peculiar situations. Modern Japanese director-playwright Hirata Oriza criticizes the negative influence of this manga series as a 'cult' (Hirata, 2004, pp. 190–6).

You have spoken about *shingeki* and the turn of the twentieth century. What about more recent and contemporary attempts to transmit Stanislavsky's practices in Japan? How conducive is the Japan theatre scene to the integration of these practices?

There are two phases in the Japanese alternative theatre movement. *Angra* (underground theatre) flourished in the 1960s to 1970s and was symbolized by a new powerful dictator – the 'playwright-director' – and by the peculiar character and physicality of its actors. The scripts originated from the director and were not only against forms of foreign drama (Nishido, 2006, p. 49) but were also critical of national politics and the unchanging nature of Confucian society in Japan. *Angra* was a kind of collective creation under a dictator.

Suzuki Tadashi and Terayama Shuji respectively, developed their special way of actor's physical training in order to visualize the strange world of *Angra*.

A new generation of alternative theatre, emerging in the 1980s, was called *shogekijo* (the little or fringe theatre). They inherited the playwright-director model, but were less political and favoured 'sub-culture'. Under the prosperity of the bubble economy and consumerism in the 1980s, they were happy to embrace commercialism – theatre activities were no longer politically motivated (Wada, 2009, p. 3). Their dramaturgies were often indebted to manga or science fiction with laughter, absurdity, and rituals considered commonplace; they were directed at a popular, like-minded audience. I find it a shame that this 'like-minded audience' sometimes does not see any other *gekidan* performances. Actors were mostly untrained, from no specific institution, performing with the self-learning method of their own playwright-director, and are expected to perform almost the same type of role in any play – type-casting is the norm.

In the framework of *shogekijo*, since the 1990s, a playwright-director Hirata Oriza created a new type of naturalistic theatre – the so-called 'quiet theatre' where there are no big events or exaggerated happenings. In Hirata's theatre, there is no leading actor but an ensemble, and many characters talk at the same time. A playwright-director, Hirata orchestrates and tunes the ensemble like a conductor. In fact, he has often referred to the Stanislavsky system in his writing and teaching at universities. Within his stream of theatre, there might be a seed of the Stanislavsky system. However, Hirata rhetorically keeps a distance from the system arguing that differences in actor's approach from inside/outside are not important for the audience (Hirata, 2004, pp. 185–7). He seems to believe that 'reality' for the audience is created by a playwright-director, but not by actors. I have to say that as long as the playwright-director dominates all aspects of their theatre, the Stanislavsky system as an actor training cannot fully prosper. It could only truly be possible if the division between a playwright and a director is reasserted.

Since the 1990s, the rise of new producers operating within building-based public theatres has changed the landscape drastically. New producers and directors have started arguing that there is no standard for actor training in Japan, there is no common language among actors – each actor has been trained differently. As a result, a demand to establish a national university for drama training has emerged among the industries. Many practitioners and critics recall the Stanislavsky system as a gold standard of actor training. However, after some decades of absence, no teachers were available, as Barter pointed out in the interview with which I started. There were, though, many foreign trainers available – especially from Russia after the collapse of the Soviet Union and from Britain.

In these circumstances, I have curated a number of short workshops with various directors and trainers for professional actors, which included Leon Rubin (on ensemble theatre), Alison Hodge (Stanislavsky and theatre of Gardzienice), Bella Merlin and Alex Delamere (Stanislavsky and the British Theatre), Chris Megson (Stanislavsky and Brecht), Jonathan Pitches (Meyerhold and Michael Chekhov), James Brining (Shakespeare in acting and education setting), and Dominic Cooke (Stanislavsky in *Noughts & Crosses* and *Macbeth*).

As there is no full-time training institute for working actors in Japan, some service organizations and *gekidan* provide training opportunities. My business is slightly unusual because many providers are apt to stick to one particular trainer or method of acting. As I said earlier, I am expected to provide various theories and practices. However, with lack of government funding for

Figure 22 Bella Merlin and Kaori Nakayama, at Meiji University, Tokyo (June 2006).

independent training and service providers, to my regret, it is getting difficult for us to continue working.

Also, as an interpreter, I have worked with Nicholas Barter, Sergei Tcherkasski, and Aubrey Mellor at Toho Gakuen Junior College of Drama and Music. The college has been keen to develop its international links and to install the Stanislavsky system into their education with the help of foreign teachers.

Given this context and this history, what do you think the future holds for Stanislavskian training in Japan?

The training opportunities for actors have increased in number. However, I must say that Stanislavsky has not reached a 'leading' position yet. In reality, when the New National Theatre founded its drama school in 2005, Stanislavsky was not installed in its three-year training course. Visibly and invisibly, Confucianism is still influential. People (actors) are educated and trained to be obedient to their authorities (directors), and manipulable within a hierarchy. Questioning why, or even making eye-contact are sometimes prohibited in education and business. In a Japanese sense, 'team-work' does not exactly mean equal collaboration. As a consequence, clarifying objectives, working as a team, and multiple leadership are core principles in my arts management education and training. I believe Stanislavsky will be in a better position when not only theatre practitioners but also theatre audiences can reconsider the definitions of what is a good actor and what is a good play. Ironically, as the number of spectators has been declining in recent years, many *gekidan* in *shingeki* and *shogekijo* have shifted their work into smaller venues – into more intimate spaces. As such, they may in the future recognize more critically the importance of Stanislavsky's system for their actor training. However, first of all, we must continue sowing the seeds and giving them water, to help achieve those changes. This must be the role and responsibility of theatre.

References

Geidankyo. (1996), 'Performer' (Magazine). Tokyo: Geidankyo. February, pp. 5–7.
Hatta, M. (1976), 'Engi-Ron-Shi' ('History of Acting Theory'), compiled for *Engi-Ron* (Theory of Acting) (1977), p.97, ed., Tsugami, Sugai, Kagawa. Tokyo: Chobun-sha.

Havens, T. R. H. (1982), *Artist and Patron in Postwar Japan: Dance, Music, Theater, and the Visual Arts, 1955-1980*. Princeton: Princeton University Press.

Hirata, O. (2004), *Engi to Enshutu* (Acting and Directing). Tokyo: Kodan-sha.

Kan, T. (1981), *Sengo Engeki* (Post-war Theatre). Tokyo: Asahi Shinbun-sha.

Kishida, K. (1932), 'Shingeki no Kara' ('Habitual Shell of Shingeki'), in (1953) *Kishida Kunio Zenshu* (Completed Works of Kunio Kishida). Tokyo: Shincho-sha.

Miyake, S. (1942), *Engeki 50 nen-shi* ('The 50 Years History of Theatre), Tokyo: Masu-shobo.

Nakayama, K. (1998), 'Engeki no Soshiki to Koyo wo Meguru Nichi-Ei Hikaku. Kenkyu' ('A Comparative Study of Theatrical Organisation and Employment in Britain and Japan'), in *Art* Management, eds Y. Miyama and F. Maeda. Tokyo: Keio University Arts Centre.

Nishido, K. (2006), 'Enshutu-ka no Shigoto' ('The Works of Directors'), in *Enshutu-ka no Shigoto – 60 nendai, angra, engeki kakumei* (The Works of Directors – 60s, angra, and Theatrical Revolution), eds Y. Wada and Japan Directors Association. Tokyo: Renga Shobo Shinsha.

Sasayama, K. (2012). *Engijutsu no Kindai* (Modern Era for Acting Technique). Tokyo: Moriwa-sha.

Sugiyama, M. (ed.) (1957), *Aoyama Sugisaku*. Published by a committee headed by Senda Koreya.

Wada, Y. (2009), 'Hakkan ni Atatte' ('Forward'), in *80 nendai, Shogekijo Engeki no Tenkai* (80s: the Expansion of Fringe Theatre), eds K. Nishido and Japan Directors Association. Tokyo: Renga Shobo Shinsha.

Watanabe, T. (2004), *Kabuki – Kata no Miryoku* (Kabuki – Beauty of Kata). Tokyo: Kadokawa Shoten.

Newsletter

Horie, S. (2014), 'Haiyu Kyoiku Zakkan: Shiteki Stanislavsky Ko' ('Miscellaneous Impressions on Actors Training; Personal View on Stanislavsky'), in *Hiroba*. Tokyo: Haiyu-za Theatre.

Part Three

Latin America

Figure 23 Stanislavsky in Latin America.

Part Three: Introduction

Stefan Aquilina

Beyond realism: Stanislavsky in Latin America

That Stanislavsky's system was developed for sole application to realistic and naturalistic play-texts is a misconception that harks back to the system's own early formulations. In fact, it was a misconception which Stanislavsky himself was aware of, one that he wanted to rectify from as early as 1911 with the staging of *Hamlet* (Benedetti, 1999, p. 189). Moreover, his choice at the end of his life to work on *Tartuffe* was similarly made 'to show that his method was universal, not limited to what is sometimes thought the "typical" Moscow Art Theatre repertoire – Chekhov and the like' (Toporkov, 1979, p. 153). Despite Stanislavsky's own efforts, however, the reading that has taken root is that the system yields effective results only when used to produce dramas such as those penned by the aforementioned Chekhov, Ibsen and, in the US, by Tennessee Williams, Arthur Miller, and the like (Carnicke, 2009, p. 2). The essays collated in this Part about Stanislavsky's influence on Latin American theatre – authored by Arlete Cavaliere (Brazil), Yana Elsa Brugal (Cuba) and Raúl Serrano (Argentina) – make reference to this reductionism and then move on to critique the realistic stress on the system made by traditional Stanislavski Studies. Consequently, these essays refer to the transformation of the system into formulas that create 'narrow' (Brugal) and 'vulgar or simplistic' (Cavaliere) realism. Theatre Director Raúl Serrano, for his part, is more positive in his reading of realism, but his development of a methodology based on 'pre-conflicts' and animal imagery was also meant to facilitate contrasting and sharper theatrical characterizations. Viewed together, the essays debunk the emphasis on realism in two ways. First, they underline Stanislavsky's final explorations in physical action and what Stanislavsky called 'the life of the human body' (Stanislavski, 2010, p. 58), to show how certain theatre practitioners and groups picked on Stanislavsky's later ideas to develop a more corporeal form of theatre. Second, they suggest a syncretism between Stanislavsky and Brecht, one that bridges the former's 'experiencing' with the latter's practices in critical distancing.

That such a syncretism between Stanislavsky and Brecht occurred in Latin America comes as no surprise when one considers that Latin American culture is intrinsically built on the blending of different cultural elements. In fact, while John King argues that the search for a common Latin American culture has indeed 'remained an elusive, somewhat quixotic ideal' (King, 2004, p. 4), Mario Vargas Llosa uses the image of the hermaphrodite to underscore one crucial element, which is the 'curious relationship of both attraction and rejecting [of foreign traditions] [but] [...] without actually denying [them]' (quoted in King, 2004, p. 5). Both Cavaliere and Brugal describe their respective contexts as ones that, in the spirit of Vargas Llosa's understanding, celebrate cultural hybridity. Brazilian culture, for example, is portrayed as being 'forged through an amalgamation of Indigenous, African and European cultures' (p. 235); in the case of Cuba, the influences are derived from Hispanic and African sources (p. 239). Both essays place cultural hybridity as a necessary contextual condition that paved the way for the integration of Stanislavskian practices in Brazil and Cuba. In other words, the fact that the two contexts are built themselves on syncretic lines facilitated the amalgamation of Stanislavsky's system with local performance practices, which included Cuban creole clowns and what Cavaliere describes, in broad terms, as the 'the Dionysian character in the Brazilian artistic way' (p. 235). The implications of such a statement should not be underestimated.

The common ground that brought together Stanislavsky and Latin American theatre was a markedly physical understanding of human life. This physical understanding is foregrounded by both Brugal and Cavaliere, with the former underlining the 'intrinsic corporeal plasticity' (p. 246) of Cuban life, and the latter remarking on 'the principle of material and corporeal life [in Brazilian culture] [and] [...] images that correspond to a vigorous display of corporeality as an expressive sign' (p. 235). The three essays emphasize the psychophysical dimension of Stanislavsky's searches and the more physical, rather than introspective, approaches to achieve it. Consequently, even when practitioners like the Cuban Adela Escartin trained at the Actors Studio, it was Stella Adler's more physical approaches rather than Lee Strasberg's Affective Memory that struck a chord. The same is evident in Serrano's essay, where he considers Strasberg's techniques as overtly introvert and conducive to 'slow and inactive' characterizations (p. 262).

In emphasizing physicality, the essays chime with Simon Murray's and John Keefe's investigation of 'the landscape of *physical theatres* and the *physical in theatre* (Murray and Keefe, 2007, p. 1; emphasis in original). Murray and Keefe expound on how the second half of the twentieth century saw a marked international increase of physical approaches to theatre, a proliferation which they locate within a wider understanding that connects performance to sport activities, dance, club culture, and '(more theoretically) with contemporary discourses that articulate and rehearse the nature of embodiment in a wide range of public, personal and intellectual spheres' (Murray and Keefe, 2007, p. 13). Their study is constructed on North American and Eurocentric lines, but they do open a window on Latin America by identifying it as an area that deserves further investigation (Murray and Keefe, 2007, p. 10). The essays collected here offer concrete contributions along the lines suggested by Murray and Keefe, by underlining, for example, how the physical approaches of Cuba's Irma de la Vega, Andrés Castro, Adolfo de Luis and Vincente Revuelta, and, also, of Serrano himself, were not pursued to the detriment of a psychophysical equilibrium. Cavaliere's exposition on Eugênio Kusnet's work, which she describes as one that was rooted in rhythm and musicality, is another particularly strong case-study that argues how the system was granted a type of contemporary and corporeal Brazilian-ness.

A possible synthesis between Stanislavskian and Brechtian approaches also emerges from the essays collated here. Cavaliere describes this synthesis as a challenge with 'which modern theatre had struggled' (p. 223) and, in fact, the delineation of Stanislavsky and Brecht as two binary opposites can be seen as symptomatic of the most narrow branch of modernism which strives to underline difference rather than points of convergence (see Introduction to Part One: Europe). Jean Benedetti describes such an opposition in the following terms: 'The polarization between emotion and reason to which Brecht objected, dominated the discussion of acting in the second half of the twentieth century and now centered round the figures of Brecht and Stanislavski' (Benedetti, 2005, p. 197). Latin American practitioners in the 1960s and after leaned towards Brecht because in his practices they found a methodology which could unite aesthetics with political intervention, a complex mix that created a 'theatre of revolution, [which] while functioning primarily on the symbolic order, also aimed at real, political change and saw itself as an important instrument in the social struggle' (Taylor, 2000, p. 176). Its reference points included, amongst many others, the Colombian playwrights Santiago Garcia and Enrique Buenaventura and the Peruvian theatre group Yuyachkani.[1] However, Stanislavsky was not forgotten, and the case-studies of Brazil and Cuba both discuss Stanislavsky's role within this socially committed theatre. Witness, for example, Brazil's Teatro Arena and its juxtaposition of protagonist roles, staged as examples of Stanislavskian 'experiencing', and the secondary roles' treatment as social masks, on the more critical and detached lines which Brecht advocated. The following case of the Uruguayan company El Galpón and its leader Atahualpa del Cioppo is another strong case in point:

> In the 1990s El Galpón remains Uruguay's major independent company, the quintessential Uruguayan theatre. Built around the personality and theatrical ideas of its director, Atahualpa de Cioppo, the group – like del Cioppo – began with its roots in Stanislavsky but evolved over several decades into a Brechtian style. At its best it blended these styles – the former more emotional, the latter more cerebral – into an effective stage reality with clear ideological content while retaining the coherence and validity of each character.
>
> Leites, 1996, p. 490

The essays collated here offer strong indications of Stanislavsky-influenced practices in Cuba, Brazil, and Argentina, but they are far from the only case-studies that could elucidate the transmission across Latin American cultures of the system. The value of these three essays also resides in the fact that they draw attention to a significant geographical area where Stanislavsky's influence is palpable but still internationally unrecognized. Theatre practitioners across Latin America have placed themselves within the Stanislavsky acting tradition, efforts that are replicated by several academic and scholarly activities that aim at unpicking Stanislavsky's work and its influence on Latin American theatre in the twentieth and twenty-first centuries. Among the practitioners, Serrano's experiments are paralleled by, for example, Juan Antonio Tribulo, an Argentinian actor, director, and teacher who, at the Theatre Institute of the University of Buenos Aires, made the system his field of 'experimentation and reflection' (Lozano, 2006). A second example is the Department of Dramatic Arts of the Universidad del Valle in Cali, Colombia, which according to Alejandro González Puche, a GITIS graduate and teacher within that same institution, develops its education in ways that 'reflect the tradition of actor training created by Stanislavski' (Puche, 2006, p. 41). Etude practice, based on trial and error in which the teacher and student create together within a workshop setting, is the favoured practice at this Department. In the case of academic research, gatherings like the 2003 conference on 'Stanislavsky in Argentina' foster an awareness of Stanislavskian practices and their application to contemporary performance (Stanislavski in Argentina website). A similar event was organized in 2013 in Peru by the Faculty of Scenic Arts of the Pontificad Catholic University. This conference invited theatre-makers and scholars to join social scientists, writers, philosophers, and psychologists to come together to research Stanislavsky's 'current influence in Peru and elsewhere' (Congreso Internacional Konstantin Stanislavski website). While opportunities for further study about the transmission of Stanislavskian practices across different cultures is evident around the whole world, such study is, perhaps, particularly prominent in relation to the Latin American world.

Note

1 For a discussion on both contexts see Taylor, 2000, pp. 177–83.

References

Benedetti, J. (1999), *Stanislavski: His Art and Life*. London: Methuen.
Benedetti, J. (2005), *The Art of the Actor*. London: Methuen.
Carnicke, S. M. (2009), *Stanislavsky in Focus 2nd ed*. Oxon: Routledge.
Congreso Internacional Konstantin Stanislavski website, http://facultad.pucp.edu.pe/artes-escenicas/eventos/congreso-internacional-konstantin-stanislavski/ [accessed 12 February 2016].

King, J. (ed.) (2004), *The Cambridge Companion to Modern Latin American Culture*. Cambridge: Cambridge University Press.

Leites, V. M. (1996), 'Uruguay', in *World Encyclopedia of Contemporary Theatre: Americas Volume 2*, eds D. Rubin and C. Solorzano. London and New York: Routledge, pp. 484–504.

Lozano, E. (2006), 'El camino de la emoción escénica. Juan Antonio Tríbulo, Stanislavski – Strasberg. Mi experiencia de actor con la emoción en escena', *Telondefondo. Revista de teoria y critica teatral*, 3, July. Downloaded from http://www.telondefondo.org/numeros-anteriores/3/numero3/ [accessed 12 February 2016].

Murray, S. and Keefe, J. (2007), *Physical Theatres: A Critical Introduction*. London and New York: Routledge.

Puche, A. G. (2006), 'Artistic Education and Profession', in *Company and Arts. Manual for Enterprise in the Arts and Creative Industries*. Colombia: Ministry of Culture of Colombia, Bogota Chamber of Commerce, British Council Bogota-Colombia, pp. 40–51.

Stanislavski, K. (2010), *An Actor's Work on a Role*, trans. J. Benedetti. Oxon: Routledge.

Stanislavski in Argentina website, http://www.alternativateatral.com/evento83-ix-jornadas-nacionales-de-teatro-comparado-stanislavski-en-la-argentina [accessed 12 February 2016].

Taylor, S. (2000), 'Brecht and Latin America's "Theatre of Revolution"', in *The Brecht Sourcebook*, eds C. Martin and H. Bial. London and New York: Routledge, pp. 173–84.

Toporkov, V. (1979), *Stanislavski in Rehearsal*, trans. C. Edward. New York and London: Routledge.

9

Stanislavsky in Brazil: Territories and Frontiers

Arlete Cavaliere

He (Stanislavsky) and I envision the solution of a task as builders of a tunnel beneath the Alps: each one advances from his own side, but somewhere in the middle, we will meet.

Vsevolod Meyerhold (quoted in Gladkov, Vol. 2, 1990, p. 240)

Stanislavsky's heritage: some key issues

The aim of this essay is to capture the development of Konstantin Stanislavsky's theatrical aesthetics in the cultural and scenic context of Brazil, throughout the twentieth and twenty-first century. Besides that, it will set the territories and frontiers in which his theatrical principles established deep and organic connections with Brazilian cultural and artistic expression.

At first glance this task may seem difficult, as it is subject to theoretical speculation about two cultural worlds that are apparently so distant, and with such pronounced specificities, as those of Russia and Brazil. It should be emphasized from the outset that the dissemination and expansion of Stanislavskian theory and its practice in the Brazilian theatre suffered the same difficulties and vicissitudes which operated in the rest of the world. The unawareness for several decades of Stanislavskian theatrical aesthetics, in Brazil and other countries, is due not only to the amplitude of his famous 'system', but also to the difficulty to access Russian and Soviet archives. It is not an easy task to know both Stanislavsky's work in its totality and the trajectory of his thinking about theatre, especially outside Russia, without having his texts in Russian and the numerous notes accompanying them. Even in Russia, many of Stanislavsky's texts were censored during the Soviet period, and became known only in recent decades, after *perestroika*, to complicate further the picture of Stanislavsky Studies.¹

Stanislavsky wrote extensively. He sought to deepen and improve his ideas until the end of his life, in order to achieve a large-scale, integrating project, whereby his experience as an actor, director, and theatrical educator could be documented according to an overarching perspective. Yet, this project was never completed. This broad Stanislavskian project should include at least eight volumes of writing, but he did not actually accomplish it in its totality. There are some parts of the whole that remained unconstructed, with books that have come to light as fragments of an evolving thought. In addition, many of his texts were fragments and outlines, sundry pieces, collected and published long after his death. In Brazil, as well as in several Western countries, the issue is even more complex because many texts were translated in a disorderly manner, especially with regard to the chronology he had proposed. An exception is the first book about the 'system', *Работа актера над собой. Часть 1: Работа над собой в творческом процессе переживания: Дневник ученика* (The Actor's Work on Himself. Part 1: Work on Himself in the Creative Process of Experiencing. The Diary of a Disciple) a single volume written entirely by him and published in Russia in 1938, a few weeks after his death. Other Russian editions were compilations organized by scholars and family members who gathered texts and notes that were in the first place considered incomplete by Stanislavsky himself. An example of such an edited and compiled volume is *Работа актера над собой. Часть 2: Работа над собой в творческом процессе воплощения: Материалы к книге* (The Actor's Work on Himself. Part 2: The Work on Himself in the Creative Process of Embodiment) which was published in Russia in 1948. The volume's editors (Kira Alekséieva, Stanislavsky's daughter, Tatiana Dorókhina, and Georgui Kristi) decided to add to the title 'Materials for a book'. Moreover, later editions also included several other fragments and outlines collected and published, therefore, long after his death.

It has been the concern of Russian scholars in recent years to establish the body of Stanislavsky's work and extract from it a possible totalizing vision, with the ultimate aim of recovering the theatrical 'system' as Stanislavsky himself might have structured it. Certainly, Stanislavsky's Russian files are inexhaustible.² An analysis of this body of work would take us to a rereading and a necessary review of those parts of the 'system' with which we are familiar. It does not come as a surprise, therefore, to note the tendency that has prevailed for a long time, where a dynamic and changeable phenomenon like the 'system', which is rooted in the constant formulation of different hypotheses, research, and ceaseless experimentation within the scope of theatre performance and of the art of the actor, was transformed into formulas of narrow realism.

The access to Russian archives and dissemination of new material and documents relating to Stanislavsky's practice and theatrical theories made possible the translation and publishing of these texts in many countries – with the most recent being Jean Benedetti's translations of *My Life in Art* (2008), *An Actor's Work* (2008), and *An Actor's Work on a Role* (2010) – but the same has not occurred so quickly in Brazil. We still do not have a substantial edition of Stanislavsky's writings in Portuguese, and many Brazilian directors, actors, teachers, and scholars became aware of his fundamental texts through indirect translations from other languages.³

The translations of some of Stanislavsky's texts, which emerged not in accordance with a possible plan established by the author, and late dissemination of his writings, are not solely responsible for the misunderstandings, deviations, or even reformulations of the Stanislavsky 'system'. In addition to his written legacy, much of Stanislavsky's heritage also spread around the world by other means. The diffusion of his ideas also took place through actors, assistants, students, and followers, Russian or others, who for various reasons separated from him and became interpreters and spokespersons in several countries of his principles and 'formulas'. They intended to bring about a complex process that, however, Stanislavsky himself considered inconclusive. He modified it incessantly at every rehearsal, at every experience and at every performance of a play. It was no different in Brazil. It is worth asking: which Stanislavsky (or is it Stanislavskies) arrived in Brazil? The answers to this question necessitate an analysis and a recontextualization of the many Stanislavskies that his heritage bequeathed to us.

It is clear that not even Stanislavsky and the Moscow Art Theatre may be considered entirely responsible for the tortuous unfolding of his teachings about the art of the actor and the 'system'. Exaggeration and even idolatry transformed a 'system', guided by theoretical precepts derived from empirical experience, to a 'method' often advocated and practiced with an extremism that elevated it to a category of true 'sacred laws', a kind of Bible of theatrical art, respected and accepted without concessions, as occurred in America and even in Europe (See Part I Introduction, Well-trodden Paths, and for more details, Carnicke, 2009, pp. 7–16). For example, the Actors Studio in New York transformed the Stanislavsky 'system' into a North American 'method' for the training of their actors, making it more oriented to the language of film and its industry. As also stated by Yuri Liubimov, one of the most significant directors in contemporary Russian theatre, 'American Theatre absorbed Stanislavsky in a strange way. It mixed Stanislavsky and made a kind of cocktail: Lee Strasberg with Freud' (Liubimov, 1994, 162). Brazil was not immune to this process of absorption and partial use of that large theatre 'system' which Stanislavsky developed, as this essay will seek to unpick. A more detailed analysis of the Brazilian case may reveal the significance and extent of Stanislavsky's aesthetic project. Of added importance is how its 'universal' character can foster a possible application and adaptation to different artistic and cultural contingencies.

Zbigniew Ziembinski and Eugênio Kusnet: the birth of modern theatre in Brazil

It would not be prudent to begin an analysis of Stanislavsky's legacy in Brazil without referring briefly to the dissemination of Stanislavsky's ideas in the United States and the West. In fact, the first translations into Brazilian Portuguese of Stanislavsky's two fundamental books on the art of the actor (*A preparação do ator* and *A construção da personagem*) were based on North American editions (Stanislávski, 2012, 2013a, 2013b).[4] Sources like Carnicke (2009) and Pitches (2006) have unpicked in detail the transmission of Stanislavsky's techniques in America, with reference consistently made to the initial role which Richard Boleslavsky had in this process.[5] I draw attention here to Boleslavsky to underline the key issue he faced and which, in a sense determines the transformation of Stanislavsky's 'system' not only in the United States, but also in the rest of the world: how is this methodology born and developed in the Russian theatrical environment transformed to fit the goals and theatrical traditions of other cultural contexts? It can be said that

Stanislavsky's 'system' underwent some changes and revisions in Boleslavsky's hands, which pointed out other ways and directions. It is in this reflective context that the analysis of the Brazilian case should be inserted, given that the North American process of disseminating Stanislavsky's work produced significant reverberations in the Brazilian theatre scene.

It was not by chance that an important signpost for the introduction of Stanislavskian practices in Brazil was a European emigre, the Polish actor and director Zbigniew Marian Ziembinski (1908–78). Ziembinski was born in Wieliczka, a small town in southern Poland near Krakow, where he made his first dramatic art studies. He started his professional life when he was only nineteen years old, and travelled to Vilnius, a Lithuanian city with a large Polish population, to return to Warsaw two years later. According to the critic Henryk Szletynski, Ziembinski became a revelation as a theatre director in Poland in 1930, because of his ability to direct actors (see Fuser, 2002).[6] He was interested in the technical aspects of psychological realism in the actor's work but also the avant-garde searches in dramaturgy and staging, which marked his homeland training. The young Ziembinski, then a war deserter, arrived in Brazil in 1941 as a result of the collapse of French forces and the German advance. He escaped from Poland a few weeks after the German invasion and tried to settle in Romania before arriving in France, where he had a brief career at the Théâtre Antoine Nouveau in Paris. Ziembinski also worked as a teacher at the Theatrical Art Institute of Warsaw, an activity which he also developed at the Dramatic Art School of São Paulo, founded in 1948, and which would become one of the pioneer schools for actor preparation in Brazil. In addition, he traveled to the Soviet Union in the 1930s, where he became acquainted with the Moscow Art Theatre and with Vsevolod Meyerhold, with whom he planned a joint production.[7]

His arrival in Brazil coincided with the emergence of the group Os Comediantes. This group was founded in 1940 and would determine the beginning of modern theatre in Brazil (Michalski and Peixoto, 1996, p. 61). Os Comediantes consisted of amateur actors who set themselves the task of aesthetic reform in the art of theatre production in Brazil. In fact, the revitalization in the 1940s of Brazilian theatre was a result of the maturation and renewed action of various Brazilian actors and amateur artists, who invested their creativity against the still incipient commercial theatre. Moreover, an aesthetic shock took place in an auspicious encounter between Ziembinski and a new national dramaturgy, represented in particular by the controversial author Nelson Rodrigues (1912–80).

The 1943 staging of Rodrigues' play *Vestido de Noiva* (Wedding Dress), directed by Ziembinski with Os Comediantes at Teatro Municipal do Rio de Janeiro, revolutionized Brazilian theatre both at the level of the actors' interpretation and at the performance level. It is an unquestionable mark in the rise of modern theatre in Brazil. The text differed radically from all previous national dramaturgies, and Rodrigues presented in this and in other plays unsuspected psychological perversions and sharp deviations in human behaviour. He shifted dramatic interest to the psychological depth of the characters. Ziembinski's direction complemented this singularity, as can be seen in several contemporary observations. For example, Gustavo Dória (1910–79), one of the founders of Os Comediantes wrote:

> We have never witnessed any director dissecting a text the way Ziembinski did. The way he knew how to justify every line of the play, which apparently would be without any intention, because of a later scene. If the cast lacked a certain theatre knowledge, this, in part, was supplied by the lessons which the Polish director offered during rehearsals, which never lasted less than five or six hours, and sometimes up to twelve. It was an entirely new system of work we had never seen before.
>
> Dória, 1975, p. 22

About the premiere of the play, Ziembinski himself wrote:

> It was a crazy show for the audience. With 174 changes of lights and the stage divided into three levels: reality, delirium and the memories of Alaíde, the heroine who was run over at Glória Square suffered a delirium over the last forty minutes of her life. Those reflectors, which were switched on and off, stunned the audience. At the end of the third act, it was the consecration [...]. A new style was then implemented. I say this without any modesty, but with us a new technique was born, which for years would fight with what was already established [...] by those who were accommodated to a certain kind of performance.
>
> Ziembinski, 1975, p. 56

Ziembinski here referred to the Brazilian professional theatre of that time, which was characterized mainly by productions of French *vaudevilles* and Brazilian *comedies of customs*. Although these productions could count on the participation of renowned Brazilian actors, like Procopio Ferreira (1898–1979), Jaime Costa (1897–1967), and Dulcina de Morais (1908–96), they represented an entirely different theatre from the more psychologically nuanced approach Ziembinski proposed for Os Comediantes. In staging *Vestido de Noiva*, Ziembinski carefully chose his cast, especially given the technical limitations of that amateur group. For the lead roles, he chose actors who seemed to have greater creative and technical potential. Therefore, the two protagonists were played by Lina Grey (pseudonym of Evangelina Guingle Miranda Rocha) and Charles Perry, who to a certain extent were both already known in the theatrical scene.[8]

Although there are few explicit references or evidence linking Ziembinski with the Stanislavsky 'system', we should not ignore the first inflows of Stanislavskian ideas in the *Vestido de Noiva* staging, brought by Ziembinski's very active theatrical practice in Europe and in his contact with European directors, especially Polish and Lithuanians. In this regard, it is worth mentioning Perry's testimony. It elucidates the aesthetic proposal adopted by Ziembinski, in which traces of Stanislavskian influence can be discerned:

> The idea of Os Comediantes was to give the performances a high artistic level, abolishing the stardom, suppressing the 'prompter'. It meant demanding from the actor an understanding of the text, respect for the aesthetic and philosophical lines imposed by the director (who was then inexistent in Brazil, as there only was at most a 'rehearse', which merely indicated the positions of the actors on stage). And also lighting, depending on the atmosphere of the performance, well-cared-for costumes, scenarios according to the line of the director, and especially, respect for the author by sticking faithfully to the text [...]. Finally, the performance showed characteristics of foreign theatres that visited us and motivated us to give Brazil something similar and valid.
>
> Perry, 1975, p. 31

Graça Melo's testimony, another Os Comediantes actor, is also enlightening in the following assertions: 'The ideas raised by Stanislavsky in Russia, which already had received support from the French and the North Americans, were amplified by the choir of our idealists' (Melo, 1975, p. 35). Ziembinski was, for Melo, at the forefront of these idealists.

However, one cannot at the same time overlook Rodrigues' dramaturgical genius, which provided Ziembinski innovative developments regarding the technique of the actor and the formulation of the play, especially if we take into account the stagnation of the Brazilian theatrical scene of the time. This memorable staging evoked the grandeur of Greek tragedy but also exhibited traces of German Expressionism (Banham, 2000, p. 126). In fact, the latter was very little known in Brazil at that time. Rodrigues himself declared: 'Old Zimba! No one has done as much as this Polish for Brazilian theatre' (Rodrigues, 1975, p. 51). Ziembinski directed many other productions for Os Comediantes, but the staging of Rodrigues' text remained a big reference point. The Polish director would continue his career as an actor and director in other Brazilian theatre companies, and performed in more than a hundred plays of Brazilian and foreign authors, as well as participated in films and TV. He would only return to Poland between 1963/4, where he would stay less than six months, after which he returned to Brazil and died in Rio de Janeiro on 18 October 1978.

Actually, it fell to Eugênio Kusnet (1898–1975), another foreigner, to accomplish the systematic and continuing dissemination of the Stanislavsky 'system' in Brazil. Kusnet, whose real name was Ievgueni (Eugênio) Shamanski Kusnetsov, was born in Kherson in the south of Ukraine. After the Russian Revolution, he began his career as an actor in the theatres of the Baltic countries (Latvia, Lithuania, and Estonia), where he acquired some knowledge of Stanislavskian theatrical practice, but without having had, until then, a direct contact with the Russian master. Kusnet speaks about this period in his career as follows:

> At the time I started working in professional theatre, that is, in 1920, there was no written Method. We knew the tendencies of the Master through some articles written by him and especially through his works accomplished at the Moscow Art Theatre, which have been very much discussed not only by critics, but also by theatre researchers. Stanislavsky's influence over all Russian theatres was already huge back then but except for his disciples, no one used elements of his Method [sic] consciously. His few known teachings and productions only awakened in every actor and director their will to practice their *metier* in a better way, to think more about their work, to personally look for ways to get closer to the results he obtained.
>
> Only much later, here in Brazil, and when I first had the opportunity to read his teachings, did I recognise, almost intuitively, elements of his Method [sic] in some details of my work of that time.
>
> Kusnet, 2003, XXI

Kusnet even declared with some modesty: 'I am no Stanislavsky expert, I was never his student, nor had the honour of a personal contact with the Master. I am only one of many researchers who look, as much as possible, to help those interested in theatre work' (Kusnet, 2003, p. XXI). Kusnet emigrated to Brazil in the late 1920s. The contact with Os Comediantes, already directed by Ziembinski, drove him to join the Brazilian theatrical life. In addition to his intense activity as actor and director, Kusnet also dedicated himself to the research, dissemination, and teaching of Stanislavsky's 'system', and did so until the last days of his career. He reported: 'When comparing the concrete experiences of Stanislavsky with mine, though timid and vague, but which appeared at that time under his influence, I can see that I conceived the idea of teaching Dramatic Art based on the Method [sic]' (Kusnet, 2003, p. XXI).

In this sense, his role as a Stanislavsky educator was of great importance to the formation of prominent Brazilian practitioners who included, among many others, Renato Borghi, Fernando Peixoto, José Celso Martinez Corrêa, and Gianfrancesco Guarnieri. Moreover, he was an active witness of the historical and aesthetic evolution of Brazilian theatre. His role was not limited to a simple transmission, but a recreation and expansion of Stanislavskian principles. Further below we shall see in more detail how this was achieved, but here suffice to say that through Kusnet, Stanislavsky's thought had a persistent and tireless spokesperson on Brazilian soil, where it found a fertile theatrical field, and where the Russian's principles would be both safeguarded but also developed.

Kusnet was able to synchronize Stanislavsky's ideas with the art of the Brazilian actor, in correlation with different aesthetic spaces and historical moments, granting to the 'Russian system' a kind of contemporary Brazilian-ness. A corporeal approach to theatre-making was central to this synchronization between the 'system' and then contemporary Brazilian-ness, as we will see below. His main contribution was to resume Stanislavskian lessons as a pedagogical practice, applicable to both the construction of characters and above all, the formation of the Brazilian actor, providing him with an extension of his expressive means. His activity is located, undoubtedly, in the construction of the narrative related to the actor's work in Brazil.[9] Kusnet sought to develop appropriate dramatic solutions in Portuguese as the Brazilian expressive language, with gestures and inflections specific to Brazilian culture, and which could correspond to a recreation of foreign theories and theatrical practices, but in national terms. Consequently, to the sentimentality and excessive spontaneity of the Brazilian actor, Kusnet opposed reasoning and discipline. His work was, moreover, never detached from the contemporary Brazilian social situation. Kusnet wanted to insert the study of the actor's technique and of theatrical creation in the flow of the historical events that determined, especially during the 1960s and 1970s, the cultural, social, and political life of the country. This socio-political contextualization was evident from 1958, with his performance in Gianfrancesco Guarnieri's *Eles não usam Black-Tie* [They do not wear Black-Tie], with the group Teatro de Arena, which was marked out as an interpretation of a labour leader, an inhabitant of a favela in Rio de Janeiro. Kusnet was worthy of being qualified as a 'Brazilian actor type'. With ironic humour, the cast of the production mentioned that the first worker on a Brazilian stage, beautifully created with absolute verisimilitude, had a slight Russian accent.[10]

With Ziembinski, Kusnet joined Teatro Brasileiro de Comédia (TBC), which for several years was the only stable theatre company in São Paulo. This is a significant moment in Brazilian cultural history, when theatrical activity shifted from Rio de Janeiro to São Paulo. This Brazilian capital became, from 1948 onwards, the biggest cosmopolitan centre of the country. Under the aegis of Italian-Brazilian patrons and foreign directors, the style and language of European theatre was instituted, through a diversified foreign repertoire that was directed to the tastes of the new São Paulo public and rising bourgeoisie.[11] Kusnet's long-term influence started at TBC, as a theatre educator rather than as an actor and director, despite his national reputation as an outstanding actor. Beyond the TBC, Kusnet's application of Stanislavsky's 'system' involved a new generation of actors and directors that created, in 1953, the Teatro de Arena. This group's aesthetic and political-ideological purposes opposed radically those of the TBC by discussing national problems on the stage, through an indigenous dramaturgy whose style and language were truly Brazilian. This meant, that the proletarian as protagonist as well as the social problems of the Brazilian working class emerged in a new dramaturgy that was articulated in an innovative aesthetic and political design, clearly delineated by playwrights like Gianfrancesco Guarnieri[12] and Augusto Boal. The latter's playwriting was influenced by American practices, and as an actor and director, he assimilated in that country the careful work on psychological truth. This was certainly a consequence of Stanislavsky's 'method', that had spread through the Actors Studio in New York, as Frances Babbage confirms: 'Boal was deeply influenced by realism and impressed by the detailed and disciplined approach to rehearsal demanded by the Stanislavsky system, which he saw practiced by at the Actors Studio in New York' (Babbage, 2004, p. 8).

The exploration of socio-political issues and theatrical expression as a popular communication phenomenon inspired new directions in the research of the Stanislavskian actor, conducted by Kusnet, which also found expression in the formation of new theatre groups of that time. These groups revolved around leftist university students and Marxist revolutionaries. The integration at Teatro de Arena of Stanislavsky's theatrical practices with those of Bertolt Brecht was a creative harmonization between different theatrical methodologies, in an unprecedented attempt to find a common ground that overcame dialectically the antitheses of realism and theatricalism with which modern theatre had struggled (Prado, 1988). Boal's key role in this context is unquestionable. He was the one who introduced Brecht's epic theatre at Teatro de Arena, and was also influenced by Piscator's *The Political Theatre*. Critical questioning implemented as a theatrical method laid the foundation to many of Arena's plays. This methodology included the playwright's criticism of his own play, the actor of his own character (with which he should not identify himself to the point of losing objectivity) and the public's critical reflection of the stage action. Stanislavsky's influence was seen in the way that Arena productions tackled the construction of the hero-protagonist, often a Brazilian national hero and the object of the fable as narrated by the play.[13] The hero-protagonist was performed by a single actor, with whom the public were to create an affective identification. A Brechtian critical detachment was applied to the other characters (which Boal called the 'social masks'), who surrounded the protagonist and who were interpreted successively by each actor in the entire cast. This practice evoked the critical spirit in spectators.[14]

Kusnet, always driven by Brazilian historical and theatrical circumstances, and motivated by his work at the Arena, emphasized a conception of an actor who was connected with social life. He assigned a political responsibility to the actor as a transforming element within society. Therefore, Kusnet stated that the only criterion for evaluating a show is its resonance with the contemporary spectators. In his last writings, brought together in the book *Ator e Método*,[15] Kusnet insisted on the effectiveness of the Stanislavskian 'system' as a process of study and research. For him, it was essential for the Brazilian actor who, stimulated by discipline and the constant exercise of his physical and emotional resources, should develop and safely master a rational and logical methodology in building a character. Moreover, in this last period of work, Kusnet also sought to incorporate his latest researches in the field of psychology and reflexology. This served not only to underpin the performance of the Brazilian actor with Stanislavskian exercises and practices, but rather as a review of his own methodology. He pointed out the importance of Stanislavsky's teachings and located their basics in the possibility of adaptation or modification that arises from the practical work, the dramaturgical material, and the scenic style proposed. The intention in Kusnet's work was not to capture a former Stanislavsky in his precise historical significance, but to find the rational, almost scientific basis of the actor's work, without losing sight of what the 'system' offers that is imperishable and indispensable.

His analytical focus fell on the necessary Stanislavskian concept of *scenic truth*, but he deepened this with a discussion about the nature and meaning of the notion of the *duality of the actor*. Kusnet seemed to be aware, at this point, of Brecht's lessons that underpinned many of the scenic researches of Teatro de Arena. Kusnet was opposed to the actor's complete identification with the character, made possible by an intervening coexistence on the scene of the actor-citizen who was capable of critical reflection in his work. Asked about what characterizes a good interpretation, Kusnet concludes:

> The absolute impression of truth. That cannot be confused with a mere imitation of reality. Because there is an eternal duality in major interpretations: the actor has to create an almost magical illusion and at the same time never lose sight that he is on a stage. There are two extremes to avoid: the actor who gives himself emotionally, absolutely, but the result of his work is aesthetically unconvincing; and the actor who lets himself go by an excess of rationality, which fully extinguishes the passion in his performance.
>
> Kusnet, 1975

At the group Teatro Oficina (another culturally influential theatre, founded in 1961 by actor and director José Celso Martinez Corrêa), Kusnet's performance as Bessemenov in Maksim's Gorki play *The Petty Bourgeois* became a milestone in the art of the actor in Brazil.[16] It was also one of the high points of his activity as a teacher and educator of the troupe, with which he would create striking theatre performances and a dramatic studio in the mould of Stanislavsky's. Even if they were successful adaptations to Brazilian reality, Oficina, TBC, and Comediantes staged productions that were seeking to remake the 'realism' of the Moscow Art Theatre. However, it is necessary to emphasize, above all, the investigative character and the opening of horizons that Kusnet provided to the 'system', especially in dialogue with Brechtian methodology that led to the development of the actor's political role. The director José Celso Martinez Corrêa describes Kusnet's vision of Stanislavsky as follows:

> He struggled very much against a badly interpreted Stanislavsky. He sought for emotion, yes, but with an agenda for the action in the text. The key word for him was action. 'Act, act, act.' José Celso confesses: I, plunged into the most beautifully hysterical emotionalism of the power of my youth, that exploded with clichés, found Kusnet, my tightrope master, who had another Stanislavsky who was different than mine. Kusnet's Stanislavsky [...]. Kusnet was a Brechtian-Stanislavskian antagonist, who brought to Oficina the years of effective action. The power of the actor occurring on stage through action was also transmitted to the power of action of the young public.
>
> in Kusnet, 2003, dust-jacket

Running parallel to the rehearsals of Oficina's productions, Kusnet welcomed actors and actresses (including professionals from other groups) for guidance in the construction of their roles according to Stanislavsky's methodology. He proposed, for example, the practice of writing in a notebook the interior monologue of a character and writing a letter addressed to some other character in the play with whom one would be acting. These and other exercises, described in detail in his books, were educational activities that became known as the 'Course of Eugênio Kusnet'. Even when the voices of Brecht, Artaud, and Grotowski were heard strongly, Kusnet methodology seemed to demonstrate an understanding, assimilation, and participation in these newer scenic proposals as well as the themes and languages of Brazilian contemporary theatre.

Physical action and Brazilian corporeality

In the mid-1970s, at the end of his life and after a 1968 study tour in the Soviet Union, Kusnet dedicated himself to researching Stanislavsky's last practices, which Kusnet denominated as the Método da Análise Ativa (the Method of Active Analysis). Actually, the title 'Active Analysis' had been coined by Maria Knebel, and the practice explained in her book *Vsiá Jizn* (A lifetime, 1967). However, it is known that Stanislavsky, at the final stage of his theatre pursuits, had added to his practices The Method of Physical Actions (fizítcheskie déistvia), i.e., physical and corporeal actions that could give rise to an organic relationship between external impulses and psychological reactions (see, especially Toporkov, 1979). The emphasis was placed on the actor's physical tasks, the 'corporeal life of the role', through which the creation of the character was pursued. The inner and outer life of the character, according to Stanislavsky, should support each other mutually.

While currently there is debate about the differences between the Method of Physical Action and Active Analysis, especially developed by Sharon Carnicke (2009, pp. 185–206) and Bella Merlin (2003, pp. 27–38), Kusnet's vision seems to integrate together the two practices. The work on physical action and the active analysis of the text as means to build the character were sustained by Kusnet through his actors' improvisations, during the process of preparing the cast for rehearsals, aiming at an 'active' approach to the play, that is, the understanding of the text through the actions executed by actors. This promoted an open-ended construction of the dramatic action. In this way, actions were seen as having the potential to incorporate the unexpected and, thus, provide the actor with creative autonomy as protagonists of the stage action. In this practice, the visual and external appearance of theatrical signs, as well as the consequent concrete materialization of the character's inner action, involve the appreciation of the actor's body (and the character) as visual and auditory elements that are essential for a scene to reach its full significance. Kusnet explains:

> Unfortunately Stanislavsky himself did not leave us systematic and concrete teachings in his written works, as he used to do previously with any new element of his 'Method'. [...] Consequently, what we can do is to continue the experiments based on what we know so far. The success or failure will depend on our ability.
>
> In what consists the method of 'Active Analysis'? As the term itself says, it is a way for actors to analyze the dramaturgical material: analyze it in action,

that is, try to understand the dramatic work through the action practiced by the interpreters of the roles [...]. Under these conditions, it is evident that the only way to execute the action of the play in the rehearsals is to improvise it in accordance with what the actors knows. [...] The improvisation of a scene represents the execution of a series of appropriate physical actions within the 'given circumstances', which automatically involves the interior action of the actor.

The permanent interdependence of these two factors was stated by Stanislavsky as a foundation for The Method of Physical Actions. Later, with only a few technical amendments, this method became what we know today as Active Analysis. About Stanislavsky's work, some theorists as K. Kristi and V. Toporkov added that through this new method, 'the actor comes to the feelings indirectly, through the organic life of the human body'.

Kusnet, 2003, pp. 100–1

Indeed, the emphasis on the 'physical means of communication', proposed by Kusnet, expanded Stanislavskian conceptions because it produced echoes in the theatrical practice of the theatre groups which emerged as scenic research centres in Brazil during the mid-1970s, and which created an enduring legacy in the wide range of scenic experiences during the late twentieth and early twenty-first century.

Kusnet's research created, although not consciously or deliberately, subliminal connections with the basics of Meyerhold's scenic poetry. Although actors, directors, and theatre scholars have placed for a long time Stanislavsky and Meyerhold in opposing theatrical fields, a closer study of Stanislavsky's physical action as developed, for example, by Kusnet, reveals that they were not radical opponents. In fact, these two wizards of the Russian theatre constitute complementary polarities. What is the most profound hybridization between these two Russian directors, in particular with regard to the concept of physical action? How, then, does this 'physicality', which seems to be inherent in the theatrical methodology of both, interact with the Brazilian artistic and cultural expression and its specificity? Kusnet's expansion of Stanislavskian concepts, in a possible dialogue with Meyerhold that is relevant to contemporary theatre in Brazil, can be located in his approach to rhythm and corporeality. As we have seen, Kusnet increasingly turned to physical goals and tasks to work on the actor's inner self and character embodiment. Therefore, each physical action should be closely attached to a certain rhythm, one of the building elements that configure the essence of the process of creation and the structuring of the character's actions. Kusnet explains:

> 'Tempo-rhythm' is one of the factors of human action. It obeys the laws governing the action itself. It has two simultaneous aspects: 'internal tempo-rhythm' and 'external tempo-rhythm'. The two rarely have the same characteristics, and the action itself rarely has the same characteristics in these two aspects. [...] How could the actor keep in mind the internal tempo-rhythm while practicing the outer tempo- rhythm? Where could he find a support for the internal tempo-rhythm? I think he could look for it in the physical actions that accompany the lines. It is sufficient that these actions are within the logic of the 'given circumstances' and correspond, by their nature, to the 'tempo-rhythm' that is being sought.
>
> Kusnet, 2003, p. 94

Even though the poetic and scenic results of their performances were different, there are unmistakable correspondences between the late Stanislavsky and Meyerhold, especially in terms of the construction of psychophysical action as the basis for the actor's work. In both systems, the solid basis on which the actor supports his work, and from which 'the feeling is born' is, without doubt, corporeality. Stanislavsky's proposals start, fundamentally, from a physical stimulus. From there it comes to 'the design of movements' as developed by Meyerhold in deep harmony with Stanislavsky's propositions: gestures, attitudes, looks, and silences establish the truth of human relations. It is the actor's task to investigate minutely the different possibilities in the relation between movement and word, always sustained by the rhythmic setting.

It is in this theatricality, marked by the overlapping of images and movement and which considers the body of the actor as the supreme expression of unusual relations between words and images, that the Brazilian scene of the last decades projects itself.

With the dissolution in the 1970s of stable Brazilian theatre companies, particularly Teatro de Arena in 1971 and Teatro Oficina in 1973, young actors mostly from São Paulo and Rio de Janeiro formed several groups, such as Mambembe, Vento Forte, Teatro do Ornitorrinco, Asdrúbal Trouxe o Trombone, Pod Minoga, Royal Bixiga's Company. These multiplied in the following decades in other parts of the country.[17] They stand out in the Brazilian theatre scene, which is usually organized as production co-operatives.

There are certainly clear differences between the creative processes and scenic results of their theatrical productions, but it is possible to unify these groups in the collective creation approach adopted and the resulting autonomy in the handling of theatrical means and techniques of expression.

Asdrúbal Trouxe o Trombone was one of the leading groups in Rio de Janeiro. The group debuted with an anarchic and irreverent production of Gogol's *The Inspector General*, which was followed by circus adaptations of Jarry's texts. National recognition occurred in 1977, with a performance titled *Trate-me Leão*, the group's first collective creation. Asdrúbal reject the protection of a traditional acting technique, in the shape of a more orthodox Stanislavskian 'system', to ground their plays in improvizations and theatre games developed in relation to the cast's personal experiences. They prefer 'to do theatre not discuss theatre', as some of its actors affirmed. The group sought to blow apart established methodologies, systems, and theories to define instead its own theatrical and collective creative process, presenting as a main axis their own individual experiences for the construction of their works' themes. In doing so they approached, what could be referred to as a more performative rather than representational acting. The scenic result proposed a type of performance based on the individual testimonies of the group's members which drew from a certain young imagery and the reality of the Southern Zone of Rio de Janeiro of that period.

The group Teatro do Ornitorrinco also worked in the 1970s, but in São Paulo. This group differed from Asdrúbal, as they defined theatrical technique and theory as the basis of their projects. Productions like *Mahagonny Songspiel* and *Teatro do Ornitorrinco Canta Brecht e Weill* called on a Brechtian inspiration for both the actor's technique and the way that the plays were composed. In *Ubu*, another production of the group, the director Caca Rosset relied on examples from the Russian avant-garde of the 1920s, especially in his conception of the montage of attractions. In this way Rosset constructed a performance that had a bias towards Meyerhold and Eisenstein, one which was strongly affiliated to the tendencies of retheatricalization of theatre, even though the work was inspired by Jarry's text and theories.[18]

Other groups working in São Paulo during the same decade, like O Pessoal do Vitor and Grupo Mambembe, exposed a dramatic inflection which was more realistic and psychological, certainly because of their strong affiliation to a more popular theatre. Their objective was to document and discuss the national reality from sociological and political points of view. In the 1980s, the group Macunaíma, achieved international renown. The group was directed by Antunes Filho, who was formed in the TBC tradition, and was one of Kusnet's many disciples. Filho became known for training young actors and creating inventive performances that marked Brazilian theatrical modernity in the 1980s. In the 1990s, the group Tapa, created and directed by the young director Eduardo Tolentino, took root in São Paulo as a stable repertory company, whose methodological inspiration, remarkably Stanislavskian, has been utilized to this day in the staging of Chekhov, Strindberg, Ibsen, Tennessee Williams, Bernard Shaw, and also Brazilian authors.

In the early twenty-first century, the legacy of the groups invested in Brazilian scenic research appears in the innovative productions of the group Vertigem, headed by actor and director Antonio Araújo. The group stages work in unconventional spaces such as churches, hospitals, and prisons. Araújo's theatrical practice is in tune with the themes and procedures of contemporary theatre and condenses in a creative manner the most varied techniques of the actor's work since Stanislavsky, Meyerhold, Grotowski, and Barba. Vertigem had a training period in Moscow with the Russian director Anatoly Vasiliev, and also presented one of its most memorable performances, *O Livro de Jó* (The Book of Job), at the Chekhov International Theatre Festival in that city (Sánchez, 2014, pp. 78–9).

As a result of these different work processes, the actor's art in contemporary Brazilian theatre inaugurates a new task for the actor: he ceases to be a simple interpreter of characters and moves away from their mere construction and theatrical embodiment. The actor becomes active and interacts with the theatrical process as a creator, mediator, and, possibly, as a critic of the character, of the performance and of himself. Therefore, contemporary theatrical aesthetics converse with the orientation of the modern scene of the 1910s and 1920s. From that scene, it is not only Meyerhold and the other Russian avant-garde that are integrated, but also important directors such as Max Reinhardt, Gordon Craig, Georg Fuchs, Adolphe Appia, and also, to some extent, Brecht. The latter's proposals for alternatives to realistic and naturalistic theatre undergo an anti-literary theatrical aesthetic, or at very least create a theatrical praxis in which words, that is, the 'literary' aspect of the drama, fulfil a very different function when compared to the tradition of Stanislavsky.

However, it is worth considering that in this contemporary reformulation of the art of the actor and theatrical phenomenon, the approaches of the 'system' are not entirely neglected. This is especially the case when we watch the reconfiguration of scenic techniques and poetry, which cannot disregard the presence of the actor on the stage, even when the first priority is given to the appreciation of gestural speech and the absence of thematic linearity.

Likewise, we cannot forget that the actor in such a spectacular, visual, corporeal, and consequently less logocentric and more somatic theatre, must possess a developed rhythmic and musical sense and transform his body and his physicality in the fundamental artistic language of theatrical art, as indeed the late Stanislavsky had emphasized. The transformation of the actor, of the man on the stage, into an artistic object signifies the transformation of the human body, with its lightness and mobility, into the essential means of stage expression, in an organic harmony with the musical and plastic rhythm of the scenic movement. Thus, the actor harmonizes the movements with the rhythmic and musical elocution and the lightness and plasticity of his body. As proposed by Meyerhold, these movements impose a virtuosity on this type of actor which is close to the acrobat's and dancer's. Therefore, within the contemporary theatrical system the scenic word compels the actor to be like a musician, because the work with pauses makes him calculate time not only as a musician, but also as a poet.

We must underline that, for Stanislavsky, rhythm was a key element for the implementation of physical actions. Thus, it is legitimate to capture not only the extension of Stanislavskian conceptions, but also their organic interaction with new practices and new poetic procedures for the actor's art, in different theatrical practices of the twentieth century and the beginning of the twenty-first century.[19] This interaction is possible because rhythm and musicality constitute an essential substrate for Brazilian culture and poetic imaginary. In many contemporary Brazilian theatre performances, these elements appear as a chain that goes beyond atmospheric application in the development of dramatic action to the expression of a profound cultural gestus. Rhythmic and musical elements, and the determining function of the actor's body as a tool for the search of a more substantial meaning of his own theatricality, allow a renewed articulation of theatrical performance and propose close connections with a specific form of Brazilian artistic expression and culture. In recent years, a re-evaluation of some forgotten aspects of theatrical tradition, from the origin of the theatre since the Greeks,[20] to the medieval autos at the fairs with their popular jugglers[21] and the commedia dell'arte and the puppet theatre with their Rabelaisians antics,[22] shows signs of some affinities with the language of Brazilian theatre, with a collective and cultural essence. Such essence is embedded in dance traditions, rituals, mime, and pantomime, and are far from a certain narrow, not to mention imported and imposed, psychological naturalism. It prevents the liberation of a popular imagery and the culture of histrionics that, to some extent, is 'natural' within the Brazilian cultural universe and its particular shaping derived from the intertwining of European, Indigenous peoples and African roots.[23]

Meyerhold's aesthetics find in the Stanislavskian 'system' one of its more important impulses. These impulses are added to modern and contemporary examples of scenic poetry. It is worth citing only a few of the most influential theatre directors, in whose work physical action is the main axis of the actor's practice, like Antonin Artaud, Jerzy Grotowski, and Eugenio Barba (Bonfitto, 2009, p. 21). This same impulse is able to fertilize the Brazilian scene with genuine and creative theatrical projects, reconcile experimentalism and folk art, modernity and tradition, formal achievements and the power of communication, and re-update at last the ritualistic connection between stage and audience. The contemporary relevance of the most essential concepts of Stanislavsky's theatrical art lies within this fertilization. His ideas and practices present potential uses even today, the consequences of which are still unpredictable.

Notes

1 The latest edition of Stanislavsky's complete works, which includes nine volumes, was published in Russia during the 1980s and 1990s. It is worth mentioning in particular the work of the Russian researchers I. N. Soloviova and A. M. Smeliansky for their research and study of Stanislavsky's archives and for the preparation of his complete works.
2 The manuscripts of Stanislavsky are at the Library of the Museum of the Moscow Art Theatre, which includes the Stanislavsky House Museum in Moscow. The Research Department of Heritage Stanislavsky and Danchenko, from the Moscow

Art Theatre School, has conducted the study of this vast personal collection of Stanislavsky.
3 A recent book organized by Aimar Labaki and Elena Vássina, *Stanislavsky: vida, obra e Sistema*, integrates direct translations from Russian of different phases of Stanislavsky's work, unpublished in Portuguese.
4 In Brazil, *Minha vida na arte* was translated from the Russian original by Paulo Bezerra (1989).
5 For an extensive analysis about the trajectory of Stanislavsky in North American Theater see Cavaliere and Vássina, 2011.
6 This source is about the trajectory of four Polish artists and war refugees: Ziembinski, Zygmunt Turkow, Boguslaw Samborski and Irena Eichlerówna (Stypinska). They gave artistic vitality to the Brazilian cultural scene and joined Brazilian theatre at that time of renewal. Of all those included in this 'group of Poland', as they became known, Ziembinski would make, without doubt, the most important contribution to the course of modern theatre in Brazil.
7 Editora Perspectiva of São Paulo will launch a biography of Ziembinski, in Brazil and in Portuguese, in 2016. It was recently launched in Warsaw by the Polish researcher Aleksandra Pluta. The book is in press.
8 For more details on this production see George, 1992.
9 It also fell to actors and directors like Augusto Boal, Sady Cabral, and Flaminio Bollini, who were also experienced in the Stanislavsky 'system'.
10 For a more detailed analysis of Kusnet's theatrical performances see Piacentini (2014).
11 Franco Zampari (1898–1966) was one of these Italian patrons. He was born in Italy, but settled in Brazil at a young age. A successful businessman, Zampari put his administrative and business experience to the service of Brazilian theatre. He invited, besides Ziembinski, several Italian directors such as Adolfo Celi (1922–86), Luciano Salce (1922–89), Flaminio Bollini (1924–78), Gianni Ratto (1915–2005), Alberto D'Aversa (1920–69), Rugero Jacobbi (1920–81) and, a little later, the Belgian Maurice Vaneau (1926–2007). Zampari's aim was to develop a national theatre revitalization project. The common background of the directors that he invited was the Second World War and economic difficulties, which facilitated the exodus of artists and intellectuals. These theatre-makers worked at TBC, in its fifteen years of existence, and contributed to professionalism and technical accuracy to Brazilian theatre, to transform simple amateur actors into relevant professional actors. The TBC also internationalized the repertoire and staged an unusual eclecticism, presenting several playwrights such as Sophocles, Oscar Wilde, Schiller, Gorky, Arthur Miller, Pirandello, Goldoni, Strindberg, Ben Jonson, and Anouilh. It should be noted that, in this theatrical process, the literary text

reigned as a sovereign, on which the actors and directors leaned in their psychological, social, philosophical, and stylistic analyses.

12 The most representative plays of Gianfrancesco Guarnieri are *Gimba* (1959), *A Semente* (1961), and *Ele s não usam Black-Tie* (1958) and, in collaboration with Augusto Boal, *Arena conta Zumbi* (1967) and *Arena conta Tiradentes* (1967).

13 It is worth remembering the anthological shows of the Arena, as *Revolução na América do Sul* (1960), *Arena conta Zumbi* (1965), *Arena conta Tiradentes* (1967). Boal was also the creator of the famous Sistema Coringa (Joker System), which made possible the unfolding of each of the actors in various characters in one performance, and simultaneously.

14 More details on Teatro Arena practices can be found in George, 1992.

15 Kusnet's most important books published in Brazil are: *Introdução ao 'Método da Ação Inconsciente'* (Kusnet, 1971) and *Ator e Método* (Kusnet, 1985, 2003).

16 Teatro Oficina's trajectory was an eclectic one. In the 1960s, it attempted stagings of psychological and scenic realism, with texts of Gorky and Kataiev, for example. It moved to a new period, the research of epic theatre (as for example, with the production of *Andorra*, by Max Fricht, that had a clear Brechtian inspiration). Oficina also attempted grotesque and comic productions, like the play *O Rei da Vela*, by the modern Brazilian author Oswald de Andrade. In the latter production, the discovery of a national means of expression, combined with the latest trends of contemporary world scene, was attempted. Kusnet was involved in these experiments, which provided Oficina's productions with a Stanislavskian basis. From the point of view of the actor's work, Oficina experienced the Stanislavsky 'system' first, and then changed from the realistic interpretation to the epic of Brecht. Later it was interested in the theories of Artaud and the practice of Living Theatre, whose troupe participated in performances at Oficina.

17 The expansion of theatre groups in Brazil in the 1980s can be seen in the Macunaíma group, directed by Antunes Filho, which became internationally renowned. In the 1990s, the Tapa group, directed by Eduardo Tolentino, gained ground in São Paulo as a stable repertoire company, and in the early twenty-first century, the legacy of the groups engaged in scenic research appears in the innovative shows of Vertigem, directed by Antonio Araújo.

18 For a more detailed analysis of the theatrical activities of these two theatre groups see Telesi and Guinsburg, 2002.

19 For a deeper reading to the subject, see the thought-provoking book of Matteo Bonfitto, *O Ator-Compositor* (Bonfitto, 2009), in which the concept of physical actions of Stanislavsky is analysed in its developments in the theories and scenic practices of V. Meyerhold, R. Laban, A. Artaud, E. Décroux, B. Brecht, M. Chekhov, J. Grotovski, and E. Barba.

20 Examples are the performances *As Troianas* (1999) and *Medéia* (2001), by Antunes Filho and *As Bacantes* (1996), by José Celso Martinez Corrêa.
21 The dramaturgy of Ariano Suassuna, in particular the play *O Auto da Compadecida*, was transposed quite recently to an innovative cinematic language. It recovers not only the innocent and irreverent universe of folk festivals in the northeast of Brazil, but also alludes to their classical origins, deepening its roots in the autos of Gil Vicente and Lope de Vega and also the satires of Cervantes.
22 A case in point is the strong tradition of popular culture of the northeast of Brazil, the mamulengos theatre (puppet theatre). It is irreverent, corporeal, and related to Carnival, from which a parodic and grotesque language has been recovered, among others, through the work of the actor, director, musician, and dancer Antonio Nóbrega.
23 The roots of Brazilian culture, forged through an amalgamation of Indigenous, African, and European cultures, are the bedrock of a particular way of being, thinking, and expressing. It will not be difficult to realize the exceptional predominance that exists at the principle of material and corporeal life, and the Dionysian character in Brazilian artistic way, which governs all imagery. It is populated by hyperbolic and hypertrophied images that correspond to a vigorous display of corporeality as an expressive sign. The artists of Brazilian modernism, especially in painting and literature, in the early twentieth century, already consciously put this physicality inherent in Brazilian culture into value. It spreads astonishingly still today, through different means of artistic expression. It is worth remembering important names in the Brazilian modernist movement of the first two decades of the twentieth century, whose aesthetic and artistic innovation dialogues with the European historical avant-gardes, while highlighting the specificities of a rediscovered Brazilian-ness cultural traits, free from Lusitanian chains. This innovation put into focus the formation of a new identity, as it appears, for example, in the prose of Mario de Andrade, the dramaturgy of Oswald de Andrade, and the painting of Anita Malfatti, Tarsila do Amaral, Di Cavalcanti, and Portinari, to cite only a few of the most important names of the Brazilian avant-garde movement.

References

Babbage, F. (2004), *Augusto Boal*. Oxon: Routledge.
Banham, M. (2000), *The Cambridge Guide to Theatre*. Cambridge: Cambridge University Press.

Bonfitto, M. (2009), *O Ator-Compositor*. São Paulo: Editora Perspectiva.
Carnicke, S. M. (2009), *Stanislavsky in Focus 2nd edn* Oxon: Routledge.
Cavaliere, A. and Vássina, E. (2011), 'A herança de Stanislávski no Teatro Norte-americano: Caminhos e Descaminhos', in *Teatro Russo-Literatura e Espetáculo*, eds A. Cavaliere and E. Vássina. São Paulo: Ateliê Editorial, pp. 199–214.
Dória, G. (1975), 'Os Comediantes', *Revista Dionysos – Estudos Teatrais*, 22. Monographic edition dedicated to Os Comediantes. Rio de Janeiro: Serviço Nacional do Teatro, p. 22.
Fuser, F. (2002), 'A turma da Polônia' na renovação teatral brasileira', in *J. Guinsburg: Diálogos sobre Teatro*, ed. A.S. da Silva. São Paulo: Edusp.
George, D. (1992). *The Modern Brazilian Stage*. Austin: University of Texas Press.
Gladkov, A. (1990), *Meierkhold* (2 vols.). Moscow: STD.
Knébel, M. (1967), *Vsiá Jizn*. Moscow: VTO.
Kusnet, E. (1971), *Introdução ao 'Método da Ação Inconsciente'*. São Paulo: Fundação Armando Álvares Penteado.
Kusnet, E. (1975), 'O mestre', *Revista Veja*. São Paulo, 14 May 1975. Interview.
Kusnet, E. (1985), *Ator e Método*. Rio de Janeiro: Instituto Nacional de Artes Cênicas-INACEN.
Kusnet, E. (2003), *Ator e Método*. São Paulo and Rio de Janeiro: Editora Hucitec-Funarte.
Labaki, A and Vássina, E. (2015), *Stanislavsky: vida, obra e Sistema*. Rio de Janeiro: Funarte.
Liubimov, I. (1994), 'Portreti na stenakh i jivie traditsi' ('Portraits on the Walls and the Living Traditions'), in *Stanislávski v meniaiuchemsia mire* (Stanislavsky in the Changing World). Moscow: MKTS, p. 162.
Melo, G. (1975), 'Testemunho', *Revista Dionysos – Estudos Teatrais*, 22. Monographic edition dedicated to Os Comediantes. Rio de Janeiro: Serviço Nacional do Teatro, p. 35.
Merlin, B. (2003), *Konstantin Stanislavsky*. Oxon: Routledge.
Michalski Y. and Peixoto F. (1996), 'Brazil', in *The World Encyclopedia of Contemporary Theatre, Volume 2 Americas*, ed. D. Rubin. London and New York: Routledge, pp. 60–82.
Perry, C. (1975), 'Reminiscências', *Revista Dionysos – Estudos Teatrais*, 22. Monographic edition dedicated to Os Comediantes. Rio de Janeiro: Serviço Nacional do Teatro, p. 31.
Piacentini, N. (2014), *Eugênio Kusnet: do ator ao professor*. São Paulo: Hucitec.
Pitches, J. (2006), *Science and the Stanislavsky Acting Tradition*. Oxon: Routledge.
Prado A. D. (1988), *O Teatro Brasileiro Moderno*. São Paulo: Editora Perspectiva.

Rodrigues, N. (1975), 'O ensaio geral', *Revista Dionysos – Estudos Teatrais*, 22. Monographic edition dedicated to Os Comediantes. Rio de Janeiro: Serviço Nacional do Teatro, p. 51.

Sánchez, J. A. (2014), *Practising the Real on the Contemporary Stage*, trans. C. Allwood. Bristol and Chicago: Intellect

Stanislávski, C. (1989), *Minha vida na arte,* trans. P. Bezerra, P. Rio de Janeiro: Civilização Brasileira.

Stanislávski, C. (2012), *A criação de um papel 17ª edição*, trans. P. Paula Lima. Rio de Janeiro: Civilização Brasileira.

Stanislávski, C. (2013a), *A preparação do ator 30ª edição*, trans. P. Paula Lima. Rio de Janeiro: Civilização Brasileira.

Stanislávski, C. (2013b), *A construção da personagem 22ª edição*, trans. P. Paula Lima. Rio de Janeiro: Civilização Brasileira.

Stanislavskii, K. (1988–99), *Sobranie Sochinenii tom 9*. Moscow: Iskusstvo.

Telesi, F. and Guinsburg, J. (2002), 'O Trombone do Asdrúbal and "Atrações" do Ornitorrinco – Uma busca de linguagem no Brasil dos anos 70', in da Silva, A. S. (ed.), *J.Guinsburg: Diálogos sobre Teatro*. São Paulo: Edusp.

Toporkov, V. (1979), *Stanislavski in Rehearsal*, trans. C. Edwards. New York: Theatre Arts Books.

Ziembinski, Z. (1975), 'Os Comediantes – Marco Novo', *Revista Dionysos – Estudos Teatrais*, 22. Monographic edition dedicated to Os Comediantes. Rio de Janeiro: Serviço Nacional do Teatro, p. 56.

Stanislavsky's Legacy in Cuba

Yana Elsa Brugal

This essay intends to create a relationship between the Stanislavskian technique and its repercussions in different moments within the Cuban theatre scene, until the present day. More than giving importance to references which are mostly historical in nature, the essay highlights important and representative instances of Stanislavsky's influence. This aim will be reached through information gathered from interviews with various actors and directors, literary sources, and the author's personal experience.

One must consider such a legacy as a set of circumstances which led to the complex integration of the system in Cuban culture. To explain this I will establish links for each moment between certain causes and their consequences. Moreover, the dates and notes given here serve as a guide and should be used as a basis to initiate future investigations about the complexity of the system's assimilation in Cuba. The Stanislavskian tradition in Cuban theatre cannot be enclosed in restricted time frames. In Cuba, the Stanislavskian tradition has been applied in performances, in teaching methods, and in the staging of performances by Russian and Soviet theatre practitioners. It was also seen in the presence of Russian touring companies. My objective is to go through a journey starting at the introduction of the system in Cuba and ending at how its presence is felt today.

Early references

In Cuba, the system has been assimilated in different ways, through different profiles, and through an identity of its own due to the integration of cultural processes which were marked by the ethnic diversity of Cuban culture. This diversity has been mostly dominated by Hispanic and African influences. The theme of syncretism as an expression of diverse traditions, a mix of local and foreign references, produces a richness that is characteristic of the Cuban theatre scene and its dramatic literature. For example, on one hand we find rituals of an African origin which have been preserved (within their logical and inevitable transformations) till the present day. Such rituals include *yoruba, palo, vodu, arara,* and *abakua. Yoruba,* also known as Regla de Ocha, is the most diffused within Cuban theatre and finds its ancestry in Nigeria. It was brought to Cuba in the seventeenth century. Witchcraft (or *Santeria,* a religion of African origin that is practiced in Cuba), is the cult towards the *orishas* or saints. It is made of particular attributes, a complex form of divination and the celebration of the occult, and is characterized by the syncretism between Catholicism and African religion. Rituals are often mixed with everyday situations within performances and plays, and one finds a reinterpretation of these rituals and everyday situations through universal codes of Western origin such as, in this case, the Stanislavskian tradition. At the essence of this marvellous synthesis one can find the Cuban human actor.

It is within this cultural map that Stanislavsky finds his place in relation to Cuba. It is necessary to clarify why Stanislavsky crossed paths with Latin America from such a distant country as Russia, during a historical period in which little cultural diffusion existed, and without many of the advancements of modern communication. Stanislavsky travelled to Cuba as part of the Moscow Art Theatre North American tour (1923–4), which made the existence of Stanislavsky's system known. He arrived to Cuba after his ventures in the United States, provoking a revolutionary impact on the Cuban theatre scene of the first half of the twentieth century. This revolutionary impact is seen in the enthusiasm of Cuban theatre-makers, who were anxious to discover and reach in their own practice the goals attained by the profound endeavour that Stanislavsky had accomplished. This focus constituted a new form of stage interpretation.

Although there is the existence of a vague reference towards a Cuban journalist who interviewed Stanislavsky in 1923 during the American tour, there exist no links between this fact and any possible consequences. According to Magaly Muguercia:

The oldest existing news regarding Stanislavsky's influence in Cuba dates back to the period of the ADADEL (1940–1943), a period during which, according to the testimonies of a number of students, the Argentinean-Hispanic teacher Francisco Martinez Allende [...] vaguely lectured certain notions which have to do with the principles of the great Russian theatre maker. Whilst basing his lessons on such principles, he used improvisation during the work with his students.

Muguercia, 1988, p. 208

According to these readings, we can conclude that Stanislavsky was introduced in Cuba at the beginning of the 1940s. Added to this, the Mexican Jose Gelada had, according to Nati González Freire,

[...] carried out during the summer of 1951 the first workshop at Havana on the general concepts of the Stanislavskian system, at the premises referred to as Nuestro Tiempo. Gelada's knowledge about this matter was accredited by attending the academy of the Japanese Seki-Sano, which was situated in Mexico after the Japanese had been Stanislavsky's pupil in Moscow.

Freire, 1961, p. 210

Seki-Sano was a very important factor in the Cuba–Stanislavsky relationship. This is because he learnt the system at the Lunacharsky Theatre Institute in Moscow during the 1930s. It was during this period that Stanislavsky was going through the last years of the creation and development of his pedagogy, on the theme of physical action. After this, Seki-Sano moved first to the United States and then to Mexico, where he eventually created a theatre academy in 1939.

First practitioners

There were various Cuban theatre practitioners who introduced the Stanislavsky system in Cuba although, really and truly, the system started being applied to stage productions and to acting seminars only at the beginning of the 1950s. Amongst these early Stanislavskian practitioners one finds Andrés Castro, Adela Escartin, Adolfo de Luis, and Francisco Morin, who all studied in the United States. I cannot ignore the great developments carried out by one of the most unrecognized creators and contributors, Irma de la Vega. As from

1953, she became associated with the promotion of Stanislavsky in Cuba, but she is never given the correct accreditation. De la Vega was a pedagogue who also studied under Seki-Sano's guidance in Mexico. Furthermore, she ran a seminar about the system, founded an acting academy, and also wrote an acting pamphlet based on the experience she had obtained from her teacher.

De la Vega's book *Técnica de actuación según Konstantín Stanislavski. Interpretactión y experiencias* (Acting technique according to Konstantin Stanislavsky. Interpretation and experiences) shows that she had assimilated an inheritance from the Stanislavsky of the last years, when the psychophysical actions were developed. Together with the exercises already introduced in the first part of the system, we find de la Vega's marked interest in muscular self-control or mind-body interrelation, action-contraction, and improvisation. De la Vega admits that this book also gathers, apart from her own exercises and Stanislavsky's teachings, other sources from theatre directors such as Evgeni Vakhtangov (De La Vega, 1967, p. 95). The author understood through her own experience the sense of holistic practice and importance of the actor: 'we consider that the structure and functioning of our body, even in its deepest psychic manifestations, can be reformed and modified, building on new psychological structures' (De La Vega, 1967, p. 7).

Another director, Andrés Castro had worked at the Actors Studio, where he was impressed by Stella Adler. He founded the theatre company Las Mascaras in 1950. Castro contributed to the knowledge of Stanislavskian precepts in Cuba and used exercises from the system with his group. According to historian Montes Huidobro, 'Andrés Castro's courses condensed lessons from the Method and were accompanied also with principles of acting technique taken from the performing concepts of Michael Chekhov' (Huidobro, 1973, p. 35). I see a relationship between Chekhov's exercise of 'imagination without words', as explained in his book *To the Actor*, when the actor is asked to transmit emotions from the body, and the essence of Castro's famous incorporation exercise which the actress Verónica Lynn describes as follows: 'Andrés would talk to us about incorporations. I remember that one of the first exercises was the task of feeling an amphora. I said: "An amphora . . . ? How does an amphora, that cold and inanimate object, think?"' (Stanislavski Siempre 2004). According to Lynn, who has been instrumental in our understanding of the Stanislavskian route, incorporations would imply work on body control, psychophysical relation, and incarnation of another object or being, in which case entailing feeling like another, thinking like another, imagining being that other being. As Lynn correctly indicates, although the association when incorporating an object would be distant, it was always a useful exercise. This I can confirm from practicing incorporation exercises with the actress Lilliam Llerena while studying acting in the Escuela Nacional de Arte (National School of Art).

Another important theatre director of the 1950s was Francisco Morin. He studied at Piscator's Dramatic Workshop and was also one of Reiken Ben-Ari's pupils, an Armenian who was also a member of the Moscow Art Theatre where he was a direct student of Stanislavsky. Ben-Ari also worked at the Habima Theatre in the 1930s. It is important to point out that Morin published articles about Stanislavsky and Ben-Ari (amongst others) in the Prometeo magazine that was founded in 1947.

The performances of the theatre group Prometeo, which was founded in 1953, left a great impact on the Cuban theatre scene. The group consisted of both actors and directors. The formalism which shaped its work stop this group from being considered as a follower of Stanislavsky and, evidently, it was not promoted as such. Despite this, the theatre critic Rine Leal states that: 'This group can be considered as the mecca of our creators with a sociological and formalist style, with a certain darkness and hushed up voices, with scenic ceremonies and communions and expressive plasticity and sobriety' (Leal, 1980, p. 127). Roberto Gacio, an actor and theatre researcher, states in an interview that 'Morin used to create a theatre which greatly stressed the formal aspects of representation but at the same time, also worked profoundly on the actor' (Gacio, 2014). In my opinion, even though he has not been tagged in history as a direct follower of Stanislavsky, one should study his influences as a director which undoubtedly drank from the fountains of his studies within the Dramatic Workshop. Such experiences must have undoubtedly left marks on him.

The Spanish Adela Escartin, who was also a student of the Dramatic Workshop at the Erwin Piscator School in New York (1947–50), arrived in Havana in 1952 and studied acting under Ben-Ari's tuition. It is also interesting to note that Escartin had also studied with Lee Strasberg and Stella Adler. The latter two interpreted the system from different points of view, and Escartin always felt more inclined towards Adler's perspectives which were based on her knowledge of physical action. Escartin was more relevant as a pedagogue and actress rather than as a director. She had a strong influence on her students. I remember her clearly during the rehearsals of Arnold Wesker's *The Kitchen* at the end of the 1960s. Adela greatly insisted on physical actions, on the meaning of the scene, and on the theatricality of the event. She was a teacher that investigated improvisation and at the same time payed attention to approaching internal states through physical movements and expressive liberty derived from profound states of concentration. She referred to rituals of origin as a way of knowing oneself. In conclusion, I can say that Escartin put together psychological and physical rules from her personal point of view which was very much shaped by her strong temperament. She could have only learnt such physical and psychological rules from the Stanislavskian system.

Two fundamental names: Adolfo de Luis and Vincente Revuelta

Mentioning these antecedents pays justice to the transmitters of Stanislavsky in Cuba, but I must mention in more detail two other pivotal names, Adolfo de Luis and Vicente Revuelta. They were two of Stanislavsky's most faithful followers and they contributed to the diffusion of his work through stage productions and their different forms of pedagogy. Both of them were invested in carrying the principle of organicity to the stage. They wanted to distance themselves from the old interpretative customs of falsehood and pomposity and which therefore lacked interior sincerity.

De Luis also studied at Piscator's Dramatic Workshop in New York, at the end of the 1940s, and was also a student under Ben-Ari and Francisco Martinez Allende. Additionally, he also received some lessons from Seki-Sano. De Luis was clearly familiar with Adler's inclinations towards physical action and the objective and superobjective, because he always mentioned these to his students during his lessons. All this emerges from an interview with Lynn. Moreover, Hernandez Díaz, a scholar of de Luis' theatre, states that:

> The method of physical actions constituted a complete negation of that mimetic and mechanic acting which Adolfo had for long witnessed its practice on our stages. This method unveiled acting as a process of creation through which the actor starts working consciously from oneself to conceive

the character from within, in order to later present on the stage a creature of true and organic existence.

Díaz, 1985, p. 18

On his arrival to Cuba, de Luis immediately began to propagate what he had learnt. His skills as a passionate defender of his point of view were put in practice to prove what he had learnt from Stanislavsky's technique. His aim was to prove the value of Stanislavsky's work in Cuba, the same Master who had impressed him by showing him the path towards the actor's organic nature.

De Luis' imprints in the history of Cuban theatre can be seen in his production processes, such as the comedy *Les jours heureux* (Happy Days) by Claude-André Puget (1951). This comedy was performed by the group Los Comediantes, with the support of Nuestro Tiempo. On this production de Luis stated the following: 'It was a great success to make the actors start from themselves, as it was to have the whole cast acting with the same line of interpretation and, above all, that the performance reached a uniform level of quality' (in Díaz, 1985, p. 31). It is important to underline two other contributions of de Luis as a theatre director. These were *Santa Camila de La Habana Vieja* (Santa Camilla of the Old Havana, 1962), written by Jose R. Brene, and *El premio flaco* (The Thin Prize, 1966), written by Hector Quintero. These two performances made the concept of dramaturgy in Cuban theatre stand out greatly. Both plays present scenes based on the most humble class of society. On *Santa Camila*, de Luis stated:

> It was important to start from the heritage of our clowns, but taken from a different perspective. We needed to work with this heritage's essence and not its form. Only in this manner could we achieve a correct stage image of the Cuban. This image was conceived as a creole, but it was deformed by its grandiosity and its emphasis on producing laughter. [...] Despite this, the clowns were more organic in their thought-gesture-word correlation than those who studied theatre academically.

in Díaz, 1985, p. 54

Lynn, who performed the title role in *Santa Camila*, provides the following testimony on de Luis:

> Adolfo asked me to join the Grupo Milanes after he had formed the group in 1961. Every rehearsal with him was a lesson [...]. I remember a great deal

of themes such as emotive memory, the magic if, the objective, the superobjective. He used to go for the details, for the small objectives of each scene [...] the subtexts were very important. He also used to talk to us about the meaning of internal and external action, that is how the actor is supposed to move in those external actions in correspondence with what is happening to him inside.

[...]

Camila was a character that I worked on a lot because I did not want it to be a sketch. [...]. For me, Camila was something else: a human being who loves above everything. The love towards her man and towards her Yoruba saints moves her. It is love above everything else.

Stanislavski Siempre 2008

In relation to the performance, the Cuban critic Rine Leal, writes:

[...] The actors manage to carry out a magnificent performance as a group, based on a great deal of naturalness as well as creole wit, turning their performance into a legitimate image of national modes and ways [...] in order to look for our universal national perspective in a more profound manner. [...] Adolfo de Luis directs *Santa Camila* [...] with great fluidity and manages to set on stage that piece of life that the author created on a base of realism and sincerity, of acute human observation.

Leal, 1967, p. 149

Recalling my opening description of Cuban culture, Brene's play thus offers an example of how the Stanislavskian tradition offers a reinterpretation of Cuban rituals and everyday life, with the Cuban human actor at the centre of this synthesis.

Another interesting de Luis experience is in relation to *El Premio Flaco*, which was staged at the Teatro Martí. In his own words:

El Premio Flaco was for us an enterprise of verifications. This was because it was a challenge to work with the unforgettable Candita Quintana, together with the well-known creole clowns (although the work was Cuban it was very far from what they were used to), and to guide them artistically without mentioning the keywords of the technique, the system, or the criteria.

in Díaz, 1985, p. 61

Such a symbiosis of 'cubanism', expressed by actors who based their success on immediate processes and a quick form of communication with the audience,

Figure 24 *Santa Camila de La Habana Vieja* (1962). Director: Adolfo de Luis, for Teatro Milanés.
Photographer: Unknown.

and combined with the rules of the Stanislavskian system, turned out to be a success for the theatrical Cuban scene of the 1960s. This is because it was an approach between what is popular from the Caribbean and from Western traditions. This unity is valuable because the person carrying out the tasks is a Cuban human being who is the product of the cultures that already have been outlined, cultures which have their own ways of doing things, a spontaneity, honesty, and intrinsic corporeal plasticity.

De Luis was also responsible for the translation from English of *An Actor Prepares*, which came out in 1970 as *Como se hace un actor*, and to which he contributed an Introduction. He asserted that he had read *An Actor Prepares* in 1940, four years after its first publication in 1936. De Luis always forwarded the existence of Stanislavsky to the people around him. He was like Stanislavsky's reincarnation in the Cuban theatre life. It is as though he decided this was his mission in life. His mission was a pedagogical one, from his first courses to the creation of the group Atelier, for young actors, in 1958, and until the mid-1980s.

While de Luis planted important guidelines in relation to Stanislavsky's teachings, the person that put in practice the main dissemination of the system in Cuba, and hence carried forward the most coherent form of the system, was Vicente Revuelta. Revuelta, a pedagogue, actor, and director, is considered to be the main artifice for the formation of actors and directors in Cuban theatre.

Revuelta's first encounter with the system dates back to 1952, when during a stay in Paris he participated in a workshop with Tania Bolachova, an integral member of the Moscow Art Theatre. This encounter unravelled a world of unusual pedagogy which was interesting and different. Revuelta explained that Bolachova emphasized 'the importance of having the objectives of the character clear and precise, the necessity to justify actions' (in Suárez, 2001, p. 76). Escartin also exerted a great deal of influence in the formation of Revuelta; the latter confessed that Escartin 'was my master, she dedicated a great deal of time to me and taught me many things, especially discipline and how to be critical and analytic' (Escartin, 2009).

Revuelta's theatrical activity is mostly linked to the publishing world. According to González Freire the theatre section of the magazine *Nuestro Tiempo* was reorganized in 1953 and put in the hands of Nora Badia and Revuelta. The *Cuadernos the Cultura Teatral* served as exponents of Stanislavsky's system, because the content was based on experiences which came out of the concepts and processes of Stanislavsky's work. Its content was also featured other directors such as Roger Vaillant, who also studied this common subject (Freire, 1961, p. 138). All these statements prove that the studies made about the system where carried out by emerging directors who adopted this practice as a route to revitalize the Cuban theatre scene.

As we can see, the people responsible for making Stanislavsky familiar to Revuelta were Escartin and de Luis. Both of them introduced him to the acting manual by Iosef M. Rapoport, written in 1936. Since Revuelta gets to know Stanislavsky through a manual, this first encounter with the system turns into a superficial one, though it was sufficient for Revuelta to absorb its exercises in order to later stage *Long Day's Journey into Night* (in Spanish *Viaje de un largo día hacia la noche*) by Eugene O'Neill. If an analysis is made of the parts which Revuelta assimilated from Rapoport's manual, one can find that he mostly took advantage of its latter aspects, such as action seen as a memory of physical actions, stage action and counteraction, and a very important element for Revuelta, justification of the stage.

A particular instance which strongly marked the pedagogical history of Cuban theatre was the renowned seminar about Stanislavsky which Revuelta organized in 1957 to coincide with the staging of O'Neill's play. It consisted of strong training sessions with actors such as Pedro Alvarez, Sergio Corrieri, Raquel Revuelta, and Ernestina Linares. The main points arising from this seminar were included in *Nuestro Tiempo*:

> We found it necessary to adapt the system [in] [...] its confrontation to the state of our theatre. It was necessary to proceed to a theoretical analysis which started off from the same base as that of the system. A base which would lead us towards an adequate development. [...] For more than seven months, we dedicated ourselves to a very deep study of the play according to the procedures included in the system. [...] For the first time ever, we managed to obtain a representation which was created by an ensemble. The daily performances in front of an audience were a decisive proof of the method's practical efficacy. A performance that was mistakenly thought out for minorities was greatly appreciated by audiences which were able to digest and appreciate a play full of psychological levels and shades which lasted close to four hours. We have recently inaugurated an adjoining academy were we hope to reaffirm and start off a new stage of higher experimentation upon the system. The most advanced members within our group will form 'laboratory' classes where we will gather students of dramaturgy and direction in order for them to work together. [...] This is a very much desired type of research which looks out for roots more than for results.
>
> Revuelta, 1958, p. 8

In one of Revuelta's last public appearances, he recalled the many experiences of the *Viaje de un largo* production:

> I was giving a seminar about *Viaje de un largo*... which is a masterpiece. As much as one tries, one is unable to reach the depth and exact intention of the

author's words. This feeling was transported into the interrelations onstage; I remember it was the first time, after a long while of doing theatre, that I finally saw actors who looked at each other. They learnt to look at each other on stage. [...] We worked on concentration, on justification, on scenic work, on objectives and superobjectives, and all of this was like being reborn.

Revuelta, 2009

In detailing the acting in *Long Day's Journey*, Leal highlights 'the sincerity of the emotions, the understanding of the text, the group work and the collective sensibility'. He adds 'the miracle of intelligence over improvisation, of seven months of rehearsals, of studies with cult-like devotion to the stage. [...] It is the most successful production of the present season' (Leal, 1967, p. 284).

As a conclusion I can say that, the introduction of Stanislavsky's system in Cuba during the 1950s made this decade significant in the development of acting. The reason behind this lies in the fact that the Stanislavsky system was introduced to Cuba during the beginning of the Salitas (Small Halls) Movement, which facilitated the emergence of new groups that brought about a transformation to the system by giving it a more professional relevance on the Cuban stage. Without doubt, such happenings set the mood and served as an artistic platform for the writing of plays by talented Cuban playwrights and the appearance of new scenic directors.

The Salitas Movement was the direct antecedent for the creation of the emblematic group Teatro Estudio. This group is greatly associated with Revuelta, who founded it in 1958 together with the director Raquel Revuelta. Teatro Estudio sustained a long process of actor and director formation, while also performing prestigious Cuban writers and classic foreign pieces. They continued the systematic study in acting technique through teaching practice and the process of staging performances. The inclination towards Stanislavsky's teachings evident in Revuelta was encouraged, and this was brought close to Brecht's dramaturgy (e.g. *The Good Person of Szechwan* and other plays) and its artistic distancing.

Contextualization and periodization is necessary when tackling the work of Revuelta as a Stanislavskian director because his theatre featured various styles and tendencies. Revuelta has always been a known experimenter, investigator, and explorer of new tendencies. He always loved the avant-garde. For Revuelta, theatre meant exploring new work processes. After setting up Teatro Estudio, he also created pedagogical projects with students and professional actors. He created the group LOS DOCE under the influence of Jerzy Grotowski. It was at this laboratory that he staged a version of Ibsen's *Peer Gynt*, with the intention of going in depth in the actor's training and in the search of oneself through the character. This demonstrates his open vocation for experimentation, which brings to mind laboratories and workshop approaches, such as the First Studio of the Moscow Art Theatre, where practitioners such as Michael Chekhov and Vakhtangov developed their experimental qualities.

It is interesting to note Grotowski's and Brecht's influences when studying Revuelta's productions of *The Three Sisters* (1972) at the Teatro Estudio. As Revuelta says, and as is supported by his actor Michaelis Cué, the production of *The Three Sisters* was particularly appreciated by its director. Revuelta had just experimented with LOS DOCE and his Brechtian montages of the 1960s. Through that production, he managed to give to his audience a theatrical experience which was the product and synthesis of his own experiences, whilst starting off from the Chekhovian essence. Cué, a LOS DOCE member and connoisseur of Revuelta's practice and direction, says that in *The Three Sisters*,

> Revuelta takes from Grotowski the professional tone, the perfecting of the actor's exercises, the person that talks with his/her own resonators, the work with internal disarmament, the presence of the actor who is involved in a performance that is also a process of research with the audience. He was attracted to Grotowski's mysticism, to the work with the actor's unconscious, and he intended the psychic world to communicate more than the actual character. [...] Interpretations of a psychological character guided by a chain of physical actions like sounds, silences, and looks impregnated with a sense of faith and a truth, were combined with interruptions occurring during the performances, declarative tones of the actors in particular moments, breaks marked by messages aimed directly to the audience. At the end of the performance there is an interaction between the audience and the actor in the singing of a song that referred to the universal dimension of the socio-political life of that moment. That way Chekhov's era became part of the present life.
>
> Cué, 2015

Figure 25 *Las tres hermanas* (1972). Director: Vicente Revuelta for Teatro Estudio. Photographer: Unknown.

It is deduced by Cué's words that under the aegis of the Chekhovian-Stanislavskian dramaturgy some Brechtian precepts were introduced that required a different form of representation, given the introduction of structures that were not strictly Aristotelian.

The arguable polarization between Brecht and Stanislavsky does not really feature in Revuelta, because in essence he was a director that searched in depth within the psychology of the actor first, irrespective of the representation that was then to follow.

A performance characterized by the construction of psychophysical actions in the Stanislavskian tradition was Alexander Guelman's *En el parque* (The Bench, 1986), which indicates the recent continuity of Stanislavskian guidelines in Revuelta's work.

The work of Revuelta and de Luis moved in two different directions. De Luis takes on a pedagogical role, in the shape of workshop situations. He does not stage regular performances. On the other hand, Revuelta adopts traditional and experimental ways of working which he then conjoins. At different moments, this conjunction results in a new and different tendency. De Luis, on the other hand, goes directly in the direction of Stanislavskian theatre. He ventures into the synthesis of Cuban theatre. De Luis stages important Cuban playwrights and facilitates the actor's work in delving in the character's psychology, while Revuelta frequently called upon world theatre and inserted in a mixture of traditions without leaving the laboratory dimension.

A number of points need to be kept in mind when evaluating the system's introduction in Cuba. The first point is that, for obvious reasons, the system was completely unknown in Cuba and that the encounter with Stanislavsky occurred through contact with his students. This encounter happened through the teachings from teacher to teacher and from creator to creator. It happened in this manner because of a lack of literature on the subject. Even though various books had already been published by the time Cuban theatre-makers visited the United States, the main introductory contact with the system still came from Rapoport's manual. The books which had been already published included *My Life in Art* (1926), *An Actor Prepares* (1936), and a version of the first part of *Building a Character* (1949). Rapoport's manual was written in the 1930s and contained theoretical aspects of theatre technique and practical elements and exercises that one can rely on when staging performance. By then Stanislavsky had already worked on Afinogenov's *Fear* (1931), Gogol's *The Dead Souls* (1932), Ostrovski's *Talents and Admirers* (1933), and Bulgakov's *Life of Molière* (1936). The manual also came about after Stanislavsky's last findings about performance and role creation. These were elemental and fundamental concepts of the Method of Physical Actions.

It is also true that Stanislavsky can be studied through his pedagogical development in the art of the actor. Such developments culminated when he worked with physical action and also in the manner with which Stanislavsky tackled scenic reality. In *My Life in Art* one can observe that as from the 1920 production of *Cain* Stanislavsky was keeping in mind that

> we should not only talk properly, with rhythm and proper timing, we should also show ourselves properly in a rhythmical manner; in order to do this and have a degree of guidance, a set of rules should exist. This discovery created an impulse inside me for a whole new series of investigations.
>
> Stanislavski, 1985, p. 415

These are the records that track Stanislavsky's arrival in Cuba. Whole generations followed his path and learnt about the art of the actor and the technique behind it.

After the 1960s

The Stanislavskian forces of the end of the 1950s and beginning of the 1960s, under the protection of the Teatro Estudio, found an opposition in some members of the collective, who felt the need to establish another kind of audience relationship. This led to the formation, in 1968, of Grupo Teatro Escambray, which later on would insert itself in the so-called movement of the new Latin-American theatre that started at the end of the 1960s. This movement incorporated Brechtian methodology because of its notorious social character and because its aim was to create a Latin-American theatre that reflected the then new ways of Latin American life.

The Grupo Teatro Escambray was fundamentally unique because its members actively participated in the creative process, from the selection of the theme to the final discussion carried out after the performance. They also understood the importance of the author's and the director's contribution in a mode of work that was named 'open structure within the work that was always modified throughout the performance process'. Stanislavskian and the so-called Brechtian traditions were in a way fused, because from its beginning the Grupo Teatro Escambray brought together actors and directors from the Teatro Estudio and the new community theatre, even though the latter had particular social aims. This had also to do directly with the fact that in a particular moment the traditional Russian theatre training in Cuba, benefiting from cultural exchange, did not have the appropriate resonance in the Cuban institutions of the 1980s.

The new generations did not know how to interpret the system, because their marked interest in new forms of expressions resulted in only a sparse understanding of the system. Confusion emerges when the system as a psychophysical apparatus to achieve the organic nature of the actor is confused with vulgar or simplistic realism. I insist that I respect the Master. The importance of his actor training methods was not always taken into consideration by pedagogues and authors that ignored or undervalued these methods, especially in a convoluted time such as the 1980s, in which experimental theatre emerged. Moreover, even if they connected with the techniques and theories of universal theatre such as those developed by Eugenio Barba, they underestimated the importance of Stanislavskian precepts that are necessary to understand theatre practice.

In any case, the relationship between Stanislavsky and pedagogy in Cuba has always been dependent on the particular teacher and the programmes that had been proposed with or without Stanislavsky, as I can confirm from my experience. To value the extent that Stanislavskian principles – applied on a case by case basis – are present in Cuban theatre art is impossible, but it is true that its fundamentals are present in the pedagogy and the theatre art of the present.

When I speak about teachings, I am referring to the fact that for the formation of actors, the most important and well-known book during these past years has been *Cómo se hace un actor* (1970), referring to the book about an actor's work upon himself. *Mi vida en el arte* was published in 1985, direct from Russian, while a year later (1986) *La construcción del personaje* came out. In the latter's case the translation was from the North American edition.

It is very important for me to promote Stanislavskian theories and practices. Because of this, in recent years, I have been trying to disseminate the system with the aim of rescuing the memory of those who practised it. I am also involved in analysing how Stanislavsky's teachings are being presently applied. I call upon participants from recent generations and in view of this, I founded the interdisciplinary programme Stanislavski Siempre [Stanislavsky Forever]. It is made of a series of analytic conferences and workshops, and has been active in Havana since 2004. The programme goes deep into the psychophysical processes of the actor's art, sustained by the system's core subjects. We have made an incursion in themes such as the relationship between the conscious and the unconscious, memory and physical actions and, more specifically, the relationship of these themes to contemporary Cuban theatre. Talking about the system's different interpretations and the forms of application that it is given by various creators of new tools and new directions is a way of connecting Stanislavsky with exponents of diverse tendencies and theatrical formulas.

The seminar is presently focusing on the different stages of work evident from the discovery of the human soul to the physical actions; I am referring to the psychophysical process which the actor does on himself up to the work on the body and on the text. Such a psychophysical process was developed with greater exactitude by Stanislavsky towards the end of his life. The seminar also unites together psychologists and psychiatrists on the understanding that the interdisciplinary connection in performance between the arts has an important role in the understanding of an artistic event as a whole. This amplifies the investigative and informational spectrum of the seminar. We have already dedicated three editions to fundamental aspects such as the conscious-unconscious relationship, memory, and physical actions.

I can mention performance moments and directors who have centred their attention on Stanislavsky, such as Miriam Lezcan with Teatro Mio and Carlos Celdrán with Argos Teatro. These people have reflected on the importance of the Stanislavskian system and the different perspectives taken by its legacy. Starting from the close relationship between the director and the dramaturg, Teatro Mio has been an important point of polemics in Cuban theatre. The detail that made this group stand out was the practice of putting characters on stage with a dominant psychological expression. Being a socially committed theatre, Teatro Mio has managed to seep into their spectators through a dramatic discourse that is full of penetrating matters about the life of their contemporaries. An example of this is *Desamparados* (1991), Alberto Pedro's version of Mikhail Bulgakov's *The Master and the Margherita*. In the case of Celdrán, his main production axis is the subtle and elaborated study of the characters' complexities, around which he directs his actors. Celdrán started his work in Image Theatre and the acuteness in his work directed him to the search of a Stanislavskian truth, with actors having physical control and in constant contact between them, as in, for example, Chekov's *Uncle Vanya* (2014) or Abel González Melo's *Mecánica* (2015).

In the case of theory, the author of this essay develops studies on Stanislavsky within the traditions of Caribbean theatre. In essence, my analysis is based on the theory of the dramatic action created by Stanislavsky and its possible application to ritual processes of African descent which – with their logical transformations – are conserved to this day. It is important to underline that acting, in all its styles and applications, always carries with it the germ of possession.

Stanislavsky's tools and analytical categories help to understand the actor's creative process in the magic-religious theatre. While it is clear that

Figure 26 *El tío Vania* (2014). Director: Carlos Celdrán for Argos Teatro.
© Alina Morante.

Stanislavsky's tradition lies in realist theatre, where a text is directly deconstructed in order to tackle the selected themes, the magic-religious theatre is driven by parameters which are related to the mythology of African origin, which transcends everyday reality. Therefore, they are different traditions. The point is not to use Stanislavskian tools to explain the original flow of acting in the Caribbean culture, but to search for the actor's spiritual state, putting it in connection with characters that are identified as divine forces. In order to do this, the theory of dramatic action developed by Stanislavsky serves as a source of comparison to the mission of the actor that interests me. Instead of isolating an essence, this research assimilates exercises and turns them into systems that compliment the studies of an ancestral culture. We have to re-formulate the system from our own practice, while keeping in mind developments made in the sciences of human behaviour.

First of all, it is important to contextualize the physical work of the ritual actor in one's physical capabilities. If nowadays we had to study from a theatrical perspective the dramaturgy of an actor of African tradition, we would see that this dramaturgy encloses the 'protagonist' in itself. Practitioners of ritualistic practices train themselves to find ancestral memories. Stanislavsky would define this as emotive memory which also helps us with other elements of his system: concentration, organic nature, the magic 'if', the sense of truth, attention, imagination, units and objectives, subtexts, the through line of action, training, given circumstances, and so on. Therefore, I am currently investigating the essential ideas of Stanislavsky's system that interact with the practices developed during the so-called 'possession', by adapting and incorporating Stanislavskian concepts of emotional and psychophysical training. Included in this research are practical demonstrations of the 'believer/possessed artist' who illustrates the state of possession with 'faith' and 'conscience'. Experiences of theatre groups are also being consulted.

In trying to uncover the factors that lead the actor to possession, I initially became aware of the timeless performer's creative action in the process behind the possession by the character. This greatly depends on the actor's preparation, on the form and style of the dramatic material which is to be internalized, and on what the director is asking for. Trance and possession happen in relation to the contact between two actors, the *orisha*, and through conscious techniques one searches for an unconscious state until full identification is achieved. As the researcher Fernando Ortiz states, 'trance is an intermediate state between the conscious and the subconscious' (Ortiz, 1981, p. 73).

Conclusion

The students of the system in Cuba experienced various acting techniques but neither of them studied directly in Moscow with Stanislavsky. Because of this, the system's introduction in Cuba was an amalgamation of resources.

And as we know, Stanislavsky's ideas arrived from the United States via such former Moscow Art Theatre figures like Seki-Sano and Ben-Ari. This makes one think that it is not possible to talk about a coherent learning regime. To this we need to add the fact that writings about the work on physical actions, on which Stanislavsky worked towards the end of his life, appeared late.

This review of Stanislavsky and Cuban theatre demonstrates the specificity of the system in Cuba, a presence that was always marked by a Cuban identity that is understood as a syncretism of diverse cultures. Moreover, Stanislavskian interpreters are post-Stanislavsky, because they developed their understanding and pedagogy within the particular tradition of their culture.

A performance by Revuelta could not have belonged to the realism that was characteristic of the first half of the twentieth century. It belonged to the reinterpretation of a man in his new circumstances. This is because the tradition of Cuban theatre is corporeal and external. Psychological theatre finds its place in the 1950s, at the same time of the Salitas Movement. This was a complex process of cultural enlightenment, but its analysis is beyond the aim of this essay.

Another factor which is seldom taken into consideration but which is very important is the strong influence from North American cinema actors. Such actors were educated in the Stanislavskian traditions and they have been slowly depositing sediments of interpretative criteria which live in a collective unconscious.

Cuban laboratories were characterized by courses and workshops which followed the experimental side of Stanislavsky that he had exhibited from the opening of the First Studio onwards. In relation to this, it is important to mention that he was always in contact with Meyerhold and Vakhtangov. These three personalities had a very complex relationship, but also fed off from each other. In fact, Stanislavsky's reflections emerged from his direct contact with his students and actors.

At the present moment, in order to continue Stanislavsky's studies, the interdisciplinary programme Stanislavski Siempre has turned into the Laboratorio Stanislavsky. This has happened to explore new forms and dimensions in the technique of the contemporary actor, starting from the Stanislavskian precepts.

References

Brugal, Y. E. and Rizk, Beatriz (2003), *Stanislavski y la posesión en el ritual afrodescendiente En: Rito y representación. Los sistemas mágico-religiosos en la cultura contemporánea cubana.* Madrid: Iberoamérica Editorial Vervuert.

Carnicke, S. M. (2009), *Stanislavsky in Focus. An Acting Master for the Twenty Century* 2nd edn. London and New York: Routledge.
Díaz, M. C. (1985), *Adolfo de Luis. Promoción y renovación del teatro Cubano*. Trabajo de Diploma, La Habana: Instituto Superior de Arte.
De la Vega, I. (1967), *Técnica de actuación según Konstantín Stanislavski. Interpretación y experiencias*. Universidad Central de Las Villas.
Escartin, A. (2009), XIII Festival Internacional de Teatro de La Habana, Panel Presencia de Stanislavski en Cuba: La Habana.
Freire, N. (1961), *Teatro Cubano (1927–1961)*. La Habana: Ministerio de Relaciones Exteriores.
Grotowski, J. (1993), 'Tú eres hijo de alguien', *Máscaras*, 3, October 1992, pp. 69–75.
Huidobro, M. (1973), *Persona, vida y máscara en el teatro cubano*. Miami: Ediciones Universal.
Leal, R. (1967), *En primera persona (1954–1966)*. La Habana: Instituto del Libro.
Leal, R. (1980), *Breve historia del teatro cubano*. La Habana: Editorial Letras Cubanas.
Mars, L. (1966), *Témoignages, essai etnophychologique*. Madrid.
Muguercia, M. (1988), *El teatro cubano en vísperas de la Revolución*. La Habana: Editorial Letras Cubanas.
Ortiz F. (1981), *Los bailes y el teatro de los negros en el folklore de Cuba*. La Habana: Editorial Letras Cubanas.
Osipovna K. María. (1967), *El último Stanislavsky*. Editorial Fundamentos: Madrid, 1996.
Rapoport, I. M. (1936), *The Work of the Actor. Theatre Workshop*. Unpublished Manual.
Revuelta, V. (1958), 'A propósito del sistema de Stanislavski', *Revista Nuestro Tiempo*, 26, November–December, p. 8.
Revuelta, V. (2009), XIII Festival Internacional de Teatro de La Habana. Panel Presencia de Stanislavski en Cuba: La Habana.
Stanislavski, K. (1970), *¿Cómo se hace un actor?*. La Habana: Colección Teatro y Danza, Instituto Cubano del Libro.
Stanislavski, K. (1985), *Mi vida en el arte*. La Habana: Editorial Arte y Literatura.
Stanislavski, K. (1986), *La construcción del personaje*. La Habana: Editorial Arte y Literatura.
Stanislavski Siempre, 1st edn. (2004), Relaciones consciente-inconsciente en la pedagogía de Konstantín Stanislavski. La Habana.
Stanislavski Siempre, 4th edn. (2008), Relaciones consciente-inconsciente en la pedagogía de Konstantín Stanislavski. La Habana.

Suárez, E. (2001), *El juego de mi vida. Vicente Revuelta en escena*. La Habana: Centro de Investigación y Desarrollo de la Cultura Juan Marinello.

Interviews

Michaelis Cué. 2015. La Habana.
Roberto Gacio. 2014. La Habana.

A Teacher's Perspective: Stanislavsky at the Escuela de Teatro de Buenos Aires in Argentina[1]

Raúl Serrano

Stanislavsky become known in Argentina during the 1940s and 1950s, through pioneers like Antonio Cunill Cabanellas, founder of the National School of Theatre, Heddy Crilla, an actress of Austrian descent, and the White Russian émigré Galina Tolmacheva. These practitioners developed different versions of Stanislavsky's work: some highlighted the ethical aspects of the acting profession, others treated the 'subtexts' and the 'sub-themes', or numbered in a disorganized manner the elements necessary for acting, such as concentration, relaxation, and imagination. There were as many different versions of the system as there were readers interested in the scarce sources available, even though Stanislavsky still appeared as a model amidst the then surviving practices of declamation and prosody.

It was against this background that I moved to Bucharest in 1957 and enrolled at the Institutul Ion Luca Caragiale. In essence, this Institute followed the pedagogic tendencies of the Soviet Institution, which I now feel confused scenic life with a superficial naturalism. Moreover, the teachers at the Institutul saw Stanislavsky's career as eclectic, with no attempt made to distinguish between opposite directions in Stanislavsky's work. I followed my student experience at the Institute with six more years as a theatre director in Romania, where I also attended a great deal of performances. Today I can say that it was from these performances that I learned my most important lessons.

I returned to Argentina in 1967. Upon my return, the first thing that disturbed me was coming face to face with a mode of acting that was called

Stanislavskian but which in reality belonged to Lee Strasberg. His was an introvert mode of acting in search of the emotional contents of a role, with the aim of unleashing what is referred to as 'sensory and affective memory'. In Argentina I attended many performances based on this technique, which felt slow and inactive when compared to what I had seen in Romania. One could not see a lot of difference between one emotion and the other. As a reaction to this scene, I started to re-read critically Stanislavsky's writings – *My Life in Art* and *The Actor's Work on Himself* – from the Romanian translations rather than Castilian which to me seemed better. I also adopted a critical stance to Strasberg, whom I considered not theatrical enough. In Romania I had given attention to the philosophy and aesthetic lectures of Marcel Breazu, who had acquired his formation with George Lukacs. To these I added my reading of such disciplines as Linguistics, Aesthetics, Structuralism, Theory of Styles, and others. It is this research which, when informed by the practical investigations I was carrying out at the Escuela de Teatro de Buenos Aires, prompted me to develop the practice titled 'Repression as a form of action', as I will discuss below.

The theoretical starting point in my investigation on Repression as a form of action was based on three critical ideas. First of all, I must point out that there was the existence of not one but two 'Stanislavskies'. The first Stanislavsky considered acting as an act that is triggered by memory. On the other hand, in 1934, the second Stanislavsky decided to change what he had been doing up till that moment and to focus instead on what he called the 'Method of Physical Actions'. From this new perspective, acting no longer needed emotional recollection. On the contrary, it proposed starting off from the 'etudes' (improvisations) to investigate a constructive process that would be more objective and interactive.

The second theoretical starting point was critical of the fact that Stanislavsky had left us with many memorable pages and examples but with little methodology or system. He treated elements related to acting separately, one by one, without me having the ability to distinguish in them a systematic nexus. After all, Stanislavsky's mode of writing was structured around the narration of different lessons, and such a mode did not really shed light onto the relationship between the elements. It was possible to conclude that Stanislavsky was in reality recommending to do everything well, together, all the time. One had to simultaneously relax, concentrate, imagine, improvise, and work on texts. Everything at the same time. The third point concerns style. It was felt that Stanislavsky comes through as unclear with regards to the problems attributed to styles. This is because in his opinion, there was only one true and great theatrical style: 'Realism'. He never really differentiated between the acting processes necessary for character identification as opposed to distancing.

Our research helped us to formulate two concepts: dramatic structure and process. The concept of structure avoids a fragmenting approach in the analysis of acting. It helps to interrelate the different elements – the surroundings, the conflicts, the main subjects, and physical action or praxis – with which the actor works. The evident advantage behind the concept of a structure is that it joins *in itself* not only the elements found in acting but also the individual work of each and every actor within the nexus that is formed amongst them. These elements create *one another* through the acting praxis, and the result is different to a mere sum of all the parts. In other words, all the elements start being generated and structured thanks to the work of the actor. They cannot be defined as pre-existing elements that are merely put side by side to each other.

Let us now discuss, in no particular order of importance, the elements of the actor's structure listed above. The surroundings. These are everything that surrounds a performance, including what happens before and outside it. It is composed of the actual space plus any given circumstances that become real through the actor's work. Conflict. There can be no theatre without conflict. Anything said about conflict should have the possibility of being executed by the actor. Wordy descriptions of emotional or social conflicts are not enough. Our technical definition of conflict derives from the actor's work: that which the actor is confronted with and which the actor fights against, in terms of one's surroundings, with oneself and with the antagonist. The actor should formulate this question: what is it that I am fighting against? Or, what is opposing me on the stage? The subject. Is this the actor or the literary subject? It is at this point that complications arise, as the subject intertwines with physical action as well as the concept of process. Initially, the subject is the actor with all his physical and mental attributes, searching for a dramatic action which is yet to be discovered or created. As the work progresses, relationships amongst the characters evolve and the relationship with the text itself starts being formed. Such relationships start producing psychological contents, which no longer belong to the actor as the subject becomes the theatrical character.

The concept of process emerged from a scene where Stanislavsky was working on Gogol's *The Inspector General*. This scene helped us identify a methodology with which to work on the subject. Stanislavsky asked two students to go on the stage and rehearse a scene. The students had not read the scene in a while and answered that they would not remember all its details. Stanislavsky says: 'Would you know what to do if, after a long train journey, you were suddenly taken hungry?' To Stanislavsky, this was a very adequate way to start investigating who and what Khlestakov is. This has a sense of methodology, a sense of doing one particular thing after another. We see the actor's work presented as a process, starting in a concrete manner and with clear tasks for him to fulfil. We sense a method of investigation, construction and work, centred on the actor as an active body, confronting a task that is not based on memory or on intellectual analysis. All these reflections are important when one considers problems related to the subject.

At the beginning of our investigations, setting the actor as the sole subject seemed enough, but as we progressed we found ourselves needing to go deeper into the matter. We were obliged to define the meaning of 'physical action'. We found help in an article written by Boris Zakhava, a Soviet director who defined action as 'all voluntary and conscious behaviour which has a determined end [result] to it'. To this we added the keywords 'transformation' and 'here and now', so that the definition read as follows: 'all voluntary and conscious behaviour aimed at transforming here and now a given target'. This definition allowed us to formulate a technical starting point for the actor. It also differentiated between action and verbs that are used to name emotions and external movements but which have no psychological content. By setting the actor as the subject, the actor not only worked to transform what was in front of him, but in the process (and this was the most important thing for us) the actor would also transform himself. The pathway which turned the actor into the character now seemed quite clear for us.

This definition of Physical Action led to great success when applied to the analysis and construction of realist scenes that had lengthy descriptions of the protagonists' physical behaviour. An example of this is the scene between Kovalski and Blanche in *A Streetcar Named Desire*. The former's physical actions are of a man who has just arrived home after a long day at work, while the latter is packing up her belongings in a stressed manner. We could deduce concrete

Figure 27 Raúl Serrano. © Escuela de Teatro de Buenos Aires.

circumstances surrounding the characters and give tasks to the actors to explore the character through physical actions. However, we also rehearsed other realist scenes which were more conversational. They might still have been conflicting and performative in nature, but these scenes seemed never ending and without any visible physical behaviour. Were we to renounce physical action? How were we to make the move from the actor to the character?

It was the practice inside the classroom that put us back on the correct path of active, psychophysical tasks. On one occasion, two students suggested working on a scene from Ibsen's *John Gabriel Borkman*, in which two sisters meet after a long time and are cross with each other because of the love they shared for John Gabriel. It is a very long scene, full of dialogue in which the possibility of physical behaviour seems impossible. Whilst reading the scene, I realized that the sisters still had a very strong desire to react violently to one another, even though they do not show this in physical action. What the sisters were oppressing was more important than what they were doing and saying.

This experience led to what I call 'repression as a form of action'. Today people are shaped from infancy to oppress their instincts, but this does not mean that they have no such instincts. The social and educational spheres substitute these instincts with dialogue, which becomes a fundamental mode of contact. Physical action is not the protagonist in everyday life, and we barely touch each other. Realist theatre essentially showed these moments of disjunction between a civilized, social, and polite conduct and another more instinctive and repressed conduct. Our conclusion was that theatre should be able to reproduce such a distinction. We became aware that the physical action which would take into account the objectives was slowly being transformed into an acceptable social conduct which repressed animal instincts. The subject stopped being a rational one and was transformed into a divided subject of great performativity, made out of instincts and impulses which were not allowed to get through ... but which still existed.

The search for a rationally conceived objective was replaced by the 'divided subject'. This is a subject which activates one's instincts when faced with conflict. It adopts the dynamics of the body without implying that there should necessarily be physical movement. In view of this, what we now refer to as 'pre-conflicts' started acquiring importance. 'Pre-conflicts' are the activities that the actor needs to carry out in order for there to be a transition from his condition and identity as a human being to the identity of a character. Students are now induced to create the 'pre-conflict': 'What does the animal inside the character feel like doing?' After this, we would add: 'Do not do it!', and from this point allowed them to take on the text. 'Pre-conflicts' are named so because they happen before and outside the scene. This physical – rather than psychological – step assists the actor in investigating the preceding scene through an instinctive corporeal impulse and not through a rational and verbal objective. Text then becomes the channel for social content which translates the unpresentable part of our impulses.

Today we are in the position to affirm that physical action is not central to the actor's work as we previously thought. Our previous mistake lay in the fact that our actors rationalized what they were going to do from beforehand and as outsiders to the given situation. Nowadays we centre our activity around the use of the body – in its totality and historicity – and that is our main tool. Our methodology has learned to improvise within the frame of dramatic texts understood as the social limits of our desires and impulses because the seemingly lack of exterior action is what makes the subjects of a conversation. We managed to decipher techniques that Anton Chekhov so desperately wanted to discover: we now understand what smoking and eating really means without losing the theatricality of such actions. Repression as a form of action helped us to work on these situations by considering the actor's body as the divided subject.

Notes

1 The Escuela de Teatro de Buenos Aires (ETBA) was opened by Raúl Serrano in 1981. He has served as its director since then. Central to the Escuela's work is the implementation of an efficient technical training that accompanies the creative and artistic development of each student. The idea of 'systematic training' for performance is actively developed. ETBA gives students the tools to practice acting in different media (theatre, film, TV), with a methodology that can be traced back to Stanislavsky's method of physical actions but which Serrano has today developed in an autonomous way. http://www.etbaonline.com.ar/nosotros.html [accessed 26 June 2015].

Part Four

Africa

Figure 28 Stanislavsky in Africa.

Part Four: Introduction

Stefan Aquilina

In between binaries and paradoxes: Stanislavsky in Africa

Scholarship about theatre and performance in Africa is often framed in ways that overshadows actor training practices on the African continent. Recurrent themes around which such scholarship is organized include applied and community based theatre and performance (sometimes referred to as Theatre for Development), socio-political playwriting, indigenous performance, and theatre companies' operation. Consequently, training histories and explorations are, in such sources, consistently conspicuous by their absence.[1]

It is the African volume of *The World Encyclopaedia of Contemporary Theatre* which, in line with its other volumes, features sections about training for some (though not all) of its entries. As expected, it is the larger countries that feature the most developed descriptions. Actor training in Africa shows a conglomeration of training approaches, from the master-apprenticeship models of indigenous performance realities (such as in the societies of Sande and Poro in Liberia and the Bambara in Mali), to state-funded or 'national' theatre schools (e.g. the Guinean School of Theatre, or Zaïre's Conservatoire Nationale de Musique et d' Art Dramatique) and the widespread practice of 'learning through doing' or 'learning on the job'. Universities are also important training centres, especially in South Africa (Ebewo, 2011). The essays on Stanislavsky in Africa within this volume, authored by Kene Igweonu (on Nigeria), Moez Mrabet (Tunisia), and David Peimer (South Africa), acknowledge these differences. While, of course, their essays cannot be considered representative of a continent which has a population of 1.1 billion people spread in 52 countries and across a vast diversity of ethnicities and cultures, the authors do offer concrete case-studies that critique would-be applications of 'Stanislavsky's system in its *unalloyed* form' (p. 282; emphasis in the original).

Recurring throughout the three essays is the awareness of a binary mode of organizing phenomena, such as colonizer/colonized, Western/African, and civilized/indigenous. These binaries were assigned by colonial forces in order to organize life in its many forms, and which post-colonial forces would then seek to critique. Homi Bhabha's work, for example, has provided 'valuable assistance in dismantling binaries (and their correlative power structures) by recognizing their inevitable ambivalences' (Gilbert and Tompkins, 2002, p. 6). Stanislavsky is caught within this colonial/postcolonial discourse. While the authors in this part do not go as far as asserting an end to binary thinking in relation to actor training – perhaps because reconciliation of diverse embodied practices within live and bodily experience is more complex than reconciliations in dramatic and staging practices – the essays do tantalizingly suggest possible future scenarios which Peimer describes as 'a notion of a possible but not yet born hybridity' (p. 310). Mrabet, for example, uses the helpful image of the 'crossroad' to place Stanislavsky within the context of contemporary Tunisian theatre which, he believes, has inherited the markedly dualistic framework of East/West, Professional/Amateur, Oral/Written, Actor-as-Creator/Actor-as-Imitator. He argues that these binaries are today being challenged at such institutions as the Institut Supérieur d'Art Dramatique, which adopts a critical approach wherein Stanislavsky's ideas are not blindly accepted but sifted through various angles that include scientific research, practical work, and historical contextualization.

A critical approach to Stanislavsky's ideas is also seen in the work of Fadel Jaïbi who, Mrabet argues, does not follow dogmatically any of Stanislavsky's tenets but actually seeks his own creative direction which, paradoxically, leads him to discover the system's principles. Such a paradoxical path also emerges in other essays. The term 'paradox' has both literary and philosophical resonances, as well as everyday uses that imply 'contradiction'. What interests me here are the startling and reconciliatory potentialities inherent in paradoxes. Chris Baldick describes paradoxes as having a sense of the unexpected, one that is 'so surprisingly self-contradictory as to provoke us into seeking another sense or context in which it would be true'. In this sense, a paradox defamiliarizes phenomena and 'challenges our habits of thought' (Baldick, 2008, p. 265). A paradox also resolves opposites, entailing the analysis of seemingly contradictory elements in order to bring forward their possible reconciliation. It is not a divisive instrument, but one that revels in incongruity and irony to create open rather than narrow interpretations (Wallace, 2011, p. 15).

The paradoxes evident in the essays not only draw attention to unexpected uses of Stanislavsky's system but also create fluidity between binary oppositions. For example, it is by employing a paradoxical methodology that Peimer transforms Stanislavsky's 'emotional memory exercises' to make them workable for his context. Theatre in South Africa, before and after the apartheid, was (and is) visibly pervaded by its context (see Hauptfleisch, 1997, p. 270 and p. 274). The paradox is evident in Peimer's recollections of the work on *Hamlet*, where instead of foregrounding the context, attention was shifted away from the lived trauma of murder in South Africa to the actors' banal everyday memories, like an accident with a cat, or the disposal of some CDs. Ironically, this led to the rediscovery of the context, and a fluidity between the apparent dichotomies of banality and depth. A second example in Peimer's essay also underlines this paradoxical appropriation (and transformation) of Stanislavsky's Emotion Memory. Whereas Stanislavsky would ask the actor to recall personal emotion memories, the example of an actor whose father had passed away sees that same actor recall 'notions of community' (p. 312), not to transpose these on the stage but to immerse himself in the character's emotions, objectives, and given circumstances. The fluidity in this case is evident in the movement from communal awareness to individual characterization, apparent binaries which, however, are brought closer together within this particular moment of praxis.[2] Igweonu, on his part, hints at a paradoxical approach when he argues that in Nigeria Stanislavsky initially featured in the White-only universities but later became a shared language and a basis on which the diversity of indigenous performance could find a common ground. Consequently, the use of the system as means to delineate hierarchies is transformed in an approach that actively seeks to find a common terminology and understanding, in a way which was also attempted by Stanislavsky himself towards the end of his life (Benedetti in Stanislavski, 2008, p. xviii).

In line with the aims and objectives of the book, the essays collected in this part also contribute to diversify the heavily Americanized line that characterized twentieth-century studies on Stanislavsky's transmission across the world. For example, Mrabet's essay on Stanislavsky in Tunisia underlines the French line and adds mileage to Marie-Christine Autant-Mathieu's own reading about French interpretations of Stanislavsky (see Part One: Europe). Both Autant-Mathieu and Mrabet signal the role played by Jean Vilar in France and, through a transmission path that was advanced by French colonization, in Tunisia. Igweonu, on his part, localizes the first traces of a Stanislavskian presence in Nigeria to Martin Banham and Geoffrey Axworthy, two British expats who had affiliations with the University of London, and then to Joel Adedeji, a 1962 graduate of Rose Bruford Training College of Speech and Drama and eventual director of the School of Drama at the University College Ibadan. In his essay on Stanislavsky's passage into the British conservatoire, David Shirley notes that Stanislavsky-informed workshops had featured at Rose Bruford from the 1950s, even though there is very little tangible information about the actual contents of these sessions (in Pitches, 2012, p. 56). A similar lack of archival information does posit a challenge in the reconstruction of Stanislavsky-informed practices on the African continent, contrasting with the plethora of material that was sourced for Pitches and Li's essay on the Shanghai Theatre Academy, for instance (see Part Two: China and Japan). An alternative research methodology is that of the oral testament, or what Yvette Hutchinson refers to as 'embodied cultural archives' which, interestingly enough, she describes as 'a way to begin breaking down some of the old binaries that have existed between oral and literary traditions, and place these in increasing dialogue with one another' (Hutchinson, 2010, p. xii). The essays in this part answer such a call in different ways and to different degrees, to posit that their main contribution to Stanislavsky scholarship lies in the critique they make of conventional binary thinking.

Notes

1 The James Currey *African Theatre* series (1999–2013) is particularly representative of these categories. Its issues have featured volumes titled *Playwrights and Politics, Women, Southern Africa, Soyinka: Blackout, Blowout and Beyond, Youth, Companies, Diasporas, Histories 1850–1950, Media and Performance, Festivals*, and *Shakespeare*. See also: Rohmer (1999), Breitinger (2003), Dugga (2002), Hutchinson and Breitinger (2000), and Igweonu (2011).

2 See also the various instances when Peimer discusses a fluidity between the contrasting poles of periphery and centre.

References

Baldick, C. (2008), *The Oxford Dictionary of Literary Terms*. Oxford: Oxford University Press.

Breitinger, E. (ed.) (2003), *Theatre and Performance in Africa – Intercultural Perspectives*. Bayreuth: Bayreuth African Studies 31.

Dugga, V. S. (2002), *Creolisations in Nigerian Theatre*. Bayreuth: Bayreuth African Studies 61.

Ebewo, P. (2011), 'Transformation and the Drama Studies Curriculum in South Africa: A Survey of Selected Universities', in *Trends in Twenty-First Century African Theatre and Performance*, ed. K. Igweonu. Amsterdam, New York: Rodopi, pp. 113–38.

Gilbert, H. and Tompkins, J. (2002), *Post-colonial drama: theory, practice, politics*. London and New York: Routledge.

Hauptfleisch, T. (1997), 'South Africa', in *The World Encyclopedia of Contemporary Theatre, Vol. 3 Africa*, eds O. Diakhaté and H. N. Eyoh. London and New York: Routledge, pp. 268–98.

Hutchinson, Y. (2010), 'Introduction', in *African Theatre Histories 1850–1950*, ed. Y. Hutchison. Suffolk: James Curry, pp. xi–xvi.

Hutchinson, Y. and Breitinger, E. (2000), *History and Theatre in Africa*. Bayreuth: Bayreuth African Studies 50/South African Theatre Journal 13.

Igweonu, K. (ed.) (2011), *Trends in Twenty-First Century African Theatre and Performance*. Amsterdam, New York: Rodopi.

Pitches, J. (ed.) (2012), *Russians in Britain*. Oxon: Routledge.

Rohmer, M. (1999), *Theatre and Performance in Zimbabwe*. Bayreuth: Bayreuth African Studies 49.

Stanislavski, K. (2008), *An Actor's Work*, trans. J. Benedetti. Oxon: Routledge.

Wallace, J. (2011), *Beginning Modernism*. Manchester: Manchester University Press.

12

Stanislavsky in Nigeria: Convergences and Counterpoints in Actor Training and Practice

Kene Igweonu

Introduction: Enter Stanislavsky

> I had been trained in Stanislavskian procedures by Robert McLaren and, as it is the nature of grand narratives to be perpetuated by their recipients, I myself began to teach and practice the psycho-system to my students.
>
> Ravengai, 2011, pp. 37–8

Although Samuel Ravengai's statement quoted above is in reference to his introduction to the Stanislavskian approach to actor training in his native Zimbabwe by McLaren – a South African dramatist who, in 1984, was appointed to teach the first drama course in the Faculty of Arts at the University of Zimbabwe long before the establishment of a formal drama department in 1992 (Plastow, 1996, p. 172) – it bears direct relevance to the advent and the place of Stanislavsky in the Nigerian theatre environment. Without a tradition of drama schools that is similar to what obtains in Britain for instance, the arrival of Stanislavsky's system of actor training to Nigeria can be traced to the establishment of the University College Ibadan (now University of Ibadan) in 1948 as a college of the University of London. Even though the School of Drama, the first academic department of its kind in Nigeria, did not open until 1962 (it was renamed in 1970 and became the Department of Theatre Arts), developments at Nigeria's premier university during the mid-1950s created the fertile ground on which Stanislavsky was introduced into Nigeria. Central to this introduction was the arrival, to the university, of British expatriates like Martin Banham and Geoffrey Axworthy to teach in the Department of English.

Driven by their interest and dedication to the theatre and encouraged by the building of the university's Arts Theatre as a concert and performance venue in 1955, both men set to work organizing and producing a number of amateur productions with active participation of the student-led University College Dramatic Society and staff-led Arts Theatre Production Group. They also organized and led a series of theatre workshops for students of the Department of English, the Department of Extra-Mural Studies, and the Institute of Education, which eventually led to a recommendation in the 1961 Visitation Panel Report into the affairs of the University College Ibadan to the effect that theatre should 'not be left any longer to "enthusiastic volunteers", but should be organized properly as an academic discipline' (University of Ibadan, n.d., para. 2).

With the inception of the School of Drama in 1962, both Axworthy and Banham were reassigned from the Department of English to the new School to serve as its founding Director and Deputy Director respectively. Both men had evidenced their strong commitment to theatre through their productions and workshops and the new School was the university's acknowledgement of the importance of drama as an academic discipline in its own right. Before founding the School of Drama in 1962, Axworthy and Banham had not concerned themselves with actor training per se. Their focus had mainly been on directing and producing the plays they organized with their group of enthusiastic volunteer actors. However, the School of Drama provided the opportunity to begin a systematic training of Nigerian actors in line with European models of actor training and thus it marks the formal arrival of Stanislavsky's system of actor training into Nigeria.

Notable in the transmission of Stanislavsky's system of actor training to students in the School of Drama was the appointment of Joel Adedeji in 1964. Adedeji attended a drama school in Britain from 1959, graduating from the Rose Bruford Training College of Speech and Drama in 1962 (now known as Rose Bruford College of Theatre and Performance). Coming from Rose Bruford, which was established in 1950 with the mission of training 'actors who could teach and teachers who could act' (Rose Bruford, n.d., para. 1), Adedeji inevitably became a key strategic conduit through which the teaching and practice of Stanislavsky's system of actor training entered Nigeria. To return momentarily to Ravengai's statement cited at the start of this essay, 'as it is the nature of grand narratives to be perpetuated by their recipients,' some of students who graduated from the School of Drama at Ibadan went on to teach and practice aspects of the system as they had learnt it as more universities were established throughout Nigeria over the years that followed. The precise details of what was taught as Stanislavsky's system is sketchy and would require further research to unpick. What is clear is that some ideas were more common than others, with those that emphasize psychological realism being more prevalent in transmission and practice than those that privilege physical actions. The attitude to Stanislavsky's arrival in Nigeria is, at least on face value, similar to what David Shirley describes in his discussion of its reception in Britain. Shirley opines that '[i]n a conventionalized theatre culture where actors' performances tended to be driven by a preoccupation with the external manifestations of "gesture" and "manners", the insistence on an "inner reality" – the source of which springs from the imagination – must have appeared extraordinarily innovative and radical' (Shirley, 2012, p. 39). Indigenous performances in Nigeria conventionally take place in communal and open space arenas, resulting in styles of acting that can be described as gestural, presentational and often melodramatic. The introduction of Stanislavsky within this environment, particularly aspects of his system that emphasizes psychological realism as detailed in his book *An Actor Prepares* (1936), provided a unique opportunity to deepen the actor's work in interpreting a role for performance. In transmission and practice, the focus on dimensions of the system that emphasizes psychological realism mainly takes the form of exercises on concentration, circles of attention, the magic 'if', and emotion memory.

Another significant development in the transmission of Stanislavsky's system of actor training to Nigeria was the founding of the School of Drama Acting Company in 1967 as resident company of the School of Drama at University of Ibadan, with Geoffrey Axworthy combining his directorship of the School of Drama with that of the new company (the company was later disbanded in 1971 and reconstituted in 1974 as the Unibadan Masques). Soon after its founding Axworthy left Nigeria and returned to England following the commencement of the 1967–70 Nigeria/Biafra civil war. Axworthy was succeeded in both positions by Wole Soyinka who was nevertheless unable to take up his appointment having been arrested and detained without trial by the then military junta of General Yakubu Gowon for his political activism aimed at averting the civil war. Soyinka was later to return to take up this appointment on his release from prison at the end of the civil war in 1970. In the interim K. W. Dexter Lyndersay, a Trinidadian émigré took on the role of director of the company. This marked another significant development in the transmission of Stanislavsky in Nigeria. Up till Lyndersay's appointment, Stanislavsky's influence had been mainly transmitted through England (Rose Bruford), but now also through America and by extension Strasberg as Lyndersay had his BFA from Chicago's Art Institute and an MFA from Yale (Gibbs, 2008, p. xi).

Today Nigeria boasts a significant number of talented actors, directors, and theatre scholars who work on the cutting edge of a creative sector that gave rise to Nollywood, often described as the second largest film industry in the world. Without prejudice to multifarious approaches to performance training and practices that are indigenous to Nigeria, Stanislavskian principles remain, by far, the most recognized and acknowledged approach to contemporary actor training and practice in the country. Thus this essay offers a reflection of some of the many ways in which those working in educational and theatre training institutions in Nigeria, as well as on the stage and film, are engaged in applying and transmitting Stanislavsky's principles through their work. As I have begun to show, the essay explores the transmission of Stanislavsky's principles for actor training to Nigeria from the mid-twentieth century, and how it has been taught, propagated, and sustained since introduction to Nigeria. It concludes by arguing that Nigerian institutions of further and higher education retain their roles as fertile grounds for the propagation of Stanislavsky today. At the same time, they reveal the many convergences and counterpoints evident in Stanislavsky's interaction with the Nigerian cultural environment as they transform, appropriate, and sometime challenge conventional ways of thinking about Stanislavsky's legacy.

Stanislavsky and the postcolonial actor

The dominance of Stanislavskian-based approaches to acting and actor training in the West throughout the twentieth century has often meant that acting and actor training are approached in terms of how to play a character in a textually based drama with an emphasis on the actor as an 'interpreter' of a role. As we well know from Stanislavsky, the process of interpreting a role engages the actor in a highly creative, psychophysical process that culminates in actualizing and 'living' or 'experiencing' that role as fully as possible on stage.

Zarrilli, Daboo, and Loukes, 2013, p. 7

In her introduction to *Actor Training*, the influential book she edited in 2010, Alison Hodge writes about Stanislavsky's 'initial project' of developing 'a single, universal system [. . .] which would contain a complete method of actor training' (Hodge, 2010, p. xxiv). However, she is quick to acknowledge that 'later practitioners resisted the notion of anything as absolute as a universally applied method' (Hodge, 2010, p. xxiv). Even though Western influences continue to pervade contemporary actor training and education in general in Africa, the idea that Western meta-narratives can be resisted or deconstructed remains a recurrent theme in African postcolonial deportment. Martin Banham, Errol Hill, and George Woodyard note, for instance,

> The influence of Western-style education continues to determine elements of theatrical form and language in much contemporary drama, but here again we can see playwrights and performers working increasingly on their own terms and asserting a powerful cultural and political identity. Theatre in many parts of Africa has been at the forefront of the anti-colonial struggle, and has not relaxed its sense of purpose in the post-independence world.
>
> Banham et al., 1994, p. 3

The search for training methodologies for the postcolonial actor gave rise to debates about the need to Africanize the curriculum in the South African context for instance (Ebewo, 2011). While this essay does not seek to engage in a discussion of the politics of Africanization and the debates that surround it, it is useful to point out that the education system in Nigeria, as in the rest of Africa, is modelled after Western prototypes. As products of the colonial enterprise in Africa, universities in their unmediated forms retain the unenviable history of privileging Western forms of knowledge over indigenous systems.

In making his case for the development of an Africanized curriculum, Ebewo acknowledges this much when he argues that South African universities 'modeled themselves on the best of the European and American ivy-league universities and benchmarked their practices based on what obtained outside the African continent' (Ebewo, 2011, p. 133). He identifies the call for Africanization of the South African school syllabus as a direct result of what he terms a 'paradigm shift from Eurocentric model to a novel model that places Africa in the centre of things' (Ebewo, 2011, p. 115). While Ebewo wrote with respect to the South African higher education context, it still remains the case that the university system in Nigeria continues to operate along the same principle as the Western institutions they derive from or were set up to emulate. However, whereas in South Africa, the country's post-apartheid government legislated against undue bias for Western systems of knowledge as part of their Africanization or transformation agenda, the same cannot be said about Nigeria where the education system continues to be modelled after their Western derivations, albeit with apparent contradictions at the level of implementation. The implication of this development for actor training in Nigeria is quite profound and accounts for the absence of an enduring methodology for actor training that is systemic in its articulation.

A key difficulty in the search for actor training methodologies most suited to those I refer to as postcolonial actors – who work with syncretic forms that are deeply influenced by Western practice – is that the exploration of such an approach is largely underdeveloped. While there is no corresponding attempt to Africanize the actor training curriculum in Nigeria, it is evidently the case that practitioners approach Stanislavsky from various standpoints that privilege numerous principles drawn from the indigenous performance milieu, as well as a range of other approaches from Brecht to Grotowski and Barba. As a result of the multifarious approach to actor training and performance in Nigeria, today one is unlikely to find practitioners, or indeed institutions, advancing Stanislavsky's system in its *unalloyed* form. Ravengai, who is one of those at the forefront of the quest to evolve an actor training methodology that speaks more directly to the African postcolonial context asks, and writes as follows: 'The question is how do acting trainers empower actors with respect to their cultural bodies?' (Ravengai, 2011, p. 36). It is however worth noting that Ravengai's work in this area is not about developing a system to rival or replace Stanislavsky's, instead it is in line with Hodge's acknowledgement that 'ultimately, practitioners have eschewed the notion of a comprehensive system in favour of identifying first *principles* within their own particular contexts' (Hodge, 2010, p. xxv).

In another essay titled 'The politics of theatre and performance training in Zimbabwe 1980–1996,' Ravengai underscores Robert Kavanagh's identification of elements of Stanislavsky's system such as 'relaxation, concentration, sincerity, observation, imagination, improvisation skills and ensemble' (Kavanagh cited in Ravengai, 2014, p. 266) as being fundamental in actor training. However, in highlighting this Ravengai puts forward a very important argument about the place of Stanislavsky in the training of the postcolonial actor who is simultaneously at one performing in indigenous as well as Western forms of theatre:

> The above list constitutes more than half of the elements of the psycho-technique, a clear testimony of the centrality of Stanislavsky in the African actor training technique. In this actor training method, the indigenous performance technique, the psycho-technique and the rehearsal run simultaneously. The result of this creative recombination of techniques is the creation of a non-actor, but an actor/singer/dancer or, in short, a performer.
> Ravengai, 2014, p. 266

It is therefore this 'creative recombination of techniques' as Ravengai puts it that characterizes the postcolonial actor. Nigerian actors clearly fall within the ambit of what I describe as postcolonial actors. Not only are Nigerian actors and actor trainers influenced by a wide range of Western approaches that includes Stanislavsky, but they also blur the boundaries further by embracing indigenous principles in the desire to make their work relevant within their particular cultural contexts.

This blurring of boundaries in the transmission of Stanislavsky through educational institutions can be traced to arrangements that came with the opening of the School of Drama at Ibadan. The admission of Kola Ogunmola as the 'first student in residence' (University of Ibadan, n.d., para. 3) saw him produce and direct the first stage adaptation of Amos Tutuola's 1952 novel, *The Palm-Wine Drinkard* in 1963. The production made use of actors who were not only encountering Stanislavsky for the first time at the School of Drama, but were in a unique position to combine this new influence with what they already knew of Yoruba folk music and dance tradition and practices. At that time in 1963 Ogunmola was already recognized as a prominent Nigerian dramatist; as an actor and artistic director of Ogunmola Traveling Theatre, which he founded in 1947. While concrete details of a Yoruba-Stanislavsky combination remains elusive, a helpful parallel with Yana Elsa Brugal's and Luis Campos' research in African-Caribbean Yoruba rituals (Brugal and Campos, 2015; see also Part 3, Cuba) gives precious indication of the synergies involved. Yoruba rituals are described as offering a dynamic mix of elements that create highly interdisciplinary events. Music and dance have a 'heightened presence', while 'man and gods' mix together 'in the magic-religious system'. Religious rituals of African origin, therefore, include 'several disciplines with the aim of achieving powerful transcendental purposes' (Brugal and Campos, 2015, p. 20 and p. 21). Yoruba practices, therefore, suggests an interdisciplinary bedrock that is not alien to the possible layering of psychophysical 'training of artists that have incorporated into their practices the cultural and theatrical heritage in which Stanislavski is a constant point of reference' (Brugal and Campos, 2015, p. 19).

Another key area for this blurring of boundaries can be seen in what Ruru Li, in her article on performance training in Beijing Opera (*Jingju*), identifies as a divergence between the concerns of Western and Eastern actor training. This divergence is most evident in Li's contention that 'contemporary Western training is concerned more with the individual actor than with set exercises for the whole group' (Li, 2012, p. 8). Like the examples used by Ruru to illustrate the training in *Jingju*, *set exercises* for the whole group within the Nigerian context manifest in the form of dance, movement, and music drawn from indigenous performance forms and practices. Because they derive directly from, and are informed by, indigenous principles these group exercises or embodied practices help to transform the actors' bodies in ways that situate their performances within the ambit of their Nigerian performative culture and background. The postcolonial actor, even when alone on the stage, is not seen as an individual but as an artistic embodiment of the collective – showcasing the transformation from a 'personal I' to a 'performer I' (Li, 2012, p. 8).

Stanislavsky in Nigeria: transmission and practice

Ravengai identifies with Diana Belshaw's concern regarding the importance of developing a framework or training model that could be useful for working with students from different cultural backgrounds. Ravengai's interest in developing a framework for actor training that speak more directly to the postcolonial actor can also be seen in his adoption of Belshaw's statement in which she asks, 'Even if she has produced work of unique quality, [...] "where was the training that made it possible?"' (Belshaw cited in Ravengai, 2011, p. 37).

The arrival of Stanislavsky in Nigeria is no doubt connected with the creation, in 1962, of the School of Drama by the then University College Ibadan. However, its persistence as a key approach to actor training derives from its perceived usefulness and relevance for the Nigerian actor. Part of the rationale is that Stanislavsky provides a useful structure for understanding and articulating the diversity of indigenous performance forms and traditions that inform the work of the Nigerian actor. This is especially significant when one considers that Nigeria is made up of well over two hundred different ethnicities. As such, for a country like Nigeria, the role and importance of Stanislavsky's system of actor training as a unifying framework for understanding and articulating the diverse principles drawn from indigenous milieus cannot be overlooked. In the Nigerian actor training context some of the fundamental features of Stanislavsky's system such as magic 'if', circles of attention, concentration, and emotional memory serve very important roles as unifying frameworks on which indigenous principles drawn from the various ethnic performance traditions hang. These features are often appropriated in ways that serve the indigenous performance principles and knowledge already developed by the actors. Some of these indigenous principles derive from training in dance, oratory, song, and masquerade traditions of various Nigerian ethnic groups. The transmission of these performance principles is often conveyed as part of group activities marking the transition from one life stage to another or of belonging to particular age, ancestral, or cultural groups.

The primary vehicles for transmitting these appropriated practices of Stanislavsky in Nigeria are the various public and private institutions of further and higher education, which remains the most productive environment for its propagation. Educational institutions across the country teaching acting today owe their existence to the establishment of the School of Drama at Ibadan in 1962 and some of the people that graduated from the School of Drama at Ibadan have gone on to teach and establish similar departments at other institutions throughout Nigeria. However, one key thing of note in the approach to actor training in most of the educational institutions is that Stanislavsky is not always clearly evident in the delivery of the curriculum. Instead it is often subsumed in the group exercises drawn from indigenous performance forms and traditions. These group exercises often take the form of improvisation exercises where students are mirroring and feeding off each other's knowledge and creativity in conveying aspects of various indigenous performance principles in a format akin to call and response. Moreover, much of the training at early stages are transmitted through participation in student-led induction rehearsals and productions, through working with senior students and staff directors in the rehearsal of departmental productions rather than through acting classes led by tutors, reminiscent of apprentice or trainee performers under the indigenous oral performance traditions.

Another important avenue for transmitting Stanislavsky in Nigeria is through the outright adoption of an apprenticeship model for actors working with theatre groups, national and state theatre troupes, as well as those working in the film industry known as Nollywood. Some of the performers working in these contexts, particularly those working with national and state theatre troupes, would most often be trained and well versed in indigenous performance practices but would not necessarily have encountered Stanislavsky in any recognizable form. However, an increasing number of theatre graduates who are taking up roles within these theatre troupes are transmitting their knowledge of Stanislavsky to troupe members through rehearsal and continuous professional development. More recently the Lufodo Academy of Performing Arts evolved out of the stage and film production company incorporated in 2000 by the renowned Nollywood couple, Olu Jacobs and Joke Silver with the vision of becoming 'the foremost acting academy in Africa' (Lufodo Academy of Performing Arts, 2015). In addition to being a much-celebrated Nollywood star, Jacobs is considered as a suitable conduit for transmitting Stanislavsky more credibly as a graduate of The Royal Academy of Dramatic Arts, London.

Even though Nollywood acting is often melodramatic, it provides an interesting contrast to what obtains in theatre productions at the various educational institutions in Nigeria. As a consequence the melodramatic acting in Nollywood movies often result in characters that are not believable and thus reinforce the view that the actors are not trained or familiar with Stanislavsky. For instance, in a recent interview with Ademola Olonilua, Nobert Young, a graduate of the University of Ibadan theatre arts course and one of the earlier generation of Nollywood actors protests, 'I have stayed away from home videos because I believe most of the actors do not have enough training. [...] Most of the newer generation of actors are very shallow. They do not know what characterization is. And if you do not know what that is, then you are not an actor as far as I am concerned' (Olonilua, 2015). On his part Noah A. Tsika laments what he considers the inclination of Nollywood actors to 'flout the determinants of realist acting, safe in the assumption that the industry's formats will do their work for them' (Tsika, 2015, p. 82). Despite their pessimism, however, it is increasingly the case that Nollywood actors are made up of theatre graduates from further and higher educational institutions in Nigeria who would have experienced Stanislavsky in one form or the other during their training. So on the contrary, I would argue that it is the nature of the cultural and commercial dynamics of the Nigerian movie industry that Nollywood actors approach character roles the way they do.

Conclusion

In Nigeria, as elsewhere in Africa, the lack of treatises on Stanislavskian actor training, particularly the practice of integrating indigenous principles, impede enquiry on the subject, but it equally presents an opportunity for a level of inquiry that goes beyond the scope of the present chapter. In his introduction to *Russians in Britain: British Theatre and the Russian Tradition of Actor Training* Jonathan Pitches identifies the three broad mechanisms of transmission as training places, theatre spaces, and documentation sources (Pitches, 2012, p. 4). While this chapter has explored the transmission of Stanislavsky to Nigeria primarily through the first mechanism, a further consideration of the other two mechanisms is necessary to build a more complete picture of the place of Stanislavsky in Nigerian actor training.

Nigerian institutions of further and higher education, theatre groups, and Nollywood retain their roles as fertile grounds for the propagation of Stanislavskian approaches. However, the dynamics of actor training in Nigeria is such that they attest to the many creative convergences and counterpoints evident in Stanislavsky's interaction with the Nigerian theatre practice as practitioners and teachers transform, appropriate, and sometimes challenge conventional ways of thinking about Stanislavsky's legacy of systemic actor training. Despite the incorporation of various indigenous principles to performance training and practices in Nigeria, the Stanislavskian approach and influence remains palpable in present day actor training and practice.

References

Banham, M., Hill, E. and Woodyard, G. (eds) (1994), 'Introduction', in *The Cambridge Guide to African and Caribbean Theatre*. Cambridge: CUP, pp. 3–14.

Bartow, A. (2008), *Handbook of Acting Techniques*. London: Nick Hern Books.

Brugal, Y. E. and Campos, L. (2015), 'A Stanislavskian Reading of Yoruba Trance on the Stage', *Stanislavski Studies*, Vol. 3, No. 1: 17–30.

Ebewo, P. (2011), 'Transformation and the drama studies curriculum in South Africa: a survey of selected universities', in *Trends in Twenty-First Century African Theatre and Performance*, ed. K. Igweonu. Amsterdam: Rodopi, pp. 113–38.

Gibbs, J. (ed.) (2008), 'K. W. Dexter Lyndersay, 1932–2006', in *African Theatre Companies*. Suffolk: James Currey, p. xi.

Hodge, A. (ed.) (2010), *Actor Training – 2nd Edition*. London: Routledge.

Li, R. (2012), 'Singing, speaking, dance-acting, and combat; mouth, hands, eyes, body, and steps – from training to performance in Beijing Opera (Jingju)', *Theatre, Dance and Performance Training*, Vol. 3, No. 1: 4–26, DOI: 10.1080/19443927.2011.646293.

Lufodo Academy of Performing Arts (2015), 'Vision and Mission'. Available at: http://www.lapanig.com/vision.html [accessed 5 February 2015].

Ogunleye, F. (2008), 'Ori Olokun Theatre & the Town & Gown Policy: Enthusiastic Amateurs, Farmers, Carpenters & School Teachers ', in *African Theatre: Companies*, ed. J. Gibbs. London: James Currey, pp. 16–26.

Olonilua, A. (2015), 'No big deal in another man kissing my wife – Nobert Young', in *Punch Newspapers,* [online] 28 March. Available at: http://www.punchng.com/feature/super-saturday-lounge/no-big-deal-in-another-man-kissing-my-wife-nobert-young/ [accessed 12 May 2015].

Pitches, J. (2012), 'Introduction: the mechanics of tradition making', in *Russians in Britain: British Theatre and the Russian Tradition of Actor Training*, ed. J. Pitches. London: Routledge, pp. 1–12.

Plastow, J. (1996), *African Theatre and Politics: The Evolution of Theatre in Ethiopia, Tanzania and Zimbabwe*. Amsterdam: Rodopi.

Ravengai, S. (2011), 'The dilemma of the African body as a site of performance in the context of western training', in *Trends in Twenty-First Century African Theatre and Performance*, ed. K. Igweonu. Amsterdam: Rodopi, pp. 35–60.

Ravengai, S. (2014), 'The politics of theatre and performance training in Zimbabwe 1980–1996', *Theatre, Dance and Performance Training*, Vol. 5, No. 3: 255–69, DOI: 10.1080/19443927.2014.944717.

Rose Bruford (n.d.), 'Our History'. Available online: https://www.bruford.ac.uk/about/our-history/ [accessed 5 February 2015].

Shirley, D. (2012), 'Stanislavsky's passage into the British conservatoire', in *Russians in Britain: British Theatre and the Russian Tradition of Actor Training*, ed. J. Pitches. London: Routledge, pp. 38–61.

Tsika, N. A. (2015), *Nollywood Stars: Media and Migration in West Africa and the Diaspora*. Indiana: Indiana University Press.

University of Ibadan (n.d.), 'History: Department of Theatre Arts'. Available online: http://arts.ui.edu.ng/historythea [accessed 5 February 2015].

Watson, I. (ed.) (2001), *Performer Training: Developments Across Cultures*. London: Routledge.

Zarrilli, P. (2009), *Psychophysical Acting: An Intercultural Approach after Stanislavsky*. Oxon: Routledge.

Zarrilli, P., Daboo, J. and Loukes, R. (2013), *Acting: Psychophysical Phenomenon and Process*. Basingstoke: Palgrave Macmillan.

13

Stanislavsky in Tunisian Theatre: a Heritage in Progress

Moez Mrabet

Where can the place of Tunisian theatre be situated on the map of the Stanislavsky System? Was Tunisian theatre able to draw benefit from the Stanislavskian 'manna', just as other theatres did? And if yes, in what way? What place would Stanislavsky's ideas occupy in contemporary Tunisian theatre? This essay will set to answer such questions and more. Any research aiming to throw light on these aspects would certainly help to penetrate the mystery of a relationship that remains obscure and tightly sealed. Given the significant role played by Tunisian theatre within the context of Arab theatre and its diverse experiences, Tunisia can certainly be considered as a privileged case-study. In spite of a history that is barely a hundred years old, but thanks to its dynamism and its ability to open up to approaches coming from both East and West, this theatre can boast of a rich, clearly-developed aesthetic and technical experience and practice. A study aiming to understand better the role played by the ideas of the 'father of modern theatre' in the development of this theatrical experience is certainly exciting, but also fraught with pitfalls.

The reference points that frame the following study are:

- The dynamics underlying the evolution of Tunisian theatre, which is based on an emulation of the founding ideas of contemporary theatre practice. At the root of the 'theatrical revolution' which marked the last century, Stanislavsky's ideas seem to be, in this respect, inescapable in the understanding of the ins and outs of this revolution.
- The attention given to the actor's work in Tunisian theatre and the search for a better understanding of the aesthetics and techniques determining

this expressive field. This led to an inevitable 'contamination' in the theatre of a Stanislavskian approach.

- Supported by an effort towards professionalizing the theatre scene, and aiming to tackle the 'excesses' and 'shortcomings' of the founding period of Tunisian theatre, the development of a theatre-training tradition since the 1950s appears, moreover, as one of the highlights of an alleged filial relationship between theatre in Tunisia and the ideas of the Russian master. The study of this aspect would undoubtedly give some form of answers to the issues that arose.

Some key ideas will emerge from this study about the convergence of Tunisian theatre and the Stanislavskian precepts. First is the connection in the tradition of French acting of Stanislavsky and the Tunisian theatre. While Stanislavsky's point of view on this 'francophiled' school of acting was both appreciative and critical, the strong impact on Tunisian theatre – especially when this was on the road to professionalization – by this school suggests a necessary mediation between this theatre and the Stanislavskian approach. The essay will argue that after having adopted, for a time, a style of acting based on the notion of 'actor-imitator', defended by Denis Diderot in his *Paradox of the Actor*, it is the notion of the 'actor-creator', dear to Stanislavsky, which seems – amongst others – to have inspired the Tunisian theatre to break with the tradition of the classical theatre in the late 1970s.

The Tunisian travels of Stanislavsky's ideas can be identified from a study of the transmission process – oral and bookish – which shaped them. This process unveils a complex topography where Western and Middle-Eastern influences are juxtaposed. Yet, while it is difficult to retrace a direct transmission (of master to student), the transmission path from the books seems to be marked better and more accessible. However, this should not divert us from a field survey to assess the direct impact of these ideas on theatre practice. Concrete examples could be used in this regard, such as case-studies.

But before addressing these questions, we will first concern ourselves with situating our study in the general context of the evolution of Tunisian theatre. We will then dwell on significant affiliations between Stanislavsky's ideas and Tunisian theatre, particularly through a reference to several significant examples such as the experiences of pedagogue Mohammed Abdelaziz Agrebi, directors Aly Ben Ayed and Fadhel Jaïbi, actors' training programmes, and scientific research.

At the crossroads

The development of Tunisian theatre, the beginnings of which are usually dated to 26 May 1909,[1] occurred at a time when Western theatre tradition was undergoing a period of intense development and change. A break with classic aesthetics (see below) was being advocated and a new practice was being established that placed the director as the 'moving force' of artistic creation, giving rise to a new thinking on the art of the actor, particularly in how to make him the main tool in the elaboration of the creative act. Russian theatre, through Stanislavsky and his experience at the Moscow Art Theatre, but also the experiences of Meiningen in Germany, Edward Gordon Craig in England, André Antoine, Jacques Delsarte, and Antonin Artaud in France, contributed to the emergence of new ideas and practices and opened the way to other 'territories' that were still uncharted within the art of the theatre.

The nascent Tunisian theatre was started by the Tunisian intelligentsia as a vehicle to engage society in the path of modernization. It seemed, however, rather distant from the 'upheaval' that Western theatre was undergoing. The major interest of this elite was to exploit theatre's capacity to mobilize the masses and use it as a means to free the people from the colonial yoke, as well as to affirm a national identity. For more than four decades, the style that prevailed on the Tunisian stages was one which showed a heavy Egyptian influence. This leaned towards the aesthetics and techniques of declamation, with an emphatic and demonstrative style. The rigid models introduced by the Egyptian troupes that toured at the end of the first decade of the last century (1908–10) promoted this 'classic' type of acting, confined within a form of amateurism that tried to hide under the elaborate phraseology of texts played in literary Arabic, and a discourse that played upon nationalism and national identity.

A pioneering figure in Tunisian theatre, Mohamed Abdelaziz Agrebi, maintained in an article published in April 1950 that 'the plays that were acted at that time [the beginnings of Tunisian theatre] pleased the people through their high linguistic level and the right diction, but disappointed them with regard to the quality of the acting' (Agrebi, quoted in Mejri, 2009, p. 41). On his part, the historian and scholar Mohamed Massoud Driss states that:

> The first generation of Tunisian actors did not have any academic training or even specific courses about the art of acting. [...] This lack seems because of a widespread approach at the beginnings of theatre practice in Tunisia, founded on the belief that the basis of this art was good diction and mastery of literary Arabic, and that these techniques and this knowledge were far more important than the mastery of movement and the interpretation of roles. [...] Could the direct influence of the Egyptian theatre, which gave more importance to singing than acting, perhaps explain this tendency?
>
> Driss, 1993, pp. 134–5

Therefore, the work of the actor – the cornerstone of the rise of theatre in Tunisia – remained neglected for a whole generation. The realization that this art could not develop without an effective approach and a professional attitude to acting struck rather late. Standing back to reflect and examine how far they had come since 1909 enabled the pioneers to steer towards ideas and ideals that placed them on the Stanislavskian path. We can refer, in particular, to the appeal that was launched in 1945 to overcome what was articulated as 'the crisis of Tunisian theatre' (Bousnina quoted in Mejri, 2009, p. 33), which insisted on the necessity of reforming theatre practice so as to attract a wider public and produce better artistic quality. Among the 'recommendations' made in this appeal, let us highlight those relating to the 'development of the approaches to mise-en-scène and the adoption of realist aesthetics'; 'to improve acting in such a way as to capture the hearts of the spectators and incite them to come back to the performance a second time'; to 'play naturally and find the right gestures for the role'; 'art for art's sake'; and the warning to actors to 'behave in a dignified manner in society, so that nobody would scorn them' (Bousnina quoted in Mejri, 2009, pp. 35–6).

This rethinking of theatre practice and the principles to achieve it bring to mind, in effect, those adopted by Stanislavsky to revolutionize the theatre of his time. When launching the Moscow Art Theatre in 1898, with his partner Vladimir Nemirovich-Danchenko, Stanislavsky tried to 'deal with the foundations of the future theatre, with questions of pure art, artistic ideals, theatre ethics, scenic techniques, planning, repertory' (Stanislavski, 1999, p. 235). These new directions were very rapidly transformed into a series of maxims: 'there are no minor roles, only minor actors'; 'Today Hamlet, tomorrow an extra, but always, even as an extra, at the service of the art'; 'all that troubles the creative life of the theatre is a crime'; 'lateness, laziness, capriciousness, hysterics, bad temper, badly-learned lines, the necessity to repeat twice the same thing; all this causes harm to the work and should be banished' (Stanislavski, 1999, p. 239).

The relationship that may be established between the mind-set underlying Stanislavsky's ideas and the reformist tendencies of Tunisian theatre cannot, however, be supported by tangible proof of direct knowledge of Stanislavsky's experience by Tunisian theatre practitioners, whether from books or through practice. Testimonies that concern the period under discussion omit, in fact, any reference to possible sources that could have nourished the dream of 'erecting the construction of the new Tunisian theatre', as Hassan Zmerli, founder member of the 'Commission for the Defence of the Tunisian Theatre', put it (Zmerli quoted in Mejri, 2009, p. 53). But these very sources allow a glimpse into the basic ideas underlying this project and the profile of the people who started it. Zmerli's sentiment for a theatrical renaissance in Tunisia was shared by a plethora of men of letters who possessed 'University degrees recognized by various European and Tunisian universities'. Their objectives included the creation of 'an Institute providing training for the theatre', 'the translation of works and plays into Arabic', 'the creation of a theatre library' (La Commission de défense du théâter tunisien) in 1954. Obviously, these choices confirm a desire to appropriate the universal theatrical heritage and the necessity to back the envisaged reform with a practical and trustworthy reference point. But if the idea of direct 'contagion' by Stanislavsky's approach remains hypothetical, it is undeniable that the values of theatre which Stanislavsky believed in and which he battled for underpinned the idea of a solid framework for theatre in Tunisia. After side-tracking into 'conventional' theatre sustained by a stereotypical and artificial type of acting, Tunisian theatre ended its 'incubation' period and showed itself ready to follow the path traced by Stanislavsky, celebrating the idea of 'an art theatre' in which 'the talented actor' is 'the sole king, the sole master of the scene' (Stanislavski, 1999, p. 488).

On the traces of the actor

The question of the actor's art and the means to develop and professionalize his/her practice was constantly brought forward as the object of principal interest in the reform that was to be carried out. In subsequent years it was the means by which various approaches and experiences searching for a theatrical 'grammar' were expressed. It is this route that we will now follow to apprehend the question of the transmission of Stanislavsky's ideas in Tunisia. The first stage of this route is the foundation, in the early 1950s, of two key institutions that spearheaded the hoped-for reform, that is, the Ecole du Théâtre Arabe (School of Arab Theatre) and the Troupe de la Ville de Tunis (Troupe of the City of Tunis).[2]

The School of Arab Theatre, founded in 1951, offered the first professional theatre training in Tunisia. Its programme focused mainly on diction and on a studied theatricalization of gesture. The syllabus recalled that of the French school, Cours Simon, where Mohamed Abdelaziz Agrebi,[3] one of the pioneers of theatre training in Tunisia, had spent three years studying classic, romantic, and modern interpretation. This training also reflected the interest of the school's director, Hassan Zmerli, who studied French theatre when in Paris (Abaza, 1997, pp. 156–7).

The tuition at the School of Arab Theatre included lessons in pronunciation, diction, analysis of texts, history of theatre, theatre themes, principles and history of staging, and physical preparation. The adoption of the French approach was inspired by the strong conviction that it was necessary to base theatre practice on the mastery of language – in this case, literary Arabic – and urged on by the increasing influence of French theatre on Tunisian theatre-makers. It was intended as a defence against archaic acting forms and as a model of high-quality artistic practice. This choice also appeared to create a sort of continuity with a tradition of classical theatre, which was still little known and badly understood by the Tunisian theatre community. Mohamed Abdelaziz Agrebi expressed this position in the following terms:

> The Tunisian actor is only concerned with gesticulating in a useless and sombre manner and in a ridiculous *cabotinage*. His ignorance of the rules of classical Arabic only worsens the situation. I do not disavow our dialectal language, but to my mind, it takes second place. The mastery of classical

Arabic is, in fact, the only way to guarantee the actor the possibility of perfecting his act in dialect. I have watched various courses in the French theatre schools and I have seen the teachers insisting on the importance of dominating seventeenth-century French. They saw this as the only means to play all roles, whether in high-flowing language, dialect or even in slang. I believe it is essential to establish Tunisian theatre on the principle of the mastery of literary Arabic and of the appropriate gesture.

in Abaza, 1997, p. 201

For Stanislavsky, who was exposed to French theatre traditions from an early age, this 'French School' was

a very complex and difficult art. It served as a starting point for my training. I went to the Paris Conservatory and that is why I can speak with authority on this subject. This art is based initially on reliving the role. The artist lives the role once or more times at home and during rehearsals. Then, having integrated the process, he learns to reproduce the results through a technique that has been carried to perfection. No Russian actor (with perhaps, the exception of Karatygine and Samoïlov, now dead) could compete in the mastery of this art with actors such as Sarah Bernhardt.

Stanislavskii, 1990, t. 9, p. 296

Even though the French school of acting was the main reference for this young professional Tunisian theatre's search for reference points which, de facto, shifted it away from the echo of Stanislavsky's ideas,[4] it is nevertheless through French theatre that the first 'formal' link between the Russian pedagogue and director and Tunisian theatre can be envisaged. This link can, in fact, be established on the one hand through Jean Vilar, the great actor and director who marked French theatre history and who fervently defended Stanislavsky's ideas and, on the other, through Aly Ben Ayed,[5] Vilar's disciple and actor and director who forged the Golden Age of Tunisian theatre in the 1960s.

Ben Ayed studied at the School of Arab Theatre, which he followed by further training at the Conservatoire de Paris and then in Cairo at the Centre for Higher Dramatic Studies. He returned to Paris in 1956 to experience a significant period with Vilar, who at the time was heading the Théâtre National Populaire (TNP). This traineeship in staging and lighting stretched over two years and coincided with the French publication, in 1957, of the first edition of *La Formation de l'acteur* [An Actor Prepares], with a preface by Vilar. The latter, who also founded the Festival d'Avignon, thus appeared as the flag-bearer, in France, of the Russian theatre-maker and, just like him, he clamoured for an 'art theatre'. Vilar also dedicated his artistic life to the idea that was dear to Stanislavsky, that of a theatre 'accessible to all', by celebrating 'the social and educational aspect' of theatre (Amiard-Chevrel, 1989, p. 18). Vilar was described as a theatre practitioner who wanted the actor to become 'the living soul of the performance. The space is offered to him almost empty. [...] Vilar's leading idea is to invent a socially unifying performance' (Roubine, 1998, p. 120).

Besides his commitment to a theatrical art at the service of society and his promotion of a realist aesthetic, Vilar was also attentive to Stanislavsky's recommendations regarding the techniques and art of the actor. For him: 'There is no authentic actor who, at one time or another, did not borrow, consciously or unconsciously, some of the paths that Stanislavsky describes so precisely in his book'. Vilar recognized in Stanislavsky an 'example for Jacques Rouché, Jacques Copeau, Appia, André Antoine and many others' and 'admit[s] to always having borne a particular veneration for this man'. With the passage of time and the works he created, Vilar's thoughts turned 'with even more fear towards this teaching' (Vilar in the preface of Stanislavski, 1986, pp. 10–11; see also Maudoues, 1989). Although Vilar retained that it was necessary to 'criticise the System [...] and to reconsider its precepts, its methods, its arguments and the very spirit it takes inspiration from', it was nevertheless true that Stanislavsky's 'style', 'example', 'school', 'training method' and 'moral lesson' would continue to influence theatre across the world (Stanislavski, 1986, p. 13).

In his article 'Stanislavsky and Vilar', Paul Puaux maintains that:

> Though Vilar at times followed paths which were different to those of Stanislavsky, and though their practices were not identical, he still shared the vision proposed by Bernard Dort with regard to Stanislavsky and Brecht [...] for a totally adult theatre – that is to be taken as a responsible creative activity, where in reproducing images and feelings, man also gives shape to himself.
>
> Puaux, 1989, p. 80

These ideas were developed and defended at the time when Aly Ben Ayed frequented Vilar and tried to soak up all that could enlighten his path in art. Ben Ayed's success at the head of the Troupe of the City of Tunis and his efforts in operating a radical change in Tunisian theatre practice, promoting the idea of an art of the theatre with improved artistic standards, suggests his emulation of Stanislavsky. The path towards Stanislavsky that Ben Ayed seems to have discovered through Vilar crossed with that of the United States, where in 1960 the Tunisian theatre-maker spent a period of study (Abaza, 1997, p. 248). Himself an actor, Ben Ayed incorporated talent and skill in his work, along with the mastery and inspiration deriving from other actors he worked with. His experience, which was raised to the level of a school, allowed the 'development of the art of the actor on inspiration, imagination and interaction with the text, and to explore the means of verbal and corporal expression' (Abaza, 1997, p. 261).

In search of the System

The transmission of a live practice like acting technique can take place in a number of ways, ranging from the embodied and direct transmission from master to disciple to other ways that are mediated through the written word or visual sources. The latter has the capacity of propagating the practice involved on a wider scale, and therefore it has an impact which cannot be neglected. The transmission of Stanislavsky's ideas across the world can only confirm this observation. The tumultuous history of the publication of his books in the United States and the subsequent fate of his work has, in fact, shaped the journey of his ideas across the world (Benedetti, 2005 and Carnicke, 1998).

For the Arab and Tunisian theatre, this story began in 1959 with the appearance in Egypt of the first Arab translation of *My Life in Art*, followed, in 1960, by that of *An Actor Prepares*. Both books were translated from English. Apart from the problems resulting from a 'second-hand' translation, doubly betraying the original text, these first Arab versions of Stanislavsky's work inherited all the defects of the 'adjustments' and suppressions made by the American translators and publishers (see Mrabet, 2012). It must be recognized that Arab theatre-makers found themselves facing texts which were, to say the least, 'indigestible' and 'disorienting'. The Syrian director, Faouez Sajer, author of a doctoral thesis in Russian entitled *Stanislavsky and Arab Theatre*, reckons that 'the bad interpretations of the System were often the source of polemics concerning its positive and negative aspects'. He specified that 'these differences were due both to the intellectual divergences between the translator and

Stanislavsky, and to the over-hasty interpretations of his method' (Sajer, 1994, pp. 63–4). In order to overcome this situation, Sajer's suggestion was to

> entrust the translation of the text from its original language to specialised translators coming from institutes of dramatic art. He believed that a translation from an intermediary language could not take into account all the details of the work of the actor on the character and the role.
>
> Sajer, quoted in Safar, 2014

Driven by this increased interest in the reconsideration of Stanislavsky's text, the Syrian director Cherif Chaker proposed, as far back as 1983, a translation of *Creating a Role*, as well as an Arab version of *Building a Character*. Chaker had already translated other important works from Russian to Arabic including, in 1979, Vsevolod Meyerhold's *On The Art of the Theatre*. He also published in 1981, a book entitled: *Le réalisme Stanislavskien dans la théorie et la pratique* (Stanislavskian realism in theory and practice). He further pursued this effort in 2002 with the publication of a translation from Bulgarian of *La Formation de l'acteur à l'école de Stanislavski* (Actor training at the School of Stanislavsky) by J. F. Christy (2002). In 2012 the complete translation from Russian to Arabic of Stanislavsky's *My life in Art* was published.

Having been absorbed by a theatrical culture largely dominated by translations from the East, these works slowly found their way to practitioners and theatre specialists in Tunisia. From then onwards, the relationship of Tunisian theatre to Stanislavsky's heritage that had long been limited to a 'superficial' reading and an 'approximate' approach, now moved towards greater attention to and a deeper knowledge of his ideas, as I will discuss below. However, apart from Arabic, the French language provided an additional springboard for the appropriation of the System. Besides the no less 'problematic' French translations of Stanislavsky's works (*My Life in Art*,[6] *An Actor Prepare*, and *Building a Character*), the French source provided research and reference writings on the Stanislavsky experience. The contributions by Bernard Dort[7] and Nina Gourfinkel (1979) in particular seem to have found an echo in the work of the young Tunisian practitioners who had trained in France in the 1970s (see Abaza, 2009, pp. 158–68). The references that can be found in the training programmes at the Centre d'Art Dramatique (Centre for Dramatic Art, CAD), which succeeded the Ecole du Théâtre Arabe, include a final year dissertation by Radka Riaskova (undated) entitled *A la Recherche de Stanislavski: la méthode de Stanislavski et son application dans le théâtre contemporain* (In Search of Stanislavski: Stanislavsky's method and its application in contemporary theatre). The existence of an original copy of this research at the bottom of the library at CAD could undoubtedly surprise us. Was this by chance or planned? We couldn't figure it out! However, the content of this dissertation gives attention to aspects such as the question of 'actor training', 'the actor's work on the role' and 'the director and the Stanislavski method'. Such research could not go unnoticed at a time when the Tunisian theatre was looking to renew itself.

However, it was only in 2005 that specific courses in Stanislavsky's approach were established, stimulated by – and stimulating – a direct interest in his ideas in scientific research. Thanks to a reform in the programmes of the Institut Supérieur d'Art Dramatique (Higher Institute for Dramatic Art, ISAD) in Tunis,[8] Stanislavsky's approach became one of the essential factors in actor training. Since then, it has been deeply used both in the practical workshops and in the theoretical courses that demonstrate its underlying aesthetics and techniques.[9] These courses aim at 'refocusing' Stanislavsky's approach to the art of the actor, placing it in its wider historical context, and teasing out the essential problems of its evolution. Stanislavsky's approach is set within the evolution of the actor's art, mainly by comparing it to Diderot's and underlining its original concepts so that participants are led onto the path of 'the work of the actor on himself from the internal process of creation' and 'the work on the role'. A beginner's level of practical courses is followed by an introduction of techniques on 'relaxation', 'concentration', 'physical control', 'imagination', 'faith and sense of truth', as well as other key concepts of the System (emotive memory, tempo-rhythm, communication . . .). A second level of this training is devoted to the practice of 'the method of active analysis' or 'action-analysis', as developed by Maria Knebel.[10]

Parallel to this training in Stanislavskian approaches, scientific research is providing a basis for reflection to raise essential questions on the appropriation of Stanislavsky's heritage. In this respect, we can refer to Sami Nasri's research on the question of 'The actor and the building of a character in Stanislavsky' (Nasri, 2000) and that on the theme of 'Stanislavsky in the American Theatre: reception, transmission and evolution of an approach to the art of the theatre'

(Mrabet, 2007). This unique case in the Arab world, this 'institutionalization' of Stanislavsky's teaching in theatre training in Tunisia, underlies better understanding of and greater attention to the ideas of the 'father' of contemporary theatre and a regeneration of the actor's practice. This teaching could safeguard, over the years, a better perception of physical training for actors; techniques enabling the development of the expressiveness of the body, voice techniques, and the concept of tempo-rhythm. It could permit, among other techniques, the actors' familiarization with 'psychophysical acting', 'scenic truth', 'emotive memory', imagination, improvisation and physical actions.

The art of the actor has in the past thirty years undergone considerable progress, transforming Tunisian theatre into a 'theatre of improvisation'.[11] However, this theatre is finding itself 'weighed down' by the model of the 'actor-creator' which it generated and which today encloses it into a mould. Nevertheless, for this theatre, Stanislavsky's 'lessons' cannot be overlooked. Whether these ideas are adopted wisely as a basis for modern theatrical art, or whether they are put at a distance, and even 'negated', in order to be better appropriated', questions on stage truth, the approach to the 'work on the role' and the 'creative powers of the actor', have unquestionably formed the cornerstone of the construction of the art of the actor in the last thirty years in Tunisia.

The test of the stage

The reception of Stanislavsky's ideas in Tunisia matured through a double influence from the West and the East and was shaped by the personal careers of the practitioners who adhered to them. There was, however, a certain diversity in the way his techniques were perceived and different positions were assumed in this regard. Apart from the 'orthodox' approach assumed by the Théâtre de la Terre under the direction of Noureddine and Nejia Ouerghi[12], which deliberately adopted a realist aesthetic in a type of play that gives prominence to the idea of 'reliving' and to a technique based on psychomotricity, other interpretations were based on the idea of 'actor-creator'[13] and the basic principles of the System as outlined in the *My Life in Art* chapter titled 'The Discoveries of Truths Long Since Known'.[14] The latter rejected all realist tendencies. The experience of Théâtre Phou (founded in 1979), directed by

Raja Ben Ammar and Moncef Sayem, focused on the body as the main tool for creativity, while that of Théâtre El Hamra, directed by Ezzedine Gannoun, explored verbal and gestural poetics. These theatres appear as typical examples of a post-Stanislavskian theatre. But in order to better understand Tunisian theatre's ability to appropriate Stanislavsky's ideas and to put them to the test of the stage, it would be useful to dwell on the experience of one of the most emblematic Tunisian theatre makers: Fadhel Jaïbi.[15]

By the end of the 1960s Jaïbi was a student of theatre and an apprentice director, and felt that his encounter with Stanislavsky's ideas was at that point 'inevitable'. However his relationship to Stanislavsky's realist art could not escape the context of the time, when the latter was highly challenged by the 'Brecht Tsunami' (Jaïbi, 2014). Jaïbi claims to have lived 'more forcefully and more passionately the challenges of the model [he] subscribed to'. According to him, beyond the rejection of all this 'bourgeois identification tripe, which did not allow one to take any distance to the object being observed', the challenge to Stanislavsky's approach involved a fundamental question which marked his beginnings in directing actors: 'Where do we look for the character? Within or outside ourselves?' (Jaïbi, 2014). This question continues to preoccupy him to this very day.

At the time, Jaïbi tried out 'all repertoires, classic, modern, tragic, comic [...] from fragments from *Woyszeck* to short scenes from Shakespeare or Molière'. In doing so, he was intuitively studying Stanislavskian ideas, confronting notions like 'affective memory', 'reliving', and the 'question of emotion', not knowing what distance to take vis-à-vis these ideas, since he felt it necessary to assume a certain distance from them. This 'passionately critical' gaze played a determining role in Jaïbi's experience and took him 'elsewhere', far from any method, towards 'synthesis', given that 'nobody held the truth' (Jaïbi, 2014). But this 'poetics of doubt', apparently 'in conflict with' Stanislavsky's approach, remained intrinsically faithful to Stanislavsky's founding idea, which in 1936 he had expressed as follows:

> It is not a question of my method or your method. There is only one method, which is of an organic and creative nature [...] and I am ready to state in writing that if a student joining our theatre finds a way to attain the laws of this nature, then I will be very happy to learn from him.
>
> Stanislavski, 1958, p. 158

It is undeniably this 'creative' direction that Jaïbi chose to follow. A rebel suspicious of all methods he 'took all sorts of liberties vis-à-vis one or the other (Stanislavsky, Brecht, Meyerhold, Craig . . .)' (Jaïbi, 2014). His own approach was the fruit of these 'encounters' and '*égarements* [losing one's path]' and led him to claim a 'retained emotion' and 'shifted play', taking as his source the actor's subconscious and creating confusion between the self and the other. Productions like *Familia* (1993), *Les Amoureux du Café Désert* (1995), *Soirée Particulière* (1997), and *Junun* (2001) reveal, in effect, an exceptional approach in this direction. While exploiting the level of the subconscious, so dear to Stanislavsky, Jaïbi constantly explored 'a dialectic of the here and elsewhere, of yesterday and today'. He fulfils his quest for 'truth, sincerity, going beyond oneself, the inexpressible, nuance, pure emotion' as a form of resistance to all schools, which leads him to constantly re-invent the aesthetic and an authentic practice of the theatrical art. 'Stanislavskian despite himself', Jaïbi has avoided a literal interpretation of the ideas of the Russian master and sought a creative direction that led him to 'rediscover' the 'principles' of the System, before integrating them within an eclectic approach which uses these principles as its backbone.

Conclusion

Tunisian theatre, formed in a spirit of contestation which marked the key stages of its history, and shaped by the search for its own identity, undeniably reveals a unique dynamic in the transmission of Stanislavsky's ideas. Initially fortuitous, this link between theatre practitioners and the teachings of the Russian theatre-maker evolved progressively to a more formal relationship where, through training and scientific research, an effort was made to apprehend his ideas. This tendency, which never ceases to re-affirm itself, and the success of Tunisian theatre to develop an acting practice that is founded on Stanislavsky and the idea of an 'actor-creator', are proof of the will to secure this theatre to the tradition that generated it.

Finally, it must be noted that in recent years Tunisian theatre has moved towards a theatrical experimentation which also appears as the fruit of the 'Stanislavskian seed'. This experimentation is the clearest expression that Stanislavsky has taken root within this theatre. These experiences, which are organized in 'laboratories', 'studios', or 'workshops',[16] reflect upon the different forms and models proposed and show the desire to 'penetrate the mysteries' of this art. This long-term effort has only just started and refers back, de facto, to the 'lifelong struggle' that Stanislavsky undertook for an art that makes practice its first source of 'knowledge'. Beyond forms and aesthetics, 'methods' and rhetoric, it is the fundamental laws of theatrical creation that are being assimilated and reappropriated, and 'truths known far longer' (Stanislavski, 1999, p. 369) that are being transcended. Stanislavsky's fundamental lesson no longer needs to be proved for Tunisian theatre. Its application remains, however, the major challenge of the act of creation and the fundamental dynamic of its evolution, requiring more research and reflection.

Notes

1 This date corresponds to the first appearance of Tunisian actors on stage. Up to then, theatre practice was reserved to the Italian and French communities which, at the time, were massively present in Tunisia. Theatre, however, was practised in numerous towns and cities in Ancient Tunisia. The Roman sites of Dougga, Sbeitla, Carthage, El Jem, and many others, testify to the importance of this art for the populations of these towns and cities.
2 This company was also called Municipal Troupe of Tunis.
3 Mohamed Abdelaziz Agrebi (1902–68), actor, director, and pedagogue. Considered as the most senior member of Tunisian theatre, Agrebi first appeared in 1919 as an actor in the company Al Chahama. Later he participated in numerous leading experiences in Tunisian theatre and was one of the founders both of the School of Arab Theatre and of the Troupe of the City of Tunis which he subsequently directed for a few years (see Khlouj, 2000).
4 As Natalia Balatova underlines: 'Stanislavsky always qualified French Theatre as "the art of representation" in comparison with "the art of reliving", which was rooted in Russian tradition. In his 1911 notes, he compares two theatre giants, the French Constant Coquelin and the Italian Tommaso Salvini, and clearly and concisely defines the difference between "representing" and "reliving". He demonstrates this by what he calls the "dispute" between Coquelin and Salvini on the actor's objectives on stage. Whereas Coquelin says: "The actor does not live, but he plays. He remains cold but his art must be perfect", Salvini replies: "The actor lives, cries and laughs on stage, but while laughing and crying, he continues to

observe his laugh and his tears. And art is born from this double life, from this balance between live and art"'. (Balatova, 2001, p. 23)

5 Aly Ben Ayed (1930–72) is an emblematic figure of the Tunisian theatre. The Director of the Troupe of the City of Tunis from 1958 to 1971, he managed to stage no less than twenty-seven productions from the classic and contemporary repertoire, including *Oedipus Rex, Hamlet, Caligula, The School for Wives, The Miser*. His talents as an actor and director earned him regional and international recognition and fame.

6 In France, the translation by Nina Gourfinkel and Léon Chancerel from the Russian version will only appear in 1934, with large cuts, and the unabridged version will only be published in 1980.

7 I refer in particular to his preface to the 1970 edition of *La Construciton du Personnage*.

8 Founded in 1982, and put under the double authority of the Ministry of Culture and the Ministry of Higher Education, ISAD is the direct inheritor of the Arab Theatre and the Centre d'Art Dramatique. This institute offers academic training, both theoretical and practical, in different specialties (the Art of the Actor, The Theatre for Young Audiences, Puppetry . . .). The course programme is at Bachelor, Master, and Doctorate levels.

9 These courses last two semesters for a BA degree and one semester for a Masters degree. Different aspects of Stanislavsky's System are tackled – historical, aesthetic, and technical – which are put into correlation with other approaches to art, such as Vsevolod Meyerhold's 'biomechanics', Michael Chekhov's 'creative imagination', and Jerzy Grotowski's 'Via Negativa'. The training programme at the Institut Supérieur de Musique et de Théâtre (Higher Institute for Music and Theatre) at Le Kef also includes a Stanislavsky Workshop.

10 Actress Maria Knebel became director in 1935, at a time when this position was rarely assigned to a woman. Stanislavsky called on her in 1936 to teach and assist him. He was then finalising the methods of 'physical action' and 'action-analysis', developed by the etudes and improvisations. See Knebel, 2006.

11 Collective writing through improvisation as a starting point for theatrical creation was promoted as a model for Tunisian theatre by the Nouveau Théâtre, the first private company in Tunisia which was founded in 1976 by Mohamed Driss, Fadhel Jaïbi, Jalila Baccar, Fadhel Jaziri, and Habib Masrouki (Abaza, 1997, pp. 170–9).

12 This theatre was founded in 1984.

13 This refers to the implicit condition for the release of artistic tensions that hinder the expressiveness of the body. 'The creation of state' which the actor aspires is supposed to give free rein to all his creative faculties.

14 These principles are 'concentration', 'the physical mastery', 'imagination', 'faith and a sense of true', 'tempo-rhythm', 'communication' and all that could be involved in creating '[. . .] the favourable terrain, the atmosphere that allow inspiration to come down into my soul more readily and more often.' See Stanislavski, 1999, p. 374.

15 Fadhel Jaïbi: author, director for theatre and film. Born in 1945, Jaïbi graduated from the Institut d'Etudes Théâtrales, Sorbonne Nouvelle, and from the Ecole Charles Dullin. Co-founder of the Nouveau Théâtre in 1976 and of Familia Productions in 1993, he has directed the Théâtre National Tunisien (National Tunisian Theatre) since August 2014.

16 Let us mention the recent experience of the Laboratoire théâtral tunisien founded in 2012, and openly engaged in theatrical experimentation, giving particular attention to the ideas and techniques developed by Stanislavsky. The leaders of the 1970–90 years, in particular the pioneers of private theatre in Tunisia (Fadhel Jaïbi, Mohamed Driss, Raja Ben Ammar and Moncef Sayem, Habib Chbil, Taoufik Jebali, Ezzeddine Gannoun, Fethi Akkari, Noureddine Ouerghi . . .) all experimented with this kind of approach, exploring the different paths of theatrical creation.

References

Abaza M. (1997), *Evolution de l'acte théâtral en Tunisie, de la naissance à la foundation*. Tunis: Centre de Publications Universitaires/Sahar Editions.

Abaza, M. (2009), *Evolution de l'acte théâtral en Tunisie, de decentralization à l'expérimentation*: Tunis, Centre de Publications Universitaires/Sahar editions.

Amiard-Chevrel, C. (1989), 'Le Théâtre Artistique', in *Le Siècle Stanislavski*, Bouffonneries No. 20/21, p. 18.

Balatova, N. (2001), 'Stanislavski et le théâtre français', in *Les Voyages du Théâtre: Russie/France*, eds H. Henry and M. C. Autant-Mathieu. Tours: Université François Rabelais. This book forms part of the collection *Cahiers d'Histoire Culturelle*, No. 10.

Benedetti, J. (2005), 'Les editions occidentales des oeuvres de Stanislavski', in *Le Théâtre d'Art de Moscou, ramifications, voyages*, ed. M. C. Autant-Mathieu. Paris: CNRS editions, pp. 79–95.

Carnicke, S. M. (1998), *Stanislavsky in Focus*. Reading: Harwood Academic Publishers.

Christy, J. F. (2002), *La Formation de l'acteur à l'école de Stanislavski*, trans. A. M. Youssef. Beirut: Nouveau Livre.

Driss, M. M. (1993), *Etudes de l'histoire du théâtre tunisien 1881–1956*. Institut Supérieur d'Art Dramatique: Sahar Editions.

Gourfinkel, N. (1979), *Le Théâtre Artistique de Moscou 1989–1917*. Paris: Centre National de la Recherche Scientifique.

Khlouj, B. (2000), *Mohamed Abdelaziz Agrebi, Doyen du théâtre tunisien*. Tunis: Centre National de communication culturelle.

Knebel, M. (2006), 'Analysis-Action', ed. A. Vassiliev, trans. by N. Struve, S. Vladimirov, and S. Paris: Actes – Sud Papiers.

La Commission de défense du théâter tunisien (1954), *Al Thuraya* 2nd year, February.

Maudoues, R. M. (1989), 'Le rôle de Jacques Rouché dans l'introduction des idées de Stanislavski en France', in *Le Siècle Stanislavski*, Bouffoneries No. 20/21.

Mejri, M. (2009), *Préoccupations fondatrices du théâtre tunisien*. Tunis: Editions Al Hurriya.

Mrabet, M. (2007), 'Stanislavski dans le théâtre américain: reception, transmission et evolution d'une approche du jeu théâtral', doctoral thesis under the supervision of M. C. Autant-Mathieu, University of Paris III Sorbonne-Nouvelle.

Mrabet, M. (2012), *Stanislavski dans le théâtre américain: Du Système à la Méthode, voyage d'une approche du jeu théâtral, Vol. I and II*. Saarbrücken, Allemagne: Presses Académiques Francophones.

Nasri, S. (2000), *L'Acteur et la construction du personnage chez Stanislavski*, Final year dissertation under the supervision of R. Boukadida. Tunis: Institut Supérieur d'Art Dramatique.

Puaux, P. (1989), 'Stanislavski et Vilar', in *Le Siècle Stanislavski*, Bouffonneries No. 20/21.

Riaskova R. (undated), *A la Recherche de Stanislavski: la méthode de Stanislavski et son application dans le théâtre contemporain*, MA Dissertation under the supervision of J. Lassalle. Paris: Institut d'Etudes Théâtrales.

Roubine, J. J. (1998), *Introduction aux grandes theories du théâtre*. Paris: Dunod.

Safar, A. (2014), 'Réédition de ses livres en arabe, le Système de Stanislavski: une nécessité créatrice', *Hinta* (Syria), No. 18, 13 May.

Sajer, F. (1994), *Stanislavski et le Théâtre Arabe*. Damascus: Commission Syrienne du Livre/Ministère Syrien de la Culture.

Stanislavski, C. (1957 and 1986), *La Formation de l'Acteur*, preface by J. Vilar, ed. O. Perrin, Paris: Pygmalion/Gérard Watelet. Republished (1957), Payot.

Stanislavski, C. (1958), *Stanislavsky's Legacy, a collection of comments on a variety of aspects of an actor's art and life,* ed. and trans. E. R. Hapgood. New York, Theatre Arts Books.

Stanislavski, C. (1960), *La Formation de l'Acteur*, trans. D. Kachaba, M. Z. Achmaoui, and M. Morsi. Cairo: Maison de la Renaissance Arabe.

Stanislavski, C. (1984), *La Construction du Personnage*. Paris: Pygmalion/Gérard Watelet.
Stanislavski, C. (1986), *La Formation de l'Acteur*, preface by J. Vilar. Paris, Pygmalion.
Stanislavskii, C. (1990), *Sobranie sochinenii t. 9*. Moscow: Iskusstvo.
Stanislavski, C. (1999), *Ma Vie dans l'Art*, trans. D. Yoccoz. Lausanne: L'Age d'homme.
Stanislavski, C. (2004), *Ma vie dans l'art, 2 volumes*, trans. D. Kachaba. Cairo: Maison Egypto-libanaise.
Stanislavski, C. (2011), *La Création du role*, trans. C. Chaker. Damascus: Commission Syrienne du Livre/Ministère Syrien de la Culture.
Stanislavski, C. (2012), *My Life in Art*, trans. N. M. Mohammad. Commission Syrienne du Livre/Ministère Syrien de la Culture.

Interview

Interview by author with Fadel Jaïbi, 10 August 2014.

14

A Director's Perspective: Stanislavsky in South Africa

David Peimer

Postcolonial thinking liberated the periphery from the centre without reducing either to itself, and it has engaged in historical explanation without crude judgement or generalisation, revealing the labour involved in sustaining the colonising project, the intersections and distances of hegemony and resistance or tradition and modernity, and the narration of counter-histories.

Ash Amin (in Sian, 2014, p. 98)

Context

After 350 years of colonization and a half century of apartheid, the contemporary situation reflects a brief moment in the ongoing South African narrative whose collective memory is forged in the racially framed binaries of primitive/civilized, superior/inferior, Western/African, and so on. A few years of the Truth Commission in the mid-1990's enabled a brief pause, a moment to reflect on a history where memory was framed by such ideological arrangements. Barely two decades into a new dispensation, there is perhaps the beginning of a small, tentative step from the 'periphery' to the 'centre'. But the overall colonial project locates all activities within this inherited, ongoing, contextual contest between the periphery and the centre.

And so with theatre-making; one can only glimpse a diverse collision of creative forces which engages with re-positioning and re-reflecting inherited legacies of 'acting' and performer training (Stanislavsky and others) from within the periphery/centre context of the postcolonial narrative. Stanislavsky re-positioned implies reflecting, transforming, appropriating, resisting, perhaps even a notion of a possible but not yet born hybridity. It is possible to observe a rough, adventurous project of how his ideas are transformed in the multiple contexts that constitute South African performance today.

It is ironic that Stanislavsky's notions were never primarily located at the 'centre' of the South African professional performances that toured the world during apartheid. Precedence was given to: Protest Theatre; Township made theatre,[1] with its attendant leaps in space and time, song, dance, dialogue, physicality, stereotypes/socially constructed character types, minimal focus on psychologically complex character or language; African ritual/storytelling; Grotowskian physicality; Brechtian socio-political characters, and their attendant historically informed narrative structures; and Workshop theatre.

Stanislavsky was, however, studied by theatre-makers in the 'Whites Only' universities or colleges and others during apartheid. This ironic tension persists and locates itself today in the overall dominant context of the Western/African binary as the constituents of memory are re-positioned in the postcolonial project, a project which ceaselessly engages with the periphery/centre fluidity of movement.

Thus, directing in South Africa today requires an awareness of this context in which the varied, at times, colliding approaches to performer training, acting, and theatre-making, take place. Re-positioning Stanislavsky's ideas in the country implies noting their presence in this uncertain migration from the periphery to the centre and back again. (Ironically, one might imagine Stanislavsky proposing this to be a dynamic verification of his Socratic, dialogical, at times dialectical aesthetic of mobilizing learning and practice.)

In this short essay I will explore certain case-studies which exhibit this fluid, self-reflexive, transforming notion involved in the re-positioning of Stanislavsky's ideas.

Stanislavsky transformed

This adventurous collision of the many performance styles alluded to above finds its expression in most contemporary South African theatre. There is no one dominant theatre genre (and associated acting theorist), but, rather, an intertextuality of the performance styles mentioned. After so many centuries of a divided socio-cultural arrangement inculcated by the colonially assigned binaries noted above, the contemporary rehearsal/theatre-making approach is to react against this in the search for a 'new' South African style of performance, a dreamed-of hybridity. This has led to at times naïve, at times creative, mixing of theoretical notions from sources as diverse as Brecht, Grotowski, Stanislavsky, African Ritual and Storytelling (with fantastical shifts in space and time, and sound and body), and multi-media – all evidenced in the current expressions of Township-made Theatre, which is the genesis of South African theatre.

This was clear when I rehearsed Heiner Müller's plays *The Task*, *Hamletmachine* and *Landscape with Argonauts*. Working on these plays illuminated less the intersection with post-modern notions of performance or theatre-making many may see a Müller play insisting upon, but rather demonstrated the dynamic, fluid mixture of peripheral/central movements in performance-making approaches; fluid movements which are located precisely in the context of the colonial/precolonial and postcolonial project noted above. Whilst we may usefully (and ironically) appropriate the post-modern term of an 'intertextuality of performance-making', it *emerges from this context* and from this we may see how Stanislavsky and other theorists' ideas are being profoundly *transformed*, not merely adapted or resisted.

Stanislavskian specifics

Emotional memory transformed (Example: 1)

While rehearsing Macbeth with South African actors, in English and Zulu, our portrayal of the characters' planning and reacting to murder tended towards the melodramatic. Then, during rehearsals, I realized I had forgotten the overall colonial and Western/African context mentioned above. Collective memory (colonization and its brutal arrangement of societal relations of self and other) and daily life (the legacy) are infused with murder in South Africa.

Thus, we thought, why not instead try banal, everyday emotional memory exercises in the transforming of this Stanislavskian idea to the cultural context?

This required removing the exercise from the lived trauma of murder in the current and historical context of South Africa. The actress playing Lady Macbeth recalled that some years before she came home one day; a hot summer day. Sweating, tired, she opened the door of her flat and her cat leapt down from a bookcase, fell on her and scratched her so hard she bled. In a moment of rage, she picked up the cat and hurled it across the room. In that moment, she 'found' her objective; to desire murder. We thought to paraphrase the philosopher Hannah Arendt – the more banal the emotional memory, the greater the connection to the objective (to murder) in the given circumstances of the play. For the actor playing Macbeth, it was recalling when his wife had thrown away his favourite music CDs, by accident. For the Stanislavskian idea to work, it needed to be transformed in such a way that the exercise had to be removed from the lived and historical contextual trauma of daily murder and employ the most banal of actor memories.

Emotional memory transformed (Example: 2)

Rehearsing *Hamlet* gave rise to a link to Stanislavsky's idea from another perspective. The actor playing Hamlet was urbanized, and had grown up in the tough Soweto Township streets. Brought up by his uncle, he had been encouraged to take on 'Western ways'. Early on in rehearsals, as he was investigating Hamlet's given circumstances and objectives, he received a late night call. The elders from his village said his father had died and that his spirit (located in the river and surrounding land) was calling him back to take his father's place as the wise man of the village. (In Africa there are few monuments as the ancestors are located in the earth.)

This is not the place to delve into the many significant cultural and historical investigations the actor's dilemma engages with. Suffice it to say, in relation to Stanislavsky, that through this experience the actor was able to immerse himself in a 'current' emotional memory and thus character objectives, given circumstances, and the 'if'. What is important is that this clearly differs from the 'banal' example illuminated above, *but nor was it psychologically based; the actor saw the memory as directly linked to a socio-cultural phenomenon rooted in cultural history and notions of community, where these phenomena are deeply embedded in the intertextuality of collective memory/community memory.* He never once mentioned his 'own' or 'psychologized' memory.

Objectives, the 'if' transformed

In rehearsing Buchner's *Danton's Death* in post-revolution South Africa, the challenge was to create a number of characters based on historical icons within a profound historical moment. The actors knew very little about this period in French history. This, and possibly parts of the script, resulted in the creation of two-dimensional, stereotyped characters. How, then, to transform Stanislavsky's ideas to help guide the actors into portraying believable, multi-faceted characters (the character's inner life in acting parlance)?

By deploying notions of precolonial African storytelling, we focused on a series of heightened physical actions to 'score' the arc of objectives. Here we discovered a useful technique: the 'Very'. By putting two, four, or five 'Very's' before a physical action, intensity was heightened, an objective achieved (without using the word) and subtle layering of complex inner life of the character created. (Later, we noted that in a shot during the film, Robespierre slowly stands on his toes, unseen behind the podium as if to exaggerate his status.) In transforming the Stanislavskian 'if', we looked to the context of how African storytellers re-enact great leaders of African history and in this way the fluid movement of the 'periphery/centre' postcolonial gaze was engaged.

Subtext transformed

When rehearsing a production of *Waiting for Godot* we tried to apply the Stanislavskian notion of beats in the subtext.[2] Subtext implies playing the beats as objectives and not focusing on the actor's feelings. This enables a focus on the dramatic action which can then lead to emotions being experienced by the audience.

Again, the Stanislavskian idea needed to be challenged and transformed by the colonial/postcolonial project. Writing only arrived in South Africa with colonization in the early nineteenth century. Prior to that, the oral tradition of storytelling and singing was dominant for thousands of years. As part of this tradition, the physicality of the performer is central, and not the conscious questioning of objectives. (Further, the actors in this example and all those given here are second or third language English speakers.) Thus the 'subtext' needed to be located as a resistance to the colonial context and transformed into a subtext of minimally verbalized physical actions, not primarily articulated objectives.

It should also be noted that few African languages originally had a word for 'theatre' as noted in the Western tradition; participation (and communitas) rather than separation between performer and spectator was the performative mode for millennia. From this series of interventions in Stanislavskian interpretations, the play emerged and attracted large audiences. As black South African spectators often noted (none of whom had heard of the name Beckett): 'we know all about waiting; we have been waiting for the white man to go for centuries!'

Rehearsal approach transformed

When rehearsing a devised piece in a rural, poor, and HIV-stricken part of Zululand, we tried many Stanislavskian ideas without referring to the colonial context. Nothing worked; the actors were starving, cold, had no shoes or jerseys, and were ill. As a last resort, I put several of Stanislavsky's ideas together but located this combination *as a way of understanding the overall situation I was rehearsing in rather than in the specifics of rehearsal itself, with specific actors*. I transformed his ideas to this: what were the given circumstances of the actors themselves, what was my objective, what was my emotional memory in trying, but not succeeding, in opening up their inner memories, what was my way of adapting his notion of the 'if'?

Putting all these ideas together we realized they perhaps wanted at least a moment of reprieve from the pain and suffering of their daily lives. Given this possible circumstance, I tried to use music to help my directing process, imagining that music might lift the actors out of their daily given circumstances, thus enabling characterization, objectives, and beats to be created via the music 'scoring' of the action, not articulated objectives. I tried every kind of African, Western, jazz, classical, pop, blues music; nothing helped. In desperation, one day I played Elvis.

Within minutes the group were focused, working together, 'scoring' the objectives (without knowing the word). The play began to take shape. Not one of the actors had heard of Elvis, most could not understand the language or genre of music, but all mentioned 'something in that voice'.

Re-positioning Stanislavskian ideas away from character/actor specifics *into the overall context of the rehearsal itself* helped me, yet again, to grasp that the overall legacy of the colonial project is always needed as the context of making theatre; a project which requires the transforming/challenging/

adapting of Stanislavsky's ideas. Then, directing by using the sounds of the Elvis voice, I could retrace my way back to Stanislavsky; character, beats, subtext, objectives (without mentioning these terms to the actors), emerged from these sounds as if they had stirred something located in a precolonial, heightened physicality of body and voice. Naturally, this is not the place to investigate the possible debates around Elvis and his music. Suffice it to note that, in a moment of cultural (and ironic) intertextuality, divorcing the name Elvis from the mythical signifying position he occupies in Western memory enabled Stanislavskian ideas to be implemented.

Conclusion

Overall, from these few examples, it is hoped that in the contemporary brief moment of the great postcolonial narrative, a South African perspective may contribute in its own small way to the profound transformation of Stanislavsky's ideas, enabling us to speak of his *notions as being in a fluid dialogue with ever changing cultural contexts, including the postcolonial 'periphery/centre' project.*

Notes

1 This is a term used to clarify theatre made in the township; it reflects theatre made by black South Africans which emerged from their forced removal into townships. It combines ancient African modes of performance, storytelling, song, dance, and sudden changes in space and time, a Poor Theatre made for economic rather than aesthetic reasons.
2 On the use of the term 'beat', also referred to as 'bit', see Carnicke, 2009, p. 214.

References

Carnicke, S. (2009), *Stanislavsky in Focus – 2nd edn.* London and New York: Routledge
Sian, K. P. (ed.) (2014), *Conversations in Postcolonial Thought.* UK: Palgrave Macmillian.

Part Five

Australasia

Figure 29 Stanislavsky in Australasia.

Part Five: Introduction

Jonathan Pitches

The autonomy of distance and theatrical ethics: Stanislavsky in Australia and Aotearoa/New Zealand

One of the landmark publications interrogating Australia's relationship to the rest of world was first published in 1966 and revised again in 2001. Geoffrey Blainey's *The Tyranny of Distance* articulated the economic challenges presented by the geographical isolation of the world's largest island country but its currency and the term itself has endured in circles far wider than those populated by economists and geographers. Indeed from the business world to the Popular Music industry, the concept of tyrannical distance appears to be equally resonant in neighbouring New Zealand or Aotearoa – the Māori term for the country.[1] Blainey's thesis is that the huge distances needed to be covered to reach Australia (and indeed to travel internally) were fundamentally obstructive to economic growth up to 1860 and, were it not for the British imperial agenda to find an isolated outcrop for its burgeoning prison population in the eighteenth century, Australia would have remained in the hands of its indigenous population much later than 1788, when the First Fleet landed in Botany Bay.[2] Subsequently, transport solutions and newly found exportable products (such as sheep, gold, and whales) went some way to ameliorating this tyranny of distance (Blainey, 1966).

Writing over forty years after the first edition, in a collection of essays published by CEDA[3], Blainey acknowledges the obvious contribution digital information technologies have made to the shortening of distance in recent decades whilst adding the disputable point that, in his view, the isolation of Australia was an economic, as opposed to a cultural, phenomenon:

> Sometimes the phrase or slogan was misused. For example, many commentators said that for a long period it was the 'tyranny of distance' which retarded the flow of new ideas to Australia. But my view – I could be wrong – was that distance had far more effect on retarding the flow of commodities and people than of ideas.
>
> Blainey, 2007, p. 2

The three essays in this Part (two from Australian scholars and one from a practitioner-academic based in Aotearoa) are all subtly embroiled in this debate about cultural transmission, isolation, and exchange. They evidence, on the one hand, that ideas cannot as easily be divorced from people as Blainey suggests, and, on the other, that the many thousands of miles between Australasia and the first locus of Stanislavskian practice in Europe were not necessarily responsible for 'retarding the flow'. Spatial distance in fact, viewed through the lens of actor training practices at least, has led to a critical distance in thinking – a healthy *autonomy* from what might otherwise be positioned as the colonial importation of Stanislavsky's system in the region.

Hilary Halba's essay 'Stanislavsky in Aotearoa: The System Experienced through the Māori World' makes this essentially political point very clearly:

> Māori theatre's espousal of aspects of Western cultural currency – such as Stanislavskian actor training and rehearsal principles – can also be read as a deliberate reaction against a neo-imperialistic cultural and theatrical hegemony. Principles are not passively adhered to, rather they are claimed for their usefulness and mobilised through a local worldview.
>
> p. 370–371

For Ian Maxwell – who takes up explicitly the idea of distanciation in his essay 'Theatrical Bowerbirds: Received Stanislavsky and the Tyranny of Distance in Australian Actor Training' – geographical distance is overshadowed in importance by a distance in *sensibility* and 'in that distance', he argues, 'lies the possibility of invention and re-invention, creative misunderstanding and innovation, even when tinged with regret at lost opportunity' (p. 345). Peta Tait examines the influential teaching of Hayes Gordon in Sydney from 1952, the most direct root in Australian theatre history to an embodied understanding of Stanislavsky (albeit via Strasberg and Meisner). Tait shares the view that cultural–geographic distance created a liberating effect in relation to Stanislavsky's influence:

This becomes far more than passing on a systematic, ethical approach to acting, as Gordon's influence in Australia points towards diverse applications of Stanislavsky's ideas within the changing socio-political context in the second half of the twentieth century.

p. 348

The two countries share a common colonial history, of course. Modern Australian history is dated as beginning in 1788 (Rubin et al., 1998, p. 40) with the first Australian piece of theatre (in the European sense) being performed in 1789 by British convicts in the Sydney penal colony (Love, 1984, p. 13). Indigenous ritual and performance, however, by Aboriginal and Torres Straight Islander cultures has persisted for tens of thousands of years. For New Zealand, the Treaty of Waitinigi was signed in Aotearoa by Māori Chiefs and British officials in 1840 with the Gold Rush of 1861 prompting the first British and North American theatre companies to tour their work, as well as companies from neighbouring Australia (Rubin et al., 1998, p. 333).[4]

Collectively, the essays of this Part represent a range of attitudes to the importation of Stanislavskian practice. These include Australian actors' enthusiastic search for a legitimate Stanislavskian practice in the 1950s and 1960s in Sydney – Hayes Gordon considered by many 'to be a type of guru with a magnetic presence' (p. 353) as Tait puts it; through the pragmatic and unacknowledged appropriation of Stanislavskian principles in the Melbourne-based Victorian College of the Arts in the late 1980s – what Maxwell calls the 'refusal to be cowed by received authority' (p. 326); to the proactive hybridization of Stanislavsky and indigenous Māori principles in the early twenty-first century, following the spirit of conversation and kinship (whanaungatanga), Halba's 'biculturalism' (p. 371). Each of these attitudes might be considered a function of the autonomy occasioned by distance. As Australian theatre critic, Katherine Brisbane, argues in relation to the early days of the Sydney penal colony: 'Distance [...] also meant the absence of supervision and at times a freedom which allowed for enterprise and self-reliance' (Rubin et al., 1998, p. 40).

Another notable meeting point across these three essays is the often-overlooked conception of ethics, recalling the influence of Stanislavsky in France, identified by Marie-Christine Autant-Mathieu in Part One. As Katya Kamotskaia has observed, there is a tendency in Stanislavskian transmission to focus on technique and to lose sight of aesthetics and ethics (Merlin and

Kamotskaia, 2011, p. 177). The evidence from these Australasian perspectives, by contrast, is that ethics, defined by Stanislavsky as that which helps 'to keep the human soul safe from corruption and which regulate[s] the mutual relations between people and whole countries' (Stanislavsky, 1984, p. 107) plays a significant part.

Hayes Gordon, influenced by the socially concerned dramaturgy of the Group Theatre and, later, by Meisner's Neighbourhood Playhouse, set out to establish similar left-leaning principles for the embryonic Ensemble Theatre of Sydney in the 1950s. Indeed, as Peta Tait outlines, Gordon wrote a whole treatise on theatre ethics, *Towards an Ethical Theatre* (1977) and along with his colleague, Zika Nester, his training was constructed along ethical lines. Both of them strove, in Tait's assessment, 'to achieve a higher standard of acting through dedicated effort and systematic technique combined with considerate behaviour offstage' (p. 350).

Doris Fitton's ethics, as described in Maxwell's historical backdrop to Australian actor training, were even more directly attributable to Stanislavsky. She modelled the principles of the Independent Theatre, founded by her in Sydney in 1931, expressly on those of the Moscow Art Theatre, as described in her 'bible', Stanislavsky's *My Life in Art*. Along with her near-contemporary, Gregan McMahon (whose attitude to Stanislavsky's work was signally more ambivalent), Fitton, Maxwell elucidates, 'was committed to the model of the "Arts Theatre" and to the ennoblement of the actor's art, to mark a decisive break from the taint of amateurism' (p. 333).

Theatrical ethics in Aotearoa are more complex and symbolize the biculturalism Hilary Halba is keen to delineate. Ethics offer a meeting point between Stanislavskian and Māori principles and protocols on several fronts: in terms of the mutuality of engagement between actors, the communion with an audience, the latent spirituality of Stanislavskian discourse and the everyday, lived spirituality of Māori culture. They even meet in the manner in which the research process was conducted for this essay, as Halba notes:

> I conducted the interviews using Kaupapa Māori (Māori platform) research principles including the kahohi ki te kanohi (face to face) contact, and a kōrero (talking) process in which connections are forged, knowledge and ideas are shared, and 'both the participants and researcher benefit from the research project'.
>
> p. 368

These are principles that underpin a Western research ethics as much as they determine the Kaupapa Māori approach: mutual benefit, respect, and dialogue. They are deeply inscribed in Stanislavsky's ethos too and specifically in his definition of an ethics of teamwork. 'Each of these people, taken separately, is an independent creator', he opined in 1907:

> To coordinate the work of many creators and preserve the freedom of each one of them separately, there have to be moral principles generating respect for the creative work of others, sustaining a spirit of comradeship in the common effort, protecting one's own and others' creative freedom.
> Stanislavsky, 1984, p. 107

In this respect at least there appears to be less distance than Geoffrey Blainey suggests between Antipodean and European sensibilities.

Notes

1. Cf. The University of Auckland Business School's 2014 seminar: 'Overcoming the tyranny of distance: Evidence from New Zealand'; The New Zealand Institute for the Study of Competition and Regulation's 2010 seminar: 'The Tyranny of Distance Prevails'; or, for a more populist example pop group Split Enz's *6 Months in a Leaky Boat* (1982), with the unforgettable lyric: 'Aotearoa, rugged individual/ Glisten like a pearl, at the bottom of the world/The tyranny of distance, didn't stop the cavalier/So why should it stop me? I'll conquer and stay free'.
2. Samuel McCulloch's book review of Blainey cites the motivation of 'timber, naval supplies and flax' (McCulloch, 1969, p. 1692).
3. Committee for Economic Development in Australia
4. The first contact between Europeans and the indigenous population was, as Hilary Halba notes, between Cook and local islanders in 1769.

References

Blainey, G. (1966), *The Tyranny of Distance: how distance shaped Australia's history*. Northwestern: Sun Books.

Blainey, G. (2007), 'Distance: a key to Australia's economic dilemma', *CEDA Growth*, Vol. 58: 6–9.

Love, H. (ed.) (1984), *The Australian Stage: A Documentary History*. Sydney: New South Wales Press.

McCulloch, S. C. (1969), 'Review of *The Tyranny of Distance: how distance shaped Australia's history*', *The American Historical Review*, Vol. 74, No. 5: 1692–3.

Merlin, B. and Kamotskaia, K. (2011), 'Revisioned Directions: Stanislavsky in the Twenty-first Century', in *Russians in Britain*, ed. J. Pitches. Abingdon: Routledge, pp.167–91.

Rubin, D., Pong, S. C., Chaturvedi, R., Majumdar, R., Tanokura, M. and Brisbane, K. (1998). *The World Encyclopedia of Contemporary Theatre: Asia/Pacific*. London: Routledge.

Stanislavsky, K. (1984). *Selected Works*. Moscow: Raduga Publishers.

15

Theatrical Bowerbirds: Received Stanislavsky and the Tyranny of Distance in Australian Actor Training

Ian Maxwell

Introducing his 2005 collection of interviews with Australian actors, Terence Crawford confesses to a 'nagging feeling [...] that Australian actors are making it up as they go along'; that 'their work processes borrow more from their life experience and the way they look at the world than from the pages of any book or the teachings of any guru' (Crawford, 2005, p. 1).

Across fourteen interviews with a carefully curated sample, Crawford's intuition is confirmed: while many of the actors are able to talk about Stanislavsky – several conflate ideas about Stanislavsky with an idea about 'the Method' – none identify themselves as working within *any* tradition. Crawford – himself a graduate of the National Institute of Dramatic Art (NIDA), of which more later, and one time Head of Acting at the now-defunct Nepean Drama School at the University of Western Sydney – concludes that these actors are 'taking fragments from very many sources, and piecing them together into what we might call "personal belief systems," or matrices' (Crawford, 2005, p. 225). The arc of their working life is a disciplined improvisation, based on 'skill and experience'; the role of training is less to inculcate in an actor a particular technique, but to provide 'the beginnings of [a lifelong] learning' (Crawford, 2005, p. 225).

Not only actors 'piece together' technique. In his memoirs, Richard Wherrett, the founding director of the Sydney Theatre Company, recounts his experiences as a teacher at E15 in the mid-1960s:

> I did have teaching skills and a passion for theatre, but I knew nothing about acting technique [...] I *could* read up a chapter on Stanislavsky the night before the class, and I *could* communicate this – improvising! – the next day.
>
> Wherrett, 2000, p. 17

This is not to disparage Wherrett as teacher or director; rather, it is to point to a certain *sensibility*: a willingness to 'have a go'; a refusal to be cowed by received authority which, I will argue, characterizes the Australian approach to Stanislavsky, and to theatrical authority in general.

In this essay, I trace aspects of this 'piecing together', the ways in which Australian actors, directors, and teachers have taken up the legacy of Stanislavsky from the first decades of the twentieth century, through the establishment of conservatory acting training institutions in the second half of that century, to more recent attempts to engage more rigorously with Stanislavskian techniques.

Shot through with a characteristic Australian suspicion of influence, this 'taking up' may be understood in terms of the behaviour of the bowerbird, an Austro-Papuan family of ground-dwelling birds, famous for their nest – or 'bower' – building practices. The male bowerbird scavenges an assortment of objects – in particular colourful objects, favouring blue – with which to decorate their bower, adorning the assemblages of woven sticks with feathers, shells, flowers, bottle tops, scraps of paper, plastic, coins, or glass, presumably in order to attract an appropriate mate. They are collectors, avian bricoleurs, building a place for themselves in the world with what they can scrounge and appropriate.

Bowerbirds constitute a compelling trope for thinking about the relationship of Australian artists, in general, to European culture throughout the twentieth century; in particular, for thinking about the ways in which Australian theatre-makers have taken up the influence of Stanislavsky. In the absence of a direct transmission of Stanislavskian practice through touring companies, visiting teachers, or even the bodies of trained actors, Australian theatre workers have, instead, assembled a received, or 'soft' Stanislavskianism, taken up as a kind of understated substrate, often with passion and high aspirations, rarely with rigour or sustained commitment.

Training

Seven or eight weeks into the first year of our actor training at the Victorian College of the Arts (VCA) School of Drama, half the class, having just completed a movement class, gathered at a studio door for the next session: 'acting'. It was early 1987. To this point, the 'acting' classes had involved work with neutral masks – embodying gods, tarot cards; later we had moved onto short scenarios: two masks waking up, encountering each other for the first time; a mask running to the end of a pier, waving a farewell.

There were forty-two of us: twenty-four acting students, three directing students, three writers, and a dozen technical production trainees. For the first months of our three years of training we were all taking the same classes: a daily rhythm of voice sessions (in the Berry tradition); movement classes (largely built upon Feldenkrais and contact improvisation); and 'acting'. The early lessons in this last set of classes had involved trust-building, motor skills development (juggling and the like), training our sensory and spatial faculties, maskwork.

The most intense session to date had been an extended focus of attention exercise, involving our teacher raising our expectations of, and then thwarting, the experience of *wanting*, in order to demonstrate to us – no, affording us the direct experience of – the way in which a range of emotional states could be elicited simply through an investment in a specific belief. We had been asked to walk, eyes shut, across the studio floor to pick up a pen, relying exclusively upon the purity of our *want*. We each repeated the task, failure after failure, experiencing frustration, anger, resentment, despair, incandescent rage, taunted and provoked by our teacher (his refrain *do you really want it?* barely masking the subtextual *are you really committed to being here; to being an actor?*) until, finally, our hand closed upon our target. A brief moment of discharge, exhilaration; a penny dropping: *it worked! That time I really wanted it, and that want drew me, blind, across the room, and I got it.*

Then the debrief: 'want' had nothing to do with it. Each time, blind chance led us across the room. We had been betrayed by this man who had, or so we had thought, initiated us into a quasi-mystical actorly metaphysic. We had believed (in) him, and now ... but then came the real lesson: acting, he explained, was this: simply wanting, with all your heart, mind and soul, something that you didn't really want, and allowing whatever happens when that want is thwarted, to happen (see Maxwell, 2010).

Our teacher, then, had form: he had shown us how easily emotional intensity might be evoked and how we had all 'survived' and moved past, moments of heightened passion. This was to be our work.

And so, a couple of weeks later, we wait outside his studio. The door opens, and the other half of the class files out in singles and in pairs, heads lowered. Behind them we see others collecting sweaters, handbags. I recall some holding each other, shoulders heaving. Those eyes we meet are puffy, red, faces pale and drawn. What on earth had happened? What were we in for?

The exercise was, again, devastatingly simple. We were to stand face-to-face with a partner, a couple of metres apart. One was instructed to raise their straightened arms to shoulder level, palms up, and to make a small beckoning gesture with the fingers of each hand. The partner was to wait until they felt ready, and then to turn away, walking the length of the studio, leaving their partner, beckoning.

Shortly afterwards – perhaps the next week – we were introduced to the major work of that first term. We were each to select the most 'x' moment of our lives – the 'x' we were to fill in for ourselves – and to spend the following weeks recalling this moment in all its specificity. Where. When. With whom. The weather; the temperature, the feeling of the air on our skin. Words spoken; actions performed. In small groups, we were to work on reproducing these moments, staging them, taking the supporting roles in each other's scenes. We did nothing else for a couple of weeks. We didn't speak of 'given circumstances'; the exercise was not framed as 'emotional recall', 'work on ourselves'. It was not legitimated by reference to any authority other than our teacher, whose credibility had already been well-established: we were deeply in his thrall. And, again, the outcomes were devastating. For several hours that Melbourne autumn, we sat, all forty of us, as each of us re-enacted our moments. Teenage selves were kicked out of home; others lost their virginity, lost loved ones, were betrayed, belittled, screamed, wept, sobbed. After each showing we hugged, consoled each other, cried, nestled in the thick fug of that studio space, hour after hour. It was the most wrenching, exhausting and, perhaps inevitably, cathartic thing I had ever encountered.

Again, afterwards: the debrief. We had learnt, we were told, the power of our recollection, supported by our mobilization of our bodily and sensory memories. Although it had taken us weeks to reach this pitch of intensity, next time it would be easier, shorter, for now we knew what was involved. Most importantly, we knew that we could face up to those memories without being harmed by them. This is what would make us actors.

It was not until well after my graduation that I read Stanislavsky, recognizing not only the provenance of the things we had been doing, but the Stanislavskian mise-en-scene: the authoritative, omniscient teacher gifted not only with knowledge of human psychology in general, but with insight into each of our individual psyches; an ability to peer deep into our souls, to elicit our deepest secrets. At College we had all but been actively discouraged from such reading, out of a concern, we were told, that had we known what was going on, it might not have had the desired impact upon us. The pen game, the beckoning exercise, emotional recall: all relied for their effect, to an extent if not on outright deception, then at least a *coup de main* revelation. The Stanislavskian mise-en-scene: students as *tabulae rasae*; credulous Kostyas falling, unwittingly, into error, and then saved, lessons hard-learnt, by the all-seeing Tortsov. The institutional imprecation was 'to do, not think'; book learning was viewed with suspicion, and as no substitute for direct, committed and, ideally, lacerative experience.

Stanislavsky was never named as the source or inspiration of the work we were doing; nor Strasberg. We did hear about Feldenkrais, largely in order, I think, to distinguish the approach taken in our movement classes from the better-known Alexander technique. The other key authority for us was Laban; in fact the only written material circulated in the course of our training was our teacher's compendium of Laban's basic effort actions. We knew, too, that another of our teachers had trained with Jacques Lecoq.

The overarching rubric for our training was, however, that of the authoritative, charismatic presence of the guru-teacher. We understood our teachers as the origin of, rather than as mediators of, the knowledge and practices into which they were initiating us. There was little, if any sense, of a tradition, or of our teachers' place in a genealogy of practice. Greater emphasis was placed upon our teachers' credibility as practitioners: artists whose work we could witness first hand.

Years later, I asked that teacher about those classes, and of the influence of Stanislavsky upon his training. Here is his account:

> Some of the work I did at the VCA, particularly the action work, came from a man by the name of Phillip Hedley. He was a protégé of Joan Littlewood's and a lot of her work came from Stanislavsky and Brecht. She visited Stanislavsky when he was quite old, I think, but she brought back with her a lot of his later work which centred around the work of Physical Action. I actually came across Stanislavsky's work after I had been acting for a while. His work influenced the acting work in England at that time but only in certain areas. Now, of course, things are quite different. However, in England there was never anything like the Method that thrived in the States. Systems and methods were very much looked down upon. Phillip had a huge influence on acting and directing in England, he had great influence over East 15 and then ended up as the Artistic Director of Stratford East which was the home of Theatre Workshop which had been founded by Joan Littlewood.
>
> David Latham, pers. comm. 19 October 2013[1]

This autobiographical sketch is something of a synecdoche, capturing the essence of the way in which the legacy of Stanislavsky has been taken up in Australia. The story is one of what we might style as 'effect at a distance': none of Stanislavsky's students taught or directed in Australia; no Australians travelled to Moscow to work in the MAT Studios; the line of apostolic succession that characterizes much of the narrative of the dissemination and cross-Atlantic translation of Stanislavskian and post-Stanislavskian ideas is entirely absent from Australian theatre history, with the noble exception of Hayes Gordon's work from the late 1950s.[2] Instead, there is a daisy-chain of influence, received ideas, accommodations, autodidactic enthusiasms, indigenizations, misconceptions, chinese whispers, shot through with characteristic post-colonial anxieties: the paradoxes of cultural cringe and anti-intellectualism; of brash, anti-authoritarianism and periphery-centre obsequiousness; a new worldish determination to do it our own way, and the anxiety of influence.

Or, as the Australian theatre director Barrie Koksy put it, somewhat more polemically:

> [...] through an appalling, watered-down, messed-up, fucked-up sort of Stanislavsky-via-the-Studio-in-New-York thing, the entire world has become obsessed with psychological profiling, which is all chitchat. That's talk you do over coffee, that's not *work* in the theatre. Don't get me wrong, there are certain things with Stanislavsky that are very valuable to an actor, personally, to *read* about. But it's of no value to me as a director to sit down

and talk about it with an actor [...] they should have done it, in some form, themselves.

in Macauley, 2003, p. 5; emphasis in original

First contact

The first Australian theatre-maker to engage with Stanislavskian aspirations, if not necessarily Stanislavskian techniques, was Gregan McMahon (1874–1941), an actor and manager who, in 1910, formed the Melbourne Repertory Company. Writing in 1978, Allan Ashbolt observed that 'he [McMahon] hoped, of course, that in time the company could be put on a durable professional basis, in much the same way as Stanislavski and Nemirovtich [sic] had developed amateur groups into the Moscow Arts Theatre' (Ashbolt, 1978, p. 329).

From the first years of the century, 'at a time when the cultural lag between England and Australia was at least ten years' as Ashbolt has it, McMahon was abreast of the latest theatrical innovations in Europe; he had 'been reading

Figure 30 Gregan McMahon, 1905–6.

Ibsen and Shaw, knew what was happening at the Stage Society in London, and speedily absorbed the influences radiating from the Vedrenne-Baker seasons at the Royal Court' (Ashbolt, 1978, p. 327). The metaphors are important: a sense of influences *radiating* out from a cultural centre; eager *absorption* in a far-flung antipodean periphery.

And yet, at the same time, Ashbolt notes an anxiety of influence in McMahon's characteristically Australian ambivalence towards – perhaps suspicion of – high cultural authority:

> [h]e had a strange parochial contempt for Stanislavski's theories. His dismissal [of Stanislavsky] was at variance with the whole pattern of his life, which had been woven out of an intelligent perception of world-wide theatrical changes [...] An Actor Prepares and My Life in Art were in the library of his office [...] but I doubt that he had more than half-read either book.
>
> Ashbolt, 1978, p. 339

However, it is apparent that McMahon had engaged in something of a proselytization of the ideas he had been absorbing. In 1918, he relocated to Sydney, founding the Sydney Repertory Company two years later. Among the actors with whom he worked was Doris Fitton, who later recalled that:

> [i]t was Stanislavsky's book, *My Life in Art* that crystallised my ideals and confirmed the teaching of Gregan McMahon. All who are interested in theatre should read this wonderful story by Constantin Stanislavsky, founder and director of the Moscow Art Theatre. It is not so much about the technique of acting as about how that great theatre was born.
>
> Fitton, 1981, p. 30

Fitton herself established a theatre – the Independent – in Sydney in 1931, following 'the guiding principles of the Moscow Art Theatre as formulated in Stanislavsky's *My Life in Art*' (Kreisler, 1995, p. 514), a book to which she referred as 'my Bible' (Fitton, 1981, p. 32). In her autobiography Fitton enumerated what she understood to be Stanislavsky's fundamental tenets:

> There are no small parts, there are only small actors.
> One must love art, and not one's self in art.
> Today Hamlet, tomorrow a supernumerary, but even as a supernumerary, you must become an artist.
> The poet, the actor, the artist, the tailor, the stage hand serve one goal, which is placed by the poet in the very basis of his play.

> All disobedience to the creative life of the theatre is a crime. Lateness, laziness, caprice, hysterics, bad character, ignorance of the role, the necessity of repeating anything twice are all equally harmful to our enterprise and must be rooted out.
>
> Fitton, 1981, p. 34

Fitton, like McMahon, was committed to the model of the 'Arts Theatre' and to the en-noblement of the actor's art, to mark a decisive break from the taint of amateurism:

> Stanislavsky's guidelines – to produce the finest plays available, to take care with every detail in production, for everyone to serve the play and for there to be no stars – were the policies adhered to by the Independent from its beginning to its end.
>
> Fitton, 1981, p. 34

Figure 31 Doris Fitton, in the 1930s.

Accounts of Fitton as a director, however, suggest that little of Stanislavsky's techniques took root in the rehearsal room. 'Everything was very "stagey", recalled one actor, involving a focus on 'diction, voice carrying, moving off on the upstage foot and acting to the audience' (Ron Falkland cited in Lowry, 2007, p. 162). Another actor explained that 'we certainly never indulged in any intellectual discussion about the play [...] she [Fitton] has a strong theatrical instinct', which she used to 'pull you up if she felt you were on the wrong track' (David Nettheim cited in Lowry, 2007, p. 162).

The exception was Fitton's production of *The Cherry Orchard* in 1944–5 which, she explained, '[w]e rehearsed for three months, following the Stanislavsky method' (Fitton, 1981, p. 53). Her gloss of that 'method' is instructive:

> [T]he cast members really grew into their parts [...] We rehearsed continuously [...] until we had all thoroughly assimilated our roles. This was very much the manner in which Stanislavsky worked, except that he sometimes rehearsed for six months.
>
> One of his precepts was not to allow the actors to put their scripts down until they knew their words. His argument was that learning a part parrot fashion caused the breaking down of interpretation. Stanislavsky insisted that the actors had to achieve complete naturalism. If they *assimilated* their parts slowly and thoughtfully, it was like drawing a cloak carefully around themselves.
>
> Fitton, 1981, p. 52

A Russian member of the company, Valentine Diakov, assisted with pronunciation, and contributed a samovar. The *Sydney Morning Herald*'s enthusiastic review observed that the play 'relies on the emotions that accompany action, atmosphere, and a completely successful detachment from theatricalism', concluding that 'Doris Fitton, who also acts in the play, has prepared this production with great thought and care in order to preserve the delicate balance between the laughter and the tears' ('L.B.' in the *Sydney Morning Herald* 29 December 1944, p. 4).

International encounters

A couple of years prior to Fitton's *Cherry Orchard*, another group of Sydney actors had experienced a more direct link with Stanislavskian technique, albeit one filtered through New York. Oriel Gray, a Marxist playwright working with the progressive New Theatre, offers a brief, rueful account of the work of a 'short, balding, unimpressive' corporal by the name of Will Lee Lubovsky, who, stationed in Sydney for a short period during the Second World War, led acting classes for the company in 1942 (Gray, 1985, p. 84). Lubovsky had worked with Clifford Odets and Harold Clurman at the Group Theatre and, as Will Lee, had appeared in several Group productions. 'Memory is the key', he told his students; Gray paraphrases his teaching: 'if you can replace the playwright's truth with something from your own experience, his lines come out with both your truths' (Lubovsky cited in Gray, 1985, p. 85).

An 'uncompromising man', however, Lubovsky did not endear himself to the right people: '[c]omments about the classes' Gray explains, 'began to be patronizing, slightly humorous, and the animal exercises brought loud guffaws' (Gray, 1985, p. 85). The more experienced members of the company stopped attending, and Lubovsky moved on without saying 'much more than goodbye' (Gray, 1985, p. 85). Gray records her disappointment: a lost opportunity to establish an Actors Studio in Sydney, sabotaged, on her account, by a characteristic Australian suspicion of cultural authority (Gray, 1985, p. 86).

The Second World War, however, had not only brought foreign servicemen to Australia; a generation of young Australian men had been dispatched across the world, among them Peter Finch. A jobbing actor prior to the Second World War, Finch had played a series of minor roles for Fitton at the Independent, where, his biographer Trader Faulkner explains, the work had involved 'mostly trying to build live characters out of virtually non-existent parts' (Faulkner, 1979, p. 55).

Stationed in the Middle East, Finch attended a Hebrew-language production of *Twelfth Night* staged by the Habima Theatre in Tel Aviv (Faulkner, 1979, p. 92). The Habima had been established in Białystok, Poland, under the auspices of the Moscow Art Theatre, the ensemble trained by Vakhtangov. The original company split during a 1926 tour of the United States, a rump of actors relocating to the Palestine Mandate in 1928, where they worked under Aleksei Dikiy, another student of Stanislavsky and Nemirovich-Danchenko. Faulkner notes that Finch also 'met a Russian actor there who had acted in London with Gielgud and had been a pupil of Stanislavsky in Moscow' (Faulkner, 1979, p. 92). (Finch's interest in things Russian had developed through his courtship of the ballerina Tamara Rechemcinc ['Tchinarova'], who had stayed in Australia following the tour of the Covent Garden Russian Ballet in 1938. The couple had married in 1943.)

Returning to Sydney, Finch embarked upon a collaboration with a German musician, 'Sydney' John Kay, who, touring Australia with a group called the Syncopators when the Second World War broke out, had been interned as an enemy alien (Vagg, 2007, p. 18). In 1946, Finch, Kay and three other collaborators – John Wilshire, Allan Ashbolt, and Colin Scrimgeour – met in The Green Parrott café in central Sydney to draft a proposal for a Sydney Art Theatre, to be named the Mercury. Among the stated aims of the company were the 'formation of an acting school and the use of students as understudies' in support of an ambitious repertory program (Vagg, 2007, p. 20). The school opened in September 1946 in a tiny theatre in the city's business district, with Finch leading classes.

In his 1979 biography of Finch, Trader Faulkner remembers 'a true theatrical jackdaw' who, 'although no intellectual', had 'read avidly and widely', and had assembled 'a glittering hoard of literary treasure' (Faulkner, 1979, p. 121). Finch had also been 'stimulated' by his encounter with Dolia Ribush, a Latvian émigré who had founded an amateur group to perform plays for the Russian Club in Melbourne in 1930–1, applying 'techniques derived from' Stanislavsky and the French actor Louis Jouvet (O'Brien, 1995, p. 500; Faulkner, 1979, p. 92).

Figure 32 Peter Finch with Diane Cilento, 1955.

Faulkner attended classes at the Mercury, and reproduces 'handwritten notes I made of words that dropped from the maestro's lips on the afternoons Finchie gave his classes' (Faulkner, 1979, p. 121).

Finch's discourse is replete with received Stanislavskianism. 'Whatever happens on stage must have a purpose', he told his students:

> When you are sitting still, and let's hope to God you are listening to the other characters on stage even if he or she is not addressing you, what are you thinking? And [what of] that golden thread of concentration in existence between you and the audience?
>
> Faulkner, 1979, p. 121

Finch was attentive to the requirement for an active inner life of the character:

> The external mobility of a person on stage does not imply passiveness. You may sit perfectly still and at the same time be charged with inner action. Frequently, physical immobility is the direct result of inner intensity and it is these inner activities that are far more important artistically.
>
> Faulkner, 1979, p. 121

He also took up the Stanislavskian aspiration to theatrical spirituality, supported by an elucidation of a tripartite topography of the actor's self:

> The essence of art is not in the external forms but in its spiritual content. Therefore it is necessary to act on stage inwardly and you automatically feel and look right outwardly. Imagination and feeling are the key to acting but there must also be 'cerebral activity'.
>
> Faulkner, 1979, p. 121[3]

At the same time, Faulkner notes that Finch was 'too volatile and too much the actor to teach as well as he should have' (Faulkner, 1979, p. 121); another biographer, Elaine Dundy, records 'boys listening spellbound and the girls crying as Peter was talking' (Dundy, 1980, p. 120). Faulkner captures the larrikin charisma, again quoting Finch:

> When you are a character speaking dialogue, it is the subtext, what you are thinking not necessarily what you are saying, but how you are feeling and saying what you thinking that separates the men from the boys and, of course, the women from the trivial, empty-headed 'sheilas' (with a big grin at a very pretty redhead in the class called Adele Romano).
>
> Faulkner, 1979, p. 121

The Mercury did not quite recover from Finch's departure in 1948. The visiting Laurence Olivier, having seen Finch play in *The Imaginary Invalid*, invited him to 'look me up' if he ever got to London. 'It was', Stephen Vagg writes, 'all the encouragement Finch needed' (Vagg, 2007, p. 23). The Mercury fell into a fallow period, re-activating briefly in 1952, and folding late the following year, having failed to establish work of sufficient quality to secure an audience.

Institutionalization

In 1949, Tyrone Guthrie was invited to visit Australia to prepare a report on the feasibility of founding a national theatre. Guthrie recommended scholarships for actors to train by 'cosmopolitan, not provincial standards' in London (Guthrie, 1949, pp. 80–1), before, as Peter Holloway has it, being 'transported back to Australia as cultural missionaries' (Holloway, 1987, p. 17). This proposal was not taken up. However, by the end of the following decade, the conservative government of Robert Menzies, guided by the advice of the remarkable H. R. 'Nugget' Coombs, had established the Australian Elizabethan Theatre Trust (the AETT) to foster the arts. Among the first of the Trust's achievements was the foundation, in 1958, of the NIDA, in Sydney, on the campus of the University of New South Wales.

Aubrey Mellor, Executive Director from 2005 to 2008, enjoyed a particularly long engagement with NIDA, first as a graduate of the technical production course in 1969, as an acting teacher from 1973 to 1978, and Assistant Director from 1983 to 1985. Mellor attributes NIDA's considerable success – alumni include Mel Gibson, Baz Luhrmann, and Cate Blanchett – to what he calls 'the Australian Method: half British communication skills and half American truth-seeking skills, with the Australian independent streak thrown in' (Mellor, pers. comm. 26 May 2014).

Indeed, NIDA may be understood as the institutionalization of the history of Australian theatrical bricolage, blending, often irreverently, sometimes obeisantly, influences from the British tradition – and in particular those of the Old Vic, the repertory system, and RADA – with autodidactically-mediated understandings of Stanislavskian techniques, and, as Mellor suggests, post-Stanislavskian method. The synergy is evident from the outset: curriculum documents for the first intake of students explicitly state that 'the method of instruction will be based upon the teachings of Stanislavsky and will include practice in a series of dramatic situations' (NIDA, 1959).[4] The syllabus is a crib from the contents page of *An Actor Prepares*:

> In the first year students will be introduced to the correct mental process of acting, will develop their powers of concentration and observation and will increase the range and vitality of their dramatic imagination. They will be taught the need of purpose in acting and truth in motivation. Their sensory and emotional memory will be trained to enable them to react naturally to imaginary stimuli in the given circumstances of the play. These inner techniques will be integrated with those learnt in movement and speech classes. By the end of the first year, it is hoped that all students will be able to act fluently, truthfully and consistently, and will be free from the inner tensions which inhibit natural talent.
>
> NIDA, 1959

Chris Puplick, two-time member of the NIDA Board, suggests that 'intellectually' the training at NIDA 'harks back to both Stanislavsky and, perhaps more significantly, the work of Michel Saint-Denis' (Puplick, 2011, p. 31), treating students as 'diamonds' whose 'accretions of bad habits' were first 'cut away, then cut and facetted, and finally polished' (Puplick, 2011, p. 31).

The tone was initially set by Tom Brown, the Institute's director from 1963 to 1969, who had trained with Saint-Denis at the Old Vic. The Old Vic connection was particularly strong, and established the 'British communications skills' to which Mellor refers: NIDA's founding director was Robert Quentin, an Englishman who, during the Second World War, had been posted to Sydney with the Royal Navy. While in Sydney, he had directed Doris Fitton at the Independent in *Mourning Becomes Electra*. Back in Sydney in 1946, he directed for the commercial producer J. C. Williamson, returning to first the Bristol, and then the London Old Vic in 1950, where he became producer/manager in 1952. At the Old Vic, Quentin had worked with Hugh Hunt; as the first director of the AETT, Hunt recruited Quentin to manage the Trust Opera Company. Observing that Australian actors had 'lived too long in the shadow of English understatement', Quentin lobbied for a drama academy to 'develop a distinctly Australian style of acting based on the natural vigour of the students' (cited in Puplick, 2011, p. 6; see also Clark, 2003).

The place of Stanislavskian ideas in the NIDA curriculum waxed and waned over the decades. His name is invoked consistently in curriculum documents, and his texts 'set' within syllabuses, often as 'recommended reading'. However, as Mellor comments, 'Stanislavsky was never ingrained in students' (Mellor, pers. comm. 26 May 2014). Concepts such as 'action playing [...] emotion memory, sense memory' he recalls, were used by Alan Edwards, another Old Vic alumnus who was Head of Acting from 1964 to 1969, but were:

> always referred to, but not credited back to Stanislavsky [...] We learned about the Moscow Arts and Stanislavsky in History of Theatre, but history of performance was rarely taught and theorists rarely credited. I really had to teach myself both Stanislavsky and Brecht.
> Mellor, pers. comm. 26 May 2014

Subsequently, under Alexander Hay, a classicist trained at RADA, Mellor recalls, 'script analysis grew stronger'; Hay was, however, 'very much of the British tradition'; although he 'had acted a lot of American works', he:

> held the view that Method Acting did little for theatre, but created great film actors. He worked with the 'W's (who, what, where, when, etc.), and used some of book two [*Building a Character*] when talking about character.
> Mellor, pers. comm. 26 May 2014

Stanislavsky's work, Mellor explains, 'did not really arrive at NIDA until George Whaley' (Mellor, pers. comm. 26 May 2014), in 1976.

Whaley's appointment as Head of Acting saw a conscious turn to Stanislavsky, and in particular to action playing. Whaley was the very model of the theatrical autodidact, his career the embodiment of theatrical bowerbirding. An engineering graduate involved in student theatre, in 1961 had founded the Emerald Hill Company with Wal Cherry, the former Director of the Union Repertory Company (URC – later the Melbourne Theatre Company) (Milne, 2004, pp. 112–14; Worby, 1987, p. 76). Cherry had introduced Brecht to the URC, and had made a series of attempts to 'form experimental theatre groups loosely based on American models, such as the Theatre Workshop and Actors Studio' (Milne, 2004, p. 112). Emerald Hill, Worby explains, 'inclined towards ideas from the Berliner Ensemble, Stanislavsky's experiments, Vilar's Theatre Nationale Populaire and Joan Littlewood's Stratford East Workshop' (Worby,

1987, p. 78). As Worby notes, however, these were 'sources of inspiration, not models for emulation or slavish imitation' (Worby, 1987, p. 78).

Around the same time that Whaley was appointed to NIDA, the influence of Stanislavsky on Australian actor training was playing out in a contrary manner in the establishment of the VCA in Melbourne. The VCA School of Drama 'began', Richard Murphet explains, in 1975, 'with a carte blanche and a vision that paralleled not the traditional British or European models, but the radical theatre scene then existing in Melbourne' (Murphet, 2011, p. 15), a scene centred on the Australian Performing Group (APG), and a confluence of specific trends:

> [a] commitment to political activism and to texts that provided a political analysis of current and historical events, a prioritizing of new Australian work that dealt with aspects of the national identity, a democratization of work practices, and a wariness of the semblance of 'trained' acting.
>
> Murphet, 2011, p. 15

VCA teaching staff was drawn mainly from the APG; the Foundation Head of Drama was Peter Oyston, an Englishman who had spent some of his youth in Melbourne, before working in the UK, setting up the Duke's Theatre in Lancaster. Prior to his appointment to the VCA, Oyston had become influenced by the community theatre movement; his vision for the new School of Drama was as an incubator: 'an intensive preparation for the formation of a series of new companies, making new work, fresh in style and purpose, and relevant to the community in which they operated' (Murphet, 2011, p. 16).

Oyston's plans, however, were at odds both with the planned philosophy for the school, and with a socio-political backlash to the perceived legacy of the liberated 1960s. The 'Educational Specifications' for the school, framed in 1974, spoke to 'a basis of classical acting technique supported by thorough voice and movement training' (cited in Murphet, 2011, p. 17), 'not', Murphet notes, 'exactly evident in the program that Oyston set up' (Murphet, 2011, p. 17). The Melbourne theatre establishment was 'dismayed' by the direction the school had taken, and lobbied for a reversion to more classical training (Murphet, 2011, p. 17). When Oyston resigned in 1984, his replacements, first Roger Hodgman and then David Latham, in Murphet's words, 'changed the curriculum over to a training that would prepare students not for making new work in the regions [...] but for work in companies such as the MTC [Melbourne Theatre Company]' (Murphet, 2011, p. 18). This was the training I encountered, as described at the beginning of this chapter.

Upon Whaley's departure from NIDA in 1981, Nick Enright, an actor and playwright trained broadly within the Strasbergian tradition at the New York University School of the Arts, took over for three years. The early 1980s saw frequent changes in direction, producing 'regular vocal protests' by students, and culminating in a review of the acting course, headed by Mellor (Lavery, 1995, p. 393). The unsettledness continued until the appointment of Kevin Jackson to the role of Head of Acting in 1990, a position he held until 2008.

Jackson was himself a NIDA graduate, and recalled the training, particularly under Alexander Hay, as involving 'teaching from anecdote': the 'just get up and do it' school of acting (Kevin Jackson, pers. corr. 11 October 2013). 'I could swear on the Bible' Jackson says, 'that I never heard the name Stanislavsky uttered throughout my training' (Jackson, pers. corr. 11 October 2013).

Jackson's stewardship of training at NIDA repeats the familiar pattern: a synthesis of influences, catalysed by key experiences, reworked through the imperatives of day-to-day practice in the studio. Key among Jackson's experiences was a period at the American Conservatory Theatre (ACT) in San Francisco, where he spent three months watching classes; there, he tells me, 'the penny dropped': he saw the concentrated, systematic, and painstaking work involved in being an actor. Upon returning to Australia, he was invited to direct a production for NIDA, and the following year was appointed as Head of Acting.

The curriculum Jackson developed drew upon the ACT 'attention to detail', a level of 'preparation and homework unprecedented' in his experience: developing extensive backgrounds and contexts for characters, identifying 'key biographical turning points' (Jackson, pers. corr. 11 October 2013). At the same time, he recalls the ACT 'rebellion against [the] emotional stuff'. From Enright he took an intense interest in encouraging young actors to the 'personalization' of roles: of owning a role 'for yourself'. While Jackson worked with first year students on improvisation and 'given circumstances', Gail Edwards focused on objectives and Tony Knight added the movement-based Yat Malmgrem technique. Specialized movement training was delivered by Keith Bain, who had trained and worked with Gertrud Bodenwieser (1890–1959), a Viennese ballet dancer, and advocate of the New Dance who, influenced by Delsarte, Laban, and Dalcroze, had established her company in Sydney in 1940 (Campbell, 2011).

In second year, students turned to scene work, described by Jackson as being driven by a combination of 'Stanislavsky and the work from last night' (Jackson, pers. comm. 11 October 2013). The final year largely involved productions and orienting students to career-readiness. Amongst other influences on the curriculum he notes Uta Hagen's *Respect for Acting*, while laughingly referring to *An Actor Prepares* as 'the most influential but least read text' in actor training as a whole.

Meanwhile, at the VCA, the curriculum moved into new territory under the direction of Lindy Davies in her role as Dean, 1995–2007. Davies is best known for her work with 'impulse' and the rubric of the 'autonomous actor', grounded in a potent blending of influences, from Feldenkrais to Peter Brook, Stanislavsky, and others. As Helen Strube observes:

> [s]he does not have a method or a system but an approach to performance. She believes strongly in the creative independence of the actor [...] Each actor works differently, since all actors are different.
>
> Strube et al., 2010, p. 58

The discourse of 'autonomous actor' remains central to what is now called the VCA School of Performing Arts, part of a claim to the 'holistic' development of the actor:

> [t]he philosophy and practice of VCA Theatre is devoted to the development of independent artists who possess a passion for theatre and a desire to contribute meaningfully to the evolution of the art form in this country. VCA Theatre employs an expansive, progressive use of the term *actor* that builds upon [the] idea of a performer who interprets existing text. Our definition also recognises the actor as an artist with agency to generate new performances.
>
> VCA website, 2014

More recent changes at NIDA, however, have seen a conscious effort to focus aspects of the training on a more rigorous Stanislavskianism. This is particularly the case with the training of directors under Egil Kipste, whose first contact with Stanislavskian ideas came during his own training as a postgraduate

Directing student at NIDA, and the visit in 1983 of Yvgeny Lanskoi from the Maly Theatre (Egil Kipste, pers. comm. 24 June 2014). Lanskoi spoke to the idea of psychophysical action; subsequently, Kipste researched Stanislavsky's 'later' ideas, largely through books such as Sharon Carnicke's *Stanislavsky in Focus* and Bella Merlin's *Complete Stanislavsky Toolkit*. Upon taking up the role of Head of Directing at NIDA, Kipste invited Carnicke as a guest lecturer, and himself visited Sergei Tcherkasski in St Petersburg. Kipste has implemented a director-training curriculum that now is grounded in working with methods of physical action drawn from his sustained research into that particular legacy.

Conclusion

Other changes have been afoot at NIDA. Chris Puplick, in the essay quoted above, expressed dismay that the 2010 brief for recruitment of the new Head of Acting did not 'mention the words "Australia" or "Australian" once' before lamenting, in a stand-alone paragraph, that '[t]he new Head of Acting, appointed in November 2011, was an American' (Puplick, 2011, p. 34). While this is not the place to rehearse the controversies attending to the restructuring of NIDA, the tenor of Puplick's essay is telling. The new appointment, indeed, is an American, although not, as Puplick claims, the first non-Australian appointed to the position (Puplick, 2011, p. 6) a claim that overlooks the contributions of Brown, Hay, and Edwards in the early years (although on a technicality it may be that they did not enjoy the title 'Head of Acting'). However, Jeff Janisheski does bring, amongst a raft of interests, experience of actor training in Moscow, where, he explains, he observed at close quarters the intensity, thoroughness and, above all, the *length of time* involved in training actors in the Stanislavskian tradition: time which, in the crowded curriculum of the contemporary drama school, is simply not available to the students he trains at NIDA (Janisheski, pers. comm. 23 October 2013).

Indeed, the controversy over Janisheski's appointment speaks to the anxiety of influence that has, as I have argued throughout this essay, shaped the Australian response to Stanislavsky. The distance that sets Australia, even in the digital age, apart from European cultural sources is as much one of sensibility as of geography. In that distance lies the possibility of invention and re-invention, creative misunderstanding and innovation, even when tinged with regret at lost opportunity.

The tension between an outward-looking obeisance – the well-noted 'Cultural Cringe' (Phillips, 1950) – on the one hand, and, on the other, a determination to do it *our* way, to cock an anti-authoritarian snoot at received knowledge, has yielded something of a dynamic synthesis. It may not necessarily be the case that there is such a thing as 'the Australian method', as Mellor claims. However, the grounds for making such a claim – the mediation of influences through an irreverent antipodean pragmatics – are well born out.

Notes

1. This anecdote is in itself indicative of the confusions and conflations that characterize Australian histories of Stanislavsky-related training. It was not Joan Littlewood from the UK who visited Stanislavsky late in life but Stella Adler from the US (in 1934 to be precise).
2. See contribution by Peta Tait in this volume.
3. Contrast with Stanislavsky's tripartite topography of Reason, Will, and Feeling.
4. This document, as well as the various curriculum-related papers to which I refer below, I accessed at the NIDA Archive in October 2013. I would like to acknowledge the assistance of the NIDA archivist, Julia Mant.

References

Ashbolt, A. (1978), 'Courage, contradiction and compromise: Gregan McMahon 1874–1941', *Meanjin*, Vol. 37, No. 3 (October 1978): 324–46.

Campbell, M. (2011), *Keith Bain on Movement*. Sydney: Currency House.

Clark, J. (2003), *NIDA*. Sydney: University of NSW, and the Department of Communications, Information Technology and the Arts.

Crawford, T. (2005), *Trade Secrets: Australian Actors and Their Craft*. Sydney: Currency Press.

Dundy, E. (1980), *Finch, Bloody Finch: A Biography of Peter Finch*. London: Joseph.

Faulkner, T. (1979), *Peter Finch: A Biography*. London: Angus & Robertson.

Fitton, D. (1981), *Not Without Dust and Heat: My Life in Theatre*. Sydney: Harper & Row.

Gray, O. (1985), *Exit Left: Memoirs of a Scarlet Woman*. Ringwood, Vic.: Penguin Books.

Guthrie, T. (1949), 'Report on Australian Theatre', *The Australian Quarterly*, Vol. 21, No. 2 (June 1949): 78–83.

Holloway, P. (1987), 'Introduction to the First Edition', in *Contemporary Australian Drama (Completely Revised 1987)*, ed. P. Holloway. Sydney: Currency Press, pp. 11–43.

Hunt, H. (1960), 'The making of Australian theatre', in *Contemporary Australian Drama (Completely Revised 1987)*, ed. P. Holloway. Sydney: Currency Press, pp. 66–71.

Kreisler, M. (1995), 'Russian influences', in *Companion to Theatre in Australia*, ed. P. Parsons. Sydney: Currency Press, in association with Cambridge University Press, pp. 514–15.

Lavery, P. (1995), 'National Institute of Dramatic Art', in *Companion to Theatre in Australia*, ed. P. Parsons. Sydney: Currency Press, in association with Cambridge University Press, p. 393.

Lowry, C. (2007), *An Independent Woman: A Re-examination of Doris Fitton's Contribution to Theatre in Sydney in the First Half of the Twentieth Century*. Unpublished PhD thesis. University of Sydney.

Macauley, A. (2003), *Don't Tell Me, Show Me: Directors Talk About Acting*. Sydney: Currency Press.

Maxwell, I. (2010), 'Do You Really Want It?', *Australasian Drama Studies*, Vol. 57, pp. 10–21.

Milne, G. (2004), *Theatre Australia (Un)Limited: Australian Theatre Since the 1950s*. Amsterdam, New York: Rodopi.

Murphett, R. (2001), *The Fall and Rise of the VCA*. Sydney: Currency House.

O'Brien, A. (1995), 'Dolia Rubish' in *Companion to Theatre in Australia*, ed. P. Parsons. Sydney: Currency Press, in association with Cambridge University Press, pp. 500–1.

Phillips, A. A. (1950), 'The Cultural Cringe', *Meanjin*, Vol. 9, No. 4: 299–302.

Puplick, C. (2011), *Changing Times at NIDA*. Sydney: Currency House.

Strube, H. et al. (2010), *Dramatexts: Creative Practice for Senior Drama Students*. Brisbane: John Wiley & Sons, Australia.

Vagg, S. (2007), 'Finch, Fry and factories: a brief history of the Mercury Theatre', *Australasian Drama Studies*, Vol. 50: 18–35.

Wherrett, R. (2000), *The Floor of Heaven: My Life in Theatre*. Sydney: Sceptre.

Worby, G. (1987), 'Emerald Hill and the ensemble ideal', in *Contemporary Australian Drama (Completely Revised 1987)*, ed. P. Holloway. Sydney: Currency Press, pp. 76–88.

16

Acting Idealism and Emotions: Hayes Gordon, The Ensemble Theatre and Acting Studios in Australia

Peta Tait

A tradition of Konstantin Stanislavsky's approach to acting developed in Australia after the arrival of American Hayes Gordon in 1952. For over fifty years a version of Stanislavsky's principles was taught at the Ensemble Studios (Studios) operated in conjunction with the actor-centred Ensemble Theatre in Sydney (ETS) founded by Gordon. While there were other applications of Stanislavsky's ideas in Australia, the ETS's productions and acting classes with Gordon and his co-teacher, Zika Nester, were the most sustained, conspicuous, and easily accessible applications. Generations of actors and other theatre practitioners attended classes at the Studios and then worked throughout Australia. While Gordon followed Stanislavsky's ideas, his background included New York actor training workshops. Accordingly then, this chapter summarizes Gordon's background and teaching, and considers this in relation to Stanislavsky's ideas and also those of Sanford Meisner and Lee Strasberg with whom Gordon took classes. It critically considers claims about real emotions across these acting approaches and, drawing on personal experience, argues that even Gordon's approach utilising psychological research affirms contradictory beliefs about whether the actor's emotional feelings rather than the dramatic circumstances should be the basis of twentieth-century realist acting. What made Gordon's approach distinctive, however, was his clear commitment to ethical acting with a socio-political purpose. Significantly, in the heyday of the 1970s, student actors were often attracted to the classes of the Studios by the ETS's reputation for theatre with social justice themes. This chapter contends that regardless of contradictory ideas on emotions, Gordon's contribution to post-war theatre history in Australia was invaluable, and among the inheritors of Stanislavsky's practices, influenced by Gordon, were political idealists and theatrical innovators. This becomes far more than passing on a systematic, ethical approach to acting, as Gordon's influence in Australia points towards diverse applications of Stanislavsky's ideas within the changing socio-political context in the second half of the twentieth century.

The emulation of an acting ensemble by founding actors and repeated evocation of Stanislavsky's concepts need to be aligned with Gordon's encouragement of a political interpretation of drama and the ETS's socio-political repertoire which are discussed in the last part of this chapter. The Studios were open to all entrants when there were limited other opportunities to study acting. As well, ETS in the round contributed to the internationalism of Australian theatre and remains an important actor-centred theatre with the third largest subscriber base in the country. While theatres in Australia grew in number during the 1970s and subsequently even adopted programs similar to that of the ETS, there is no other theatre in Australia so closely associated with contemporary realist theatre over decades. The longevity of the ETS might in part be due to its realist repertoire and its advantageous lower North Shore location in Sydney, but it remains a remarkable achievement since it has never been part of the Australia Council government arts subsidy system despite acclaimed productions, and it continues to be maintained largely by its box office income.

Realist drama might sustain the theatre industry and theatres like ETS but its importance is questioned in theatre scholarship. For example, Richard Hornby (1992) challenges an ideological dichotomy of realist versus nonrealist arguing that realism should be considered as only one theatre form among numerous forms. Yet realism was the dominant twentieth-century form in theatre and it delivered socially complex perspectives; relevant scholarship includes Elin Diamond's (1997) theoretical critique of how Brechtian realism might fix ideas of reality. Jonathan Chambers (2010) points out that there are comparable ideological implications in nonrealism for actors although the inherent patterns of social power relations might be more opaque. While Stanislavsky's legacy crosses theatrical forms and political movements, Sharon Carnicke (2010) explains that his work including actor training became associated with realism in the USA in part because of the Soviet Government's control of international tours, and she points out that understanding of his artistic scope is still restricted outside Russia. Given that Stanislavsky's approach conveys a fundamental precept that an actor must continue to experiment, the system and its subsequent variants might locate realistic acting in dialectic relation to nonrealist acting and avant-garde performance rather than in opposition to them. The principle of experimentation remains relevant to actors trained in Stanislavsky's ideas with Gordon and who subsequently went on to create performer-derived texts, often with a political purpose.

Influences and legacies

While politics and political events impacted on Stanislavsky's approach (Whyman, 2008), they also influenced the dissemination of Stanislavsky's ideas from the outset, even in Australia. During the 1930s prior to the English language publication of Stanislavsky's writing, Dolia Ribush, a Russian Jewish refugee, interpreted Stanislavsky's ideas in the productions that he directed in Melbourne mostly with non-professionals although several went on to work in professional theatre and notably the director, Irene Mitchell (Parsons, 1995, pp. 500–1, 371). (A history of individual teachers influenced by Stanislavsky's books in Australia including the founder of Sydney's important Independent Theatre, the director, Doris Fitton, is outlined in this Part in 'Theatrical Bowerbirds' by Ian Maxwell). Actor-singer Gordon came to Australia in 1952 to evade the increasingly restrictive policies and employment practices championed by Senator McCarthy in the USA against anyone with left leaning sympathies (Durrant, 1997). Gordon had been a labour organizer for fellow actors in New York during the 1940s.

Gordon started working informally with his fellow actors in Australia soon after he arrived in Sydney (Durrant, 1997, p. 90). This gathering turned into weekly classes by 1956. But it was an invitation from Fitton, that began to formalize the process of acting classes in 1957, and by 1958 some of Fitton's students had formed the ETS in North Sydney with Gordon – probably to her consternation (Durrant, 1997, pp. 103, 107, 110).[1] Together with a group of professional actors from these classes, Gordon founded the long running ETS

Theatre in Sydney to present contemporary international plays. Australian theatre was yet to undergo the transformation brought about by the socio-political change of the late 1960s–70s with a proliferation of theatre companies focused on Australian identity in new drama (Meyrick, 2002; Wolf, 2008; Filewood and Watt, 2001). Gordon's approach to theatre was visionary in two ways. He perceived a paucity of studio training appealing to the idealism of professional actors, as well as an absence of actor ensembles. But Gordon sought more than Stanislavsky's (1994) ethical theatre striving to achieve a higher standard of acting through dedicated effort and systematic technique combined with considerate behaviour offstage. Significantly, the ETS was dedicated to building on ethical acting through a repertoire in which populist productions with box office appeal alternated with plays presenting current social justice themes often to controversy. The content of a play mattered.

When Gordon was working as a performer in New York, he took acting classes first with Sanford Meisner, and then with Lee Strasberg. Gordon's classes in Australia became associated with the Method although Gordon, only overtly acknowledges the influence of Stanislavsky on his work. Moreover his first formative classes in Boston were with Robert de Lany who followed Boleslavsky and Ouspenskaya (Durrant, 1997, p. 14). Gordon was taking workshops in New York at a time when Stanislavsky's teaching was pre-eminent and before even Strasberg had acquired a widespread reputation for teaching at the Actors Studio. Instead Gordon and the Russian-speaking Nester interpreted Stanislavsky's key principles in workshop practice – see chapters 3–7 and 9, 14 in *An Actor Prepares* – for several thousand actors and students in Australia who studied with them.

Certainly Gordon's way of working emulated the weekly workshop processes of New York training but it was not merely an importation of existing techniques, as Gordon synthesized his own training and performance experience and even invented terms; for example, 'tacking' based on sailing terminology for interpreting a character's subtextual shifts to achieve an objective in a dialogue sequence (Gordon, 1992, p. 66). By 1959 there were 150 students attending weekly classes with him (Durrant, 1997, p. 118). Nester was a music performer when she began attending classes in the 1950s, and she took his weekly classes for eight years. It was Nester who was chosen to teach classes when Gordon was away performing. A Russian refugee who could follow Stanislavsky's works in

Russian, the young Nester had also worked with a Shanghai director, Zoya Arkkadava Prybiskava, who is said to have worked with Stanislavsky; Nester performed in Russian, French, and English (Durrant, 1997, pp. 139, 178).[2] She and Lorraine Bayly went to the Moscow Art Theatre in 1972. Nester became the other major acting teacher at the Studios over decades and she brought a more organized approach to classes and the payment of fees. Weekly classes were turned into a three-year course at the ETS and in city premises with a one-year minimum for a claim to have studied there. By the mid-1970s a student could take classes in a full range of training techniques including acting, voice, movement, mime, even fencing, and in both realist and nonrealist performance forms with leading practitioners, some of whom trained in Europe.

Acting classes were a component of the ETS's approach from the outset. The Declaration of Policy of Ensemble Theatre Company describes: 'a professional institution with a resident company' that seeks to provide sustainable incomes from employment opportunities and 'the improvement of prestige of the "method" trained actor' (Durrant, 1997, p. 243, Appendix B). The newly formed theatre valued specialist, systematic knowledge of acting because it improved theatre.

Gordon had actually studied science. While scientific precepts and Ribot on emotion can be found to have influenced Stanislavsky's work (Pitches, 2006; Whyman, 2008), Gordon's scientific education no doubt contributed to his capacity for analysis. Certainly his use of psychology and allied studies of emotion is unmistakable (Gordon, 1992, pp. 76–7, 147).

Gordon began taking acting classes and working in community theatre as an adolescent and in musicals, and studied science and pharmacy at college graduating in 1941 (Durrant, 1997, p. 22). After moving to New York, his singing voice led to regular professional work and he was able to change from retail pharmacy to music theatre and was selected as a performer when drafted into the Army Air Force. At this time Gordon was introduced to Meisner and took acting classes at The Neighbourhood Playhouse. After a marriage break up, Gordon also engaged in psychotherapy which he described as an invaluable experience (Durrant, 1997, p. 54). By 1948 Gordon was starring in musicals and working with the American Veteran's Committee for performers. While Gordon continued working in commercially produced musicals, through producer, Cheryl Crawford, he attended the classes with Lee Strasberg that

Crawford set up in 1947 and would turn into the Actors Studio. While working for CBS radio music programs in 1951, Gordon opted to join the protest against signing a disclaimer about Communist Party membership in the contract, and subsequently found difficulty obtaining work (Durrant, 1997, p. 73). An offer to perform in Cole Porter's *Kiss Me, Kate* in Melbourne and later Sydney brought Gordon to Australia in January 1952 (Durrant, 1997, pp. 79–80). He made his home in Sydney and it is worth noting tangentially that Gordon may have introduced New York psychodrama to Sydney when he volunteered at Concord Hospital, and after his initial invitation to work on television as a singer, he also instigated a show with doctors talking about health, seemingly the first of its kind (Durrant, 1997, pp. 98–9).

In New York, Gordon seemed to have taken classes with Meisner when his work schedule permitted (Durrant, 1997, p. 63). Meisner was a founding member of the Group Theatre in the 1930s and involved in the development of a performance style based on Stanislavsky's approach. He contributed to its major productions and started teaching in 1935, spending his working life teaching actors. The argument between Strasberg and Stella Adler about Stanislavsky's approach to acting that led to their divergent approaches after 1934 also facilitated the third approach of Meisner. He emphasized the importance of working to and with another actor and carrying out an action in the moment with justification and particularization (Meisner and Longwell, 1987, p. 16, 142). Meisner's distinctive point of difference was the encouragement of an 'actor's "reactions" in performance' to another or others rather than an actor's internal purpose or 'self-will' (Stinespring, 2000, p. 98). Meisner uses some of Stanislavsky's principles including the belief that an actor embodies a character and, 'When you do something, you really *do* it rather than pretend that you're doing it' (Meisner and Longwell, 1987, p. 24 (italics in original)). Importantly, Meisner advocates that an actor's imagination can deliver 'emotional aliveness' because his or her own experience is limited (Meisner and Longwell, 1987, p. 78). Through Meisner's connection with the Group Theatre and The Neighbourhood Playhouse, Gordon encountered professional theatre that was co-operative and different to the commercial theatre in which he worked. Co-operative practice reflected Gordon's personal values.

The process of training actors to draw on their own inner experience is attributed to Strasberg and the use of an actor's private moments and affective or emotional memory applied to an interpretation of a character. These techniques remain controversial in actor training and its scholarship (Krasner, 2000). Yet emotion memory is one of Stanislavsky's techniques and the argument against emphasizing it arose because Stanislavsky seemed to have reversed his approach by prioritizing physical actions (Carnicke, 1998; Merlin, 2003, p. 29). While there was a range of techniques evident in Strasberg's approach, training focused on the qualities of the actor rather than dramatic circumstances. The dynamic between teacher and student was central in this pedagogical process which means that the undue influence or judgement of the teacher becomes questionable.

Rosemary Malague (2012) investigates the power imbalance and distortions in Strasberg's and Meisner's teaching, and particularly in exchanges with female student actors. Malague argues that Strasberg's approach bordered on a form of quasi-psychotherapy and finds that this contributed to the more troubling aspects of his approach. Similarly Gordon's interest in psychoanalytical and psychological processes was personal and professional, and his teaching could also cause consternation and possibly anxiety. Nester recounts crying after classes with Gordon when she received 'The Treatment' (Durrant, 1997, p. 139). But she argued with Gordon and also recalls the male actors being under comparable pressure. The founding group of ETS actors considered Gordon to be a type of guru with a magnetic presence (Durrant, 1997, pp. 112, 138), in part because of his capacity to explain ideas – and especially Stanislavsky's ideas – to actors. The ETS documents enshrine how the Governing Director has the final decision about all the productions despite the co-operative ETS ideal, and it was Gordon who made the artistic decisions (Durrant, 1997, pp. 113, 243). Clearly Gordon was the dominant figure behind the ETS and the Studios over decades.

Nester's contribution to the Studios, however, was very important and it offsets some of the criticisms about male dominance that Malague makes about Strasberg or Meisner. Nester's knowledge of Stanislavsky's ideas made her an important acting teacher. Her classes significantly expanded the capacity of acting classes at the Studios beyond one teacher and this was necessary because Gordon continued working away from the ETS as a performer and as a director at the ETS and elsewhere. Gordon's teaching was only one aspect of his theatre work, which seems to have mitigated another issue that Malague identifies with Gordon's teachers. At the same time classes with Gordon became highly valued because of his legendary reputation in theatre in Australia, and his somewhat limited availability.

Actors acknowledge Gordon's considerable capacity as a teacher. Lorraine Bayly became a household name during the 1970s for her high-profile television roles, and she first attended Gordon's classes in 1956 when actors paid a token fee. She remained associated with the ETS for four decades. Bayly recalls that Gordon, 'encourages, he provokes, he inspires, he gives; you grow' (Durrant, 1997, p. 136). Bayly is adamant that he was an inspiring teacher.

Intersections and divergences

Gordon developed an open-ended approach to learning to act closely aligned with Stanislavsky's principles. Gordon's teaching about the acting of emotions and emotional feelings also grapples with the issues arising from inner emotions in Stanislavsky's acting (Tait, 2002). For example, Gordon claims like Strasberg that an actor aims to 'truly' feel grief or despair and actors and audience members can tell when an emotion is real or indicated (Gordon, 1992, p. 78). Yet Gordon contradicts this assertion in other examples that suggest externalization and which correspond with Stanislavsky's later work. Perhaps this reflects the inherent difficulty in acting, as Stanislavsky sought to reconcile external and internal modes over decades (Pitches, 2006, pp. 1–2). Nonetheless Gordon's claims for emotions also confirm longstanding contradictions within twentieth-century realist acting.

One of the founding members of the ETS, Don Reid, remembers studying acting with Gordon using sensory exercises and describes 'action playing' focusing on the transitive verb and detailing the character's intentions (Durrant, 1997, p. 105). The alignment with Stanislavsky's techniques is unmistakable (Stanislavsky, 1989, pp. 35, 111–26). Gordon notes the influence of Moscow Art Theatre's style of acting on his ideas of 'the emotional colouration through a single active verb with an adverb attached' (Gordon, 1992, p. 63). A material interpretation of the 'if' or the 'magic if' is crucial (Stanislavsky, 1989, p. 46; Whyman, 2008, p. 34; Gordon, 1992, p. 99).

There is a manual of Gordon's (1992) instruction with workshop exercises that details his approach and advice. While its verbatim style explains some of its anecdotal limitations, the manual contains numerous practical examples encompassing imagined situations and specific roles across all forms including musicals and film. As well as improvisation, Gordon definitely uses the characters in the dramatic circumstances to illustrate how to act. He first acknowledges Stanislavsky (and Machiavelli) in the prologue (Gordon, 1992, p. ii), and the direct influence of Stanislavsky's techniques on Gordon's teaching is repeatedly specified with only a brief mention of Meisner and Strasberg. The chapters are divided into 'Acting' and 'Performing' and cover 'Sensing', 'Thinking', and 'Feeling'. The chapters on imagery, imagination, and sensing techniques correspond with ideas in Stanislavsky's *An Actor's Prepares* (Gordon, 1992, pp. 15–23; 35–7; Stanislavsky, 1989, pp. 54–71), and Gordon emphasizes the 'magic if' as a fundamental principle that encourages belief and for converting 'a creative idea into a creative deed' (Gordon, 1992, p. 47). An actor should break down each scene into manageable smaller components and 'particularise' each one and this facilitates imagining and the use of 'if' (Gordon, 1992, p. 99). Gordon recounts a second-hand story about the Moscow Art Theatre actors in New York explaining to American actors that they break scenes into 'bits', and this was misunderstood and became 'beats' in Method acting (Gordon, 1992, p. 63). He finds the latter useful because of its rhythmic associations and bits because it makes acting possible. Gordon explains how the actor plays a series of 'bit actions' (units) compiled into scene action (objective) which eventually create the 'spine' of the play (superobjective) – the terms in brackets come from Elizabeth Hapgood's (Stanislavsky, 1989; 1994) translations of Stanislavsky first published in 1936 and 1949.

Whyman explains that, above all, Stanislavsky was primarily concerned with how to constantly reinvigorate acting (Whyman, 2008, p. 1). Gordon focuses on the acting problem of anticipation and 'anticipating the wrong expectations' for actors (Gordon, 1992, p. 67). He writes: 'That is, they anticipate what they know happens to the character according to the script because they read it, rehearsed it, and play it. When one anticipates what actually happens in a play, the scene becomes stale.' (Gordon, 1992, p. 67). The strategies for counteracting this problem involve making the objective personal to the actor rather than related to the circumstances of the play – this seems to correspond with the Method or Strasberg's and possibly Meisner's approach. An actor needs to be mentally quick and to play supplementary or minor actions that provide detail in a performance.

Is Gordon's approach influenced by Strasberg's ideas of the Method in particular? Probably not, although Gordon starts with the senses and sensing (Gordon, 1992, pp. 19–37). Marc Gordon (2000) argues that Strasberg's use of emotions needs to be clarified with more accuracy, since he advocates remembered emotion rather than (somehow) delivering actual feeling during performance. This distinction adheres to Stanislavsky's point that an actor experiences sensations and body memory but must not be lost in the emotional experience during performance. Strasberg's teaching style, however, focused on personal development and the actor's self, which is open to criticism when a subjective response to the quality of his or her expression is the substance of the interaction. David Krasner points out that Strasberg was also influenced by Vakhtangov, who advocated that an actor's inspiration and immediateness could be achieved independently of the character and dramatic circumstances (Gordon, 2000, p. 29). An actor's *'experiencings'* becomes the important source (Whyman, 2008, p. 159). By contrast Meisner focuses on imagining. Crucially Marc Gordon points out that Strasberg shifted the emphasis from remembering the emotion to remembering the sensory circumstances of sight, sound, taste, and touch surrounding an emotive memory (Gordon, 2000, p. 53). Hayes Gordon emphasized 'sense memory' like Strasberg, but he also specified Meisner's idea that emotions could not be summoned at will (Gordon, 1992, pp. 138, 81). Gordon only acknowledges Strasberg as one of a number of people, and while he does probe ideas of acting emotions like Strasberg, Gordon repeatedly utilizes dramatic circumstances.

Gordon's approach appears to juggle the contradictions in how actors perform emotions and how they feel emotions. Certainly his manual (Gordon, 1992) makes his instruction focus on what is required for a role and this is more indicative of Stanislavsky. Yet Gordon (1992) shows an understanding of the complexity of emotions and he distinguished these from feelings in ways that correspond with later twentieth-century psychological, anthropological, and philosophical definitions, those which separate emotions as socially recognizable signification from emotional feeling (Parkinson et al., 2005). In the language of acting technique, Gordon summarizes physiological and experiential aspects of feelings as: 'ambivalence' as the actor acting the effort to stay in control; 'kaleidoscopic' as acting shifts and rapid fluctuations between emotional feelings in the moment; and 'retention' as not suddenly changing but acting a continuing effect of heighted emotional expression such as tears and anger since the biochemical residue of feelings is known to remain (Gordon, 1992, p. 78). He contends that it is impossible to summon most emotional feelings at will, although he agrees that social expressions can be manipulated – a distinction evident in Stanislavsky's work (Tait, 2002).

When Gordon claims that emotions are part of universal language, he also acknowledges that 'an emotional reaction' or feeling changes become evident in 'body-signals' (Gordon, 1992, p. 75). In a well-tested workshop exercise, one participant opens a box and reacts silently to the spider or doll inside, as other participants guess the unseen contents with some accuracy. This demonstrates a shared cultural understanding of nonverbal expression of the emotions, and one possibly acquired from cultural familiarity with acting – this is not necessarily confirmation of universality. Interestingly, while Gordon suggests that feelings can be known to others, he recognizes that this depends on 'the acuity of the person who is "reading" us' (Gordon, 1992, p. 76). Gordon draws on ideas from psychology and makes a distinction between instincts, reflexes, and primary and secondary emotions, and mentions how emotions have been politicized (Gordon, 1992, p. 77). Further, Gordon distinguishes 'complex feelings' and 'shades upon shades of emotional nuances, each of a different weight and duration, each constantly on the move and interweaving with others' (Gordon, 1992, p. 77). He draws on several psychological studies of emotions, indicative of comparatively recent knowledge about emotions.

The proposition that an actor should draw on his or her inner remembered emotions or sense memory of them is offset in Gordon's approach by claims that emotional feelings impact on body language and the actor needs outward manifestations. Gordon writes of actors: 'Feelings – both the character's and our own – need to be regulated as deliberately and artistically as actions, voice and kinetic behaviour' (Gordon, 1992, p. 80). These are external expressions that can be analysed and thoughtfully controlled and presented through technique. An actor needs to produce external signs for inner experience. Yet this also implies a different type of imitation in adherence to cultural expression inclusive of theatrical practices. In Gordon's framework, an actor needs to study emotions in social interaction and in theatre.

Real feelings or belief?

Despite the emphasis on social interactions, Gordon still refers to the 'real feelings' of the actor which Stanislavsky advocated and which became so significant in Strasberg's Method (Gordon, 1992, pp. 78, 81). How is it possible to act real feelings? As a young actor, the author of this article experienced difficulties with the directive to reproduce real emotion even in workshops. While Gordon's and Nester's teaching was practical and could be logically applied and was immensely useful, the instruction and discussion of acted emotion proved problematic. In hindsight, it became clear that this was about the discourse describing acted emotions rather than the practical process of acting emotions. A gulf between the experience of emotional feeling and its interpretation, and acted expressions of emotional feeling seemed to exist; emotions were surrounded by contradictory and irreconcilable language. A demand for the expression of real emotion potentially inhibited the acting for the following reasons. First, there was a discrepancy arising from language describing acted emotions as real when these were not actual personal feelings but believable outer signs of inner emotional feelings on cue and, significantly, in accordance with social expectations. Secondly, there were unquestioned assumptions around what a character would feel in given circumstances especially female characters. Thirdly, there were norms and expectations about how inner emotion was acted and expressed, regardless of rhetorical claims that stereotypical patterns should be avoided.

Despite some acknowledgement of the separation of expressed emotion in acting and the physiology of feeling, Gordon's approach became caught up in the twentieth-century acting problem of how to make socially recognizable emotions seem like the personal feelings of a character. This is particularly important for realist drama. There is an erroneous assumption that these should be the personal feelings of the actor remembered or otherwise. Gordon understands some of the complexity when he explains that an actor needs a motivation technique to change delivered emotions and achieve a particular emotional colour, and that an actor's belief in selected circumstances could assist this delivery (Gordon, 1992, pp. 88, 92, 100). A process of belief seems to accompany the acted expression of feeling. Hence an actor who believes that he or she is acting his or her feeling might be particularly convincing – arguably, he or she is replicating a culturally acquired set of embodied signs that are socially understood to represent inner emotion.

Certainly Stanislavsky and his successors developed mental strategies and processes including thinking about emotion to facilitate an actor's focus in the present moment of a performance. Nonetheless, a discursive belief that the actor can and does act his or her experienced feeling crept into twentieth-century actor training discourse accentuated by loose interpretations of Strasberg's approach. Cultural expectations of displays of personal and private individualized emotions seem to shape theatrical explanations of emotions and especially in realist forms supported by claims that an individual actor is interpreting these from his or her experience. Such adherence to belief that emotion in acting is intrinsic continues despite anthropological study since the 1980s revealing culturally specific experience that disputes modernist beliefs in the universality of emotions, and which challenges ideas of individualistic natural feeling (Lutz, 1988).

The high degree of visibility of female actors and the prominence of female characters makes issues of gender identity more complicated in theatre especially where gender difference manifests through emotional expression (Tait, 2002). Malague compares Adler's approach to actor training which was centred on analysis of drama and character with the approaches of Strasberg and Meisner which focused on the actor and implicitly then on the actor's emotional expression. She suggests that quasi-therapeutic dimensions of their teacher–student exchanges were applied differently for female and male actors and questions the dominance of the male teacher's personality. Significantly, questionable practices seem to arise from emotional exchanges between teacher and student in this model of actor training. The gendered consequences of Strasberg's and Meisner's teaching pertain to emotions and emotional feelings and expose the complexity of demanding real feeling from actors in training situations in which there are no given parameters other than the teacher's assessment of the realness of the expression. As Suzanne Burgoyne, Karen Poulin with Ashley Rearden (1999) show, training in emotions has personal impact and remains particularly fraught. Alternatively, Malague suggests that Adler's pedagogical approach using the play text, offset highly subjective emotional interactions in classes by exploring emotions in relation to the social circumstances given in the drama. In addition, this approach to acting drama would facilitate change in actor training over time as the content of newer drama and the social experience of its characters came to reflect changing social worlds and values.

To some extent, the divergent gender difference in the emotional expression in acting began to unravel in the late twentieth century; for example, male actors were increasingly expected to cry in roles rather than simply act out anger. Nonetheless while the equity imbalance in the work practices of theatres could be addressed by the inclusion of female directors, playwrights, and other practitioners, complex concerns remain with gendered performance of emotion that influence the acting of female identity. It is pertinent to challenge an assumption that socially realistic emotional acting is somehow the actor's real emotional experience, and especially with female actors. My difficulty following the directive about real emotion supports an understanding that the acting of interiority should be contingent on the character's experience in the dramatic circumstances.

Enacting socio-political ideas

The ETS's productions remained responsive to changes in social values and arguably contributed to that change in Australia through innovative realist productions. The repertoire of the ETS confirms this commitment and, as outlined here, dramatic themes, characters, and concerns change noticeably over the decades. Actor training processes should be expected also to respond to this progressive development, especially since emotional interactions are invariably implicated in theatrical depictions of changing social relations. The close association of the ETS and its productions and the Studios suggests comparable development in the teaching of acting.

Gordon was always a leading advocate for how professional theatre should present socio-political issues and, significantly, he argued that actors should hold ideals and be concerned with issues of social change during the 1950s–60s. Although social commitment was not unique to the ETS's actors and directors, upholding this purpose over decades distinguishes it. For example, while the left leaning worker's theatre and new theatre movement was well-established in Sydney (Milne, 2004, pp. 77–8), an association with members of the

Australian Communist Party may have become a disadvantage in Australia in the 1950s. Although the ETS opted to produce plays that were tried out elsewhere, a number of potent productions confronted socio-political issues and the ETS became known for this intention from the outset.

Two productions in 1958 established the ETS's reputation for compelling and powerful realistic acting and attracted national attention: Tennessee Williams' *Orpheus Descending* and an American thriller *The Man* by Mel Dinelli that became a long running production (Durrant, 1997, p. 116). A pattern of balancing two types of production would subsequently typify the ETS, with an artistically accomplished play on a social theme followed by a genre with wide audience appeal such as a play by Neil Simon or Alan Ayckbourn. While the choices reflected a recognizable twentieth-century canon of drama,[3] and some plays received productions elsewhere in companies and venues that were short-lived (Milne, 2004), ETS's lasting stability set it apart. Gordon's commitment was central to its success. For example, Gordon directed Ibsen's *An Enemy of the People* in 1968 and Tom Stoppard's *The Real Inspector Hound* in 1969 while he was starring as his most famous role, Tevye in J. C. Williamson's production of *Fiddler on the Roof*, which ran from 1967 to 1970 touring Australasia.[4]

In his history of post-Second World War Australian theatre, Geoffrey Milne (2004) summarizes the purpose of the ETS Theatre but somewhat sidelines its achievement with inclusion in a description of all the theatres started in the geographical location of Sydney's northern suburbs (Milne, 2004, pp. 95–6). This lack of particular attention can be explained by the ETS's production of international plays until the 1980s – 50 per cent American and 25 per cent British (Milne, 2004, pp. 95–6) – at a time when the New Wave theatres set out to reflect Australian identity in drama. The ETS produced realist plays by male writers from North America, England, and Europe between 1957 and 1981, but expanded its repertoire to include Australian plays by male and female writers and Australian identity after 1981.[5] With a couple of exceptions, the ETS did not produce classics or even Shakespeare because these were produced elsewhere, and the inclusion of Australian drama followed developments forged in other Australian theatres during the 1970s (Meyrick, 2002). Arguably, by 1981 Australian drama was comparable to any international drama but with an Australian political purpose.

The political responsiveness of the programming becomes unmistakable over time although it was part of the ETS's conception of the theatre from the outset. A production of John Herbert's *Fortune and Men's Eyes* directed by Brian Syron, an Aboriginal Australian, early in 1968 was about prison, homosexuality, and the failings of the justice system in Canada, and it attracted considerable media attention about prisons in Australia.[6] As Australia's involvement in the Vietnam War was attracting increasing public protest and dissent, the ETS produced two antiwar plays in the 1970s; Clive Exton's *Have You Any Dirty Washing Mother Dear?* and Joseph Heller's *We Bombed in New Haven*, directed by Gordon.

As well as training leading actors for the main stage and television, the Studios attracted acting students interested in making socially relevant performance, and a number who passed through the ETS and the Studios subsequently forged new directions in theatre and worked on controversial issues.[7] In one well-known example, during the 1970s the leading actor, Reg Livermore, left the ETS and applied his experience in the creation of some of the most potent queer characters in Australian and international theatre (Pender, 2013). Certainly actors from the ETS and Studios engaged in the provocative area of identity politics and in performer-devised performances and these required expanded depictions of emotions.

An external project in 1970 confirms an unmistakable wider political purpose. Gordon was commissioned to work with Ken Colbung and direct a major national outdoor spectacle of the re-enactment of Cook's landing in Botany Bay on 19 April, and they set out to make sure that Aboriginal people were represented and participated as performers (Gordon, 1977, pp. 167–8). While their intention was positive, there were a number of protest interventions that caused problems on the day of the performance. The first Aboriginal play at the ETS was Jack Davis's *The Dreamers* directed by Andrew Ross which transferred there in 1983.

Broader issues of gender equity in the composition of the ETS's production teams would eventually be fully addressed. The Studio's open access meant that the backgrounds of ETS practitioners did reflect Australia's cultural diversity by the late 1970s. The ETS produced Australian plays by 1981, and plays by female playwrights: the first female director was Patricia Jones in 1968, and then Jane Oehr in 1982. The director Sandra Bates, who became associated with the ETS Theatre over decades had a play produced in 1981 and directed her first production, *The Marginal Farm* by Alex Buzo in 1985. Gordon or Bates directed most productions between 1985 and 1989 and Bates was the main director until the 2000s. The feminist play, *The Heidi Chronicles* by Wendy Wasserstein was produced in 1992, directed by Adam Cook. Shifts in ETS personnel as well as its repertoire reveal the ETS's responsiveness to the socio-political values of the time either concurrently or in advance of changes elsewhere in Australian theatre.

A number of directors worked with Gordon over the years and Australian directors working on Australian plays are central to the ETS Theatre program by 1989 when Peter Kingston directed *Daylight Saving* by Nick Enright, and Rhys McConnochie directed Enright's *Mongrels* and *The Christian Brother* in 1991 (Pender and Lever, 2008). This Australian component becomes an important part of the programming in subsequent decades with plays by Australia's leading playwrights, David Williamson and Katherine Thomson. A production of Shakespeare's *Hamlet* in 2006, however, reveals that the ETS's programming eventually accommodated international, national, historical, and contemporary plays.

Gordon (1977) explains how the initial impetus for the ETS Theatre came from a group of actors with about six years' experience disillusioned by the existing opportunities and wanting to control and run their own theatre in 1957. The type of roles and the content of the plays mattered to ETS who aspired to develop theatre in Sydney that produced 'Ethical' plays (Gordon, 1977, p. 28). Gordon declares that an actor must take responsibility for the impact of dramatic roles on the community. ETS was well known for this purpose, and it continues to respond to social and theatrical changes in Australia.

Conclusion

The ETS has outlasted comparable theatres and remains an important contributor to the theatre industry in Australia. Its significant influence may have been underestimated, in part because of preoccupation with Australian drama and a lack of comprehensive scholarship on actor training in Australia to date, but also because Brechtian-influenced theatre scholarship polarizes

Stanislavsky-influenced realist work and even condemns these acting approaches (Krasner, 2000). Hundreds of actors in the theatre industry in Australia, however, have actively sought out and sustained Stanislavsky-derived training and the success of the ETS and the Studios.

The Studios were an important development in the history of actor training in Australia with students studying Gordon's and Nester's interpretation of Stanislavsky's principles. The contradiction in explaining acted emotion as if it is intrinsic personal feeling is indicative of unquestioned twentieth-century modernist ideas of universality and accompanying ideas of an individualistic self and its psychology. The legacy of these problems continues in discourse about acting, especially for female actors.

Australian actors taking acting classes with Gordon and Nester developed reputations for highly accomplished realist acting although their impact on Australian theatre was far wider encompassing nonrealist performance and work with socio-political intention. Actor training classes with Gordon and Nester aligned with the ETS's expectation that actors would be committed to ethical theatre with social justice values.

Notes

1 Some of the leading actors who studied in Gordon's classes from this time were founding members of the ETS Theatre (Durrant, 1997, p. 111), and included Lorraine Bayly, Jon Ewing, Don Reid, Reg Livermore, Patricia Hill, Sophie Kranz, Brian Young, Henri Szeps, Max Cullen, Max Phipps, and Brian Syron. Gordon worked with the following performers away from the ETS: Lorrae Desmond, Judi Farr, Nancye Hayes, and numerous other well-known performers (Durrant, 1997, p. 152).

2 Additional information about Zika Nester is based on an interview for the Australia Research Council funded project, 'The Players: The Lives and Works of the Actors for National Theatre 1950–2012' undertaken by Anne Pender. Nester was born in Harbin, Northern China of Russian, Jewish heritage. The family moved to Shanghai when Zika was eight and she lived there until she was twenty-five. She married there, and moved to Australia in 1953. Nester studied piano and dance and was playing with a symphony orchestra by age eleven. Zika Nester died on 10 July 2014.

3 The ETS Theatre produced the work of leading modernist playwrights such as

Eugene O'Neill, Friedrich Durrenmatt, Jean Anouilh, Sean O'Casey, Arthur Miller, Brian Fiel, John Osborne, Terrance McNally, Christopher Hampton, David Hare, Harold Pinter, Michael Frayn and Pam Gems, and Athol Fugard, but few classic texts such as, for example, those of Bernard Shaw. Instead there were more contemporary choices such as plays by Maurice Valency, William Inge, Landford Wilson, Peter Ustinov, John Steinbeck, and D. H. Lawrence.

4 The author remembers seeing Gordon on tour in New Zealand in her youth.
5 See http://ensemble.com.au/about-us/ensemble [accessed 21 September 2016] for a PDF of the Ensemble Theatre Repertoire with directors and actors from 1957 to 2014.
6 Katharine Brisbane's review in *The Australian* recognized its achievement and the importance of this type of example for theatre in Australia.
7 The author observed these values among fellow acting students. I had worked professionally before studying acting with Gordon and Nester at the Studios 1976-7 and I also took workshops with Don Reid in 1977 in a tertiary institution. Although I began making theatre about women's issues in 1975, I was involved in collaborative theatre productions about gender experience in 1981-4 with other performers who had studied at the Studios.

References

Burgoyne, S. and Poulin, K., with Rearden, A. (1999), 'The Impact of Acting on Student Actors: Boundary Blurring, Growth, and Emotional Distress', *Theatre Topics*, Vol. 9, No. 2: 157-79.

Carnicke, S. M. (1998), *Stanislavsky in Focus*. Amsterdam: Harwood Academic Publishers.

Carnicke, S. M. (2010), 'Stanislavsky and Politics: Active Analysis and the American Legacy of Soviet Oppression', in *The Politics of American Actor Training*, ed. E. Margolis and L. T. Renaud. New York: London.

Chambers, J. (2010), 'Actor Training Meets Historical Training', in *The Politics of American Actor Training*, ed. E. Margolis and L. T. Renaud. New York: London.

Diamond, E. (1997), *Unmaking Mimesis*. London: Routledge.

Durrant, L. (1997), *Hayes Gordon: The Man and His Dream*. Sydney: Hale and Iremonger.

Filewood, A. and Watt, D. (2001), *Worker's Playtime*. Sydney: Currency Press.

Gordon, H. (1977), *Toward An Ethical Theatre*. Sydney: A Saturday Centre Supplement.

Gordon, H. (1992), *A Complete Compendium of Acting and Performing*. Sydney: Ensemble (Theatre) Press.

Gordon, M. (2000), 'Salvaging Strasberg at the Fin de Siècle', in *Method Acting Reconsidered*, ed. D. Krasner. New York: St Martin's Press.

Hornby, R. (1992), *The End of Acting*. New York: Applause Theatre Books.

Krasner, D. (2000), 'I Hate Strasberg: Method Bashing in the Academy', in *Method Acting Reconsidered*, ed. D. Krasner. New York: St Martin's Press.

Lutz, C. (1988), *Unnatural Emotions*. Chicago: University of Chicago Press.

Malague, R. (2012), *An Actress Prepares: Women and "the Method"*. Abingdon, Oxon: Routledge.

Meisner, S. and Longwell, D. (1987), *Sanford Meisner on Acting*. New York: Vintage Books.

Merlin, B. (2003), *Konstantin Stanislavsky*. London: Routledge.

Meyrick, J. (2002), *See How It Runs: Nimrod and the New Wave*. Sydney: Currency Press.

Milne, G. (2004), *Theatre in Australia (Un)Limited: Australian Theatre since the 1950s*. Amsterdam: Rodopi.

Parkinson, B., Fischer A. H. and Manstead, A. S. R. (2005), *Emotion in Social Relations*. New York: Psychology Press.

Parsons, P. (ed.) (1995), *Companion to Theatre in Australia*. Sydney: Currency Press.

Pender, A. (2013), 'Eat, Pray, Laugh!': Barry Humphries, Reg Livermore and Cross-Dressed Australian Burlesque!', *Australasian Drama Studies*, Vol. 63: 69–83.

Pender, A., and Lever, S. (eds) (2008), *Nick Enright: An Actor's Playwright*. Amsterdam: Rodopi, 2008.

Pitches, J. (2006), *Science and the Stanislavsky Tradition of Acting*. London: Routledge.

Stanislavsky, C. (1989), *An Actor Prepares*, trans. E. Reynolds Hapgood. New York: Routledge/Theatre Arts Books.

Stanislavsky, C. (1994), *Building A Character*, trans. E. Reynolds Hapgood. New York: Routledge/Theatre Arts Books.

Stinespring, L. M. (2000), 'Just Be Yourself: Derrida, Difference and the Meisner Technique', in *Method Acting Reconsidered*, ed. D. Krasner. New York: St Martin's Press.

Tait, P. (2002), *Performing Emotions: Gender, Bodies, Spaces in Chekhov's Drama and Stanislavski's Theatre*. Aldershot: Ashgate.

Whyman, R. (2008), *The Stanislavsky System of Acting*. Cambridge: Cambridge University Press.

Wolf, G. (2008), *Make it Australian: The Australian Performing Group, the Pram Factory and New Wave theatre*, Sydney: Currency Press.

Stanislavsky in Aotearoa: The System Experienced through the Māori World

Hilary Halba

Introduction

An open space – a bare stage – the dimming theatre lights illuminate a woman's haunted face. Wordlessly she makes a decision to walk into the ocean to end her life and to return to the spirit world of her ancestors.[1] The moment is alive, the actress engaging, beautiful, moving, determined, defeated and the clarity of her intention is limpidly apparent. Stanislavsky himself might have given his approbation to this moment as one in which *'the life of the human spirit'* is communicated to us *'onstage in an artistic form'* (Stanislavsky, 2008, p. 19, italics in original). Nevertheless another layer of signification complicates the moment, situating it between theatre and life-world experience. The lights dim as the woman takes her last steps and the eerie strains of a chanted karakia[2] (incantation, sometimes translated as 'prayer') are heard faintly; this karakia closes the door to the world of the dead, removing the tapu (sacred, subject to restriction) associated with death, and has a material significance in the Māori[3] world. Indeed in Māori thought, theatre itself arguably occupies a blurry site between representation and lived experience, and this chapter focuses upon how the training and directing of actors in Māori or bicultural contexts account for this sense of in-betweenness.

Anne Salmond calls for 'studies of cross-cultural encounters that do justice to the ancestors on both sides, and the potent perilous pae – the edge between them' (Salmond, 1997, p. 513), and this study seeks to respond to that wero (challenge). This chapter charts a journey through time and cultural connections, and in it I investigate ways in which aspects of Stanislavsky's System have been synthesized with Māori customary practices, life-world idioms and performativities. I focus in particular upon three case-studies: rehearsal and performance processes of Kilimogo Productions in Dunedin; Tawata Productions in Wellington; and actor training at Toi Whakaari o Aotearoa: New Zealand Drama School. Interviews that form the basis of the chapter were carried out with ten performing arts practitioners associated with each organization who employ aspects of tikanga (customary cultural practices), kawa (protocols) and other Māori-centric principles in their theatre work. I conducted the interviews using Kaupapa Māori (Māori platform) research principles including kahohi ki te kanohi (face-to-face) contact, and a kōrero (talking) process in which connections are forged, knowledge and ideas are shared, and 'both the participants and researcher benefit from the research project' (Kana and Tamatea, 2006, p. 10). Te Kawehau Clea Hoskins remarks, 'In every social setting, from welcoming, to meetings, to fighting, to political alliances, a face-to-face encounter is considered supremely important' (Hoskins, 2010, p. 9). Interviews were recorded so participants' voices can be legitimately represented. Moreover, the possibility that each participant's own practice might be assisted or developed by the research was kept alive in the kōrero. Participants sanctioned the use of their words after this chapter was completed.

In each kōrero, I look at ways in which the Māori concepts of whanaungatanga (the creation of relationships), manaakitanga (allowing receptiveness) and tikanga find congruency in the Stanislavskian notions of communion/communication, the magic 'if', spiritual connection, and active approaches to training and rehearsal practices. This is not to say that the Stanislavskian concepts mentioned above can be applied without mediation to te ao Māori (the Māori world), but that similarities generate a sense of notional kinship, and this similitude could be seen as the birthplace of an acting sensibility mobilized through a Māori worldview. Moreover, although the Active Analysis process which Stanislavsky developed in his later career is not daily currency *in toto* in Aotearoa's theatre practice, Māori and bicultural theatre's focus on community and the imbrication of life-world practices and customary protocols into performance processes has meant that training and rehearsal methods often involve connection and playfulness, and by extension the 'here, today, now' (Merlin, 2003, p. 35) spirit to which Bella Merlin refers as key to Active Analysis. It should also be noted that the claims made in this chapter are not necessarily true for all Māori actors nor in all Māori theatre contexts.

Beginnings

Like many countries with a history of colonial incursion, Aotearoa[4]/New Zealand experienced a cataclysmic sea change wherein a myriad of ideas, belief systems, technologies, flora, fauna, people, and cultural practices were imported from Europe – mainly from the British Isles – and transplanted from the time of first contact with Europeans. British explorer Captain James Cook, in search of the fabled Terra Australis Incognita, made landfall in Aotearoa in October 1769 and presented a local man with 'trinkets' (Gore 1769, cited in Salmond, 1991, p. 127); from that time interchange between these two worlds – to use Salmond's term – has not ceased. In many cases, indigenous forms were put under pressure from the encroachment of the new; Māori cultural practices and language were eroded, and land was arrogated. Contact with Europeans meant that the holistic Māori universe, whose vertical strands of whakapapa (genealogy) could be traced back to deities and cosmic beginnings, was eroded in favour of horizontal categorizations of Western thought. A Māori worldview was called into question as the full impact of imperialism's 'cultural bomb' (Thiong'o, 1986, p. 3) was felt. Nevertheless, Māori sovereignty has been constantly re-asserted from the time of very early contact with Pākehā (non-Māori New Zealanders, usually taken to mean New Zealanders with European ancestry). In te ao Māori, art is part of the fabric of daily life (King, 1992a), and in a pre-contact context, songs, chants, and other performative forms interwove with and governed a myriad of daily activities. However when traditional epistemologies and ontologies collide with those of the newcomers, misunderstandings invariably arise. Salmond details a formal encounter between Cook's sailors and local Māori in Northland in 1769 in which she suggests Cook's men may have misinterpreted the Māori women's ceremonial weeping, 'an element in any Maori ceremonial of encounter' (Salmond, 1991, p. 231), and duly gave the women gifts to 'put them in a better humour' (Banks in Beaglehole (ed.) 1962, cited in Salmond, 1991, p. 231).

Salmond remarks, 'If these were ritual tears, the women would have been extremely surprised to be given gifts to cheer them up' (Salmond, 1991, p. 231). Such performative actions undergird many activities in the Māori world, and Nathan Matthews and Karyn Paringatai note that '[the performing arts] are present in almost all ritual and ceremony associated with Māori culture.' (Matthews and Paringatai, 2004, p. 103). In this chapter I argue it is this very performativity that has given rise to vibrant and potent Māori and bicultural theatre practices in rehearsal and performance. Indeed, actor training in general in Aotearoa draws from a wide range of practitioners and approaches. Loosed from the boundaries of exacting adherence to one style or form, training methods typically display freedom, dynamism, and energy.

Speaking back

Arguably, Stanislavsky's approach to actor training and rehearsal is another tool of cultural imperialism, of limited relevance to conditions of life, performativities, and modes of representation in Aotearoa. Theatre can be seen as a means by which settlers preserved or recalled an image of, as it were, 'England's green and pleasant land', and through which they laid claim to the new country, arguably viewing Māori as 'almost the same, but not quite' (Bhabha, 1994, p. 86) Europeans. Settler histories imagined the colonized land as a 'blank slate' onto which imported forms and ways of being could be inscribed, and theatre – including Stanislavsky's System – is one of these forms. Rose Whyman remarks that Stanislavsky makes subjective assumptions in his writing that what is true for him must also therefore be true for all actors (Whyman, 2008, p. 264). Such a critique, which seeks to dismantle assumptions based on universalist values, supports a post-colonial assessment of Stanislavsky as yet another dead white male, brought from Europe and installed in a colonized country without cognizance of the local situation, promulgating a performative representation of response and affect that arguably had little to do with te ao Māori. Moreover, researcher and performance historian Te Ahukaramū Charles Royal's assertion that, 'Mimesis is not present in [traditional] Māori culture' (Royal, 1998, p. 12) further complicates the issue. However Māori theatre's espousal of aspects of Western cultural currency – such as

Stanislavskian actor training and rehearsal principles – can also be read as a deliberate reaction against a neo-imperialistic cultural and theatrical hegemony. Principles are not passively adhered to, rather they are claimed for their usefulness and mobilized through a local worldview. The post-colonial world bears witness to the energy and productiveness resulting from these encounters, and to the possibility of multiple competing truths. Blended or hybridized social and performative forms are generated through such encounters.

Biculturalism

In Aotearoa, this blending has come in the form of the concept of biculturalism, a notion which has underpinned much political and social discourse in this country since the mid-to-late twentieth century. Indeed, the conceptual roots of biculturalism can be traced back to Aotearoa's founding document the Treaty of Waitangi, formulated in Māori and English, and signed by representatives of the British Crown and by more than forty Māori chiefs in 1840. However, significant differences in meaning between the Māori and English versions of the Treaty have led to debate and protest as to its interpretation. Nonetheless, the Treaty – especially the Māori version – provides a way of operating socially and politically between two cultural contexts. Some of the principles of the Treaty, which were drawn from the Māori world, have since been blended with non-Māori forms in a variety of public and political contexts, including some theatre. As far as theatre goes, for theatre-maker and commentator Roma Potiki 'you don't get a true bicultural form until you get equity and equality right down the line.' (in Pavis, 1996, p. 175). Biculturalism in practice often struggles to achieve this sense of equity as the pervasive effects of colonialism are still apparent. Additionally, and although it is beyond the scope of this chapter to explore, it is important to note that the concept of biculturalism has been complicated and extended by the addition of a number of other world cultures to the social and cultural make-up of Aotearoa.[5]

When she was appointed director of Toi Whakaari o Aotearoa: New Zealand Drama School[6], Annie Ruth built on the work of her predecessors who had sought to promote a bicultural approach to actor training and bicultural development within the School's community. Andrew Noble (head of the School from 1988 to 1989) had worked hard to further the biculturality of the School and it was during his tenure that the Māori prefix had been adopted in addition to the school's existing nomenclature; George Webby (head of the School from 1974 to 1987) had also espoused this principle and sought to teach his students about acting in New Zealand rather than Western acting in general (Guest, 2010, p. 117). In her turn, Ruth closely adopted principles drawn from Māori tikanga in both her approach to training actors at Toi Whakaari but also in the modus operandi and modus vivendi of the school, as a whole. As noted earlier in this chapter, tikanga are customary Māori cultural practices. Tānia Ka'ai and Rawinia Higgins characterize the concept as:

> a system of protocols that are observed within *te ao Māori*, based on cultural traditions, practices, values and beliefs. The word tika means right or correct, therefore the extension of the word to *tikanga* implies an appropriate or customary way of behaving within Māori contexts.
>
> Ka'ai and Higgins, 2004, p. 18

Tikanga is regarded as a dynamic concept, available to adapt to contingent circumstances yet rooted in tradition, lore, and ancestral knowledge. Behaviour, and hence the embodiment of tikanga, is significant. The synthesis of tikanga with essentially Western acting methods, to which Ruth refers, resulted in a bicultural fusion which disrupts a wholly 'Western' conceptualization of actor training. Ruth developed a bicultural approach because the external, somatic focus of tikanga 'doesn't make you go inside yourself' (Ruth, 2014). For Ruth, in addition to inviting actors to concentrate their focus outside themselves, tikanga also means 'you're doing what you're doing in service of something' (Ruth, 2014). Although Ruth does not consider herself a Stanislavskian adherent, there are nonetheless evident similarities between her approach and Stanislavsky's experiments with the concept of 'Communion'. There, he also sought to focus his actors outside of themselves, to encourage them to appreciate 'the wealth of information that they could glean from each other just by allowing the space between them to be "alive"' (Merlin, 2003, p. 22), to focus their attention on creating a genuine connection with their scene partner, and to hold that partner in their 'grip' (Stanislavsky, 2008, p. 251). Communion thereby serves scene, play, and audience.

Māori performativity and Stanislavsky's System

Sharon Marie Carnicke draws her readers' attention to Stanislavsky's term 'experiencing' (translated from the Russian *perezhivanie*) which she describes as 'an actor's unbroken concentration on the events of the play during performance' (Carnicke, 2009, p. 133). The actor who is demonstrating this sense of experiencing 'embod[ies] the ephemeral and improvisational creative act itself' (Carnicke, 2009, p. 140) in a seemingly oxymoronic 'theatrical reality' (Carnicke, 2009, p. 145), a condition in which emotions 'are neither authentic or inauthentic' (Tait, 2002, p. 170) but where moment-by-moment living by-play generates an authentic instance onstage. A similar principle applies in Māori performativity where moment-by-moment participant and audience engagement is a crucial constitutive force in any performance. This is the case in Māori Performing Arts, a combination of haka (posture dance), waiata (song), and forms such as poi[7] and ti rākau[8], as well as in performative rituals such as the pōwhiri or ritual of encounter. Nathan Matthews and Karyn Paringatai analyse Māori performative forms and outline ways in which they provide a means for audiences and performers to 'experience' a performance. Although the term 'Māori Performing Arts' describes a performance form distinct from theatre, elements of this form – as well as Māori ceremonials – are at times interwoven into theatrical performance,[9] and the principles underlying Māori Performing Arts can inform Māori theatre. Matthews and Paringatai examine the tripartite concepts of ihi, wehi, and wana. These notions are applied to performances which are deemed excellent, in which the potent qualities of engagement, connection, and presence are evident, and hence fulfil the essential functions of performance in the Māori world (Matthews and Paringatai, 2004, p. 114). Matthews and Paringatai describe ihi as 'a combination of authority, charisma, essential force' whose projection can in turn elicit ihi in an audience (Matthews and Paringatai, 2004, p. 114). For Tamati Kruger, ihi in a performer consequently 'commands the respect, attention and empathy of the audience' (Kruger, 1984, 230). Matthews and Paringatai characterize the term wehi as 'a strong spiritual and emotional response' which can be felt by both performers and audience members even 'long after the completion of the performance' (Matthews and Paringatai, 2004, p. 114). Stanislavsky perceives a strikingly similar phenomenon, stating, 'Theatre lives by the exchange of spiritual energy, which goes continuously back and forth between audience and actor', uniting them with 'invisible threads' (Benedetti, 1990, 199). Matthews and Paringatai define wana as 'a thrilling feeling' that audience members experience during a performance that 'is directly linked to an active performance' rather than to an inanimate artwork (Matthews and Paringatai, 2004, p. 114). Principles to do with ihi, wehi, and wana suggest that emotional identification and empathy are generated in the living moment of 'experiencing' onstage, and are consequently perceived by both performers and spectators. Wehi, in particular, it could be concluded, involves the educing of empathy in actors and also in members of the audience. Experiencing, for Stanislavsky, is also not confined to the stage alone, and he considered the audience 'the "third artist"[10] in the theatre' (Carnicke, 2009, p. 157). Carnicke reminds her reader that Stanislavsky wanted the audience to 'take from us [the actor] and like a resonator they return to us our vital human sentiments' (Carnicke, 2009, p. 157). Instead of ignoring the audience, as is popularly espoused by the American Method version of the System, Stanislavsky understood the vital relationship between performer and audience (Carnicke, 2009, p. 157). In Stanislavsky's reckoning performers' and audience members' emotional identification arises when 'the actor creates the role anew at every performance in full view of the audience', when acting 'remains essentially active and improvisatory' and when it 'infects' the audience 'with the artist's emotion' (Carnicke, 2009, p. 217). In other words although a performance is rehearsed, it remains engaged, immediate, seemingly spontaneous, emotionally alive, and present. In many aspects of Māori theatre practice, the concept of experiencing for both performers and spectators is generated in the dynamics between Western theatrical training systems (to do with action, connection, empathy, and emotional identification), and Māori performativity (with its locus in tikanga).

Certainly this principle is central to the practice of Rangimoana Taylor (Ngāti Porou[11]), one of the first Māori students to study at the (then) New Zealand Drama School, and later the school's kaumātua (respected elder). A central figure in Māori theatre, and a founder-member of bicultural theatre collective Kilimogo Productions, Taylor talked with me about the way in which 'experiencing' has governed his conceptualization of Stanislavsky's mobilization through te ao Māori. Brought up in close association with the Māori world,

Taylor was introduced to theatre in adulthood (Halba, 2007, p. 210) so his point of reference to do with performance was located in his knowledge of things Māori. He first encountered Russian drama in general, and Stanislavsky's approach to acting in particular, in the summer of 1973 as he was about to enter drama school. He recalls Downstage Theatre in Wellington undertaking a Russian play.[12] Having gone to a Russian Cultural Attaché for advice on the Russian psyche, members of the theatre were told that in order to find the 'expansion [...] of thought, of spirit' (Taylor, 2014) required for the piece, they need look no further than Māori culture. This experience led Taylor on a quest to understand how this idea intersected with theatre in his own land, a journey that began with him buying a copy of *An Actor Prepares* in 1974 and forty years later sees Taylor as one of the country's preeminent proponents, and a pioneering initiator, of Māori theatre. Taylor was struck by the fact that in the Russian theatre he had seen in those early years, underneath the trappings of Realism – huge cherry orchards and life-like rooms – lay something else, something experientially 'real'. For him the outwardly-focused, experiential actor embodies the Māori concept of manaakitanga or 'a sense of reciprocity, of giving and receiving' (Reilly, 2004b, p. 68). Simply translated, manaakitanga is taken to mean the sense of hospitality shown to a guest or visitor, and is considered to be one of the most crucial conventions in the Māori world, especially in the traditional marae (traditional assembly site)[13] setting. For Taylor manaakitanga combines the concept of mana (prestige, influence, status) with 'aki [...] to encourage [...] So when you manaaki people you encourage their mana, not yours, theirs' (Taylor, 2014). Moreover Māori rituals of encounter, in literal or symbolic form, have been included in numerous Māori and bicultural plays and performances, and even non-Māori plays with a Māori sensibility have included an indication of such rituals. Manaakitanga underpins such ritual elements.

Kinship through manaakitanga and whanaungatanga

The deployment of manaakitanga also produces a reciprocal sense of empathy, that is the 'cognitive capacity to take the perspective of another person' (Blair after Lamm, 2009, 98–9). Although Rhonda Blair notes that empathy does not mean that the boundaries between self and other dissolve (Blair, 2009, p. 99), it is fair to assume that they are nevertheless porous. One cannot fully come into being without connection with the other, and Michael P. Shirres notes that in the Māori world 'the real sign of a person's *mana* and *tapu* is [...] that person's power to *manaaki*' (Shirres, 1997, p. 47). To this end, Taylor goes on to remark that the 'actor on stage [should] [...] mihi [acknowledgement, salutation] to the other actor', that is to say 'to make them look better' (Taylor, 2014). Rawinia Higgins and John C. Moorfield state that in Māori terms the mihimihi (informal speech-making, salutation) 'facilitates connections' (Higgins and Moorfield, 2004, p. 83). Taylor also uses the practice to this end as a rehearsal technique wherein actors are assigned a fellow performer at random at a rehearsal's conclusion, at which point the actor is required to articulate specifically something positive and constructive their assigned partner did in that rehearsal. Taylor requires the mihimihi to be specific, and actors do not know to whom this salutation will be made until the conclusion of each rehearsal, meaning that it is essential that the actors' focus is partner-centric throughout rehearsals.

For Taylor the actor is rangatira (respected leader) – 'the one who weaves the people together: ranga, to weave and tira [a group of] people' (Taylor, 2014). These concepts represent core ideals in Māori contexts, and are especially important for theatre actors as weavers of this connection. In Stanislavsky's reckoning, too, the creative act is not experienced in isolation, but in ensemble and with an awareness of 'how characters on the page relate to each other and confront each other in performance' (Carnicke, 2009, p. 212). This highly interactive approach demands 'deep communication between partners' (Carnicke, 2009, p. 121). One of the functions of Māori rituals of encounter is to effect this deep communication. Michael Reilly explains that in Māori terms this sense of communication is understood as whanaungatanga or the elucidation of kinship relations both human and, in a broader sense, between humans and the world – and greater cosmos – in 'a vast and interlinking family tree' (Reilly, 2004a, p. 10). Kin-like groups, exhibiting the core traits of whanaungatanga, can include Māori performing groups (Reilly, 2004b, p. 70). The invisible, yet ontologically significant changes that occur to an individual through the processes of whanaungatanga and the attendant concept of manaakitanga further correspond to Stanislavsky's ideal of the actor's experiential transformation as the result of an onstage encounter. Annie Ruth views the ritual of encounter as a model for actorly connection, stating, '[it's] a ritual so it's structured, but within the ritual it's completely improvised. So [...] you have to be on your feet; you [...] have to know what's happening [...]. Especially on the marae [...] you can see those negotiations going on [...]. That's how I structure performance now' (Ruth, 2014).

For Stanislavsky, experiencing is also arrived at through technique. Tortsov tells Kostya '[f]irst technique, the[n] experiencing, not the other way around' (Stanislavsky, 2010, p. 252). Similarly, for Taylor, whanaungatanga and manaakitanga are arrived at first through an adherence to the fundamental operative framework of tikanga. Whanaungatanga can be seen as congruent with the creation of a collaborative ensemble. Former Head of Acting at Toi Whakaari Jonathan Hendry sees an enactment of whanaungatanga, manaakitanga, and principles located in a Māori understanding of the world as beneficial to trainee actors as it 'enable[s] the student to put themselves in the learning, [...] [to] constantly look to be in response to other[s] rather than [saying] "this is what I do and this is what I know." [...] where every moment is alive with an attempt to create connection' (Hendry, 2014).

From life-world to the world of representation

Cindy Diver (Kāi Tahu), actor, director, acting tutor for young people, and co-founder of southern bicultural theatre collective Kilimogo Productions,[14] discussed congruencies between her Stanislavskian training and her deep-seated relationship with the Māori world and Māori theatre during my kōrero with her. Diver recalls an occasion when, as a young drama student having difficulty in rehearsal, she was encouraged by director and Theatre Studies lecturer Lisa Warrington into a moment of 'acting as if' (Diver, 2014), which led to a sense of experiencing the role. Rhonda Blair reminds the reader that before the term 'as if' was adopted by contemporary neuroscience, Stanislavsky used it to describe how the actor ought to 'have an empathic connection with the character – a capacity to engage the character's experience imaginatively while at the same time maintaining a sense of self that is separate from the character.' (Blair, 2009, p. 100) For Diver that experience of Stanislavsky's 'magic "if"' signalled 'the first time I really remember [acting] working' (Diver, 2014). In this moment of experiencing, Diver also found congruencies with the performativity of the marae that she had known as a child (Diver, 2014). She recalls:

> the events, the gatherings, the kai (food) and the drama, oh, the drama. It was theatre, absolute theatre, especially for a young kid growing up in that environment [...]. It made you very much an observer [...] and [you learn] what role you have to play at certain times [...]. Those are such great skills aren't they? [...] Reading somebody else and reacting?
>
> Diver, 2014

Another defining moment of Stanislavskian experiencing – and of Māori ihi and wehi – came for Diver when she was an audience member at a 1990 performance of John Broughton's monodrama *Michael James Manaia*. She recollects:

> There was an element of the wairua [spirituality] and the strength and the power of that play that made me want to go 'tihei mauri ora'[15] [...] It connected to me and it made me think [...] this is the kind of stuff I want to do.
>
> Diver, 2014

After studying drama, Diver wrote her first play about a Māori tangihanga (funeral and mourning rites) and was told by an older Māori woman whom she 'really respected tikanga-wise' that she could not depict a dead body onstage (Diver, 2014). For Diver:

> the Western theatre part of me [thought] it's acting; I can have a body on stage. There won't be a body, it's just a coffin; we're not having anyone in it. And this beautiful wahine [woman] was like 'no, you're bringing bad stuff in'. And I'm clashing these two worlds now.
>
> Diver, 2014

Diver came to appreciate the adherence to Māori tikanga and kawa, experienced in the liminal space of Māori theatre, and this became embedded in her own approach. She duly sought to create 'Maori theatre that keeps people safe but still uses [...] Western theatre technique as a carriage to help tell the stories' (Diver, 2014). In her later work with Kilimogo Productions, Diver further sought to integrate Māori life-world practice with theatre, using the form of rituals of encounter – especially as they are enacted in the southern parts of Aotearoa – as a template for rehearsal and performance processes. Diver acknowledges that within and beyond such blendings, the creation of new forms and approaches is inevitable. For her a sense of 'cultural purity' is not inherent in Māori theatre, itself a hybrid form resulting from 'generations of colonisation and [...] culture changes' (Diver, 2014). Having said this, the Stanislavskian concept of 'as if' that Diver had first been exposed to as a student resonated with her Māori understanding of the world, and she applied this sense of congruence to Māori characters she has played with Kilimogo Productions. In these performances she worked on the principle that 'your character is separate from your [own] mana; it's separate from your wairua [spirit]' (Diver, 2014). Here the actor is not applying her own emotion memories to the role, but asking 'what if ...?' Diver also discussed ways in which the principle of manaakitanga interwove with her application of Stanislavskian principles. Like several of the practitioners to whom I spoke, for Diver manaakitanga meant that the actor 'always [had] that sense of kind of openness to somebody else' (Diver, 2014). Most especially her formative theatrical and life experiences meant that the cultural safety of actors and audience members became a defining feature of Diver's theatre practice.

Weaving together actor and audience into the embodied experience of the play typifies theatre academic and practitioner David O'Donnell's experience of Māori theatre both as an actor and director. He explains that by fusing Māori tikanga with Stanislavskian rehearsal principles, performances he has worked on with Kilimogo Productions – and later with Taki Rua Productions in Wellington – 'genuinely communicate with an audience.' (O'Donnell, 2014). For O'Donnell, Stanislavsky's concept of communion was embodied in Māori plays he has directed and performed in with these companies through a commitment to whanaungatanga and through the imbrication of Māori spirituality. He says, 'when you're performing a Māori play in a Māori context [...] it's about being part of a circle of concentration with an audience where everybody's committed to the storytelling [...] and [to] a shared belief in the storytelling in the moment.' (O'Donnell, 2014) O'Donnell also notes that the 'spiritual aspect' (O'Donnell, 2014) of Māori theatre practice gives a sense of potency. Bella Merlin remarks on the 'spiritual absence' in Benedetti's translation of Stanislavsky (Merlin, 2012, p. 1). Filtered through te ao Māori, that sense of spirituality has perhaps re-emerged; rehearsal and performance principles are informed by 'a genuine deep cultural history where acknowledging ancestors and Gods and spirits is totally, totally valid and [...] just part of everyday life' (O'Donnell, 2014) yet indicate an additional level of signification in the performance. This sense of slippage between representational and life-world frames that O'Donnell identifies means that, in Māori terms, that which is tapu (restricted, prohibited) in the real world is also tapu in performance. As Cindy Diver registered, death and anything associated with it are held to be tapu in the Māori world; Rawinia Higgins and John C. Moorfield remind us that '[t]he continual reference to the dead in Māori rituals highlights their importance in cultural paradigms' (Higgins and Moorfield, 2004, p. 86). A cognizance of tapu in this slippage between frames is in evidence in playwright Harry Dansey's account of his play *Te Raukura: The Feathers of the Albatross*. Dansey discusses one of his actor's responses to a mourning scene in the play, saying, '[o]ne of the women said to me, "I tangi [weep, mourn] for those dead *real* each night"' (Dansey in King, 1992b, pp. 112–13). The concept of spirituality, which governs such instances, is also dealt with by Stanislavsky repeatedly in his work, and provides a 'powerful, but invisible affectivity, which can springboard us as actors into all sorts of creative experiences' (Merlin, 2007, p. 47). In Māori terms, wairua 'crosses between the physical and spiritual dimensions and includes the various levels of consciousness that drive certain behaviour in particular situations' (Ka'ai et al., 2004, p. 18). It is not simply ephemeral but is also visceral, and focused on the world and an individual's relationship with each observable and unviewable part of it. Wairua is linked with the concept of mauri which Ka'ai and Higgins translate as 'a life-force or life principle and ethos of all objects both animate and inanimate within the universe' (Ka'ai and Higgins, 2004, 18), and which perhaps finds a congruence with the notion of 'soul' in Hapgood's translation of Stanislavsky. Theatre kaitiaki[16] (guardian) and playwright Rua McCallum (Kāi Tahu, Kāti Māmoe, Waitaha, Rapuwai) discusses the principles of life-force and spiritual connection in the Māori world. She says:

> it's not necessarily a physical connection [...]. [It] happens across time and space in a spiritual dimension [...]. And that, of course, goes back again to whanaungatanga and to the marae because [...] the first thing that happens in the pōwhiri is that a spiritual voice is [heard] [...]. A physical voice is heard but that physical voice is representational of the spiritual voice, and

the connections made between the physical humans and the [...] wairua of the humans and their ancestors.

McCallum, 2014

Like the 'rays' about which Tortsov teaches Kostya's class (Stanislavsky, 2008, p. 246), this spiritual dimension is deemed to be palpable and hence is available to the actor as a mechanism for connection.

Tawata: 'ourselves in action'

The concept of slippage between frames of enunciation wherein Western acting methods, rooted in Stanislavsky's legacy, are interwoven with Māori lifeworld practices and values is present in other Māori theatre-makers' practice. Cook Islands Māori playwright and director Miria George (Te Arawa, Ngāti Awa, Rarotonga, and Aitu, Cook Islands) characterizes her practice with her Wellington theatre company Tawata Productions as a 'determining of ourselves in action' (George, 2014), but George also sees the concepts of whanaungatanga and communion as foundational to a sense of connection that focuses such self-determination. She says, 'we're never going to be able to sustain that action if the whanau (family, extended family) isn't healthy, if our communion and our connection with each other isn't a healthy one' (George, 2014). As an emerging director, George sought to work in a culturally appropriate way in the rehearsal of her own play *Sunset Road*, preferring a method whereby the action of the play and relationships between characters were explored actively on the rehearsal room floor (George, 2014), ensuring actors' 'thought processes' were not 'disengaged from their physical and emotional resources' (Merlin, 2007, p. 197) in a process similar to Carnicke's description of Stanislavskian Active Analysis where 'acting generates its own experiential dimension' (Carnicke, 2009, p. 145).

Tawata, co-directed by George and award-winning playwright and theatremaker Hone Kouka (Ngāti Porou, Ngāti Raukawa, Ngāti Kahungunu), provides a productive illustration of Hami K. Bhabha's 'double vision' (Bhabha, 1994, p. 88), a concept which is exemplified in the company's ventures in Māori theatre, in a similar way to Kilimogo in the south. In part, Tawata's work has been buttressed by actor training methods including those of Stanislavsky, aspects of which

Kouka himself studied theoretically and comparatively at university (Kouka, 2014). Kouka sees Stanislavskian techniques as providing 'an understanding [about] what these basics are' and creating theatre from 'a base of experience' (Kouka, 2014). In this context actors are present 'in action' meaning the Tawata company is, for Kouka, 'on a cusp of something different' (Kouka, 2014) – an ambivalent 'third' space (Bhabha, 1994) where codes of life-world and theatre are dismantled. By way of example, Kouka discusses Tawata's commitment not only to the development of emerging practitioners but to the Māori practice of enfolding of whanau into the group's daily operations which develops 'an environment of leadership and [...] creates sustainability' (Kouka, 2014).

Actor and director Erina Daniels (Ngā Puhi), who has worked extensively with Tawata Productions, cites respect for leadership and communities (of theatre-makers and the wider community) as well as for tikanga and traditional knowledges – and 'see[ing] that in action' – as being central to her work (Daniels, 2014). Conversely her experiences of an over-reliance on round-the-table analysis or emotion memory have presented her with impediments as an actor. For example, she recounts an instance when she worked with a theatre director who used round-the-table analysis extensively. Daniels recalls that she and the young Māori actors in the cast had 'our own little games and stuff but none of that was on the floor' (Daniels, 2014), meaning that any live, embodied interaction was, in effect, blocked from the stage. The dual consciousness aspect of Stanislavsky's System (Carnicke, 2009, p. 143) also comes into play when one coins the term 'Māori actors'. This serves not simply to describe the actor's ethnicity but, more importantly, to signal the cultural currency that actor brings to bear upon the role and the process of acting, contiguously – or perhaps simultaneously – operating in the life-world context of te ao Māori and the role-playing context of Western theatricality. Since, in Stanislavsky's reckoning, the latter is predicated upon 'experiencing', these contexts act in a way in which both systems operate at once, yet resist fixity by the very fact of this operation. Daniels also recollects that 'I remember for the longest time relying on emotional resonance', and describes her choice to seek further training as an actor 'to learn some skills to wrap around this thing of emotion [...] because it's just useless trying to repeat something every night if you are going to go for emotion because it's unreliable' (Daniels, 2014). Stanislavsky, too, acknowledges the problem that feelings 'won't take orders' (Stanislavsky, 2008, p. 273). Daniels' current preferred practice, as an actor and director working predominantly in Māori theatre is 'to use better do-able actions that I can do [...] *physically* do [...]. That's the way I like to roll' (Daniels, 2014).

Toi Whakaari: tūrangawaewae and Koiwi

For Toi Whakaari tutor Heather Timms, Stanislavsky's practice has a place in a modern drama school because it provides a core foundational language for actors and theatre practitioners, a language of action as well as terms to describe things (Timms, 2014). However, the central principles undergirding Toi Whakaari's practice are located within a distinctly Māori frame of reference and hence provide a counter-discursive site for understanding the foundational language to which Timms refers.

Timms, after reflecting on these ideas, developed a document outlining the philosophy of the School's acting programme. Entitled *The Responsive Actor – Turangawaewae*, this document uses the Māori construct of tūrangawaewae as its underlining principle. Tūrangawaewae is defined as 'the very source and origins of a person's whakapapa, sometimes referred to as one's "roots" or place of belonging' (in Kai'ai et al., 2004, p. 18). Beginning with the question 'who are you, and what are all the things that you bring?', the initial stages of the Toi Whakaari training concentrate upon 'the individual within a group' (Timms, 2014), and move outwards in the three years students spend at the school (Timms, 2013, p. 3). The first year of training centres on 'turanga' – which can be translated as 'positioning' – and upon the individual, encouraging actors to look 'inwards [...], and introduc[es] questions of stance, position and offer, freeing habitual patterns, releasing creative fluency and building foundational skills' (Timms, 2013, p. 1). Characterized as 'raranga' or 'weaving', the second year 'reorients the relationship outwards – Centralising [sic] questions of listening, the nature of the collective, reading the live moment and applying individual skills to the group with increasingly complex variables' (Timms, 2013, p. 1). Finally, the third year – focused upon waewae[17] – encourages the trainee actor to function as an 'independent artist' with the increasing ability to 'self navigate [sic] diverse performance contexts and build relationships with arts practitioners.' (Timms, 2013, p. 1). Although based upon Māori-centric processes, tūrangawaewae, as it is conceptualized by the School, bears striking similarities to aspects of Stanislavskian actor training that itself echoes the teaching of Ramacharaka to which Stanislavsky was introduced in 1911 by his son's tutor and which he began to adopt in his own shifting approach as early as 1912 (Carnicke, 2009, pp. 172–3). For Ramacharaka 'the internal world must be conquered before the outer world is attacked' (in Carnicke, 2009, p. 173), and Stanislavsky re-states this idea even in the original title of his acting manual: *An Actor's Work on Himself*; Benedetti's translation of the first two years of training – 'Experiencing' and 'Embodiment' – further reflect this precept. Alongside the principles located in *The Responsive Actor*, the conceptual practice of Koiwi is employed as a foundational means for the Toi Whakaari's staff and students to share and interweave experience and 'experiencing'. Koiwi are twice-weekly assembly sessions which act as 'platforms for vertical learning which engage students across years and disciplines' (Timms, 2013, p. 8). The word 'koiwi' translates as 'bones', and these sessions form the bedrock of the school through their collaborative approach, and the interpenetration of Māori values and practices with Western actor training. Traditional hierarchies are re-evaluated as students often take leadership roles in Koiwi. The Koiwi concept represents an 'in-between' (Bhabha, 1994, p. 1) space which provides 'the terrain for elaborating strategies of selfhood – singular and communal – that initiate new signs of identity, and innovative sites of collaboration, and contestation' (Bhabha, 1994, pp. 1–2). A new site – Koiwi – destabilizes binary oppositions and hence provides a productive space rather than one that hinges on slavish adherence to past forms. Although his pedagogical practice was clearly hierarchical, nonetheless Stanislavsky may well have given his endorsement to this concept, too, because for him 'Human life is so subtle, so complex and multifaceted, that it needs an incomparably large number of new, still undiscovered "isms" to fully express it' (in Carnicke in Hodge, 2010, p. 6).

Conclusion

Stanislavsky often slips in unnoticed in contemporary Aotearoa, some of his techniques, ideas and teachings having become abbreviated into a generalized currency of *bon mots* for the actor ('what's your motivation?'; 'listen, respond';

'don't act by yourself'). Of greater interest to this study is that a number of his principles have entered into a complicated, even complicitous, relationship with Māori life-world principles and practices where both conscious distancing from and engagement with Stanislavskian ideas simultaneously take place creating a hybrid articulation of acting in certain contexts in Aotearoa. This chapter has sought to uncover and to highlight ways in which relationships (articulated in te ao Māori as whanaungatanga) can produce vital forms of rehearsal and performance practice. In kōrero with practitioners, I have not found an emphasis on difference; instead the focus was often on discovering the joy of kinship in both affinity and individuality. Hone Kouka sees the uniqueness of these encounters, stating 'no one has a view-point like you [...] no one sees the angle of the sun like you do' (Kouka, 2014). The Cultural Attaché who spoke to Rangimoana Taylor in 1973 also saw traces of this sense of kinship. There is an open-endedness to these encounters, wherein specific situational contingencies are accounted for and even celebrated, where community and family are preeminent concerns, where connection and communion are indubitably manifest and transformative phenomena, where wairua and mauri exist as palpably as action, and where an integrated and properly focused creative state can 'create a continuous line of action', a 'core which brings all the elements together in service of the basic goal of the play' (Stanislavsky, 2008, p. 587). Indeed, te ao Māori serves to re-infuse Stanislavsky with the 'spirit' and 'soul' absent in Benedetti's translations and in many contemporary reckoning of Stanislavsky's practice (Merlin, 2012, pp. 12–18). I argue that aspects of Stanislavskian training can coexist in dynamic interplay with the structured yet improvisatory operations of Māori ritual, performative and life-world practices wherein the actor's 'body, imagination, mind, emotions and spirit' (Merlin, 2012, p. 18) are 'harnessed together holistically' (Merlin, 2007, p. 197). Hybridity is not a distant and abstracted concept; instead it is rooted in very specific articulations of action and is contingent upon embodiment.

Rhonda Blair reminds the reader that 'How we construct our sense of identity and self is greatly affected by the particular semantic categories of social values and the dominant cultural metaphors with which we are raised' (Blair, 2007, p. 55). These values and cultural metaphors can also be recuperated and reformulated into productive, amalgamated forms through many voices in a cultural exchange. Kouka articulates this exchange as a 'flow' stating 'we keep the thing flowing, constant flow, we understand that flow' (Kouka, 2014). One of those voices in that flowing aggregation, perhaps humming low but distinctly, is Stanislavsky's.

Notes

1. *Ngā Tāngata Toa* by Hone Kouka, Kilimogo Productions, Globe Theatre, Dunedin, 1997, directed by Rangimoana Taylor and Hilary Halba.
2. Translations from Māori to English are drawn from the *Ngata Dictionary* (online) or are made by the author. In a conscious strategy of linguistic integration, I have chosen not to italicize words in te reo Māori (the Māori language).
3. First nation people of Aotearoa/New Zealand.
4. Māori place-name for New Zealand, sometimes taken to be the place-name for only the North Island with the South Island sometimes referred to as Te Waipounamu, Te Waka o Aoraki, and by other names. The North Island, too, is sometimes referred to by other names such as Te Ika a Maui. For the purposes of this essay, Aotearoa will refer to New Zealand as a whole.
5. Immigrants from the British Isles have come to Aotearoa/New Zealand since the early nineteenth century, and they represented the largest number of migrants until after the Second World War. However, Chinese migrants also came to partake in the gold rush from the 1860s onwards, and Dalmations for work in the gum fields in the mid-nineteenth century. After the Second World War, migrants from the British Isles and The Netherlands were given an assisted passage to Aotearoa/New Zealand. From approximately the 1960s onwards, people from the Pacific Islands, and further waves of migrants from China arrived. Later waves of immigrants arrived from India, other parts of Asia, the Middle East, Europe, and Africa.
6. One of Aotearoa/New Zealand's pre-eminent actor training institutions and the country's oldest. The school was originally called the QEII Arts Council Drama Training School (Guest, 2010, p. 18), and it went through several incarnations before it was re-named and re-focused as Te Kura Toi Whakaari O Aotearoa: New Zealand Drama School in 1989 in response to the perceived need to acknowledge actively to the country's developing bicultural ethos. The school celebrated its fortieth year of operation in 2010.
7. Performance form involving swinging small balls on strings in complicated patterns.

8   Short sticks used in performance.
9   This is the case, for instance, in Hone Kouka's play *Waiora* in which the chorus of tīpuna (ancestors) perform waiata, haka, and other traditional forms alongside the more naturalistic action of the play.
10 The first two artists are the author and the actor (Carnicke, 2009, p. 157)
11 An individual's iwi (tribal) affiliation is typically given in parentheses after their name.
12 Probably *The Dragon* by Yevgeny Schwartz, produced by Downstage Theatre in 1973 (Smythe, 2004, p. 468).
13 This traditional Māori assembly site encompasses a meeting house and attendant buildings such as a dining hall, as well as the ceremonial open ground (the marae ātea) where rituals of encounter typically take place. Strictly, the marae ātea is the marae, but in contemporary vernacular, the term 'marae' is now taken to mean the assemblage of land and buildings as mentioned above.
14 For further informations about Kilimogo Productions see Halba, 2008.
15 A metaphorical concept to do with the infusion of the life principle; literally translates as 'the sneeze of life'.
16 The concept of kaitiakitanga (guardianship, stewardship) is important in the Māori world. Kaitiaki (guardians) are responsible for resources, ensuring they are 'not [...] impacted by people's actions' (Williams, 2004, p. 50). The concept has been applied to theatre by Kilimogo Productions, as well as by other Māori and Bicultural theatre groups and companies.
17 Literally, the foot, but in this case it perhaps should be read symbolically as taking a foothold.

References

Benedetti, J. (1990), *Stanislavski: A Biography*. London: Methuen.
Bhabha, H. (1994), *The Location of Culture*. London and New York: Routledge.
Blair, R. (2007), *The Actor, Image and Action*. New York and Oxon.: Routledge.
Blair, R. (2009), 'Cognitive Neuroscience and Acting: Imagination, Conceptual Blending and Empathy', *TDR*, Vol. 53, No. 4, pp. 93–103.
Carnicke, S. M. (2009), *Stanislavsky in Focus: An Acting Master for the Twenty-First Century (2nd edn)*. Oxon. and New York: Routledge.
Guest, B. (2010), *Transitions: Four Decades of Toi Whakaari: New Zealand Drama School*. Wellington: Victoria University Press.
Halba, H. (2007), '"Let Me Feel the Magic": Hilary Halba Interviews Rangimoana Taylor', in *Performing Aotearoa: New Zealand Drama and*

Theatre in an Age of Transition, eds D. O'Donnell and M. Maufort. Brussels: P.I.E Peter Lang.

Halba, H. (2008), 'Conversations Between Cultures: Aspects of Bicultural Theatre Practice in Aotearoa/New Zealand'. *alt theatre*, Vol. 6, Number 2, December 2008, pp. 14–19.

Higgins, R. and Moorfield, J. C. (2004), 'Tangihanga: Death Customs', in *Ki Te Whaiao: An Introduction to Māori Culture and Society*, eds T. M. Ka'ai, J. C. Moorfield, M. P. J. Reilly, and S. Mosley. Auckland: Pearson Education New Zealand, pp. 85–90.

Hodge, A. (ed.) (2010), *Actor Training (2nd edn)*. Oxon. and New York: Routledge.

Hoskins, T. C. (2010), *Māori and Levinas: Kanohi ki te Kanohi for an Ethical Politics*. PhD thesis, University of Auckland.

Ka'ai, T. M. and Higgins, R. (2004), 'Te Ao Māori: Māori World-view', in *Ki Te Whaiao: An Introduction to Māori Culture and Society*, eds T. M. Ka'ai, J. C. Moorfield, M. P. J. Reilly, and S. Mosley. Auckland: Pearson Education New Zealand, pp. 13–25.

Ka'ai, T. M., Moorfield, J. C., Reilly, M. P. J., and Mosley, S. (eds) (2004), *Ki Te Whaiao: An Introduction to Māori Culture and Society*. Auckland: Pearson Education New Zealand.

Kana, F. and Tamatea, K. (2006), 'Sharing, Listening, Learning and Developing Understandings of Kaupapa Māori Research by Engaging with Two Māori Communities Involved in Education', *Waikato Journal of Education*, Vol. 12, 2006, pp. 9–20.

King, M. (1992a), *Moko: Maori Tattooing in the 20th Century*. Auckland: David Bateman.

King, M. (1992b), *Te Ao Hurihuri: Aspects of Maoritanga*. Auckland: Reed Publishing Group.

Kouka, H. (1997), *Waiora*. Huia Publishers.

Kruger, T. (1984), 'The Qualities of Ihi, Wehi and Wana', in Mead, H. M. *Nga Tikanga Tuku Iho a te Maori: Customary Concepts of the Maori*. Wellington, Department of Māori Studies, Victoria University of Wellington.

'Learning Media Ngata Dictionary'. http://www.learningmedia.co.nz/ngata [accessed 21 September 2016].

Matthews, N. and Paringatai, K. (2004), 'Ngā mahi a Tāne-rore me Te Rēhia: Performing Arts', in *Ki Te Whaiao: An Introduction to Māori Culture and Society*, eds. T. M. Ka'ai, J. C. Moorfield, M. P. J. Reilly, and S. Mosley. Auckland: Pearson Education New Zealand, pp. 103–15.

Merlin, B. (2003), *Konstantin Stanislavsky*. London and New York: Routledge.

Merlin, B. (2007), *The Complete Stanislavsky Toolkit*. Drama Publishers.

Merlin, B. (2012), '"Where's the spirit gone?" The Complexities of Translation and the Nuances of Terminology in *An Actor's Work* and an Actor's Work', *Stanislavski Studies*, Issue 1, February 2012, pp. 43–86.

Pavis, P. (ed.) (1996), *The Intercultural Performance Reader*. London and New York: Routledge.

Reilly, M. P. J. (2004a), 'Te Tīmatanga Mai o Ngā Atua: Creations Narratives', in *Ki Te Whaiao: An Introduction to Māori Culture and Society*, eds T. M. Ka'ai, J. C. Moorfield, M. P. J. Reilly, and S. Mosley. Auckland: Pearson Education New Zealand, pp. 1-12.

Reilly, M. P. J. (2004b), 'Whanaungatanga: Kinship', in *Ki Te Whaiao: An Introduction to Māori Culture and Society*, eds T. M. Ka'ai, J. C. Moorfield, M. P. J. Reilly, and S. Mosley. Auckland: Pearson Education New Zealand, pp. 61-72.

Royal, Te Ahukaramū C. (1998), *Te Whare Tapere: Towards a Model for Māori Performance Art*. PhD thesis, Victoria University of Wellington.

Salmond, A. (1991), *Two Worlds: First Meetings Between Maori and Europeans 1642-1772*. Auckland, N.Z.: Viking.

Salmond, A. (1997), *Between Worlds: Early Exchanges Between Maori and Europeans, 1773-1815*. Auckland, N.Z.: Viking

Shirres, M. P. (1997), *Te Tangata: The Human Person*. Auckland: Accent Publications.

Smythe, J. (2004), *Downstage Upfront: the First Forty Years of New Zealand's Longest-Running Professional Theatre*. Wellington: Victoria University Press.

Stanislavsky, K. (1956), *An Actor Prepares*, trans. E. Reynolds Hapgood, New York: Theatre Arts Books.

Stanislavsky, K. (2008), *An Actor's Work: A Student's Diary*, trans. J. Benedetti. London and New York: Routledge.

Stanislavsky, K. (2010), *An Actor's Work on a Role*, trans. J. Benedetti. London and New York: Routledge.

Tait, P. (2002), *Performing Emotions: Gender, bodies, spaces, in Chekhov's drama and Stanislavski's theatre*. Burlington, VT: Ashgate.

Thiong' o, N. W. (1986), *Decolonising the Mind: The Politics of Language in African Literature*. Portsmouth, N.H: Heinemann.

Timms, H. (2013), *The Responsive Actor – Turangawaewae*. Toi Whakaari: New Zealand Drama School.

Whyman, R. (2008), *The Stanislavsky System of Acting: Legacy and Influence in Modern Performance*. Cambridge and New York: Cambridge University Press.

Williams, J. (2004), 'Papa-tuā-nuku: Attitudes to Land', in *Ki Te Whaiao: An Introduction to Māori Culture and Society*, eds T. M. Ka'ai, J. C. Moorfield, M. P. J. Reilly, and S. Mosley. Auckland: Pearson Education New Zealand, pp. 50-60.

Interviews

Daniels, E. Personal interview, Museum Hotel, Wellington, 22 January 2014.
Diver, C. Personal interview, Macandrew Bay, Dunedin, 17 January, 2014.
George, M. Personal interview, Museum Hotel, Wellington, 23 January 2014.
Hendry, J. Personal interview, Toi Whakaari, Wellington, 21 January 2014.
Kouka, H. Personal interview, Lido Cafe, Wellington, 23 January 2014.
McCallum, R. Personal interview, University of Otago Staff Club, 14 August 2014.
O'Donnell, D. Personal interview, Martinborough, 20 January 2014.
Ruth, A. Personal interview, Museum Hotel, Wellington, 22 January 2014.
Taylor, R. Personal interview, Museum Hotel, Wellington, 22 January 2014.
Timms, H. Personal interview, Toi Whakaari, Wellington, 23 January 2014.

Part Six

India and Bangladesh

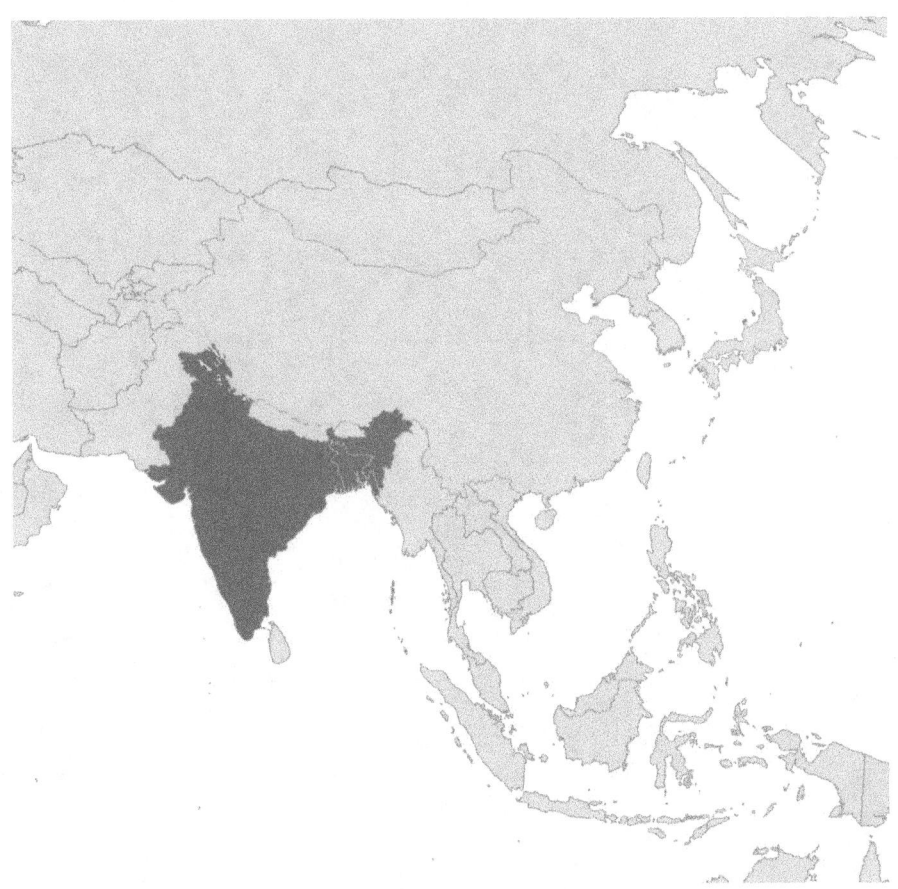

Figure 33 Stanislavsky in India and Bangladesh.

Part Six: Introduction

Jonathan Pitches

Two poles of hybridity: Stanislavsky in India and Bangladesh

The ex-Director of the National School of Drama (NSD) in New Delhi, Anuradha Kapur, suggests that there have been three phases to the history of modern acting in India: i) acting in traditional theatre; ii) acting in the Parsi theatre, inspired by the actor-manager model of colonial Britain; and iii) acting in the institutionalized theatre:

> By which I mean theatre taught and learned in institutions that see themselves as part of the educational systems of the modern world – universities, schools and other academies.
>
> Kapur, 1996, p. 43

Kapur sees this third stage in Indian acting methodology as 'conceptually different' (Kapur, 1996, p. 43) from the traditional theatre, with its *guru shishya* traditions (master–disciple transmission). In institutional training embodied learning is moved out of the domestic, family-oriented domain into a more systematic and strategically organized context of acting pedagogy. The two essays that comprise this Part – a historical analysis of NSD's developing curricula in India from 1959–95 and an examination of three productions with differing attitudes to Stanislavsky staged in Dhaka University, Bangladesh – are both examples from Kapur's third phase of acting.

Writing as a theatre academic working in Dhaka University, Syed Jamil Ahmed, argues, following Edward Said, that one of his country's 'conditions of acceptance' (Said, 1983, p. 227) of the Stanislavsky system is inherently tied up in this idea of the institution: 'Such engagements' with the system, he posits, 'have been possible only in academic circles, where the students can, in ideal conditions work and dream of theatre 24/7' (p. 438). This is true for JooYeoul Ryu, also, who draws on fieldwork, interviews, and curriculum papers to examine the development of India's most prominent training institution – the NSD. Founded in 1959, a dozen years after Indian Independence in 1947, the first two directors of the NSD, Satu Sen (1959–62) and Ebrahim Alkazi (1962–77), were physical embodiments of these conditions of acceptance. Both had experienced training in Western institutions – Sen with Boleslavsky in the United States and Alkazi at RADA in the United Kingdom. And both sought to integrate elements of Stanislavsky's psychotechnique with traditional forms of Indian theatre, Bharata (from the father of Indian theatre and author of the ancient manual of performing arts technique, *Natyashastra*[1]), along with other oriental traditions of performance from Japan and China.

Just as there are 'conditions of acceptance' so there are 'resistances' in Said's model of travelling theory and its fourth phase, where 'the full (or partly) accommodated or (incorporated) idea is to some extent transformed by its new uses, its new position in a new time and place' (Said, 1983, p. 227) is the most interesting in the context of this study. This brace of essays offers two very different answers to the question of transformation and as such they occupy polarized positions on what might be called a continuum of hybridity in Indian and Bangladeshi responses to Stanislavsky.

Before expanding on this idea, one or two caveats are necessary. The first is to stress the partiality of the picture in this section. As with the other Parts in the book, there is no attempt here to be broadly representative of South Asian theatre practices, or for that matter of Indian and Bangladeshi theatre traditions. These are more than numerous and form what Rakesh Solomon calls 'the extraordinary variety of theatrical genres that flourished in Indian languages' in the second millennium (Solomon, 2004, p. 207). Farley Richmond, Darius Swann, and Phillip Zarrilli, attempted to organize this multiplicity of forms over a quarter of a century ago in *Indian Theatre* (Richmond et al., 1990), coining the term 'spheres of performance genre' and determining five interlocking kinds: Ritual, Classical, Devotional, Folk/Popular, and Modern (p. 10).[2] Here our focus is naturally on Modern theatre and performance: work that utilizes twentieth-century stage techniques, spaces, and technologies. As such, and with a concentration on the training *institution*, both of these essays focus on urban practices from the capital cities and commercial centres of both countries. However, as Richmond et al. point out, these spheres of influence are in 'constant interplay' (Richmond et al., p. 11) with classical forms making use of modern technology and contemporary directors, playwrights, and choreographers drawing on traditional folk forms.[3]

The extent to which this interplay is evident in the two essays relates to my earlier point on hybridity. Always a multivalent term, hybridity in this context is helpfully defined by Lo and Gilbert via Homi Bhabha:

> Hybridity offers an effective way of resisting the replication of Manichean binaries and the discourses of cultural purity which underpin colonialist relations. But as Homi Bhabha warns, hybridity 'is not a third term that resolves the tension between two cultures'; that is, it is not a simple fusion of differences but rather a volatile interaction characterised by conflict between and within the constitutive cultures of a colonised society.
>
> Gilbert and Lo, 1997, p. 7

Ahmed's essay identifies two strands in the modern theatre of Bangladesh: i) the dominant mode of simplified realism which 'developed from the colonial encounter out of which "modern" Bengali theatre in 19th century Kolkata emerged' (p. 420); and ii) a 'counter-mode of acting [...] appropriating and assimilating the System to fashion hybrid acting' (p. 430). For the former he analyses productions of *A Doll's House* and *Three Sisters* directed by Israfeel Shaheen, himself a graduate of the NSD in New Delhi. In these two productions with MA students at Dhaka University, Shaheen drew on his training in the Stanislavsky system from NSD, immersing the students in detailed readings of *An Actor Prepares* and *Building a Character* as well as of the Ibsen and Chekhov scripts. Ahmed uses recent interviews with some of the key personnel in these productions, originally staged in the late 1990s, to provide a vivid picture of the assimilations and adjustments needed to explore the resonances between Russian culture at the turn of the twentieth century and Bangladeshi culture at the turn of the twenty-first. The 'magic if' and Emotion Memory are two of the key mechanisms used to 'transcend [...] physical geography delimited by time' (p. 428). For the latter, hybrid, form (evidenced in successive productions of *Behular Bhasan* in 2004 and 2005) Ahmed describes a more agile and critical attitude to Stanislavsky, the actors operating 'as subversive explorers of the playful condition of "acting", who were prepared to selectively borrow from it because of expedience' (p. 432). Here, in Ahmed's own production, states of possession experienced in traditional contexts in rural Bangladesh rubbed shoulders with Stanislavskian ideas of concentration and attention; tempo-rhythm was induced by indigenous music and detailed and unitary characterization gave way to a Brechtian co-presence of role and self; the complexities of Bhabha's hybridity, and the mobile appropriation of both colonial and indigenous influences is, Ahmed reasons, bringing about a paradigm shift in contemporary Bangladeshi performance.

For Ahmed this hybrid collision offers a 'middle way' (p. 438) recalling, perhaps, Bhabha's 'third space'.[4] For Ryu and his elucidation of teaching at NSD, no such dialogue between colonial and indigenous sources ever really occurs – despite attempts by many influential directors and teachers at the only national academy in India to manufacture their meeting. Sketching a history of the NSD with reference to the place of Stanislavsky and the *Natyshastra*, 'shows that the two practices have been consistently kept apart rather than actively brought together' (p. 400), Ryu argues. This is notwithstanding the shifting personnel at the helm and the changing attitudes of each School Director. Indeed, as Ralf Yarrow suggests in *Indian Theatre* (Yarrow, 2001): 'the appointment of Directors and other faculty reflects the different periods of the post-Independence quest for cultural identity [...] NSD has gone through most phases of the anti-colonialist – intracultural – intercultural debate' (p. 167). Ryu's history, then, based on what is a narrow data set of curricula, interviews and School documentation, nevertheless illustrates wider cultural and political trends in India: Ebrahim Alkazi's eclecticism and urge to improve pedagogical standards and programme coherence, Karanth's emphasis on traditional theatre forms, Kirti Jain's diversification and respect for horizontalism, and the concurrent shift to a pragmatic, means-to-an-end, application of theatre techniques.

It is difficult to see this longitudinal separation of sources at the NSD as anything but a missed opportunity, not because the utility of Stanislavskian practice was at times overlooked, and not because the School seems to have been particularly vulnerable to the buffetings of external and internal forces – what Yarrow calls its 'chequered history' (Yarrow, 2001, p. 166). It is a missed opportunity because the productive collision of different sources, captured in Bhabha's notion of hybridity seems not to have ever taken place (or at least not in the period addressed here). The possibility for a radical interculturalism and a conscious repurposing of Stanislavsky in an Indian context (as just one of the many colonial sources imported from the British theatre) is similarly compromised.

The two essays in this Part, then, both offering a localised institutional microhistory, stand at different ends of a continuum of hybridity, with only the Bangladeshi case-study reaching the Saidian 'fourth phase' of a travelling idea: one that in its incorporation is 'to some extent transformed by its new uses, its new position in a new time and place' (Said, 1983, p. 227).

Notes

1. Literally meaning, 'drama science' the Natayashastra is 'the most important text of dramaturgy that ancient India produced' which has 'exerted a profound influence over the formation and structure of successive theatre genres throughout India' (Richmond et al., 1990, pp. 34–5).
2. Solomon's historiographical critique of India theatre histories considers this formulation an 'important' (Solomon, 2004, p. 217) contribution to the challenges of fairly representing the breadth of Indian performance forms, a history which also includes Bangladeshi theatre, of course, before its own independence from Pakistan in 1972.
3. Two outstanding examples of contemporary training institutions in India, which draw on traditional forms, are Adishakti (in Pondicherry) and Attakalari (in Bangalore).
4. Revisiting in an interview his essay 'Signs Taken for Wonders', Bhabha offers two examples of this third space or what he calls 'something [that] opens up as an effect of this dialectic, something that will not be contained within it, that cannot be returned to the two oppositional principles' (Mitchell, 1995, pp. 80–4). See also https://prelectur.stanford.edu/lecturers/bhabha/interview.html [accessed 13 September 2016].

References

Bhabha, H. (1985), 'Signs taken for wonders: Questions of Ambivalence and Authority Under a Tree Outside Delhi, May 1817', *Critical Enquiry*, Vol. 12, No.1, pp. 144–65.

Gilbert, H. and Lo, J. (1997), 'Performing Hybridity in Post-Colonial Monodrama', *The Journal of Commonwealth Literature,* Vol. 32, No. 1: 5–19.

Kapur, A. (1996), 'On Acting', *Seagull Theatre Quarterly,* issue 12, ed. A. Katyal. Calcutta: Seagull Foundation for the Arts.

Mitchell, W. J. T. (1995), 'Interview with Cultural Theorist Homi Bhabha', *Artforum,* Vol. 33, No. 7: 80–84.

Richmond, F., Swann, D. and Zarrilli, P. (1990), *Indian Theatre: traditions of performance.* Honolulu: University of Hawaii Press.

Said, E. W. (1983), *The World, the Text, and the Critic.* Cambridge, Mass.: Harvard University Press.

Solomon, R. (2004), 'When did Brahma Create Theatre? And other Questions of Indian Theatre Historiography', in *Writing and Rewriting National Theatre Histories,* ed. S. E. Wilmer. Iowa: University of Iowa Press.

Yarrow, R. (2001), *Indian Theatre: Theatre of Origin, Theatre of Freedom.* Surrey: Curzon Press.

Websites

Adishakti: http://adishaktitheatrearts.com [accessed 13 September 2016].

Attakalari: http://www.attakkalari.org [accessed 13 September 2016].

18

Between Stanislavsky and Bharata: Actor Training at the National School of Drama in New Delhi

JooYeoul Ryu with Stefan Aquilina

Introduction

In her account aimed at positioning Stanislavsky as 'an acting master for the twenty-first century', Sharon Marie Carnicke unpicks the various levels that coexist within the Stanislavskian technique known as 'the through-line' of a role. These levels include elements of work which have become part and parcel of what Christopher Balme calls 'acting in dramatic theatre in the Western tradition' (Balme, 2008, p. 18), such as 'the line of events', 'the line of a scene's bits, tasks, desires' and 'the line of characterization' (Carnicke, 2009, p. 2). However, the 'through-line' of a role also includes two entries that can be traced back to an alternative theatre tradition, one which Robert Leach refers to as 'Eastern, specifically Hindu yogic, sources' (Leach, 2003, p. 79). These two 'Eastern' entries are 'the line of *prana* and its movement' and 'the line that sends forth and receives rays of energy', which Carnicke references as 'a concept [...] derived from Yoga' (Carnicke, 2009, p. 2). The System, it would seem, was intended by Stanislavsky himself as an open and malleable practice that allowed for cross-cultural hybridity, a statement which this article places at its core and tries to unpick by focusing on the work of the National School of Drama (NSD) in New Delhi, India. On paper, the NSD appears as an ideal place for the integration of Stanislavskian elements with techniques found in the *Natyasastra*, the classical Indian text about the performing arts, which traditionally has been attributed to Bharata Muni. The teaching philosophy and methodology of NSD were concretely influenced by these two systems, both of which emphasize a process of rigorous preparation to sensitize the actor psychophysically. However, and notwithstanding this common ground between Stanislavsky's System and the *Natyasastra*'s teachings, a history of the NSD shows that the two practices have been consistently kept apart rather than actively brought together. This chapter will expound on the cultural as well as personal reasons for this distance by outlining developments in NSD training under five of its Directors, namely: Satu Sen (1959–62), Ebrahim Alkazi (1962–77), Babukodi Venkataramana Karanth (1977–82), Brij Mohan Shah (1982–4), and Kirti Jain (1988–95).

The early years of the NSD (1959–62)

NSD's first syllabus was structured as a two-year diploma course in what was referred to as 'Dramatics'. Its aims included: 'to impart knowledge of acting, both in theory and practice, and of producing and directing plays'; 'to equip the students with the literary history of drama and to acquaint them with the fundamentals of script-writing'; and 'to run special short-term courses on specified subjects'. The course consisted of three divisions, namely Dramatic Literature, Acting, and Production. Acting pedagogy during the first year aimed to help actors 'express the poetry of emotions' after the investigation of 'the actor's media, e.g. mechanism of voice, its scale and range and of the body and its gestures and movements'. The emphasis was therefore on the individual's work on the self. The students began working on character in the second year. Collective work was also given attention, in the context of textual 'interpretation and projection of character' for 'achieving mutual response', such as the 'relation of [an] individual actor to the ensemble and its impact on the audience'. Stanislavsky was included under the remit of 'acting theories', alongside Bharata and others.[1]

The earliest applications of Stanislavskian practices at the NSD are symptomatic of broader difficulties encountered in the transmission of a technique that has been obfuscated by time, partial original sources and mythological clouding, leading to what Katya Kamotskaia refers to as an 'uncertainty about the specifics of Stanislavsky's "system"' (Kamotskaia and

Merlin, 2012, p. 173). Kamotskaia's analysis of 1970s Soviet training in the System exposes a detachment between the acting theories as elaborated in Stanislavsky's books and their application in the studio and on stage. This led her to experience a sense of ambivalence: whereas Stanislavsky was presented to her as the key methodological reference, the value and potential of his practices remained elusive: 'I now understand that there was no explanation [of the exercises choices made] because our tutors did not necessarily have one. They were taking their exercises directly from Stanislavsky's books with (as yet) very little direct questioning or interpreting of his "system"' (Kamotskaia and Merlin, 2012, p. 169). Similar difficulties were encountered during initial training in Stanislavskian techniques at the NSD, which was led by Sheila Bhatia:

> She had her own understanding of Stanislavsky['s System] and began to teach it from the very beginning. She focused on his theories of acting but it was not related to the practice. She had [the idea of] physical exercises on the basis of improvisation but there was no connection between the theories of Stanislavsky she had been teaching. [...] That didn't give any idea of why we should do this and [...] what we should do particularly. [...] We simply started to read *An Actor Prepares* and Ms. Sheila Bhatia taught us a certain psychological acting with [reference to] *An Actor Prepares* for two years.
>
> Sharma, 2005

Bhatia's choice as the Stanislavsky teacher at the NSD is a curious one, particularly when one considers that Satu Sen, the School's first Director, had already come under the direct influence of Richard Boleslavsky at the American Laboratory Theatre in New York. While the specifics of Sen's training with Boleslavsky remain ambiguous,[2] it is clear that his foreign sojourns (1925–32) coincided with the Laboratory Theatre's years of activity (1924–32). Kironmoy Raha introduces Sen in the *Oxford Companion to Indian Theatre* as follows:

> Pioneering technician of Bengali theatre [who] [...] proceeded to New York and joined the American Laboratory Theatre. He nursed his love of theatre there by study, hard work and an indefatigable will to learn the many aspects of production and direction under Richard Boleslavsky, former associate and disciple of Konstantin Stanislavsky. Sen became assistant production manager and assistant technical director of the institute and produced there and later at the newly started Woodstock Playhouse many plays, directing

some of them. In his subsequent travels to Europe he met and saw such renowned producers and directors at work as Vsevolod Meyerhold, Max Reinhardt and Gordon Craig.

Lal, 2004, p. 429

At the NSD, however, Sen took charge of the set-cum-lighting design courses rather than the acting classes. It is perhaps appropriate to assume that there were few technicians in those days who could deliver detailed knowledge of stage and light and that therefore it was more urgent for Sen to prioritize that over acting. The onus to integrate the grammar of Stanislavsky's System with Bharata-influenced traditional instruction therefore fell on Bhatia, but interviews with some of the NSD's first graduates reveal that the Bharatian concept of Rasa was only dealt with in the Dramatic Literature class as a theory of poetics and not referred to as an acting practice (Karanth, 2002; Kaushal, 2002; Sharma, 2005). The performative value of the *Natyasastra*, therefore, seemed totally absent in her acting class, a condition that would remain at the NSD for some years to come.

The contributions of Ebrahim Alkazi (1962–77)

Ebrahim Alkazi's directorship of the NSD was marked by a strong effort to improve the School's pedagogical standards. Training in a broad array of techniques in order to prepare actors for a varied and eclectic career became imperative. According to the 1966–7 syllabus the course programme was extended to three years and restructured to feature four specializations: Acting, Direction, Stage Craft, and School (as in with school children) Dramatics. The overall thrust of working on the self during the first year and on the character during the second was, however, retained. The third and final year of study was allotted to various acting theories and practices, which included acting in Sanskrit, Classical Greece and Rome, Chinese and Japanese theatres, Bhavai, Jatra and other folk forms, Commedia dell'Arte, Elizabethan acting, and Realism and Epic Theatre. Stanislavsky's name was featured in the syllabus as an example of 'a great actor' (like Garrick, Duse, Olivier, and others) about whom students were expected to be aware, but it is clear that, beyond this simplistic referencing, many of his practices became an integral part of the new course programme.

Stanislavsky's techniques were central to the second year of study as:

aids to coax feelings and creative approach to building [a] character: atmosphere, psychological gesture and tempo-rhythm; the character analysis and the design of a role: the actor's personal analysis from the point view of positive qualities, disabilities and limitations; the acting in crowd scenes.

1972–3 syllabus

These techniques built on the general objective of the aforementioned 1966–7 syllabus, which was then already inflected towards 'the objective of the actor's art: [the] creation of character'. Alkazi attached great value to the inner technique of the actor. Consequently, terms that are associated with Stanislavsky and the psychological dimension of acting repeatedly appear throughout the 1963–77 Acting curricula. These terms include: concentration of attention, observation, relaxation, imagination, sensory and emotional memory, communion and adjustment, and given circumstances. The acting training programme shared much with Stanislavsky's ideas: 'relaxation' is essential to both training process and performance; participants have to accept the 'given circumstances' of the play as completely as possible; and the actor, in the vein of the 'sensory and emotional memory', identifies with the character by the 'Imagination', leading to thought and feeling as if he, i.e. the actor, is playing the role in the circumstances of the play. The students were taught the ability to focus on the objective that the character is struggling to attain, while being enclosed in the 'circle of attention' and fixed on a definite point by will and choice, which means 'concentration'.

This is not to say that the NSD pedagogy during these years gave no attention to the physical dimension of the actor's work, but it seems that Alkazi searched for physical paradigms in other, non-Stanislavskian sources. The 1966–7 curriculum makes it clear that the physical and vocal culture of the School was developed during Alkazi's years via a regimen of 'Yoga, Dance Movement & Mime, Improvisation, Judo, Manipuri Martial Arts, Modern Dance for the body; Speech, Music, Voice Production, Interpretation, Performance in Plays for the voice; and Make-up, Kathakali exercises for the face'. Several of these approaches, especially ones like Judo, Martial Arts and the Kathakali face exercises make evident the School's consistent technical training, one that while informing performance work can be considered as

Figure 34 The NSD first year Acting class focusing on the actor's work on self (Lecturer: Abdul Latin Khatana, 2005).

being effectively detached from the staging of plays. This contrasted with Alkazi's application of Stanislavskian techniques, which was never dissociated from the rehearsal and production of theatre performances. Therefore, practice in the System was situated in the relatively long and research-oriented process of 'reading' a play. In other words, the grammar of Stanislavsky's System was mainly transmitted to students while analysing the character and the play during the rehearsal or before the rehearsal began. Alkazi asked students to examine backgrounds for designing the set, costume and stage properties, as well as when working on the character. K. M. Sontakke, a graduate of 1966, describes the rehearsal process as follows:

> At times, every student researched some aspect of the work. [...] We started from the understanding of Stanislavsky['s] method [sic] about how to analyze textual and sub-textual meanings and how the psychological excavation arrives at audiences via [a line of] the words. What is the use of the concept[s], objective, super-objective, given circumstances, motivation and so on? Stanislavsky['s] method [sic] suggested to us the idea how to deal

with the text. And so we became dramaturge[s] and researched the period and style of the play, author, language, theme. [...] Alkazi showed paintings, films and also brought in guest lecturers who are knowledgeable about the play. He guided us to visit museums or galleries or other locations that would give us ideas for visualizing the play. [...] I remember that we rehearsed a play more than three months.

Sontakke, 2003

These practices recall Stanislavsky's Round-the-Table Analysis work which he actively pursued in the 1910s and later in order to 'unravel a playtext and its characters' (Merlin, 2003, p. 16). While Stanislavsky discontinued such approaches in the 1930s to make way for his experiments in physical action, play analysis at the NSD under Alkazi's direction took root as a rigorous rehearsal model in historical research and character nourishing. This is confirmed by Anuradha Kapur, a recent NSD Director whose term ended in 2014: 'Pedagogically, the NSD of the early 1960s took up the Stanislavskian method of building a character and made an intervention by creating actors who brought a new realism to the Hindi stage' (Kapur, 1996, p. 44). To Alkazi, the potential of Stanislavsky's techniques was, therefore, in the process of play production rather than as a pedagogical and formative process and, as a consequence, there was little serious attention given to the methodological approach of the System towards the work of the actor upon himself in the sense of modern actor preparation. The actual operation of the Acting curriculum was often, in reality, taken away from the classroom and subordinated to the production.

The emphasis on Stanislavsky's techniques as a rehearsal approach meant that an integration of his approaches to Bharata's phenomenological perspective on the character and the play (e.g. Pravrtti and Vrtti) could make little advance. While the *Natyasastra* was included vaguely in the 1959–77 syllabi as 'teaching material', its position remained predominantly that of a 'metaphorical' and 'traditional' work which a modern acting student would relate to with difficulty. It was only a marginal document, as Suresh Awasthi and B. V. Karanth argue, particularly because Alkazi's knowledge of the *Natyasastra* was at best minimal (Karanth, 1981). Any practice which the students might have had in Bharata was restricted to occasional lecture-demonstrations that were 'organised [...] in an ad hoc manner [without them being] incorporated in the teaching programmes' (Awasthi, 2001, p. 48). While Alkazi's approach did expose students to traditional performing arts – he, in fact, convened workshops with experts like Shivarama Karanth from the Yaksagana Kala Kendra Centre in Udipi and encouraged research in ancient Sanskrit theatre – his emphasis was clearly elsewhere. However, Alkazi can be credited with initiating a necessary 'beginning' step towards the implantation of Bharata's theory and practice into the NSD training programme. As R. G. Bajaj put it, Alkazi was the man to propose the 'idea' of the concurrent use of indigenous and modern theatre practices, but not the 'dynamic individual to give those ideas a shape' (Bajaj, 1981).

Stanislavsky's disappearance from the NSD (1977–82)

Babukodi Venkataramana Karanth followed Alkazi as the next School's Director. His term lasted between 1977 and 1981. Rather than building on Alkazi's work, about which he was particularly critical, Karanth opted to emphasize the traditional forms of Indian theatre, which entered the curriculum at the expense of Stanislavskian techniques. In fact, the latter all but disappeared from both the syllabus and the actual training and production work carried out at the NSD. Karanath saw Alkazi as 'an excellent teacher' who was 'so capable himself that he could take every class' (Karanth, 1981). He was a teacher and director with a charismatic personality but who prevented the School from experimenting in diverse practices and its students from developing their own individual approaches. Bajaj supports such a reading, adding that Alkazi's years were marked by 'one mode in which people acted [...] [and] one method to which they got exposed' (Karanth, 1981). Karanth was also critical of the lack of serious effort made in the application of Bharata's *Natyasastra* to the training programme. His direction of the School coincided with a struggle between a Euro-American realistic mode of doing theatre and a conscious reconstruction of Abhinaya, the ancient Sanskrit acting technique for transferring Bhava ('an emotion or state of being' [Richmond et al., 1990, p.469]) to the audience in order to lead them to evoke the relish of Rasa (the ultimate aesthetic, sentimental, and imaginative experience). Realism was seen as a colonial import that needed to be resisted and a search for alternatives was encouraged to make Sanskrit classic theatre part of the modern performance arena (Dharwadker, 2005, p. 93). Karanth was strongly inclined towards the

Figure 35 The NSD second year Improvisation class (Lecturer: Tripurari Sharma, 2005).

latter and insisted that the NSD must apply Bharatian approaches to the actor training and exploit its full potential. Stanislavsky's System, seen then as a technique that was only suitable to realistic plays and for developing truthful characterization, became caught on the wrong side of this tug-of-war and its application at the NSD therefore lost valuable ground.

Karanth's application of Bharata's techniques to the training programme was attempted in two ways. First, he invited qualified artists, experts, and scholars from eminent backgrounds and institutions to the School in order to train students in traditional theatre forms. According to the Academic Council Reports of 1978–81, these workshops usually lasted between three to five weeks, and they included sessions in Kathakali, Chhau, Kutiyattam, Yaksagana, Bhavai, Jatra, and Nautanki, and also in martial arts like Kalaripayattu and Thangta. In all fairness, such classes had already been introduced by Alkazi, but under Karanth training in traditional forms became more common and, as from 1978, an integral part of the School's syllabus. Karanth also invited tutors who could contribute with more theoretical inputs and thus support the practical pedagogy in that manner. These included names like Adya Rangacharya and the aforementioned Suresh Awasthi who, with others, elaborated on the conventions of traditional theatre forms, Sanskrit plays, sculpture, mural paintings, and ancient Indian History. The second way in which Karanth exposed students to traditional forms of Indian theatre was by setting up in 1980 the scheme known as the Traditional Theatre Workshop. This scheme allowed students to travel to regional training centres for periods of forty-five days in order for them to gain experience of pre-modern training systems such as the Guru-Sishya tradition.

Students taking the Traditional Theatre Workshop scheme were encouraged to focus on traditional aesthetics and techniques with a view to incorporate them in modern plays, and under the supervision of a modern director. The aim behind this approach was to evolve a fresh theatrical idiom that interwove modernity with tradition (Jain, 1995, p. 17). This emerges from the syllabus. Whereas the headings resonate with conventional Western pedagogies, the actual content was shifted to traditional theatre by Karanth, who asserted that 'a lot of work needs to be done on Bharata's *Natyasastra*. Who else [will] take it up if not NSD? Who else is more qualified or more privileged?' (Karanth, 1981). Of particular value was the idea of the self-sufficient actor, freed from the dependency on literature and director, which Karanth traced back to Bharata (Karanth, 2002). The syllabus was revised with the major purpose of discarding the concept of specialization and introducing an actor-oriented integrated theatre course. The idea of an 'all round education' thus became important. This was evident in the vast number of subjects studied, which in the compulsory first two years were structured in four divisions, namely: (i) Dramatic Literature – Traditional Drama, Classical and Contemporary Indian Drama, Western and Asian Drama; (ii) Theatre Technique – Scenic Design, Lighting, Theatre Architecture, Costumes, Make-up, Carpentry, Property, Mask and Model Making; (iii) Acting – Voice and Speech, Acting, Improvisation, Movement in different styles, Music, Yoga, Martial Arts, Acrobatics, Mime; and (iv) Play Production (1979–80 syllabus). In the third year, students were required to take a series of short-term courses, providing an advanced level of training in the subject of their choice, mostly from Acting and Theatre Technique. A short dissertation (Honours) on an important aspect of theatre arts under the guidance of a faculty member also had to be compiled.

The integration of Stanislavskian and Bharatian techniques remained undeveloped during the terms of the NSD's first three Directors. Alkazi underscored rehearsal and production work in terms arising from Stanislavsky's System, but in a way that precluded serious research in traditional forms of Indian theatre. Karanth, on the other hand, can be seen to have taken the opposite road and emphasized '[r]esearch, interpretation and definition of the *Natyasastra*' (Karanth, 1981). Some components of the System, like the Super-Objective, the Through-Line-of-Action, Units and Moment-by-Moment Action, did remain as a means to analyse character motivation, but then *An Actor Prepares* and *Building a Character*, continuously referred to as the primary text during Sen's and Alkazi's years, simply disappeared from the 1978–81 syllabus. S. Raghunandana, a graduate of 1981, says that 'no teacher recommended at all the acting manual of *An Actor Prepares* or *Building A Character* or others, so I, for one, never even thought about looking into Stanislavsky's method [sic] in my school time' (Raghunandana, 2005). Ram Gopal Bajaj, who had trained under Alkazi and would later serve as the NSD's Director between 1995 and 2001, is described by Raghunandana as an acting teacher whose 'classes generally began with the text analysis right away' (Raghunandana, 2005) and who tentatively made use of certain Stanislavskian techniques like the super-objective and the through-line-of-action without, however, attributing these to Stanislavsky or the System. Such appropriation of Stanislavsky's techniques without a routing back to their origin and exposition about how they developed would remain a staple of NSD's practice, as I will discuss below.

B. M. Shah (1982–4) and Kirti Jain (1988–95): Stanislavsky within horizontal training approaches

The production-based pedagogy adopted at the NSD, whether it was approached via an application of Stanislavskian techniques (as evident during Alkazi's years) or through more Bharata-influenced traditional approaches (as in Karanth's), was not without its critics. Brij Mohan Shah, for example, who followed Karanth as the next NSD Director, believed that too much attention was being given to play production, to the detriment of the School's research and experimental ethos. Moreover, play production was also seen as damaging to the students' long term formation: 'In the first year itself students had started doing massive productions and these big plays gave some false notions to the students [that] they thought that they had become big time actors' (Shah, 1981). Shah experienced these difficulties first-hand, having trained with both Alkazi and Karanth. His term as a school director would see the acting class becoming independent of production work, as well as a renewed interest in Stanislavskian methodologies. Consequently, *An Actor Prepares, Building a Character*, and *Creating a Role* were reintroduced in the classes.

The aims of the Acting class were expressed in the 1982–3 syllabus as follows:

> [To] draw out, mould and reinforce each individual talent by extending the actor's apparatus of body and voice, sharpening his imagination and sensibility and tapping his emotional recourses; [...] increasing the student's general awareness of his environment, experience and personality; providing him with a foundation of technique and skills in acting; and placing at his disposal major codified theories and methods of acting.

These 'theories and methods of acting' included Stanislavsky's System and Bharata's techniques which were now seen, at least in theory, as having important common principles. Stanislavsky's dictum of 'reaching the unconscious through the conscious' chimes with Bharata's continued emphasis on the need for a highly disciplined mastery of technique that helps the actor find stimuli of the 'immediate-sentiment-spring' and guides the audience to evoke or create Rasa (Bharatamuni, 1961, XXI: 121–2).

Stanislavsky argued that a systematically composed acting approach pushes the actor on towards the 'truth', and that it is the feeling of truth that best awakens emotion, imagination, and creativity. For Stanislavsky, inspiration arrives to the actor when in the Creative State, and the right use of technique makes this State accessible (Stanislavski, 2008, pp. 260–2). Similarly, Bharata's concept of Abhinaya is not a mere imitation (Anukarana) of the character but the 'imaginative' and 'explorative' imitation (Anukirtana) of being (Avastha) of the character (Gnoli, 1968, pp. xix–xx, 41). For him, a well-coordinated management of the fourfold Abhinaya, i.e. Vacika (verbal), Angika (physical), Sattvika (psychological, mental, or emotional), and Aharya (make-up, costume,

Figure 36 Solo performance, 'Karna' of a NSD student (the present writer) for his final examination (Duration: 90 minutes, 16 May 2004, NSD).

properties), generates 'a power of communication (avagamanasakti)' (Gnoli, 1968, p. 31) capable of stimulating Manas (mind-consciousness), Sattva (emoting consciousness), and Hela (passion) interactively to make accessible the actor's creative state. Indian theatre traditions were taken into the classroom not only for attaining physical and vocal skills but also as a means to explore the actor's inner processes that develop artistic imagination and creativeness. Shah realized the necessity of techniques that stimulate the actor's inner state, but his years, as well as those of the Directors who followed (including Kirti Jain, discussed below), saw the treatment of Stanislavsky and Bharata as *alternative* rather than complementary approaches towards the actor's inner state. Even so, Shah's years do underline a development in the application of Stanislavsky, wherein his techniques are not applied strictly to the rehearsal room but they are also valued for the actors' technical formation. More than directing, it is the training dimension of Stanislavsky's practice that is highlighted.

Shah was part of a group of Directors who led the School for the relatively brief period of two years. Similar short terms include those of Mohan Maharishi (1984–6) and Ratan Thyam (1987–8). In line with the School's desire to continuously revise and improve its practices, a review committee was set up in 1989 which, amongst others, suggested the extension of the Director's tenure to five years because, it was argued, a two-year term had 'made the Director's position very vulnerable to all kinds of manipulation and pressures' and 'might also encourage the director to take ad hoc and make-do decisions' (4, the Report of the Review Committee). Kirti Jain was the first Director to be appointed under this recommendation and her term started in 1988.

Jain's tenure was characterized by an even broader diversification of the training. Under her directorship, actor training at the NSD developed along horizontal rather than vertical lines. Instead of a deep and exclusive engagement with one training practice and, very often, one master, student-actors undergoing horizontal training are exposed to a variety of models, leading to what Jonathan Pitches refers to as 'the synchronous borrowing from a range of parallel sources and practices' (Pitches, 2014). Symptomatic of the horizontal approach taken at the NSD is the increase of visiting staff from fourteen (in 1990–1) to fifty-six (in 1993–4) and then again to sixty-four (in 1995–6). The workshops, which typically lasted from four to six weeks, featured both Indian (e.g. the theatre and film director Satyadev Dubey) and international teachers (e.g. Cicely Berry, the then Voice Director of the Royal Shakespeare Company). Horizontal training within the workshop setting became not only common but also institutionalized as the School's working method, particularly during the third year of studies:

> Once again you only get to know one kind of theatre, one way of working, which was the problem in the earlier training mode at NSD. But in today's world there is so much diversity and so many things happening at the same time, [that] I think people need to be exposed to a larger number of approaches and methods and styles and way[s] of working. I think it's only in the institutional mode that that can happen in a systematic manner, apart from giving him [the actor] the basic skills and competence to handle the task of acting or design. Otherwise it will take 30–40 years for a person to train with three different people and learn their way of working. [...] What we want to achieve in three years from the basic training of theatre, basic awareness of theatre and the basic learning of the education system is to equip them [NSD students] to deal with any of these kinds of theatre.
>
> Jain, 1995, p. 19

What ensued in the application of Stanislavsky at the NSD was that, similar to what had happened during Alkazi's years, some fundamental precepts of the System were readily adopted in the training but without acknowledging, or indeed attempting to develop, the original source. Consequently, students were introduced in the first semester to an awareness of the 'self' and its constituents like concentration, attention, imagination, trust, and belief, but without these being specifically introduced as the grammar of Stanislavsky's System. In the second semester students were introduced to scene work and rehearsal approaches pertinent to modern realistic texts, and it is here that Stanislavsky's methodologies were seen as fitting best. A shift away from Shah's application of the System as Acting preparation and return to Alkazi's reading of Stanislavsky as a rehearsal paradigm is therefore to be noted. In other words, the System was processed during Jain's term not as an open-ended practice but as a means towards a very specific end, that of textual study. The reduction of specific techniques to equally specific ends seems to have become a recurring mode of operation at the NSD. For example, acting in Classical Greek drama was treated as training in animal and mask work, chorus, story-telling, and verse speaking, while acting for Shakespearean text was primarily valued as a preparation for performance on open stages. The *Natyasastra* was similarly given a specific application, and in this case it became a Mime and Movement source to explore 'postures and movements as agents of expression of human experience and activity[,] both mental and physical[;] [and] relative stance and projection[,] which are the essential features of traditional movement in practice' (1994–5 syllabus).

Conclusion

The history of actor training at the NSD during the years covered is one that highlights the accumulation of practices, thus creating a baggage of appropriated and abridged techniques which precluded the possible development of a Stanislavskian-Bharata hybrid in a way that Stanislavsky himself had envisaged when he first experimented with Yoga and Prana. The lack of integration at the NSD of two such diverse approaches raises a fundamental question: which space best facilitates the integration of disparate training and acting techniques? The NSD was clearly established and run on the conservatoire and drama school model, where day-to-day training was set against clear work structures like a syllabus, binding timeframes (time-tables, semesters, and workshops duration) and an institutionalized grading and degree-awarding system. Its running recalled the operation of the Moscow Art Theatre's Second Studio, which was also treated as a training institution from which graduating students tended to join the main Theatre. A syllabus based on the System was also at the core of its teaching and 'the full course was three years' (Edwards, 1965, p. 123). Therefore, the work ethos at the Second Studio was markedly different from the more research-oriented frame adopted at the First Studio, particularly during its first years of activity under Leopold Sulerzhitsky's direction. Participants of the First Studio were, for example, encouraged 'to create their own exercises, scenic innovations and theatrical visions' (Gordon, 1987, p. 43). It was within this research environment that Stanislavsky investigated the application of Yoga and Prana because the context allowed for error-prone experimentation. Training at the NSD, on the other hand, was more concerned with preparing students for varied and eclectic careers rather than researching new and untested acting techniques, thus highlighting the difficulties of the school model as a space to create theatre and performance training hybridity.

Notes

1 All quotations taken from the Annual Report 1959–60 of the Sangeet Natak Akademi and the syllabus 1959–60 of the NSD.
2 There are opposite points of view about Satu Sen's work. While H. V. Sharma and Kironmoy Raha appreciate his contribution to Indian theatre and the School, Suresh Awasthi devalues it: 'He had acquired some experience in the stage lighting in the US in the 40s [...] [but] he had absolutely no knowledge of the theatrical traditions of the country and of [the] contemporary situation' (Awasthi, 1981).

References

Awasthi, S. (1981), 'Suresh Awasthi' (interview) in *Enact*, No. 172–4, ed. R. Paul. New Delhi: Pauls Press.
Awasthi, S. (2001), *Performance Tradition in India*. New Delhi: National Book Trust.
Bajaj, R. G. (1981), 'Ram Gopal Bajaj' (interview) in *Enact*, No. 172–4, ed. R. Paul. New Delhi: Pauls Press.
Balme, C. (2008), *The Cambridge Companion to Theatre Studies*. Cambridge: Cambridge University Press.
Bharatamuni, (1961), *The Natyasastra, Vol. II*, trans. M. Ghosh. Calcutta: Manisha.
Carnicke, S. M. (2009), *Stanislavsky in Focus, 2nd edn*. Oxon: Routledge.
Dharwadker, A. B. (2005), *Theatres of Independence – Drama, Theory, and Urban Performance in India since 1947*. New Delhi: Oxford University Press.
Edwards, C. (1965), *The Stanislavsky Heritage*. London: Peter Owen.
Gnoli, R. (1968), *The Aesthetic Experience According to Abhinavagupta*. Varanasi: ChowKhamba.
Gordon, M. (1987), *The Stanislavsky Technique: Russia*. New York: Applause.
Jain, K. (1995), 'Perspectives on the National School of Drama' (interview) in *Seagull Theatre Quarterly*, issue 6, ed. A. Katyal. Calcutta: Seagull Foundation for the Arts.
Kamotskaia, K. and Merlin, B., (2012), 'Re-visioned directions: Stanislavsky in the twenty-first century', in *Russian in Britain*, ed. J. Pitches. Oxon: Routledge, pp. 167–91.

Kapur, A. (1996), 'On Acting', in *Seagull Theatre Quarterly*, issue 12, ed. A. Katyal. Calcutta: Seagull Foundation for the Arts.
Karanth, B. V. (1981), 'B. V. Karanth' (interview) in *Enact*, No. 172-4, ed. R. Paul. New Delhi: Pauls Press.
Lal, A. (ed.) (2004), *Oxford Companion to Indian Theatre*. Oxford: Oxford University Press.
Leach, R. (2003), *Stanislavsky and Meyerhold*. Bern: Peter Lang.
Merlin, B. (2003), *Konstantin Stanislavsky*. Oxon: Routledge.
Richmond, F. P., Swann, D. L., Zarrilli, P. B. (eds.) (1990), *Indian Theatre: Traditions of Performance*. Honolulu: University of Hawaii Press.
Shah, B. M. (1981), 'B. M. Shah' (interview) in *Enact*, No. 169-71, ed. R. Paul. New Delhi: Pauls Press.
Stanislavski, K. (2008), *My Life in Art*, trans. J. Benedetti. Oxon: Routledge.

Unpublished materials

An interview with B. V. Karanth at Guwahati on 5 January 2002.
An interview with J. N. Kaushal at New Delhi on 18 March 2002.
An interview with K. M. Sontakke at Mumbai on 9 January 2003.
An interview with Kirti Jain at New Delhi on 11 April 2005.
An interview with S. Raghunandana at New Delhi on 17 September 2005.
An interview with H. V. Sharma at New Delhi on 12 December 2005.
An interview with R. G. Bajaj at New Delhi on 29 December 2005.
Pitches, J. (2014), 'From Vertical to Horizontal: the future of Russian actor training in a digital age', in Russian Theatre Symposium, organized by the Russian Theatre Research Network (UK).
'Report of the High-Powered Committee: Appointed to Review the Performance of the National Akademis and the National School of Drama', an official document of the Department of Culture, Ministry of Human Resource Development, Government of India (July, 1990).
'Report of the Review Committee', a confidential document of the NSD (1989).
The Academic Council Reports for the years from 1978 to 1981, NSD documentation.
The Annual Reports of Sangeet Natak Akademi from 1956 to 1960, from 1971 to 1972, the printed documentation of the Sangeet Natak Akademi.
'The Memorandum of Association', an official document of the NSD (1959).
The syllabuses for the years from 1959 to 2010, NSD academic documentation.

Stanislavsky in the Modern Theatre of Bangladesh: A Mapping of Postcolonial Appropriation and Assimilation

Syed Jamil Ahmed

If the performance mode of realism that surfaced at the juncture of Western industrial modernism is characterized as one that seeks to articulate 'a psychological exploration of man [sic] and his relations with other men' in a darkened auditorium by adopting performance conventions that confine a play inside a box set, and 'turn[s] the audience into eavesdroppers who peer through an invisible fourth wall into the lives of real people' (Carnicke, 1977, p. 43), then the entire mechanics of such a mode have rarely been employed both in the mise-en-scène and the acting technique of the 'modern'[1] theatre in Bangladesh since it emerged in 1972. Today, more than pursuing the ideological project of realism, 'the distinguishing marks of which lie in its character as rhetoric, its ways of using theatrical production – conventions of acting, design, direction – to naturalize a particular relationship between the dramatic fiction and the offstage world of the audience' (Worthen, 1992, p. 14), the modern theatre in Bangladesh appears to be taken up by the presentational mode of the traditional (indigenous) theatre aesthetics that challenges the ideological project. Nevertheless, if Stanislavsky is recognized as a deep explorer and a subversive instigator of the playful mode known as 'acting', and not a prophet of a hallowed Truth, and if his System is acknowledged as a historically conditioned process that seeks coherence and organization in the conscious preparation and rehearsal of a role, so as to generate conditions of spontaneous and intuitive creation, then indeed the System has been a usefully enabling tool in the modern theatre of Bangladesh.

This theoretical endeavour is informed by the argument produced by Edward Said (1983, p. 226) that the 'travelling' of theories and ideas, from the point of origin where the theory came to birth and entered discourse, to a new historical period and national culture that is altogether different from the point of origin of the theory, is never unimpeded. The impediment, which arises because the processes of representation and institutionalization at the point of implantation are different from those at the point of origin, inevitably leads to transformation, appropriation, and assimilation of the theories. Informed thus, this endeavour seeks to demonstrate that a unique condition has emerged in Bangladesh, where the System, articulated in *An Actor Prepares* (Stanislavski, 1980), *Building a Character* (Stanislavski, 1968) and *Creating a Role* (Stanislavski, 1981) as the theory at the point of origin, is being appropriated and assimilated to produce a form of 'hybrid acting' (Schechner, 2002, p. 173) in the transplanted location of the postcolony of Bangladesh. In working towards this objective, this undertaking argues its case by means of qualitative research. It draws on primary data collected by the author as a participant observer in directing plays and attending performances, by semi-structured and structured interviews of fifteen actors and directors who served as key cultural consultants and through focus group discussion (FGD) with a group of thirty-eight actors and directors; and secondary data collected from archival documents, scholarly and popular publications. Critical analysis of the data has been presented in three parts: the first relates the notion of the System that is current among the theatre practitioners, in the context of the 'normative' mode of representation and institution of theatre production that exists in Bangladesh today; the second is a brief account how the System was applied in two productions that came closest to the intent of the theory at the point of origin; and the third demonstrates how the System as the theory at the point of origin, is being appropriated in academia to produce a form of 'hybrid acting' that seeks a bold new postcolonial terrain. The essay ends by looking back to the encounter of the indigenous theatre with colonial modernism in the nineteenth century, so as to ascertain the 'conditions of acceptance or, as an inevitable part of acceptance, resistance' (Said, 1983, p. 227) that has impelled the postcolony to appropriate and assimilate the travelling theory of the Imperial centre.

The institution of theatre production and 'normative' mode of representation

No commercial or professional institutions of theatre production exist in the modern theatre of Bangladesh today. Full-time professional theatre in the country exists in the indigenous (traditional) theatre performed mostly in the rural and semi-urban areas, and bears a history of at least a thousand years. In the urban areas, 'Group Theatre' is the dominant mode of organization for producing theatre performances. Such organizations distinguish themselves from both the amateur groups, which, as the exponents of the Group Theatre movement claim, fail to reach up to the professional standard and the professional companies, which, they assert, pander to profit and commerce and hence cannot aim for artistic excellence at the cost of box-office failure.

Group Theatre emerged as an artistic movement concurrently with the emergence of Bangladesh immediately after a horrendous civil war fought against Pakistan in 1971. Today, over 250 such non-profit city-based organizations of theatre practitioners operate in urban locations of Bangladesh, such as Dhaka and Chittagong. These organizations (or 'groups' in popular parlance), produce plays entirely in Bengali, emphasize collectivity and egalitarianism against the dominance of celebrity performers, inculcate professionalism in the work that they produce and are run by voluntary contributions of its members, box-office receipt, revenue accrued from adverts published in souvenirs, and occasional grants and sponsorships received from the government, national and multinational industrial and trading houses. The practitioners are mostly made up of middle-class students and professionals belonging to the media, advertising agencies, teaching, and other private services. They devote their 'surplus time' extracted from the economics of their livelihood to produce performances that illustrate an acute awareness of the socio-political actuality of contemporary Bangladesh.

Most of the performers of the Group Theatre ensembles are not formally trained in acting. An excellent example of such home-schooled yet successful actors is Ferdousi Majumdar. As she testifies, she learnt acting from the daily-life performances of her father, who would feign silent anger in order to discipline his children, and emoting from her mother, who, when hurt, would draw her veil and weep in muted stillness (Kundu, 2013). Nevertheless, a few theatre-makers have indeed studied theatre abroad and some of them have produced their students, mostly from graduate and postgraduate programmes in theatre and performance studies at the University of Dhaka (DU) and the Jahangirnagar University (JU). Although a strong wave of 'university theatre' has emerged because of plays produced at five public universities in Bangladesh, most of the students who graduate from these institutions are unable to sustain themselves by working full-time in theatre because the economics of the stage performance is not viable enough. Occasionally, a few actors, directors, and designers, are paid, but it is not enough to sustain a body of full-time theatre practitioners. On the other hand, the Group Theatre practitioners are increasingly finding it difficult in a globalizing neoliberal world to devote their surplus time to training, rehearsing, and performing, so as to attain professional as well as artistic excellence they profess to be their goal.

The mode of acting that exists in Bangladesh theatre today is underpinned by simplified realism. Briefly, the mode may be explained in terms of the following four characteristics: (i) emoting of the actor articulated by means of the face (primary) and hands (secondary) in a way that strikes the 'right' balance between 'art' and 'life', and does not appear as overtly dramatic (or melodramatic); (ii) the emoting, drawing on the actor's personal experience, is based on him/her believing in the emotion; (iii) clarity and modulation in speech that veils technique by supporting the projected emotion; and (iv) an approach to characterization that is best described as *dwaitā-dwaita* (lit., 'two and not-two'), in other words, the actor in appropriate costume and makeup projects a heightened state that is both the 'I' (i.e., the actor) and 'not-I' (the character) at the same time. As it will be evident in the concluding section, these four characteristics have developed from the colonial encounter out of which 'modern' Bengali theatre in nineteenth century Kolkata emerged. At this point, suffice it to say that hardly any theatre practitioner in Bangladesh follows the entire gamut of the System as it emerged at its point of origin.

An eminent actor and director in Bangladesh theatre and the media, Mamunur Rashid asserts that the System's greatest strength is that it impels the actor to build his/her creativity by means of discipline, instead of floundering aimlessly, relying upon vague inspiration. He looks back to the late 1960s as the time Stanislavsky was introduced in erstwhile East Pakistan through *My Life in Art* and *An Actor Prepares*, and asserts that the actors of earlier generations applied various elements of the System intuitively and instinctively. As the venerable master Stanislavsky himself acknowledges, Rashid notes, the System 'is based on the laws of nature' (Stanislavski, 1968, p. 287). The discipline underpinned by the laws, according to Rashid, is most effective in the construction of character biography based on given circumstances, observation and imagination.[2]

Interviews with faculty members teaching acting at the Department of Theatre and Performance Studies (DU) and the Department of Drama and Dramatics (JU), as well as students who have passed out of these institutions reveal that they have mostly adopted ten elements of the System. These are action (along with 'magic if' and given circumstances), observation, imagination, emotion memory, concentration of attention, adaptation, communion, tempo-rhythm, super-objective, and truth and belief. With these, some teachers also add relaxation of muscles, units, and objectives and through-line of action. Clearly, academia in Bangladesh has adopted most of its Stanislavskian ideas from *An Actor Prepares*, and has generally disregarded *Building a Character* and *Creating a Role*.

The received tradition of the System prevalent among the Group Theatre actors also relies heavily on selections from *An Actor Prepares*. In a FGD held on 13 March 2014 with thirty-eight actors based in Dhaka city, it emerged that only one actor consciously applies all the ten elements of the System mentioned above and finds them extremely effective. For the rest, 'magic if', observation, emotion memory, and concentration of attention are the elements that they find useful. Besides these, one participant acknowledged that conscious application of imagination was useful, another credited truth and belief as expedient and three others found the through-line of action to be extremely valuable. There was a consensus that observation of life and living is a very helpful tool for actors. One participant added that for plays built around times and spaces other than that of the actors, audio-visual and written materials drawn from archival and documentary sources prove to be useful. Two others underscored the extra-normative in daily life as the observed material that they value and employ.

Three images of playing a role that emerged from the FGD and interviews were that (i) the actor is immersed in the role (চরিত্রে ডুব দেয়); (ii) the actor is possessed by the role (চরিত্র ভর করে); and (iii) the actor bears the role (চরিত্র ধারণ করে). As Dr A. K. M. Yusuf Hassan Arko, Professor, Department of Drama & Dramatics (JU) insists, it is futile for the actor to walk along the bank of a pool; it is necessary to be immersed in the water. It is only then that an engrossed state is achieved, which is indispensable for creating a role. Anisul

Haque Barun, a director who also participated at the FGD, sought to provide a reasonable explanation of how the engrossed state is achieved. He says, the actor begins by gathering information given at the point of inception of a play, identifies the point of termination (the super-objective in Stanislavsky's parlance) and traverses the distance between the two by gathering further information given throughout the play and filling up the gap of what is not given by imagination. The engrossed state is nothing more than the 'auto run' state where the actor is inevitably propelled from the point of inception to the point of termination. While none asserted that the actor 'becomes' the role, a few participants offered to explain that the actor is 'possessed' by the role, or that s/he 'bears' the role, but many sharply disagreed. One argued that it is not possible to be possessed by the character. Another asserted that if there is any 'possession', it is not by the role but the philosophy or the worldview underpinning the role.

In sharp contrast to these appropriations of the System, five actors offered to explain their performance by the notion of dual consciousness, echoing Stanislavsky in *Building a Character* (Stanislavski, 1968, p. 21). Tariq Anam Khan, an eminent actor and director in theatre as well as the media, and an alumnus of the National School of Drama (New Delhi, India), discards the notion of submersion in the role. He asserts, an actor cannot perform without a dual consciousness. One continues as the self, the other as the role. Titas Zia, an alumnus of the Department of Theatre and Performance Studies (DU), currently a faculty member at the department and the winner of the National Film Award 2013 for best actor, also finds the notion of divided consciousness essential in acting. However, he argues, at heightened moments of performance, where the actor reaches an altered state of consciousness, the division disappears. Pavel Azad, artistic director of a leading group in Bangladesh known for its innovative approach to performance, unhesitatingly acknowledges dual consciousness during his performance. Portraying a role, for him, is a struggle where the self is very much present along with the character. It is only at certain moments that the consciousness of the self disappears completely. At other times, the actor is only left with the mechanics of the body and voice to interpret the role. Riaz Mahmud Jewel, an actor whose work traverses the stage, television, and film, employs the metaphor of the 'gardener' and the 'garden' to explain his process of portraying a role. He asserts that during a performance, he is aware of the self (as the gardener) as well as the character (as the garden). Nevertheless, there are moments, he realizes later, when the 'gardener' disappears altogether. Mohsina Akhter, an emerging director and an alumnus of the Department of Theatre and Performance Studies (DU), employs the metaphor of the musical instrument (the role) and the instrumentalist (the actor) to explain. Although the instrumentalist always 'plays' the instrument, an on-going interaction between the two continues throughout the performance. By consciously applying herself to the given circumstances of the role, and by charging these with personal experience, she derives aesthetic delight, which in turn enlivens her performance each night.

The System applied in performance

The closest that Bangladesh theatre came to fashioning productions by employing the System of the point of origin and the performance mode of modern realism can be best exemplified by two plays produced by the Department of Theatre and Performance Studies (DU). These are, Henrik Ibsen's *A Doll's House* (directed by Israfeel Shaheen in 1998) and Anton Chekhov's *The Three Sisters* (directed by Israfeel Shaheen in 2005). Importantly, the director of these productions never attempted to rigorously follow the definitional parameter of Carnicke cited at the beginning of this essay. Indeed, he delved into psychological exploration of characters in relation with other characters, but not by confining them entirely inside a box set. Both the productions were played at the department's studio theatre that houses a tiny proscenium stage thrusting out into an extended apron. *A Doll's House* was played on this stage, with the spectators facing the proscenium arch. The mise-en-scène of *The Three Sisters* extended beyond the thrust stage into the auditorium and the spectators were seated on the three sides of the extension. The conception of a 'picture-frame' was abandoned altogether for this production. Nevertheless, the performers of both the plays succeeded in turning the spectators into witnesses who vicariously experienced the lives of fictive characters and their action, in a manner that the 'as if' of fiction bore remarkable resemblance with the 'as is' of everyday life.

Shaheen, trained in direction with the System as a core component at the National School of Drama, devoted thirteen months to staging *A Doll's House*

Figure 37 A scene from *A Doll's House* (Act 1), showing Golam Farida as Mrs Linde (far left), Sahana Ferdous as Nora (right of centre) and Nurur Rahman as Dr Rank (far right).
Photograph by Altaf Hossain.³

with a group of MA students at the Department of Theatre and Performance Studies (DU). As Nurur Rahman, then a student who played the role of Dr Rank recounts, after completion of a very comprehensive study of *The Doll's House*, *An Actor Prepares* and *Building a Character*, they began the actual journey with the play, which can be best described as '"consciously arriving at an unconscious state". At that time, we certainly didn't realize that the journey could be so extensive and significant in terms of all concerns of naturalistic performance technique that is known as the System!'

Shaheen embarked upon the journey by engaging the actors in self-exploration. He asked them to narrate the story structured in the plot, sought out the external facts of the plot to identify the physical action, had the plot broken down into units, and then had the actors narrate the actual incidents from their lives, which incidents bore similarity with the play. By having the actors frequently execute the actual incidents by means of improvisation, Shaheen sought to let them arrive at the state of 'I am thus', imbued with truth and belief. The following example demonstrates how one such improvisation not only led the actors to truth and belief, but also enhanced the meaning of the dramatic text. The end of Act Two is given thus in the dramatic text:

> Nora: [*Standing for a moment as if to collect herself, then looking at her watch*]:   Seven hours till midnight. Then twenty-four hours till midnight tomorrow. Then the tarantella will be over. Twenty-four and seven . . . thirty-one hours to live.
> Helmer: [*At the door on the right*]:   But where's my little sky-lark?
> Nora [*Going to him with arms outstretched*]:   Here she is!
>
> Ibsen, *Doll's House*, Act Two; 1965, p. 206

The scene, developed out of improvisation, showed Nora saying the line 'thirty-one hours to live' and then discovering the key to the letterbox lying on the table. Jubilant, she jumps in joy and throws the key in the air. Helmer, who enters the room at that point, says 'But where is my little sky-lark?', and snatches the key from the air. Then he asks her to join the others for dinner and goes back to the dining room. Nora is plunged back to desperation as the lights fade.

When the characters were firmly anchored in the psyche of the actors, Shaheen gradually introduced the text and sought to transfer the state of 'I am thus' into 'I am the character'. As Ahasan Khan, then a student who also played the role of Dr Rank recounts, he found physical characterization specially challenging, even as he applied the notion of 'magic if'. He ascertained the 'given circumstances' and identified a correlation with the loneliness of his role and that he experienced as a person, having lost his wife a few months back. He found it useful to walk back home alone, often late in the evenings in order to latch firmly on to the psychological state of the role. Having vigorously correlated himself with the psychological state, he applied his imagination to articulate the physical characterization. Dissatisfied with what he had achieved, he spent time observing quite a few doctors at work in hospitals, and devoted himself to a meticulous study of consumption of the spine that Dr Rank suffers from. It was this study of consumption and the subsequent application of the study to his role that helped him achieve truth and belief.

The cumulative effect of all the initial rehearsals bore fruit in the run-throughs. Nurur Rahman describes the effect of one such run-through thus:

> I was entirely centred, and completely focused on my role, so much so, that I did not waver even for a moment. When the run-through ended, I felt so

completely involved with my role that I became aware of a different kind of vibration in my body. It took me awhile to return to my 'normal' physical and psychological state.[4]

When the performance of *The Doll's House* opened on 26 October 1998 at the department's studio theatre Natmandal, the result was stunning. The spectators were completely engrossed in the performance, as the actors had effectively situated them in the 'time present' of the fictional universe of *A Doll's House*. As a reviewer commented, the production rigorously followed the realist-naturalist acting style and each performer clearly bore imprint of concentration and diligence. He further observed, *A Doll's House* demonstrates unequivocally as to why it is necessary for the actors engaging with the realist-naturalist style to work on him/herself in the creative process of experience as well as physical characterization (Kabir, 2002, p. 306).

Perhaps one of the finest moments of the performance was created in the scene in Act Three, where Dr Rank bids Nora and Torvald goodbye, and proceeds to 'shut himself up to die' (Ibsen, *A Doll's House*, Act Three; 1965, p. 219). Towards the end of the scene, Torvald offers Rank a black Havana cigar, and Nora offers the light.

Nora [*striking a match*]:   Let me give you a light.
Rank: Thank you.
[*She holds the match while he lights the cigar.*]
Ibsen, *A Doll's House*, Act Three; 1965, p. 217

In the performance directed by Shaheen, Rank attempted to light a cigarette, but, due to his extremely fragile mental state, repeatedly failed. Nora realized his inner turbulence and came forward to help him light the cigarette. Her eyes were transfixed upon Rank's and his hands held her clasped palms holding the fire. Eyes upon eyes, and hands upon hands – the actors created a magical moment of communion that engulfed the spectators in a breathtaking silence. A renowned actor of Bangladesh stage and television, Fazlur Rahman Babu, commented after the performance, 'I was really feeling very distressed, especially because of my sympathy for Dr Rank's misfortune.'[5]

The finest proof of eating the proverbial pudding was a performance of the play at the open-air theatre of JU. Performances at this theatre always risk being challenged by a highly critical body of student-spectators, who never shy away from voicing their slightest displeasure. Hence, the actors approached this performance with extra caution, and believed that if they could maintain their focus on their roles, the spectators would be bound to be attentive. During the performance, the indirect communion with the spectators was so gripping that Professor Selim Al-Deen, known for his intellectual distance from naturalism, was heard to whisper: 'Excellent, superb!'

Following a rehearsal process quite similar to that of *A Doll's House* but spread over a more condensed time span of five months, Shaheen worked on *The Three Sisters* with another group of MA students at the Department of Theatre and Performance Studies (DU). As with *A Doll's House*, the work on *The Three Sisters* was a part of the MA programme in acting that focused on the application of the System. At the same time, both the plays were taken up because they were regarded as extremely relevant to contemporary urban life in Bangladesh. Looking back on the process of work undertaken by Shaheen, Dr Abdul Halim Pramanik (then a student and now Associate Professor at Jagannath University) observes, creating the character of Andrei was quite complex and daunting. On the one hand, the given circumstances of Russia were far removed from his experience, and on the other, his personal experience resonated strongly with Andrei. In overcoming this complex situation, 'magic if' proved to be extremely helpful. In his journey from the conscious to the unconscious, he began to locate his state of 'I am thus' by articulating the 'I' underpinned heavily by his personal experience: a youth living in a village who loves to listen the birds and dreams of going to Dhaka (Moscow) to become a university professor. Firmly anchored at this point, he began to adapt the other aspects of the character and the play. In the chain of events that develop throughout the plot, Pramanik employed imagination to the given circumstances to identify the action of each unit, and thence the through-line of action. For physical characterization, he incorporated into his physique the signs of age, profession, class, family background, and related notions entwined with the social reality of Chekhov's Russia. As Pramanik recounts:

> In the early rehearsals, my 'self' and Andrei appeared as distinct entities. However, after about two months of rehearsals, the 'self' began to appear quite unknown to myself. During the run-throughs, there would be distinct clash between my 'self' and Andrei in Act One. By Act Four, though, the question of 'if I were Andrei' disappeared completely; instead, 'I' would

become *almost* Andrei. I would feel that the Andrei that he played transcended physical geography delimited by time.

Indeed, Pramanik was most eloquent in playing the role of Andrei at the very end of *The Three Sisters*. The dramatic text ends the play thus:

> *The music is growing fainter and fainter; Kulygin comes in, happy and smiling, with Masha's hat and cloak; Andrei is wheeling Bobkins in the pram.*
> Chebutykin: (*sings quietly*):   Ta-ra-ra boom-di-ay. I'm in the soup today. (*Reads the newspaper.*) It makes no difference. No difference at all.
> Olga: If only we knew! If only we knew!
> <div align="right">Chekhov, <i>The Three Sisters,</i> Act IV; 1973, p. 158</div>

Shaheen changed the end by cutting Chebutykin and Olga's lines. He had Chebutykin exit muttering inarticulate words, as Olga stood silently with Masha and Irina, facing Andrei. An image of the disintegration of the Prozorov family was thus visualized by having the four siblings face each other for the last time. Masha was the first to leave, after Kulygin brought her hat and cloak. After a little while, Irina departed, but she went in another direction. Finally, it was Olga's turn. Andrei was left all alone, standing helplessly, silently clutching the perambulator as the lights faded.

Initially, Pramanik found it difficult to perform this scene convincingly. Then, advised by the director, he applied emotion memory. He recalled a crisis that had erupted eight years ago, when the joint family of his parents, his two married brothers, himself, and two younger sisters broke down because of economic strain. His father had retired from service a year ago and the family economics was dependent entirely upon the earnings of the two married brothers. Unable to bear the strain, especially of educating the two sisters and Pramanik, the eldest brother and his wife decided to leave. It was morning. The eldest brother was busy loading the van with his belongings. His father sat watching, numbed in silence. His mother was desperately making futile attempts to persuade her eldest son to stay. Pramanik and his younger sisters could only stand and watch them go. A sense of utter helplessness, which he had never known before or after, seeped in through his sinews and veins. The air seemed too thick to breathe.

The application of this bit of emotion memory was absolutely successful for Pramanik. He would recall the sense of helplessness he had experienced in his teenage years, as he watched his eldest brother leave with his wife and child. This is how he recalls the inner process of thought during the scene:

> Thus is erased all traces of happiness. I (Andrei) do not want them to leave. But I can only watch them go. My perambulator halts. I feel numb. Inside me (Andrei), a desolate gust of tears tear away. I *must* suppress all pain, my jaws clench – but why do my cheeks feel wet? My shoulders feel heavy. A morning in the month of August in 1997. Here I stand, watching my brother go. Now, I am empty. All is void. Life is a desolate landscape – a half-broken door banging against the walls of an abandoned house as the storm lashes relentlessly.[6]

The performance of *The Three Sisters* opened on 3 April 2005. The spectators were engrossed as they watched, sitting on the three sides of the performance space, the performers play in a space defined by selective-realist scenography,

Figure 38 Abdul Halim Pramanik as Andrei in *The Three Sisters* (Act 4). Photograph by Kamaluddin Kabir.

further nuanced by the audiographic ambience of live music on the violin. Critical appraisals of the production were in full praise for the emotive power it evoked. According to a critic, in contrast to most of the plays performed on Dhaka stage, where the acting is dressed and masked by scenography, this play mobilizes acting as the prime driver of the performance (*Daily Sangbad*, 2005, p. 21). Many spectators found the characters of the play to be familiar, as though drawn from their daily-life experiences. Hence, most of them found it easy to empathize with them almost completely. Theatre critics agreed that the production was extremely relevant in Bangladesh – a country where agrarian mode of production, rural society, and institution of family were undergoing radical transformation as unplanned and imitative urbanization were generating complications and crises in human lives at an exponential rate (Moishan, 2005, p. 16).

The System adapted and assimilated: seeking new directions

Moving away from the normative mode of acting underpinned by simplified realism and the concomitant exertion towards the System at the point of origin, a counter-mode underpinned by a strong postcolonial discourse that seeks to challenge the peripheral relation of the postcolony to the Imperial centre is emerging in modern theatre of Bangladesh today. The counter-mode is traceable back to the early 1990s, when a few Group Theatre practitioners and university academics produced plays such as *Chaka* (1991), *Bishad Sindu* (Parts 1 and 2, 1991 and 1992), *Koinya* (2001), *Araj Ali Charitamrita* (2001) and *Behular Bhasan* (2004, 2005, and 2010).[7] In these, the practitioners and the academics sought to challenge some of the foundational assumptions of the ideological project of realism by attempting to articulate a counter-mode of acting. Curiously, this counter-mode is appropriating and assimilating the System to fashion 'hybrid acting', by subverting the rhetoric of realism and seeking ways and means to jump or elide its frame with performance techniques drawn from storytelling, trance, epic theatre, and the indigenous theatre of Bangladesh. Consequently, Bangladesh theatre appears to be at a crossroads where a paradigm shift in acting is noticeably being mobilized by a body of actors and directors who are attempting to transcend mere imitation or impersonation.

The paradigm shift was most noticeable in *Behular Bhasan*, a performance based on a collation of six medieval narratives composed in verse known as the *Manasa-mangal* (literally, 'auspicious poetry' or 'poems of well-being' in honour of Manasa, the serpent deity). The third movement of the narratives recount the marriage of a virtuous maiden named Behula to Lakshmindar (the son of Chad Saodagar, the antagonist in the narratives), Lakshmindar's death by snake-bite inside the bridal chamber, and the sailing of Behula on a raft in a desperate attempt to revive her husband. During the journey, she overcomes various forms of masculine snares ranging from brother's love to attempted rape. At the end of her journey, she arrives at the abode of the gods, where she has to dance for the pleasure of Shiva. Finally, in a bargain struck with the serpent deity, Behula's husband is restored back to life after Chad agrees to resolve his antagonism to the deity by making an offering with his left (i.e., 'unclean') hand.

The performance of *Behular Bhasan* was structured in seven parts prefaced with a song of invocation and suffixed with a benedictory song. It retained Behula's setting off with the dead body of her husband on a raft. However, it also challenged the patriarchal discourse embedded in the medieval narrative by recounting her encounter with a series of male stereotypes during the journey, only to be disillusioned as she is gradually forced to concede that even her dead husband is as much the vehicle of power of patriarchal social relation as all the males she encountered in the journey. The performance ends by Behula's questioning whether it is worthwhile to revive her husband back to life.[8]

The first two versions of *Behular Bhasan* (2004 and 2005) had entirely abandoned the ideological project of realism, as well as its concomitant conventions of acting and mise-en-scène, that confines a play inside a box set and coaxes the spectators to play as eavesdroppers. Instead, these versions drew heavily from the presentational mode of the traditional (indigenous) theatre aesthetics. For example, both were presented on an 'empty' platform (12 feet square), lit by stark white light, with the spectators seated on four sides. Although the third version was presented on a proscenium stage, it called the artifice of the picture-frame into question by removing all the wings and borders, and deploying a second frame that stood centre stage and spanned halfway across the breadth.

All the three versions adopted the indigenous theatre aesthetics, by employing live music, song and dance, such that a narrator (*gayen*) 'told' parts of the 'story' in prose, as well as in song (party by narrating in her own person, and partly by assuming the character other than her own), while other parts were represented by characters performing the action in first person. All these performers played throughout the performance with the support of a group of choral singers and musicians who remained in full view of the spectators, and produced music, sang choral accompaniment to all the songs sung by the narrator and the characters, and also danced to the narrator's songs connecting all the episodes. Importantly, the application of the indigenous theatre aesthetics did not remain an empty shell, for the performers had drawn from 'extra-daily techniques' applied by the performers of the indigenous theatre, and the process by which they worked on the pre-expressive levels to articulate the quality of their scenic existence.[9]

The rehearsal process of *Behular Bhasan* was underpinned by an implicit acknowledgement that the System is not the hallowed Truth but a historically conditioned process. The actors approached it as subversive explorers of the playful condition of 'acting', who were prepared to selectively borrow from it because of expedience. Their goal in approaching the System was to ensure coherence and organization in the conscious preparation of roles, so that conditions of spontaneity and intuition would be generated in them. Hence, despite drawing on the aesthetics of indigenous performance, the director (this author) as well as the performers had a clear understanding of the super-objective they were working towards when they began to rehearse. They had broken down the dramatic text into units, identified the action and objective of each unit and strung the actions into a through line. By concentrating on the action of each unit and remaining focused on the action, the performers attained a level of truth and belief that in no way attempted to 'naturalize a particular relationship between the dramatic fiction and the offstage world of the audience' (Worthen, 1992, p. 14). Instead, their truth and belief drew upon the indigenous aesthetics, which teaches the performers that the 'truth' of a character of a tale necessarily effuses out of the philosophy, system of belief, values, and manner of perception that underpin the collective psyche and the social ethos of a people (Arko, 2015, p. 115). The element of tempo-rhythm was deployed not so much as the external signs generating from a character, but by the music and songs played and sung by the performers. The musical score was carefully selected from the vast repertoire of the indigenous theatre, specifically with the objective of evoking the particular rhythm of a scene, and its concomitant range of emotions. It was the live music and songs that were responsible, to a great extent, for generating intense emotional experience in the performers, as well as the patterns of their gestures, moves, and physical actions.

Particularly memorable was the scene of lamentation in the first episode, where Tania Sultana in the role of Behula convincingly played the loss of Lakshmindar by drawing upon the elements of 'magic if', emotion memory, and imagination from the System, as well as the indigenous technology of commemoration known as *bilāp* (aptly described as a public performance of lament presented by means of 'tuneful texted weeping', Wilce, 2002, p. 159).[10] Consequently, the performers' construction of imagination operated not in a rationally coherent world one is able to connect empirically and analytically, but in a mythopoetic space where '"make believe" and "make belief" converge[d]' (Schechner, 2013, pp. xi and xii). The operation in the mythopoetic space made it possible for the performers as well as the spectators to connect with the archetypical figure of Behula inhabiting their collective unconscious, and emote with profound exuberance as seen in numerous indigenous performances.[11]

Some of the actors, particularly Tania Sultana and Taskin binte Siddique (who played Behula in the 2004 and 2005 versions, respectively), employed the elements of 'magic if', concentration of attention, imagination, and truth and belief in their roles, but at the same time, elided the parameter of the rhetoric of realism by inducing in them a state of obsession (ঘোর), which bordered on the trance state seen in women possessed by spirits (*djin*) in traditional rural society of Bangladesh.[12] After they had put on their costume and makeup, and took up their place in the performance space immediately before the spectators entered, it would be difficult to communicate to them. As the performance commenced, they appeared to be far removed from their daily-life 'selves'. When the performance ended, they were so completely drained of strength that for a while their bodies appeared utterly exhausted and drained.

Whereas the roles of Behula and the seven male stereotypes required the performers to play these in the first person, that of the *gayen* or the narrator required the performers to deploy elements drawn from the System, as well as narrative techniques sourced from the indigenous theatre and storytelling

Figure 39 A scene from *Behular Bhasan* showing Farida Akhter Lima as the narrator (top), and Tania Sultana as Behula (bottom).
Photograph by Kamaluddin Kabir.

techniques from Europe and the US. Importantly, the narrator employed a fixed and memorized (verbal) text, and performed in an ensemble project that deployed elaborate set, costumes and props (more so in the third version than in the first two), and thus was removed from contemporary Euro-American storytelling models that emphasize individual endeavour, minimal set, costumes and props, and fluid and improvised (verbal) text (Wilson, 2006, p. 46).[13] Nevertheless, s/he remained in direct communion with the spectators even as s/he remained completely focused on the onstage action. Thus, the narrator transcended the System's dictum never to extend the actor's 'circle of attention' in the auditorium (Stanislavski, 1937, p. 75), and at the same time, to remain in direct communion with self, persons, and objects on stage, and only in indirect communion with the spectators (Stanislavski, 1937, p. 208).

As a result, the narrator in *Behular Bhasan* was able to perform two tasks at once, which, according to Carol Birch, can be seen in the most interesting of storytellers. By the first, the narrator was able to 'wear' different characters by mobilizing verbal as well as nonverbal signs, so as to bring out large and small nuances of the characters, 'and direct the point of view of an audience toward the characters' (Birch, 2000, pp. 20–21). By the second task, the narrator refused to submerge his/her own *self* in service of character, as demanded by the rhetoric of realism; rather, they remained visible, engaged, and fully present at the time of telling, such that that the spectators were viscerally involved. In such a state of visible 'self', they communicated, as Euro-American storytellers, their 'judgment of, and responses to, the characters in a story' (Birch, 2000, p. 21), but less by the verbal text and more by the intonation of voice and attitude of the body.

Importantly, these techniques are not uncommon in the indigenous theatre of Bangladesh, and hence, the performers were very familiar with it. Consequently, they were able to go beyond the Euro-American storytellers, whenever necessary. For example, in the first episode, while narrating the grief of Lakshmindar's mother when she discovers that her son has died of snake-bite, the narrator played the full potential of the role and its concomitant physical as well as mental aspects, although she continued to refer to the action of the mother in first person. The same was true in the third episode, when describing the plight of Behula's mother upon her learning that her daughter has undertaken the perilous journey in a raft. In all such cases, the roles were co-present with the performance persona of the narrator. Like a sphere revolving in space, the narrator revealed different sides of his/her persona co-present with the roles of the narrative. Although s/he always remained the same 'sphere', the roles s/he created for brief instants remained rooted in the 'sphere', and drew from the collective psyche and the social ethos. Each role was present only so much as the narrator was not, and each absent only so much as the narrator was present. Framed within the presentational mode of indigenous theatre aesthetics, the effect produced a blurring of demarcation of one role from another in terms of physical appearance but at the same time etched their features in distinct shades of emotions.

The act of the narrator 'telling' the story of Behula with the support of the choral singers-musicians-dancers, was accomplished by mobilizing the entire

Figure 40 Farida Akhter Lima as the narrator (left), Nahida Sultana Sati as the charlatan sage (centre) and choral singers in the fourth episode of *Behular Bhasan*. Photograph by Kamaluddin Kabir.

body in movement that was 'capable of affecting the mind outside of all representation', for the body invented 'vibrations, rotations, whirlings, [...] dances or leaps which directly affect[ed] the mind' (Deleuze, 2005, p. 9). Together with the performers playing the various roles of the story as first-person representation, *Behular Bhasan* successfully produced, borrowing from Walter Benjamin, 'a structure whose site [was] not homogeneous, empty time, but time filled by, the presence of the now [Jetztzeit]' (Benjamin, 1969, p. 261).

This is well affirmed by the reviews it received after the performance of the play at a festival in Delhi. *The Hindu* observed:

> This production from Bangladesh would be remembered for long. [...] There is no false and pompous theatricality in [Ahmed's] production. The silence he creates at places evokes profound sense of pathos. The dance movements, the singing, the sense of timing appear to be flawless. In this nearly two hour-long show, the action flows in a seamless manner, touching the emotional chord of the audiences.
>
> Bajeli, 2010

The Telegraph in Kolkata testified that *Behular Bhasan* was a 'revelation' if only because the performers' 'non-stop energy and power were incredible, whether in acting, singing or dancing' (Lal, 2010). Finding it to be 'a compelling journey', *The Indian Express* in Kolkata added, 'even though it's steeped in tradition, *Behular Bhashan* never shies away from embracing modernism. There is a hip-hop like vibe to the choreography of most dance sequences. The movements and mudras are distinctly Indian, but the energy and zest with which the actors take the stage is very Western' (Biswas, 2010). Many of the spectators commented after the performance that they were involved in it with remarkable immediacy, and were engaged fully in and with the characters. The visual, auditory, kinesthetic, and emotional faculties of the spectators aroused in many the perception that the fictive world of the story populated with the characters was alive and immediate. If the proof of the proverbial pudding is in its eating, then the endorsements cited above are enough to believe that the hybrid acting employed in *Behular Bhasan* by the appropriation and assimilation of the System has set Bangladesh theatre off on a bold new postcolonial terrain.

Biogenesis of the System: conditions of acceptance and resistance

The System, after it travelled to the postcolony of Bangladesh by entering the discourse of theatre in the late 1960s, and transplanted quite rigorously into academia in 1998, is now being appropriated and assimilated to produce a form of 'hybrid acting' that is seeking to elide realistic acting with techniques drawn from performances of storytelling, trance, epic theatre, and indigenous theatre of Bangladesh. This raises an inevitable question: why so? If Said's postulation of the travelling theory has any currency, then the answer may be obtained by ascertaining the 'conditions of acceptance or, as an inevitable part of acceptance, resistance' (Said, 1983, p. 227) that has impelled the postcolony to appropriate and assimilate the travelling theory of the Imperial centre.

One of the 'conditions of acceptance and resistance' must be sought in the institutions of theatre production currently prevailing in Bangladesh. These institutions of the Group Theatre and of academia have no room for full-time professional actors and repertory companies. The extra-theatre means of livelihood that the Group Theatre practitioners are impelled to engage in leaves hardly any surplus time to engage fully with the System. Such engagements have been possible only in academic circles, where the students can, in ideal conditions work and dream of theatre 24/7. However, even academia has been crossing troubled water of late, as neoliberal economic order increasingly exacts its stranglehold of 'personal responsibility' and 'self-care' (Lemke, 2001, p. 203). Mamunur Rashid confirms this view by observing ruefully that in the current socio-economic condition of Bangladesh, it is not possible to pursue Stanislavsky's System in its entirety.[14]

The second 'condition of acceptance and rejection' needs to be sought in the historic contingency of the 'colonial crucible out of which Bengali modernity originated' (Chakrabarty, 2000, p. 148). It was in this 'crucible' of nineteenth century Kolkata, that the indigenous tradition of Bengal encountered European modernity. Consequently, the institution of theatre production of colonial Kolkata, as exemplified by the most dominant figure of late nineteenth and early twentieth century Bengali stage, Girishchandra Ghosh (1844–1912), embraced a creative hybridity. Particularly in mythological plays that gained overwhelming popularity, Ghosh 'combined versified dialogue, music, stylized action and declamatory melodrama' from the indigenous performance tradition of the Jatra, 'with conversational dialogue, an-action driven plot, realistic characterization, reversals and dramatic conflict from Western theatre' (Allana, 2013, p. 15). In his own words:

> My mythological plays have followed the middle way between Jatra and realistic theatre. [...] The structure and tightness of the mythological plays are controlled by the principles of Western drama, but their emotions are all taken from the Indian mythological world. It is the union, and at times the opposition between the realism of Western theatre and the spirituality of our own theatrical tradition that surfaces in these plays.
>
> cited in Allana, 2013, p. 15

The new grammar of modern realistic acting that Gosh fashioned laid emphasis on the physical appearance to be activated by 'appropriate costume and makeup, along with body movement, deportment and facial expression', such that the outer appearance was to '*arise from* the inner feeling' (Allana, 2013, p. 14). Underscoring the importance of dialogue delivery and the tune of the actor's voice,[15] Ghosh (2013) insisted that the actor be adept in the faculties of 'imagination, proper recollection and focused attention' (Ghosh, 2013, p. 23). Advising them to internalize the playwright's depiction of the character and 'render[ing] it through their mannerism' (Ghosh, 2013, p. 27), Ghosh argued that 'the actor must be immersed in the role, yes, but he [sic] must also be a spectator of himself' (Ghosh, 2013, p. 26).

At about the same time when Ghosh was riding high by staging his mythological plays, Rabindranath Tagore had attended a performance of *Hamlet* by Henry Irving during his visit to England. For Tagore, Irving's performance in romantic-realist style was only a 'sweat-weltering exercise', because he was attempting 'to mimic the truth instead of revealing it' (Tagore, 1355, pp. 505–6, author's tr.). Rejecting the European mode of representation outright, Tagore valorized Jatra because it eschews complicit passivity insisted by the 'fourth wall' of the illusionist theatre, and instead insists upon active participation 'in which there is hardly any distance between the actors and the spectators' in the imaginative construction and operation of the 'here and now' of the fictional universe unravelled in the play (Tagore 1347, p. 451, author's tr.).

Nearly a century after Ghosh and Tagore, another iconic figure of Bengali theatre, Sombhu Mitra (1915–97) also voiced the necessity to find an organic relation between the mode of representation articulated by naturalism and that of poetry. As he says:

> If the passion of love that we experience deep in ourselves had a language of its own, it would be this language: the language which we cannot speak and yet which is the language of our deepest passions—the language of poetry. Acting should attune itself to express naturally the poetry of passion. It cannot be accomplished through a naturalistic style alone. We must find a way to pass easily from the naturalistic plane to the subjective. Exterior and interior life should rub shoulders with each other and remain organically related [...].
>
> Mitra, 1971, p. 204

The paradigm shift in acting that is in the process of being mobilized in Bangladesh theatre is transpiring because it too seeks 'a middle way' between an 'organic unity' of the indigenous and the 'Western' modes of representation. Even as it employs the System, it is simultaneously keen in tapping into 'the spirituality' of indigenous theatrical tradition that Girishchandra Ghosh so successfully accessed, and the 'language of poetry' which Mitra so boldly employed.

Summing up then, the two conditions of acceptance and resistance, i.e., the institutions of theatre production currently prevailing in Bangladesh, and the mode of representation rooted in the colonial crucible of nineteen century Kolkata, have impelled the postcolony to appropriate and assimilate the travelling theory of the Imperial centre.

Notes

1. For the purpose of this chapter, the 'modern' is to be read as the antonym of 'tradition'. It is underpinned by the notion of 'modernity', which may be 'defined overwhelmingly by/as that initial moment of rupture from indigenous tradition brought about by colonialism, one that contains all subsequent disjunctions as extensions of the original breach' (Dharwadker, 2008, p. 143).
2. Interview with Mamunur Rashid held in Dhaka on 18 March 2015.
3. The frame seen in the middle ground is the proscenium arch of Natmandal (the studio theatre of the Department of Theatre and Performance Studies, University of Dhaka). Mrs Linde, Nora, and Dr Rank are playing on the extended apron of the proscenium stage.
4. Written response received from Nurur Rahman, sent by email on 18 April 2015.
5. Written response received from Nurur Rahman, sent by email on 22 April 2015.
6. Based on a written response received from Dr Abdul Halim Pramanik by email on 22 April 2014.
7. *Chaka* was directed by this author and produced by Dhaka Theatre in 1991; *Bishad Sindu* (Parts 1 and 2) was also directed by this author and produced by Dhaka Padatik in 1991 and 1992; *Koinya* was directed by Pavel Azad and produced by Prachya Nat in 2001; *Araj Ali Charitamrita* was directed by Tariq Anam Khan and produced by Natya Kendra in 2001; and *Behumar Bhasan* was at first directed by the author in 2004, and subsequently revived in two different versions in 2005 and 2010, by the Department of Theatre and Performance Studies (DU).
8. For further details, see Ahmed, 2015, pp. 23–43.
9. Akhter's research has confirmed that the extra-daily techniques, which Barba claims to be transcultural recurring principles (Akhter, 2012, 1995, p. 15), are indeed valid for the indigenous theatre of Bangladesh.
10. The performance of *bilāp* is gradually disappearing in Bangladesh as it enters the vortex of globalization and neoliberalism. In rare instances where it can still be seen, the performance usually induces a woman or a group of women

(uncommonly, also a man recognized as 'mad') 'to sing, wail, and verbalize grief and outrage' (Wilce, 2002, p. 161). For further details on *bilāp*, see Wilce, 2002, pp. 159–85.
11 Indigenous performances where mythopoetic spaces make it possible to literally unleash emotive exuberance are *Rayani Gan, Nam Kirtan, Lila Kirtan, Jari Gan* of eastern Mymansingh, and *Manipuri Ras Nrtya* (Ahmed 2000, pp. 31, 50, 124, 182–9).
12 For further details on shamanism and spirit possession in Bangladesh, please see Karim, 1988, pp. 290–1 and 299–300.
13 In all fairness to the Euro-American storytelling model, Wilson (2006, p. 46) points up the distinction between 'acting' and 'storytelling' as false. Nevertheless, the distinction is deployed in this essay because he acknowledges it to be the commonly held view.
14 Interview with Mamunur Rashid held in Dhaka on 18 March 2015.
15 For example, Ghosh would insist that 'every emotion is tied to a tune' (Ghosh, 2013, p. 26).

References

Ahmed, S. J. (2000), *Acinpakhi Infinity: Indigenous Theatre of Bangladesh*. Dhaka: University Press Limited.
Ahmed, S. J. (2015), 'A Passage to [India] South Asia through Religion and Gender: The Case of Behulār Bhāsān in Bangladesh', *Shilpakala: Annual Journal of Bangladesh Shilpakala Academy*, 22: 23–43.
Akhter, M. (2012), Dwaitadwaitabada Shilpatattwer Aloke Bangladesher Lokanatye Drishta Barnatmak Ritir Abhinay Bishleshan, *Bangla Academy Patrika*, Vol. 55, No. 1–2: 81–96.
Allana, A. (2013), 'The Birth of Realism and the Training of the Actor', in *The Act of Becoming: Actors Talk*, ed. A. Allana. New Delhi: National School of Drama, pp. 10–17.
Arko, Y. H. (2015), *Ovinoyriti: Bangla Bornonattok O Pashchattya Prosongo*. Dhaka: Bhashachitra.
Bajeli, D. S. (2010), 'A Dhaka Delight', in *The Hindu*. Retrieved from http://www.thehindu.com/todays-paper/tp-features/tp-fridayreview/a-dhaka-delight/article789552.ece [accessed 22 September 2016].
Barba, E. (1995), *The Paper Canoe: A Guide to Theatre Anthropology*, trans. R. Fowler. London: Routledge.
Benjamin, W. (1969), *Illuminations: Essays and Reflections*. New York: Schocken Books.

Birch, C. L. (2000), *The Whole Story Handbook: Using Imagery to Complete the Story Experience*. Little Rock: August House Publishers.

Biswas, P. (2010), 'Hope Floats', in *Indian Express*. Retrieved from http://archive.indianexpress.com/news/hope-floats/592367/3 [accessed 22 September 2016].

Brook, P. (1972), *The Empty Space*. Harmondsworth: Penguin.

Carnicke, S. M. (1977), 'Naturalism to Theatricalism: The Role of Symbolism', *Ulbandus Review*, Vol. 1, No. 1: 41–58.

Chakrabarty, D. (2000), *Provincializing Europe: Postcolonial Thought and Historical Difference*. Princeton: Princeton University Press.

Chekhov, A. (1973), 'The Three Sisters', in *Selected Works, Volume 2: Plays*, trans. Kathleen Cook. Moscow: Progress Publishers.

Deleuze, G. (2005), *Difference and Repetition*, trans. P. Patton. London: Continuum.

Dharwadker, A. (2008), 'Mohan Rakesh, Modernism, and the Postcolonial Present', *South Central Review*, Vol. 25, No. 1: 136–62.

Ghosh, G. (2013), 'Girishchandra Ghosh: The Garrick of Bengal' (English translation of 'Obhinoy o Obhineta'), in *The Act of Becoming: Actors Talk*, ed. A. Allana. New Delhi: National School of Drama, pp. 18–27.

Ibsen, H. (1965), 'A Doll's House', in *The League of Youth, A Doll's House, The Lady from the Sea*, trans. P. Watts. Harmondsworth: Penguin Books, pp. 145–232.

Kabir, K. (2002), 'Moncho '98: Asha-nirashar Itibritto', in *Bangla Desher Theatre*, ed. N. Saha. Kolkata: Dey's Publishing, pp. 301–8.

Karim, A. (1988), 'Shamanism in Bangladesh', *Asian Folklore Studies*, Vol. 47, No. 2: 277–309.

Kundu, A. K. (2013), 'Aparajita Ferdousi Majumdar: An Interview', *Daily Samakal*. Retrieved from http://www.samakal.com.bd/print_edition/details.php?news=28&action=main&option=single&news_id=350657&pub_no=1437&view=archiev&y=2013&m=06&d=13 [accessed 22 September 2016].

Lal, A. (2010, 27 March), 'Scenes from the Neighbourhood', *The Telegraph*. Retrieved from http://www.telegraphindia.com/1100327/jsp/opinion/story_12265652.jsp [accessed 22 September 2016].

Lemke, T. (2001), '"The birth of bio-politics": Michel Foucault's lecture at the Collège de France on neo-liberal governmentality', *Economy and Society*, Vol. 30, No. 2: 190–207.

Mitra, S. (1971), 'Building from Tagore', *The Drama Review: TDR*, Vol. 15, No. 2: 201–4.

Moishan, S. (2005), 'Bak o Bidirnota', *Daily Prothom Alo*, 22 April: 16.

Said, E. W. (1983), *The World, the Text, and the Critic*. Cambridge, Mass.: Harvard University Press.

Schechner, R. (2002), *Performance Studies: An Introduction*. London: Routledge.

Schechner, R. (2013), 'Foreword', in *The Act of Becoming: Actors Talk*, ed. A. Allana. New Delhi: National School of Drama, pp. xi–xiii.
Stanislavski, C. (1968/1950), *Building a Character*, trans. E. R. Hapgood. London: Eyre Methuen.
Stanislavski, C. (1980/1937), *An Actor Prepares*, trans. E. R. Hapgood. London: Methuen.
Stanislavski, C. (1981/1961), *Creating a Role*, trans. E. R. Hapgood. London: Eyre Methuen.
Tagore, R. (1347 [1311] Bengali Era), 'Rangamancha', in *Rabindra-rachanabali, Vol. 5*. Kolkata: Visva-Bharati, pp. 449–53.
Tagore, R. (1355 [Bengali Era]), 'Antar Bahir', in *Rabindra-rachanabali, Vol. 26*. Kolkata: Visva-Bharati, pp. 502–7.
Thomson, P. (2000), 'Brecht and Actor Training: On whose Behalf do We Act?', in *Twentieth Century Actor Training*, ed. A. Hodge. London: Routledge, pp. 98–112.
Wilce, J. M. (2002), 'Genres of Memory and the Memory of Genres: "Forgetting" Lament in Bangladesh', *Comparative Studies in Society and History*, Vol. 44, No. 1: 159–85.
Wilson, M. (2006), *Storytelling and Theatre: Contemporary Storytellers and their Art*. Houndmills: Palgrave Macmillan.
Worthen, W. B. (1992), *Modern Drama and the Rhetoric of Theater*. Berkeley: University of California Press.

Notes on Contributors

The editors

Stefan Aquilina is a lecturer within the Department of Theatre Studies and Director of Research of the School of Performing Arts (University of Malta). His research areas include the work of Stanislavsky, Meyerhold, and post-Revolutionary amateur theatre in Russia. Aquilina runs the research projects 'Performance Lineage: the Russian Tradition of Actor Training' and 'Cultural Transmission of Embodied Practice' – both projects are supported by the University of Malta Research Committee. His essays have appeared in *Studies in Theatre and Performance*; *Theatre, Dance and Performance Training*; *Stanislavski Studies*; *Theatre Studies International* and *Journal of Dramatic Theory and Criticism*.

Jonathan Pitches is Professor of Theatre and Performance at the University of Leeds in the School of Performance and Cultural Industries. He specializes in the study of performer training and has wider interests in intercultural performance, environmental performance, and blended learning. He is founding co-editor of the journal of *Theatre, Dance and Performance Training* and has published several books in this area: *Vsevolod Meyerhold* (2003), *Science and the Stanislavsky Tradition of Acting* (2006/9) and *Russians in Britain* (2012). In addition to the current volume, he is working on two new books, *Great Stage Directors Vol. 3: Komisarjevsky, Copeau, Guthrie* (Bloomsbury, 2017) and *Performing Landscapes: Mountains* (Palgrave, 2018).

The contributors

Part 1: EUROPE

Marie-Christine Autant-Mathieu is Director of Research at the National Centre for Scientific Research (CNRS), Assistant-director of Centre

Eur'ORBEM (CNRS/Paris-Sorbonne). Historian of Theatre and specialist of Russian and Soviet Theatre, her research is concerned with cultural transfers (tours, circulations of Acting Theories); the history of the Moscow Art Theatre and genesis of Stanislavsky's System; and Russian dramaturgy. Among her last publications are: *Le Théâtre soviétique après Staline*, Paris, I.E.S., 2011; *Stanislavski. La Ligne des actions physiques*, Montpellier, L'Entretemps, 2007; *Créer, ensemble. Points de vue sur les communautés artistiques* (ed.), Montpellier, L'Entretemps, 2013; *The Routledge Companion to Michael Chekhov*, (ed. with Yana Meerzon), London/New York, Routledge, 2015. For more information, see her website: www. autant-mathieu.fr

Ina Pukelytė is Associate Professor of the Department of Theatre Studies, Faculty of Arts, at Vytautas Magnus University in Kaunas, Lithuania. In the period 2003–7 Pukelytė was the Head of Kaunas State Drama theatre. She did her Masters degree at the Paris Sorbonne Nouvelle University and defended her doctoral thesis at the University of Leipzig in 2002, with the publication of her thesis under the title *Funktionen der Bildmedien in Theaterinszenierungen der neunzigerJahre des 20.Jahrhunderts* (Functions of visual medias in theatre performances of the nineties in the twentieth century). Among the articles she has published is a piece dedicated to the promotion and development of Mikhail Chekhov's theatre system in Lithuania (Paris, CNRS, 2009). Her other research interests are theatre history, theatre management, and cultural policies.

Maria Gaitanidi is a Greek-born actress, director, and pedagogue based in London. In 2011 she founded the ensemble We Are Raw Material, creating a programme of performances, laboratories, and workshops that explore the rawness of the space, the text, and the performer as creator. Her work explores classical and modern texts, breaking clichés and developing her own artistic research on 'the vertical actor'. Her approach combines different elements of her training and research, including 'ludic structures' (inspired by Plato's texts and developed by Anatoli Vassiliev), and 'active analysis' developed by Maria Knebel. In 2008, Gaitanidi became Assistant to Russian director Anatoli Vassiliev (Epidaurus Festival), with whom she also completed her training as an actress, director, and pedagogue. In 2013 she completed her Practice as

Research thesis at the University of Kent. For more information visit: http://www.wearerawmaterial.net

Franco Ruffini graduated in Physics in 1964, and entered the theatre world through Odin Teatret's production *Ferai* (1970). In 1975 he met Jerzy Grotowski at Wroclaw's University of Research of the Theatre of Nations. Barba and Grotowski were the two main reference points for his study of twentieth-century theatre. In 1980 Ruffini contributed to the creation of ISTA, and in 1986 he was one of the founders of the *Teatro e Storia* journal. His publications on twentieth-century theatre include: *I teatri di Artaud*, (Bologna, 1996); *Stanislavskij. Dal lavoro dell'attore al lavoro su di sé* (Roma-Bari, 2003 and 2005); *Craig, Grotowski, Artaud. Teatro in stato d'invenzione* (Roma-Bari, 2009); *The Empty Room. Studying Grotowski's Towards a Poor Theatre* (in Paul Allain ed., *Grotowski's Empty Room*, London-New York-Calcutta, 2009); *I libri di Jerzy Grotowski* (in Zbigniew Osinski, *Jerzy Grotowski e il suo laboratorio*, Roma, 2011); *Theatre and Boxing. The Actor who Flies* (Holstebro–Malta–Wroclaw–London–New York, 2014).

Part 2: CHINA AND JAPAN

Ruru Li acquired her BA and MA at the Shanghai Theatre Academy and her doctoral degree in Drama and Theatre at the University of Leeds, UK. She was brought up in a Beijing Opera actress family, and received some basic training when she was ten. Her research interest lies in performance art, comparative and intercultural theatre studies. She also performs Beijing Opera and runs various workshops. She regards regular contact with the theatre as essential to her academic work.

Siyuan Liu is an associate professor of Theatre at the University of British Columbia. His published books include the *Routledge Handbook of Asian Theatre* (2016), *Performing Hybridity in Colonial-Modern China* (Palgrave Macmillan, 2013), *Modern Asian Theatre and Performance 1900-2000* (co-author, Methuen, 2014), and *The Methuen Drama Anthology of Modern Asian Plays* (co-editor, 2014). A former President of the Association for Asian Performance, he has also published over two dozen journal articles and book chapters.

Kaori Nakayama is a producer, international coordinator, translator, policy-maker, and theatre historian. In addition she teaches arts management and cultural policy. In particular, Nakayama is devoted to human development *in* and *through* theatre, in collaboration with a host of international directors and educators. Her publications include, 'Theatre and Society – A Social History of British Theatre 1843–1997', 'The Twelfth Chapters Searching for Drama Education' and 'International Arts Briefing No.1 Japan' (Arts Council England). Also as a theatre translator, Kaori brought 'The American Pilots', 'The Monster in the Hall', 'Yellow Moon' (David Greig), 'Hanna and Hannah' (John Retallack), and 'Noughts & Crosses' (Dominic Cook) to the Japanese stage. Since 1998, Kaori has been running a charitable organization *Theatre Planning Network*, and in 2012 was appointed as the first drama officer of the Japan Arts Council in its history.

Part 3: LATIN AMERICA

Yana Elsa Brugal (La Habana, Cuba) studied at the Instituto Estatal de Teatro, Música y Cine de San Petersburgo (State Institute of Theatre, Music and Cinema, St Petersburg, 1984), where she also obtained her PhD in Art Sciences. She studied acting at the Escuela Nacional de Artes de Cuba (National Arts School of Cuba, 1966–70). Brugal has published numerous articles in specialized journals and theatre collections. She was co-editor, with Beatriz Rizk, of the book *Rito y Representación Los sistemas mágico-religiosos en la cultura cubana contemporánea (Compendio de ensayos críticos)* (Ritual and Representation: the magical-religious systems in contemporary Cuban culture. [Collection of critical essays]). Dr Brugal has delivered courses and workshops in several arts institutions. Currently, she is a researcher, teacher, and director of Laboratorio Stanislavski (Stanislavsky Laboratory) and Registro de la memoria de rituales sagrados y profanos (Register of memories of sacred and secular rituals).

Raúl Serrano was born in Tucumán, north of Argentina, in 1934. He started practicing theatre at an early age, despite some years studying law and philosophy. In 1957, Serrano joined a group of actors at the Argentina Youth Festival in Moscow, and then settled in Bucharest where he joined the Caragiale Academy of Theatrical Arts and Cinematography. In total, he has staged more than seventy performances. His main published books are: *Dialéctica del trabajo creador del actor* (Dialectics of the actor's creative work), *Tesis sobre Stanislavsky* (A Thesis on Stanislavsky) and *Nuevas Tesis sobre Stanislavsky* (A New Thesis on Stanislavsky). Currently in press is Serrano's next book *Lo que no se dice – Una teoría de la actuación* (What is not said – A Theory of Performance).

Arlete Cavaliere is Professor of Russian Theatre and Russian Culture and Literature at the University of São Paulo (Brazil) in the Faculty of Philosophy, Languages and Human Sciences (FFLCH-USP), where she is coordinator of the Graduate Programme on Russian Language and Russian Literature and also coordinator of the Laboratory of Russian Studies – LERUSS. She was a Visiting Professor (2002–3) at Moscow State University (MGU), in Russia. Her research areas include the Art and Russian Theatre (acting theories of Stanislavsky and Meyerhold), Russian Vanguards and classical and contemporary Russian drama. Her major books include *The General Inspector of Gogol/Meyerhold: a spectacle-synthesis* (1996), *Russian Theatre: itinerary for a study of the parody and the grotesque* (2009), *Russian Theatre: literature and spectacle* (2011), and *The Theatre of Gogol* (2009). She is also a Russian literature translator and has published in Portuguese several Russian authors such as Gogol, Chekhov, Bunin, Mayakovsky, and Vladímir Sorokin.

Part 4: AFRICA

Kene Igweonu is Director of Knowledge Exchange for the Faculty of Arts and Humanities at Canterbury Christ Church University, UK. He is a member of the editorial boards of *African Performance Review* and *South African Theatre Journal*. Igweonu is founding convener, and currently co-convener of the African and Caribbean Theatre and Performance Working Group of the International Federation for Theatre Research. His research and practice interests are in actor and performance training, theatre directing, black British theatre, theatre and performance in Africa and its Diasporas, as well as cultural and performance theory. In addition to journal publications and book chapters, he has also edited a number of books including, *Trends in Twenty-First Century African Theatre and Performance* (2011) and a three-volume collection published under the general title *Performative Inter-Actions in African Theatre* (2013).

Moez Mrabet is General Director of the International Cultural Center of Hammamet and Director of the International Festival of Hammamet (since March 2016). He holds a Doctorate in Theatre and Performing Arts from the Institut des Etudes Théâtrales, Paris III, Sorbonne Nouvelle. His thesis – defended in 2007 – was titled: *Stanislavsky in American theatre: Reception, transmission and evolution of an approach to theatrical work*. As an actor, he has participated in many productions by the Theatre Director Fadhel Jaïbi, and his own recent productions include *Striptease – The Feast of Rats* (2013) and *L'Escale 32* (2015). He is founder and artistic Director of The Arab Laboratory of Danse-Theatre (2009) and The Tunisian Laboratory Theater (2012). An activist in civil society, Mrabet is founder and President of the Tunisian Association of Graduates from the Higher Institutes of Dramatic Arts (since 2011), Executive Director of the Live Art Association (since 2012), and member of the Executive board of the Dramatic Arts Syndicate (since 2013).

David Peimer is Professor of Drama and Head of Performing Arts at Edge Hill University. He has also worked at the University of the Witwatersrand in Johannesburg, and New York University (Global Division). Peimer was the first English-speaking director in Prague's Vaclav Havel's theatre, and also directed contemporary and classical work, from Shakespeare to modern European performances and South African work, in London and parts of southern Africa. Peimer, a Fulbright Scholar at Columbia University, was involved and was arrested for being part of anti-apartheid theatre in the 1970s and 1980s. He contributes to the Pinter Centre for Performance and Creative Writing at Goldsmiths in London as a Theatre Director and Research Associate and has presented work in the EU Parliament's Culture Department in Brussels.

Part 5: AUSTRALASIA

Hilary Halba is a teacher, director, actor, producer and dramaturge with over 25 years' experience in New Zealand theatre and education. Her research interests include: bicultural theatre in Aotearoa/New Zealand; the study of acting methodologies; actor training; verbatim and documentary theatre; New Zealand post-colonial theatre. Hilary studied acting and the teaching of acting at the Neighborhood Playhouse in New York City. She contributes to international theatre journals and presents regularly at national and international conferences. In 2009, she was guest co-editor of the *Australasian Drama Studies* journal special edition (issue 55), focusing on the theatre of Aotearoa and the Pacific. She is a founder member of the southern bicultural theatre collective Kilimogo Productions, and has directed a number of works for this company.

Ian Maxwell is a graduate of the Victorian College of the Arts School of Drama, where he majored in Directing. Subsequent to that training, he embarked upon academic work at the University of Sydney, where he completed his PhD – an ethnography of Hip Hop culture in the suburbs of Sydney in the 1990s – in 1997. He has published extensively on a range of topics, including his 2003 book, *'Phat Beats, Dope Rhymes': Hip Hop Down Under Comin' Upper* (Wesleyan), chapters in several collections, and a number of journals. An Associate Professor in the Department of Theatre and Performance Studies at the University of Sydney, Maxwell is currently researching the influence of Jerzy Grotowski on Australian performance, and in particular the impact of Grotowski's visits down under in 1973 and 1974.

Peta Tait, Theatre and Drama at La Trobe University, is an academic scholar and a playwright. She is a Fellow of the Australian Academy of the Humanities and a visiting Professorial Fellow at the University of Wollongong. She has written sixty scholarly articles and her recent books include: *Fighting Nature: Travelling Menageries, Animal Acts and War Shows* (Sydney University Press, 2016); the co-edited *Routledge Circus Studies Reader* (Routledge, 2016); *Wild and Dangerous Performances: Animals, Emotions, Circus* (Palgrave MacMillan, 2012); *Circus Bodies* (Routledge, 2005); *Performing Emotions* (Ashgate, 2002). She is currently working on emotion and affect in performance, and editing the first volume in the Great Director Series on 'Stanislavsky, Antoine and St Denis' (Bloomsbury Methuen). Her most recent play, *Eleanor and Mary Alice*, about Eleanor Roosevelt meeting with Mary Alice Evatt was first staged at the Heide Museum of Modern Art in 2014.

Part 6: INDIA AND BANGLADESH

Syed Jamil Ahmed is a theatre director and designer, and Professor at the Department of Theatre and Performance Studies, University of Dhaka in Bangladesh. He trained at the National School of Drama (India), and was awarded an MA in Theatre Studies by the University of Warwick (UK) and his PhD by the University of Dhaka. He founded the Department of Theatre and Music at the University of Dhaka in 1994 and served as its Chair till 1997. He has published extensively in research journals at home and abroad. His book-length publications in English are *Acinpākhi Infinity: Indigenous Theatre in Bangladesh*, *In Praise of Niranjan: Islam, Theatre and Bangladesh*, *Reading Against Orientalist Grain: Performance and Politics Entwined with a Buddhist Strain*, and *Applied Theatrics: Essays in Refusal*. Ahmed has directed and designed plays in Bangladesh, Pakistan, India, and the USA, has received two Fulbright fellowships, serving as visiting faculty in the US, UK, and India.

Joo Yeoul Ryu is Lecturer of Drama at Trinity College, University of Melbourne. His research expertise is in the area of psychophysiological acting process and he is currently interested in how actor training methods can be applied to the rehabilitation of neurocognitive disorders. As an actor, one of his performances, 'Seduction' (1996, La MaMa) was acclaimed by the New York Times as 'deadly power struggles and transient glory'. He also worked at MBC, a Korean public television and radio network, as an overseas marketing executive. His work in theatre and media have been enriched by the opportunity to carry out extensive research and training in India between 2000–9.

Index

Accademia d'Arte Drammatica 36
Actors Studio 4, 40, 60, 70, 137, 209, 216, 223, 241, 340, 350, 352
Adedeji, Joel 274, 278
Adler, Stella 4, 8, 209, 241, 242, 243, 345, 352, 359
Agrebi, Mohammed Abdelaziz 291, 292, 295, 304
Akhter, Mohsina 423
Al-Deen, Selim 427
Alekséieva, Kira 214
Alexander Technique 329
Alexandrinsky Theatre 135
Alkazi, Ebrahim 394, 396, 400, 402–6, 407, 409, 410, 413
Alvarez, Pedro 248
Amateur theatre 108, 114, 120
American Conservatory Theatre (ACT) San Francisco 342
An Actor Prepares 36, 38, 44–9, 58, 64, 81, 103, 113, 121, 146, 149, 151, 152, 166, 190, 199, 246, 252, 254, 279, 296, 298, 332, 339, 343, 350, 356, 375, 395, 401, 409, 410, 418, 420, 421, 424
An Actor's Work (on Himself) 35, 36, 38, 40, 44–9, 51–4, 58–9, 64, 81, 103, 113, 121, 146, 149, 151, 152, 166, 190, 199, 246, 252, 279, 296, 298, 332, 339, 343, 350, 375, 395, 401, 409, 410, 418, 420, 421, 424
Andreou, Vassilis 134
Antoine, André 64, 75, 144, 292, 297; Théâtre Libre 144
Antorova, Konkordia 54
Aotearoa (New Zealand) 21, 27, 319–23, 367–90
Appia, Adolphe 55, 230, 297
Aquilina, Karmenu 117
Araújo, Antonio 230, 234
Arbuzov, Alexei 106
Arendt, Hannah 312

Argentina 20, 207, 210–12, 261–7; Escuela de Teatro de Buenos Aires 262, 267; National School of Theatre 261; Theatre Institute of the University of Buenos Aires 211
Arko, Yusuf Hassan 421
Armenis, Giorgos 130
Artaud, Antonin 12, 83, 192, 225, 232, 234, 292
Ashbolt, Allan 331, 332, 336
Australasia 14, 21, 317, 320, 322, 361
Australia 21, 319–23, 325–46, 347–66; Ensemble Theatre Sydney (ETS) 347, 348, 350; National Institute of Dramatic Art (NIDA) 325, 338–45; Sydney Theatre Company 325; Victorian College of the Arts (VCA) School of Drama 327, 330, 341, 343; Melbourne Theatre Company (MTC) 340, 342
Awasthi, Suresh 405, 408, 415
Axworthy, Geoffrey 274, 277, 278, 279
Ayckbourn, Alan 361
Azad, Pavel 422, 440
Azzopardi, Karmen 115–16
Azzopardi, Mario 107, 109, 113, 117, 121

Babu, Fazlur Rahman 426
Badia, Nora 247
Bain, Keith 342
Bangladesh 21, 391, 393–7, 417–43; Department of Drama and Dramatics (JU) 421, 426; Department of Theatre and Performance Studies (DU) 421, 422, 423, 424, 427, 440; Group Theatre 419–20, 421, 430, 437–8
Banham, Martin 274, 277–8, 281
Barba, Eugenio 12, 55, 56, 57, 119, 230, 232, 234, 254, 282, 440
Barter, Nicholas 196, 197, 202, 203
Bartet, Julia 69

Bates, Sandra 362–3
Batti, Gaston 127
Bayly, Lorraine 351, 354, 364
Beaumarchais, Pierre 67, 99
Beecher-Stowe, Harriet 95
Belasco, David 3
Ben Ammar, Raja 302, 306
Ben Ayed, Aly 292, 296, 297, 298, 305
Ben-Ari, Reiken 242, 243, 257
Benedetti, Jean 4, 17, 59, 163, 209, 215, 379, 385
Berliner Ensemble 64, 340
Bernard Shaw, George 230, 365
Bernhardt, Sarah 28, 71, 296
Berry, Cicely 327, 413
Bhabha, Homi 272, 381, 395, 396, 397
Bharata 394, 399, 400, 402, 405, 406, 407, 408, 409, 410, 412, 414
Bhatia, Shelia 401, 402
Binet, Alfred 69
binte Siddique, Taskin 433
Blainey, Geoffrey 319, 323
Blair, Rhonda 375, 377, 385
Blake, Shirley 118
Blanchett, Cate 338
Boal, Augusto 222–3, 233, 234
Bodenwieser, Gertrud 342
Bolachova, Tania 247
Boleslavsky, Richard 42, 166, 190, 216–17, 350, 394, 401
Bolsheviks 71, 73, 76, 77, 83, 95, 103
Borghi, Renato 221
Boris Shchukin Institute 170–1
Brando, Marlon 117
Brazil 20, 207–10, 213–37; Asdrúbal Trouxe o Trombone 228, 229; Dramatic Art School of São Paulo 217; Grupo Mambembe 228, 229; Os Comediantes 217–21, 225; Pod Minoga 228; Royal Bixiga's Company 228; Teatro Brasileiro de Comédia (TBC) 222, 225, 230, 233; Teatro de Arena 210, 222–4, 228, 234; Teatro do Ornitorrinco 228, 229; Teatro Oficina 224, 225, 228, 234; Teatro Municipal do Rio de Janeiro 218; Vento Forte 228
Breazu, Marcel 262
Brecht, Bertolt 40, 64, 84, 119, 131, 135, 145, 188, 191, 202, 208, 209–10, 223, 224, 225, 229, 230, 234, 249, 250, 251, 253, 303, 310, 311, 330, 340, 348, 363, 396
Brene, Jose R. 244, 245
Brining, James 202
Bristol Old Vic 107
Bristol University Drama Department 107
Brook, Peter 12, 13, 119, 152, 343
Broughton, John 378
Brown, Tim (T-profile) 17–18
Brown, Tom 339, 344
Buchner, Georg 313
Buenaventura, Enrique 210
Building a Character 44, 49, 58, 153, 154, 163, 252, 254, 299, 340, 395, 409, 410, 418, 421, 422, 424
Bulgakov, Mikhail 252, 255
Buzo, Alex 363

Camilleri, Frank 111, 112, 120
Cao Yu 152, 153
Capitalism 8, 108
Carnicke, Sharon Marie 1, 2, 4, 5, 6, 7, 8, 9, 15, 103, 216, 226, 315, 344, 348, 373, 374, 381, 399, 423
Castro, Andrés 209, 240, 241
Cauchi, Manuel 118
Celdrán, Carlos 255, 256
Centre for Higher Dramatic Studies (Cairo) 296
Chaker, Cherif 299
Chekhov, Anton 56, 73, 74, 106, 128, 130, 131, 133, 150, 151, 207, 230, 251, 267, 395, 423, 427
Chekhov, Michael 3, 70, 81, 83, 87, 92–6, 100–1, 102, 103, 131, 166, 202, 241, 250, 305
Chekhov, Mikhail *see* Chekhov, Michael
Chen, Mingzheng 172, 176, 178, 179, 185, 190
Cherry, Wal 340
China 16, 20, 141, 143–6, 149–65, 166–95, 274, 386, 394; Beijing People's Art Theatre (BPAT) 146, 149, 152, 153, 154, 162; Central Academy of Drama (CAD) 150, 154, 168, 170, 171, 173, 174, 180, 184, 185, 186, 190, 192; Cultural Revolution (1966–76) 145; huaju (spoken drama) 143, 149, 150, 162, 166, 191; *jingju* (Beijing Opera) 150, 181,

284; Shanghai Theatre Academy (STA) 168, 169, 170–3, 175, 176, 177–8, 180, 185, 190, 192; *xingxiang* (image) 151; *xinxiang* (mental image) 149, 151, 163; *xiqu* (indigenous Chinese theatre) 181
Chmara, Grigori 81
Clurman, Harold 4, 335
Colbung, Ken 362
Colonialism 19, 105, 371, 440
Communism 8, 103, 167, 200
Cómo se hace un actor see *An Actor Prepares*
Cooke, Dominic 216
Copeau, Jacques 29, 32, 38, 42, 55, 64, 75, 81, 83, 119, 127, 190, 297; Vieux-Colombier 29, 75
Coquelin, Benoît-Constant 28, 68, 69, 71, 83, 153, 162, 163, 304
Corrieri, Sergio 248
Costa, Jaime 219
Craig, Edward Gordon 55, 56, 81, 144, 147, 190, 198, 230, 292, 303, 402
Crawford, Cheryl 351, 352
Crawford, Terence 325
Cremona, Vicki Ann 110
Crilla, Heddy 261
Cruciani, Fabrizio 30, 55, 56; Founding Fathers 55, 56
Cuba 20, 207–10, 238–60, 284; Argos Teatro 255, 256; Escuela Nacional de Arte 242; Grupo Teatro Escambray 253; LOS DOCE 250; Prometeo 242; Regla de Ocha (Yoruba) 239; Salitas Movement 249, 258; Teatro Estudio 249, 250, 251, 253; Teatro Mio 255
Cué, Michaelis 250, 251
Cunill Cabanellas, Antonio 261

d'Amico, Silvio 35, 36, 37, 38, 39, 40, 53
Dalcroze, Emile 198, 343
Daniels, Erina 382, 383
Dansey, Harry 380
Davies, Lindy 343
Davis, Jack 362
Davydova, Alexandra 93
De la Vega, Irma 209, 240, 241
De Lany, Robert 350
De Luis, Adolfo 209, 240, 243–7, 251, 252
De Morais, Dulcina 219

De Niro, Robert 117
De Pirro, Nicola 39
del Cioppo, Atahualpa (El Galpón) 210
Delamere, Alex 202
Delsarte, Jacques 292, 343
Diaghilev, Serge 71, 83
Diakov, Valentine 334
Diderot, Denis 28, 38, 40, 64, 69, 82, 83, 291, 300
Dikiy, Aleksei 335
Dinelli, Mel 361
Diver, Cindy 377–9, 380
Doboujinski, Mstislav 95
Dongli, Guo 172, 176, 185, 190
Dória, Gustavo 218
Dorókhina, Tatiana 214
Dostoevsky, Fyodor 73
Doughty, Marvic 109
Driss, Mohamed Massoud 293, 305, 306
Dubey, Satyadev 412
Dullin, Charles 81, 306

Earley, Michael 119
Edwards, Alan 340, 344
Edwards, Gail 342
Eisenstein, Sergei 229
Enright, Nick 342, 363
ensemble 17, 28, 29, 31, 64, 75, 78, 81, 91, 96, 125, 129, 132, 136, 201, 202, 248, 283, 348, 350, 376, 377, 434
Escartin, Adela 209, 240, 242–3
Euripides 133, 135
Evangelatou, Katerina 135
Exton, Clive 362

Farrugia, Lino 115, 118, 121
Feldenkrais, Moshe 327, 329, 343
Ferreira, Procopio 219
Filho, Antunes (Macunaíma) 230, 234, 235
Finch, Peter 335–8
First Studio 6, 42, 56, 66, 88, 89, 93, 95, 102, 132, 250, 258, 414
First World War 88, 101, 124
Fitton, Doris 322, 332, 333, 334, 335, 339, 349
Florian, Stephen 108, 112, 116, 120, 121
folk 129, 130, 232, 235, 283, 394, 395, 402
Fomenko, Piotr 107, 114

France 20, 27–8, 63–86, 120, 127, 143, 217, 274, 292, 299, 305, 321
Free Stage (Jiyu Gekijo) 20, 197
Fuchs, Georg 230

Gabrėnas, Antanas 97
Gacio, Roberto 242
Galan, Jaroslav 99
Gannoun, Ezzedine 302, 306
Garcia, Santiago 210
Gelada, Jose 240
Gémier, Firmin 65, 81
George, Miria 381
German Expressionism 76, 84, 144, 220
Gest, Morris 73
Ghosh, Girishchandra 438, 439, 441
Gibson, Mel 338
Gielgud, John 335
GITIS 32, 87, 97, 99, 103, 107, 132, 170, 211
globalisation 14, 30, 112, 143, 440
Gogol, Nikolai 28, 229, 252, 264
Goldoni, Carlo 74, 75, 150, 233
Goncharov, Andrei 3
Gordon, Hayes 21, 320, 321, 322, 330, 347–64
Gorki, Maxim *see* Gorky, Maxim
Gorky, Maxim 73, 74, 79, 99, 149, 152, 154, 224, 233, 234
Government Inspector, The 51, 93, 103, 185, 229, 264
Greece 20, 27, 31, 124–39; National Theatre (Athens) 125, 131, 132; Royal Conservatory (Athens) 125; Royal Theatre (Athens) 125; Theatro Technis 31, 127, 129, 131
Grey, Lina 219
Gromov, Viktor 93, 95, 102
Grotowski, Jerzy 12, 35, 54–7, 60, 100, 119, 130, 192, 225, 230, 232, 250, 282, 305, 310, 311
Group Theatre 322, 352, 419, 421, 430, 438
Grybauskas, Juozas 96, 103
Guarnieri, Gianfrancesco 221, 222, 234
Guelman, Alexander 251
Guerrieri, Gerardo 30, 35, 40, 48–52, 57, 59
Gureev, G.N. 170, 171, 173, 174, 186, 191
Gurevich, Liubov 42, 48, 69

Guthrie, Tyrone 338

Habima Theatre, Tel Aviv 242, 335
Hamlet 93, 102, 103, 147, 207, 273, 294, 305, 312, 332, 363, 439
Hapgood, Norman 43, 44
Haque, Anisul Barun 422
Hatta, Motoo 199
Hay, Alexander 340, 342, 344
Heller, Joseph 362
Hendry, Jonathan 377
Herbert, John 362
Hervé, Florimond 64
Hijikata, Yoshi 198
Hirata, Oriza 146, 200, 201
Hodge, Alison 202
Hodgman, Roger 341
Horn, Pantelis 124
Hu, Dao 172, 177, 192
Huang, Zuolin 145, 188, 190
Hunt, Hugh 339
hybridity 18, 144, 208, 272, 310, 311, 385, 393–7, 399, 415, 438

Ibsen, Henrik 14, 74, 125, 126, 128, 130, 137, 144, 146, 150, 182, 198, 207, 230, 250, 266, 332, 361, 395, 423, 425, 426
Ichikawa, Sandanji II 146, 197
Il Dramma (The Drama) 39
India 21, 386, 391, 393–7, 399–416, 437, 438; National School of Drama (NSD) 393, 399–415
Inspector General, The see Government Inspector, The
Institutul Ion Luca Caragiale (Bucharest) 261
interculturalism 18, 22, 397
Irving, Henry 439
Italy 6, 20, 27, 30, 31, 35–62; Court of Bari 30, 45, 47, 48, 52, 58; Einaudi (publishers) 51, 52–3, 59; Laterza (publishers) 45, 46, 47, 48, 50, 51, 52, 54, 58, 59; Piccolo Teatro di Milano 40, 107
Ivanovna, Galina 170

Jackson, Kevin 342, 343
Jaïbi, Fadhel 272, 292, 302, 303, 305, 306
Jain, Kirti 396, 400, 412, 413

Jakševičius, Algirdas 92, 93, 96, 102, 103
Janisheski, Jeff 344
Japan 19, 20, 141, 143–6, 150, 182, 191, 196–204, 240, 274, 394, 402; angra (Underground theatre) 200–1; *gei* (actions) 198; *gekidan* (actors' membership groups) 198–9; Jiyu Gekijo (Free Theatre) 20, 144, 197; *shingeki* (modern theatre movement) 144, 197, 198, 199, 200, 203; *shogekijo* (little/fringe theatre) 201, 203; *yoseijo* (drama school) 199
Jarry, Alfred 229
Jewel, Riaz Mahmud 422
Jiang Qing (Madam Mao) 187
Jiao, Juyin 144, 146, 149–63, 186
Jones, Patricia 362
Jouvet, Louis 75, 81, 336
Judic, Anne 64, 82
Juknevičius, Romualdas 87, 93, 96, 97, 100
Jurašas, Jonas 100

Kabuki 182, 197, 198; *kata* (trained gestures) 198
Kachalov Group (Kachalov, Vasily) 72, 89
Kačinskas, Henrikas 96, 103
Kahn, Ahasan 425
Kaiser, Georg 144
Kallergis, Lykourgos 128, 137
Karanth, Babukodi Venkataramana 396, 400, 405–9, 410
Karanth, Shivarama 406
Karatzas, Dimitris 135
Katrakis, Manos 132
Katselis, Pelos 124
Kay, 'Sydney' John 336
Khan, Tariq Anam 422, 440
Khrushchev, Nikita 2, 100
Kiasashvili, Niko 106
Kingston, Peter 363
Kipste, Egil 343–4
Kiveli, Andrianou 124
Knebel, Maria 130, 133, 134, 137, 138, 226, 300, 305
Knight, Tony 342
Koiransky, Aleksandr 42
Konski, Grigori 98, 100
Kotopouli, Marika 124, 125
Kougioumtzis, Mimis 130

Kouka, Hone 381, 382, 385, 386, 387
Koun, Karolos (Theatro Technis) 31, 125, 127–31, 132, 133, 136
Krėvė, Vincas 90, 102; *Šarūnas* 90, 91, 92, 93, 102
Kristi, Georgui 214
Kulnyov, Boris 145, 146, 149, 154, 155, 156, 159, 162, 168, 170–80, 185, 189, 191
Kusnet, Eugênio 209, 216, 220–8, 230, 233, 234

La construcción del personaje see *Building a Character*
La formation de l'acteur see *An Actor Prepares*
La mia vita nell'arte see *My Life in Art*
Laban, Rudolf 234, 329, 343
laboratory 20, 132, 248, 250, 252, 401
Lan Ma 154
Lanskoi, Yvgeny 344
Lao She 152, 158, 163
Latham, David 330
Lavoro dell'attore see *An Actor's Work (on Himself)*
Lavoro dell'attore su se stesso see *An Actor's Work (on Himself)*
Lazanis, Giorgos 130
Lecoq, Jacques 329
Leikov, Y.W. 170, 171, 173, 174
Lensky, Aleksandr 42, 66, 82
Lermontov, Mikhail 132, 133
Lesli, Platon Vladimirovich 168, 170, 171, 173, 174, 186, 191, 192
Lezcan, Miriam 255
Ligizos, Hector 135
Linares, Ernestina 248
Lipkovskaya, Yevgenia 145, 168–71, 174, 185, 190, 192
Lithuania 20, 27, 29–30, 87–104, 217, 219, 220; Acting Studio 89, 90; Hebrew Acting Studio 90, 95, 102; Klaipėda State Theatre 96; National Theatre 87, 88, 89, 91, 92, 93, 95, 96, 97, 101, 102; Vilnius National Drama Theatre 97; Young Theatre (Jaunųjų teatras) 95
Liubimov, Yuri 216
Livathinos, Stathis 125, 131–4, 135, 136
Liverpool Institute of Performing Arts 107
Llerena, Lilliam 242

Lo Gatto, Ettore 40
London Drama Centre 6
Lü, Fu 183, 184
Lubovsky, Will Lee 335
Luhrmann, Baz 338
Lunacharsky State Theatre Institute 105, 190, 240
Lvov, Giacomo 36, 58
Lyndersay, K.W. Dexter 280
Lynn, Verónica 241, 242, 243, 244

Ma vie dans l'Art see *My Life in Art*
Mackevičiūtė, Antanina 97
Mademoiselle George 71
Maeterlinck, Maurice 71, 144
Maharishi, Mohan 412
Majumdar, Ferdousi 419
Mallia, Alfred 113
Malmgrem, Yat 342
Malta 20, 27, 29, 105–23; Atturi Theatre Productions 106, 109, 115, 116; Curtain Raiser Productions 109; Groups for Human Encounter 109, 112, 117, 121; Koperatturi 109; Lemonhead Productions 109; MTADA (Manoel Theatre Academy of Dramatic Art) 106–7, 117; Politeatru 106, 107, 109, 118; Teatru 111, 109, 112, 120; Valletta European Capital of Culture (2018) 119
Mao, Zedong 166, 183, 187
Markov, Pavel 113
Marshall, Albert 105
Martinez Allende, Francisco 240, 243
Martinez Corrêa, José Celso 221, 224, 225, 235
Marxism 8, 187, 223, 335
McCallum, Rua 380–1
McConnochie, Rhys 363
McIntyre, Gail 188
McMahon, Gregan 322, 331, 332, 345
Mei, Lanfang 168, 188
Meisner, Sanford 4, 320, 322, 347, 350–3, 355, 356, 359
Melik-Zhakarov, Sergei 14
Mellor, Aubrey 203, 338, 339, 340, 342, 345
Melo, Abel González 255
Melo, Graça 219
Merezhko, Viktor 106
Merlin, Bella 7, 9, 202, 226, 344, 369, 379

Method, The (*see also* Lee Strasberg) 4, 8, 70, 114, 118, 131, 180, 200, 216, 220, 221, 223, 241, 330, 340, 350, 351, 355, 356, 358; Australian Method 338, 345
Meyerhold, Vsevolod 3, 55, 59, 71, 72, 81, 82, 83, 96, 119, 130, 171, 191, 202, 217, 227, 228, 229, 230, 231, 232, 234, 258, 299, 303, 305, 402
Mi vida en el arte see *My Life in Art*
Milano, Paolo 38, 40
Miller, Arthur 207, 233, 365
Miuchi, Suzue 200
Molière 66, 67, 83, 302
Mollica, Fabio 56
Morin, Francisco 240, 242
Moruo, Guo 156, 158
Moscow Art Theatre (MAT) 1, 2, 3, 6, 14, 15, 17, 20, 27, 28, 29, 31, 36, 39, 40, 42, 63, 65, 67, 70, 71–2, 74, 75, 76, 77, 78–80, 83, 88, 93, 98, 99, 103, 105, 106, 128, 129, 132, 147, 150, 152, 170, 171, 183, 207, 215, 217, 220, 225, 239, 242, 247, 250, 257, 292, 293, 322, 330, 331, 332, 335, 340, 351, 354, 355, 414
Moundraki, Irini 132
Mounet-Sully, Jean 69, 71
Müller, Heiner 311
Muscat, Bryan 115
My Life in Art 8, 12, 36, 38, 41, 42, 43, 48, 49, 51, 52, 53, 59, 64, 121, 129, 137, 146, 215, 252, 254, 262, 298, 299, 301, 322, 332, 420

Nafpliotou, Maria 134
Natyasastra 16, 394, 396, 399, 400, 402, 405, 406, 408, 409, 414
Nemirovich-Danchenko, Vladimir 1, 22, 37, 77, 78, 79, 80, 83, 150, 151, 152, 293, 335
Nester, Zika 322, 347, 350, 351, 353, 358, 364, 365
New Zealand (Aotearoa) 21, 27, 319–23, 367–90; Kilimogo Productions 368, 374, 377, 378, 379, 386, 387; manaakitanga (allowing receptiveness) 368, 375, 376, 377, 379; Tawata Productions 368, 381–3; tikanga (customary Māori cultural practices); 368, 372, 374, 377, 378, 379, 382; Toi Whakaari o Aotearoa:

New Zealand Drama School 368, 371, 386; whanaungatanga (spirit of kinship) 321, 368, 375–7, 376, 377, 379, 380, 381, 385
Nigeria 20, 239, 271, 273–4, 277–89; Lufodo Academy of Performing Arts 286; Nollywood 280, 286, 287; School of Drama (University of Ibadan) 274, 277, 278, 279, 283, 285, 287
Nivoix, Paul 66
Noble, Andrew 372
Noreika, Laimonas 87, 97

O'Neill, Eugene 96, 144, 248, 365
Odets, Clifford 127, 335
Oehr, Jane 362
Ogunmola, Kola 283
Oikonomou, Thomas 31, 125–6
Okakura, Shiro 199
Oleka-Žilinskas, Andrius 30, 87, 88–96, 100, 101, 102, 103
Olivier, Laurence 338
organic life/organicity 36, 56, 96, 130, 136, 144, 213, 226, 231, 243, 244, 253, 257, 439
Orlov, Vasilii 98, 101
Orlova, Marja 98, 101
Osanai, Kaoru 20, 146, 147, 197
Ostrovski, Alexander 28, 252
Ouerghi, Nejia 301
Ouerghi, Noureddine 301, 306
Ouyang, Yuqian 184, 186
Oyston, Peter 341

Pacino, Al 114
Pagnol, Marcel 66
Pavlov, Ivan 70
Pavlova, Tatiana 35, 36, 37
Peixoto, Fernando 221
Perry, Charles 219
Piscator, Erwin 223, 242, 243
Pitches, Jonathan 121, 127, 202, 287, 412
Pitoëff, Georges 81, 127
Politis, Fotis 31, 124, 126–7
postcolonialism 272, 281, 311, 313, 330, 370, 371, 440
Povoledo, Elena 45
Prague Group 89, 105
Pramanik, Abdul Halim 427, 428, 429, 440

Prybiskava, Zoya Arkkadava 351
Puche, Alejandro González 211
Puget, Claude-André 244

Quentin, Robert 339
Quintero, Hector 244

RADA (Royal Academy of Dramatic Art) 6, 196, 198, 286, 338, 340, 394
Ragauskaité, Aurelija 97
Raghunandana, S. 409
Rahman, Nurur 424, 425, 440
Rapoport, Iosef M. 247, 248, 252
Rashid, Mamunur 420, 421, 438, 440, 441
Raubaitė, Birutė 87, 97
Real Escuela Superior De Arte Dramatico Madrid 107
Rebellato, Dan 14, 113
Reid, Don 354, 364, 365
Reinhardt, Max 126, 230, 402,
representation 28, 64, 68, 69, 70, 82, 84, 229, 242, 248, 251, 304, 367, 370, 377, 380, 418, 419, 436, 439, 440
Revuelta, Raquel 248, 249
Revuelta, Vincente 209, 243, 247–52, 258
Reynolds, Elizabeth 30, 43–8, 49, 50, 52, 53, 58
Riaskova, Radka 300
Ribot, Théodule 69, 70, 351
Ribush, Dolia 336, 349
Richards, Thomas 57
Ripellino, Angelo Maria 53, 59
ritual 132, 255, 256, 310, 311, 321, 370, 373, 375, 377, 385, 394
Robbins, J.J. 42
Rodiris, Dimitris 124
Rodrigues, Nelson 218, 219, 220
Rose Bruford College 6, 107, 119, 274, 278, 280
Ross, Andrew 362
Rosset, Caca 229
Rouché, Jacques 81, 297
Royal Central School of Speech and Drama 107
Rubin, Leon 202
Ruth, Annie 371, 377

Saint-Denis, Michel 6, 339
Sajer, Faouez 298–9

Sano, Seki 240, 241, 243, 257
Sayem, Moncef 302, 306
Schembri-Bonaci, Giuseppe 107, 110
Schildkraut, Joseph 4
Schranz, John J. 105, 112, 117
Scrimgeour, Colin 336
Second Studio 98, 414
Second World War 6, 15, 30, 40, 87, 96, 97, 125, 233, 335, 336, 339, 361, 386
Sen, Satu 394, 400, 401, 415
Senda, Koreya 199
Serov, Georgy 81
Serov, Gueorgui 81
Sevastikoglou, George 127, 137
Shah, Brij Mohan 400, 409–12, 413
Shaheen, Israfeel 395, 423, 424, 425, 426, 427, 428
Shanzun, Ouyang 152
Shchepkin, Mikhaïl 28, 68
Shimomura, Masao 199
Shirley, David 6, 274, 279
Simon, Neil 361
Simonov Theatre 107, 110
Slavutski, Aleksander 106
Smeliansky, Anatoly 3, 4, 5, 15, 190, 232
Socialist Realism 2, 8, 15, 43, 80, 97, 167, 199
Sokolov, Vladimir 81
Soloviova, Inna 105
Soloviova, Vera 95, 103
Song, Tingxi 172, 185, 190
Sontakke, K.M. 404
Sophocles 135, 233
South Africa 20, 271, 273, 277, 281–2, 309–15
Soviet Union 42, 97, 99, 145, 146, 154, 166, 167, 183, 191, 202, 217, 225
Soyinka, Wole 279, 280
Sruoga, Balys 30, 88, 89, 90, 91, 93, 95, 101
Stalin, Joseph 2, 8, 79, 80, 97, 99, 100, 103
Stanislavsky Electrotheater 135
Stanislavsky Studies 8, 56, 168
Stanislavsky, Konstantin; Active Analysis 9–10, 133, 226, 227, 300, 368–9, 381; Affective Memory 8, 9, 70, 82, 209, 262, 302; Characterization 28, 66, 114, 207, 273, 287, 314, 396, 399, 407, 420, 425, 426, 427, 438; Concentration 28, 175, 176, 177, 178, 243, 249, 257, 261, 279, 283, 285, 300, 306, 339, 373, 379, 396, 403, 413, 421, 433; embodiment 41, 64, 82, 209, 227, 384, 385; Emotion Memory 28, 29, 70, 113, 180, 188, 200, 257, 262, 273, 279, 285, 311, 312, 314, 339, 340, 353, 356, 382, 395, 403, 421, 428, 433; ethics 28, 29, 31, 63, 90, 98, 137, 146, 294, 319, 321–3; everyday life 114, 115, 134, 191, 245, 273, 311, 322, 380, 423; experiencing 38–9, 41, 51, 64, 66, 69, 82–3, 149, 151, 153, 171, 178, 186, 190, 208, 210, 281, 356, 373, 374, 378, 382, 384; Given Circumstances 19, 69, 70, 98, 132, 133, 153, 154, 159, 169, 188, 189, 227, 228, 257, 263, 273, 312, 314, 328, 339, 342, 403, 404, 421, 423, 425, 427; imagination 10, 29, 98, 113, 130, 175, 176, 177, 178, 257, 261, 283, 300, 301, 306, 337, 355, 385, 403, 410, 413, 421, 422, 433; 'magic if' 245, 354, 355, 395, 421, 425, 427, 433; Method of Physical Action 9, 40, 51, 155, 226, 227, 243, 252, 262; psychophysicality 8, 96, 118, 129, 155, 208, 228, 241, 251, 254, 255, 257, 284, 301, 344; subtext 56, 70, 132, 159, 245, 257, 261, 313, 315, 327, 337, 350; tempo-rhythm 65, 228, 300, 301, 306, 403, 421, 432. See also *An Actor Prepares, An Actor's Work (on Himself, Building a Character, My Life in Art*
Stoppard, Tom 361
Strasberg, Lee (see also The Method) 4, 8, 121, 209, 216, 242, 262, 280, 320, 329, 342, 347, 350–6, 358, 369
Strehler, Giorgio 59, 107
Strindberg, August 230, 233
Suda, John 117
Sulerzhitsky, Leopold 71, 88, 89, 90, 102, 414
Sultana, Tania 433, 434
Suzuki, Tadashi 36, 201
Syron, Brian 362, 364

Tairov, Alexander, Chamber Theatre 71, 76, 88
Taviani, Ferdinando 30, 56, 57
Taylor, Rangimoana 374–7, 385, 386
Tcherkasski, Sergei 5, 203, 344

Teatrin (Light or Diminutive Theatre) 106, 109, 112, 120
Terayama, Shuji 201
Terzopoulos, Theodoros 135, 136
Theatre Arts Books 45, 46, 47
Théâtre des Champs-Élysées 73, 75, 77
Third Studio 95, 98
Thomson, Katherine 363
Thyam, Ratan 412
Tian, Han 158
Timms, Heather 383
Tolentino, Eduardo (Tapa) 230, 234
Tolmacheva, Galina 261
Tolstoy, Alexei 73, 74
Tolstoy, Lev (Leo) 79, 127
Toporkov, Vasily Osopovich 40, 57, 115, 226
transmission 2, 4–7, 13, 16–21, 22, 27–32, 40, 101, 105, 124, 132, 144, 166, 167, 168, 170, 172, 173, 189, 210, 211, 216, 221, 273, 274, 278, 279, 280, 283, 284, 285, 287, 291, 295, 298, 300, 303, 320, 321, 326, 393, 400
Treniov, Konstantin 79
Tribulo, Juan Antonio 211
Tunisia 20, 32, 271–2, 274, 290–308; School of Arab Theatre (Ecole du Théâtre Arabe) 295, 296, 299, 304; Théâtre de la Terre 301; Théâtre El Hamra 302; Théâtre Phou 301; Troupe de la Ville de Tunis 295, 297, 304, 305
Turgenev, Ivan 73, 74
Tutuola, Amos 283

universality 12, 13, 15, 21, 68, 72, 207, 216, 239, 245, 250, 254, 281, 294, 357, 359, 364, 370

Vaillant, Roger 247
Vaitkus, Jonas 100, 103
Vakhtangov, Yevgeny (Vakhtangov Theatre) 3, 71, 91, 96, 102, 107, 130, 132, 133, 154, 171, 241, 250, 258, 335, 356
Vancevičius, Henrikas 97, 100
Varnaitė, Regina 97

Vassiliev, Anatoli 132, 133, 136, 137
Vilar, Jean 64, 81, 274, 296–8, 340
Vitez, Antoine 81
Vlasova, Vera 105

Warfield, David 4
Warrington, Lisa 377
Wasserstein, Wendy 363
Webber Douglas Academy of Dramatic Art 107
Webby, George 372
Wesker, Arnold 243
Whaley, George 340, 341, 342
Wherrett, Richard 325, 326
White Army 72
Whyman, Rose 6, 118, 370
Wilde, Oscar 144, 233
Williams, Tennessee 207, 230, 361
Williamson, David 363
Williamson, J.C. 339, 361
Wilshire, John 336
Worms, Gustave 69

Xia, Chun 159, 163
Xu, Qiping 172, 177, 185
Xue, Mu 172, 185

Yamada, Hajime 199
Yashin, Sergei 106
Young, Norbert 286
Yu, Shizhi 153, 157, 160, 163
Yusupov, Prince Felix 78

Zakhava, Boris 170, 264
Zelčius, Leonardas 87, 97, 103
Zelwerowicz, Alexander 14, 22
Zhang, Min 183
Zhao, Ming 183
Zhao, Qiyang 152, 154, 156
Zhou, Bing 172, 176, 191
Zia, Titas 422
Ziembinski, Zbigniew 20, 216–20, 221, 222, 233
Zmerli, Hassan 294, 295

www.ingramcontent.com/pod-product-compliance
Lightning Source LLC
Chambersburg PA
CBHW052111010526
44111CB00036B/1662